CONVERSATIONS IN
FOOD STUDIES

CONVERSATIONS IN FOOD STUDIES

Edited by
Colin R. Anderson, Jennifer Brady,
and Charles Z. Levkoe

Foreword by Mustafa Koç

UMP
University of Manitoba Press

University of Manitoba Press
Winnipeg, Manitoba
Canada R3T 2M5
uofmpress.ca

© The Authors 2016

Printed in Canada
Text printed on chlorine-free, 100% post-consumer recycled paper

20 19 18 17 16   1 2 3 4 5

Cover design: Jess Koroscil

Library and Archives Canada Cataloguing in Publication

Conversations in food studies / edited by Colin R. Anderson,
Jennifer Brady, Charles Z. Levkoe.

Includes bibliographical references.
Issued in print and electronic formats.
ISBN 978-0-88755-787-3 (pbk.)
ISBN 978-0-88755-544-2 (pdf)
ISBN 978-0-88755-542-8 (epub)

1. Food. 2. Nutritional anthropology. I. Levkoe, Charles Z., editor II. Anderson,
Colin Ray, editor III. Brady, Jennifer, 1978–, editor

GN407.C658 2016   641.3   C2016-903162-4
                                        C2016-903163-2

This book has been published with the help of a grant from the Federation for the Humanities
and Social Sciences, through the Awards to Scholarly Publications Program, using funds
provided by the Social Sciences and Humanities Research Council of Canada.

The University of Manitoba Press gratefully acknowledges the financial support
for its publication program provided by the Government of Canada through the Canada
Book Fund, the Canada Council for the Arts, the Manitoba Department
of Culture, Heritage, Tourism, the Manitoba Arts Council,
and the Manitoba Book Publishing Tax Credit.

Contents

Foreword

Mustafa Koç

When the editors of *Conversations in Food Studies* first informed me about their plans to pursue this project well over two years ago, I could see that it was not going to be a typical edited volume. The way they planned to work collaboratively with an impressive group of scholars to design, write, and edit the chapters, made this an exceptional project. Traditionally, edited volumes avoid new and unconventional research topics and writing styles and limit participation to well-known writers to secure marketability. The conventional advice offered is to publish in well-established disciplinary journals with high-impact scores, avoid edited volumes, and stay with "safe" topics. *Conversations in Food Studies*, however, is an edited volume of scholarly contributions written by a group of emerging and senior scholars who collectively inquire into new directions in food studies, an emerging interdisciplinary field of scholarship. It is new, exciting, inspiring, and unconventional.

The field of food studies is informed by analytical and critical insights and methodologies of disciplines in the social sciences and humanities. It examines the interconnections that make up the food system as a whole. Despite its relatively short history in Canada, this has been an impressive decade for food studies research and interdisciplinary collaborations. There have been a number of Canada Research Chairs in food-related fields as well as several projects funded by the Social Sciences and Humanities Research Council of Canada (SSHRC) and Canadian Institutes of Health Research (CIHR) that have brought researchers in academia and community organizations together. Among the examples of this bountiful harvest, there are now two Canadian scholarly journals emphasizing interdisciplinary research in food studies: *CuiZine: The Journal of Canadian Food Cultures / Revue des cultures culinaires au canada* and *Canadian Food Studies/ La Revue canadienne des études sur l'alimentation*. Further, there have been a plethora of special journal issues, books, and articles highlighting the contributions of Canadian scholars in social sciences and humanities focusing on food. *Conversations in Food Studies* adds masterfully to this bounty.

As a relatively new field of inquiry, food studies is characterized by its interdisciplinary focus, systemic perspective, and dedicated commitment to change. Continuing in this tradition, this book reminds us of the importance of critical inquiry, collaboration, and conversations in transgressing boundaries for cross-disciplinary and inter-epistemological inquiry. Its authors underline the importance of cooperative and collective engagement among researchers, practitioners, activists, policy makers, and other stakeholders and demonstrate how food studies can contribute to this critical conversation.

Food studies seeks to examine the complex web of practices, processes, structures, and institutions in which we humans engage with one another and with nature in defining and transforming part of that nature into food. This is a complex process involving not only certain tasks and procedures such as production, distribution and consumption but also cultural codes, ideologies, and politics.

Going beyond a traditional sector's specific thinking, the authors of this volume organize their intellectual inquiry and conversation around four themes: representing, governance, undoing, and learning. This unconventional classification provides a chance to look at the practical, social, and political implications of how knowledge about food is represented and how these representations might reveal and conceal new possibilities. It looks at how both state and non-state actors shape and control contemporary food systems, how food studies can organize and transform the structures that bolster the dominant food system, and how transformative learning in food studies can contribute to individual and collective food system change.

This book is one of the early outputs of the new generation of scholars of the Canadian Association for Food Studies/ l'Association canadienne des études sur l'alimentation (CAFS/ACÉA). When CAFS/ACÉA was established in 2005, the founding group of university- and community-based researchers all agreed about the need for establishing a research network to promote critical, interdisciplinary scholarship in the broad areas of food production, distribution, and consumption. We had all hoped that the new association would be a space for promoting interdisciplinary scholarship and exchange among researchers who are committed to not only understanding how the food system works but also to finding ways to contribute to its transformation. Exceeding our expectations, CAFS/ACÉA has become a school for promoting critical inquiry and scholarly exchange. This book is one of the best examples of this critical inquiry and collaboration—a very daring volume in its approach to scholarship. It is disrupting disciplinary boundaries, questioning the institutions and structures of our modern food system, and critically engaging with some of the "conventional" critical inquiry.

Conversations in Food Studies is a snapshot of the scholarship in food studies in early-twenty-first-century Canada. It not only reflects the existing body of literature but also critically engages with it and will provide us direction for decades to come. This book takes an important step forward in defending and defining interdisciplinary critical inquiry. It shows us how food studies can be an interdisciplinary, inter-epistemological, and pedagogical tool for building a more socially just and ecologically sustainable world. It is an invitation for collaboration and cooperation among researchers, practitioners, activists, policy makers, and other stakeholders. I hope it will push us to go beyond interdisciplinary engagement and seek ways for inter-epistemic collaboration.

Like Frances Moore Lappé and Joseph Collin's *Food First* (1977), Don Mitchell's *The Politics of Food* (1975), the People's Food Commission report *Land of Milk and Money* (1980), or Brewster Kneen's *From Land to Mouth* (1989), I would recommend that you hold on to this book. For a future voyage in the sociology of knowledge, some years from now you may want to pick up this volume to see where our food systems thinking was in the early twenty-first century.

CONVERSATIONS IN FOOD STUDIES

Toward an Interdisciplinary Food Studies: Working the Boundaries

Charles Z. Levkoe, Jennifer Brady, and Colin R. Anderson

Why has the study of food attracted so much attention in the last decades? Perhaps the reason is that it is instantly relatable and engages our emotions in both personal and collective ways. Or maybe it is because food is deeply implicated in many of the societal challenges that we face today, including climate change, hunger, malnutrition, rural decline, and social inequality. Food invites us to work together on wider issues such as poverty, environmental sustainability, and social justice in ways that cross the disciplinary boundaries that shape our thinking and often limit our imagination. *Conversations in Food Studies* seeks to engage with current debates on food by placing a spotlight on interdisciplinary collaborations among scholars from different theoretical, methodological, epistemological, and pedagogical traditions.

Similar to the other interdisciplinary fields such as women and gender studies, queer studies, and cultural studies, food studies has become a broad and dispersed field of inquiry, yet it is still relatively young in its evolution. Food studies scholars have examined a range of social (Atkins and Bowler 2001; Gottlieb and Joshi 2010; Alkon and Agyeman 2011), economic (Mintz 1985; Norberg-Hodge et al. 2002; Weis 2007), political (Nestle 2002; Patel 2007; Tansey and Rajotte 2008), cultural (Counihan and Van Esterik 2012), and environmental (Sage 2011; Weis 2014) issues related to food and food systems. Food studies draws together multiple perspectives to examine the complex web of relations, processes, and structures that make up the harvesting and production, distribution, preparation, consumption, and disposal of food.

The innovative potential of food studies is derived from the coming together of diverse perspectives to inform a more holistic and nuanced understanding of food and food systems as well as the transformation, evolution, and deconstruction of disciplinary silos. Contributing to this transformation requires not only the coexistence within food studies of different disciplines, or multidisciplinary approaches, but also the integration of disciplines in interdisciplinary collaborations. Even more radical work in food studies involves the transgression of disciplinary boundaries through integration of different knowledge systems such as those of farmers and fishers, Indigenous peoples, and scientists.

At the same time, disciplinary silos are deeply entrenched within, and beyond, the academy and aspirations toward interdisciplinary research in food studies have only partially been realized. While in some cases, knowledge boundaries are generative and have resulted in a depth of knowledge and expertise in particular areas, in other cases, boundaries limit how we perceive and respond to challenges. This is particularly pertinent in the context of food, which is entangled in complex social, cultural, and political dynamics that demand more integrated approaches to research (Koç, Winson, and Sumner 2012). In many cases, the structures and outputs of food studies (e.g., books, conferences, ongoing research projects) have been a space where multiple disciplinary perspectives coexist and are exchanged, but often with little opportunity for the substantial integration of theory, methods, and learning. In order to ensure that food studies can develop further as an interdisciplinary field of inquiry, there is still much work required to interrogate and transgress the boundaries that have been developed over time.

The development of *Conversations in Food Studies* began with the intention to create forums to confront, question, and transgress the boundaries that limit food studies. This project builds on a number of recent volumes that have mapped the expanding field of food studies (e.g., see Atkins and Bowler 2001; Power and Koç 2008; Koç, Winson, and Sumner 2012; Guptill, Copelton, and Lucal 2013; Murcott, Belasco, and Jackson 2013; Goodman and Sage 2014). The chapters in this book demonstrate the generative potential of practising food studies as a border-crossing collaborative process to develop new approaches and methodologies, and to ask new questions that bring multiple disciplines and perspectives to bear on pressing issues related to food. The book is the result of a three-year process that brought together over forty scholars and practitioners from diverse disciplinary backgrounds in an interactive approach, which we describe below. Through this project, we have attempted to make visible the research and writing behind this work in order to produce more rigorous, critical, and relevant outputs. It is in the spirit of forging new cross-boundary collaborations that *Conversations in Food Studies* was conceived.

We describe this process, which undergirds our vision for the future of food studies, as "working the boundaries." Working the boundaries is conceived in this book as the antithesis of what Gieryn has called "boundary work" (1983, 781). Boundary work describes the effort of one group to erect boundaries between themselves and others for the purpose of maintaining power and authority. In contrast, working the boundaries describes our effort to critique or dismantle these boundaries to achieve a particular goal. These approaches are based on a claim that boundaries are political and often perform in ways that impede the emergence of knowledge and action that can enable progressive social, cultural, economic, and environmental change. Working the boundaries also draws on Michelle Fine's (1998) notion of "working the hyphen." With this concept, Fine calls for an alternative to the processes of "othering," which are rooted in the problematic relationships among researchers and the researched that constructs unequal access to self-definition and power based on imagined, rigid categories of identity. She writes, "Eroding the fixedness of categories, we and they enter and play with the blurred boundaries that proliferate" (72). Similarly, disciplinary and epistemic boundaries contribute to the unequal distribution of power among different individuals, knowledge, and ways of knowing. Similarly, working the boundaries is a process of crossing and blurring borders and working at the productive edges between the range of often segmented disciplines, epistemologies, political stances, actors (e.g., consumers vs. producers, researchers vs. practitioners) and focus areas (e.g., fisheries vs. agriculture, waste vs. food) to develop new knowledge and power relationships. Working the boundaries does not disregard the importance of disciplinary training, but invites us all to question the effect of our disciplinary and epistemic assumptions on our research, writing, and practice in order to see problems from new perspectives and transgress the limitations of the boundaries that shape our own thinking.

The desire to transgress the limits of our own disciplinary silos invites a lifelong practice of reflexivity, learning, and self-transformation. Moreover, working the boundaries is enhanced through collaborative processes that involve the discussion and negotiation of different perspectives and approaches. In this case, working the boundaries requires a critical reflexivity that is not only an inward and individual process but is relational and contingent upon the maintenance of ongoing constructive yet critical exchange among food studies practitioners. Here, individual researchers and the broader field, are continually constructed through dialogue that pushes scholars to adapt our conceptual commitments and disciplinary experiences. Using a collaborative, interdisciplinary approach, which is reflected in the ensuing chapters, this book is an important part of that reflexive practice.

Collaboration and Critical Inquiry

Conversations in Food Studies was developed on the overlapping premises of collaboration and critical inquiry. First, fostering new collaborations creates the conditions for working the boundaries, which enables new forms of knowledge to emerge. We contend that it is essential for diverse scholars, practitioners, and government stakeholders, as well as food harvesters, producers, manufacturers, and consumers to be engaged in the co-production of knowledge that will inform the pathway to a more socially just and ecologically sustainable food future. New collaborations form the basis of new conversations and debates that require researchers to share, negotiate, and integrate their research approaches to generate new hybrid outcomes. In this book, hybrids are formed where chapters bring together different disciplinary approaches and substantive focus areas, as well as through the integrative analysis of results from previous research projects. Collaboration demands sharing knowledge and ideas, negotiating differences and building consensus and, when effective, contributes to the creation of democratic learning communities.

Over the last decade in Canada, the community of interdisciplinary food studies practice has had a strong and growing presence. In 2005, the Canadian Association for Food Studies/l'Association canadienne des études sur l'alimentation (CAFS/ACÉA) was established to encourage interdisciplinary collaboration between researchers from different disciplinary backgrounds and between community-based researchers and organizations (Power and Koç 2008). CAFS/ACÉA has become an important platform for exploring and supporting interdisciplinary collaboration through providing a physical space to meet face-to-face at annual assemblies and through providing support for its members. The Association's main objective has been to facilitate researchers from diverse disciplines within the social sciences and humanities working at universities as well as public and community-based organizations to meet, identify priorities, and to share research findings on diverse issues with respect to food. CAFS/ACÉA has also become a testing ground to experiment with research collaborations in the broad area of food systems, for example, by providing an arena within which this book project could emerge (e.g., by providing financial support, providing space at meetings for the related workshops, and for helping to build its profile through various communications platforms).

The chapters in this volume involved new collaborations between authors using different approaches, methods, and ideas to develop joint writing projects and create new insights on a range of issues. Many of the chapters were forged through conversations between distinct empirical and theoretical research projects to generate novel insights and cross-case, inter-contextual knowledge. In some cases this involved a synthesis and/or comparison across completed research projects. In other cases it involved new writing projects that emerged from the coming together of two or more authors for the first time. Far greater than the sum of their parts, these fusions drew out deep insights that were only made possible through the cross-examination and integration of analyses generated through the collaboration of multiple authors.

As a second overlapping premise, the book's authors were committed to critical inquiry as an integral part of working the boundaries of food studies. Working the boundaries is as much about questioning the power relations among the various stakeholders that are impacted, either directly or indirectly, in our work as it is about breaking down disciplinary silos. Research that critically examines and challenges the logics of the dominant food system (and neoliberalism more broadly) is prominent in food studies in Canada and beyond. Working the boundaries demands examining the power dynamics that are tied up in cultural practices. Adopting a critical stance as a basis for working the boundaries involves questioning established norms and, more importantly, negotiating pragmatic and utopian proposals for new possibilities that move us toward a more socially just and ecologically sustainable food system.

Conversations in Food Studies

Conversations in Food Studies aims to advance the field of food studies through an investigation of long-debated themes as well as emerging and under-represented topics of inquiry. Whereas a number of texts have examined the breadth of food studies, this book presents a collection of chapters that provide an in-depth exploration of key topics—in many cases probing less developed areas at the edges of food studies. The structure of the book reflects the collaborative nature of the writing and publishing process where authors engaged in new partnerships to co-produce chapters.

Teams of authors were encouraged to focus on their mutual strengths and to emphasize aspects of their inquiry that worked the edges created between the different disciplinary positionings as well as their topical focus.

The book was initially developed through an open-topic call for collaboratively written papers based on empirical research, critical reviews, conceptual models, methodologies, reflective essays, and case studies from across the humanities and social sciences. As the book took shape, the chapters clustered around key themes explored in each of the four sections of this volume. The emergent nature of the process lent a structure that avoided some of the more common tropes explored in food studies (consumption, production, political economy, etc.), resulting in a book that cuts across standard ways of thinking about food studies and brings interdisciplinary writing into conversation within the four themed sections: "Re-presenting Disciplinary Praxis"; "Who, What, and How: Governing Food Systems"; "'Un-doing' Food Studies: A Case for Flexible Fencing"; and "Scaling Learning in Agri-food Systems." Each section is synthesized by a critical commentary written by a leading food studies scholar who places the section's chapters into conversation and further locates the chapters and the theme within the broader debates in and beyond food studies.

The first section of the book, "Re-presenting Disciplinary Praxis," includes four chapters that examine the practical, social, and political implications for how food and food issues are represented in a range of contexts. The chapters each interrogate the ways that food and food practice are represented in and beyond textual form and the power relations that are bound up in the different processes of representation. These chapters provide new insight into how knowledge about food, and the creation of that knowledge, are represented and how these representations might reveal and also conceal new possibilities. Text dominates as a mode of representation in food studies, however new mediums and strategies of communication are emerging that are making new ways of representation possible. Transmedia forms of communication hold an inchoate potential to give new voice to represent knowledge (e.g., through art, performance, video, and social media) and simultaneously to make the products of food studies more accessible and understandable to a wide range of actors (e.g., through the use of images, interactive web platforms, etc.) (Anderson and McLachlan 2015).

In Chapter 1, Cadieux, Levkoe, Mount, and Szanto draw on three case studies that use visualizations in interdisciplinary academic, public, and teaching contexts to explore how visual methods can be used in food scholarship to translate between methods and representations as well as evaluate different processes. In Chapter 2, Szanto, Wong, and Brady use Skype as a tool to experiment with performativity (i.e., acts of doing and/or making within felicitous environments) as a way to illuminate the blurred boundaries between "head work" and "hand work," between self and other, between production and consumption, and between many of the conventional dualities within food scholarship (and academic practice in general). The chapter demonstrates the challenges of translating action into text, including the temporally stabilizing effects that writing has on lived experience and the ways in which text is a form of performance, just as any other act of doing and reporting on food practices.

In Chapter 3, Brady, Millious, and Ventresca cross-examine literature on the study of milk from social science and humanities approaches. The authors contrast different analyses that trouble milk as a mundane and known object. The interconnections among these analyses are then probed, demonstrating the potential of integrating the insights offered by the author's different disciplinary perspectives and highlighting the importance of transgressing epistemological and disciplinary boundaries. In Chapter 4, Green and Bunn deconstruct the different ways that food issues are represented in debates over agriculture and food systems through the concept of "food talk." Their chapter examines how the politics of planning and the contested preservation of agricultural lands around urban centres are shaped by competing discourses. Through an examination of the contested issue of the Agriculture Land Reserve in British Columbia, they demonstrate how the different discourses are linked to broader cultural, political, and geographic tensions around food production, distribution, and consumption.

Penny Van Esterick's section commentary considers the intersections between disciplinary positioning and representation as well as the relationships between representation and practice. She argues that it is vital to understand the intention and context of representation in food studies research by "linking the little and the large."

The second section, "Who, What, and How: Governing Food Systems," includes three chapters that examine different processes and discourses that are brought to bear on the informal and formal governance of food and food systems. Beyond the more common emphasis on the role of government policy, these contributions add nuance to our understanding of how both state and non-state actors shape and control contemporary food systems. These chapters provide new insight into questions about who has power, how power is negotiated, and the wider implications for communities connected through different foodscapes.

In Chapter 5, Lowitt, Mount, Khan, and Clément cross-examine research on local food systems governance with the longer-standing literature on governance of fisheries to identify common challenges and opportunities across these realms. Drawing on a cross-case analysis of the governance of local food systems in China, Canada, and Ireland, the authors provide new insights into pressing governance questions for local food systems. The chapter demonstrates the importance of the different governance structures that emerge based on the contingencies of place and nation and the implications this has for the future development of sustainable local food systems.

In Chapter 6, Détolle, Jennings, and Nash examine the history of "Bring Your Own Wine" restaurants in Montreal and discuss how the governance surrounding the regulation of alcohol is shaped by the motivations of different stakeholders. Their chapter focuses on issues of thrift, profit, and distinction to exemplify the complexity of food governance, which is shaped by wider regulatory and consumptive processes, and to demonstrate how liminal spaces of food consumption can be both implicated in, and become victims of, wider process of neighbourhood gentrification. In Chapter 7, Martin, Mundle, and Rideout use a case study of public policy within public health in British Columbia to examine the tensions between food safety and food security. Synthesizing interdisciplinary and community-based research, they explore the paradigmatic differences between two competing discourses that divide public health professionals: food safety and food security. The tensions that arise between these often overly polarized perspectives can undermine the development of more sustainable food systems. The authors discuss how these perspectives can begin to be reconciled by fostering mutual understanding between proponents of both camps through processes of communication and collaboration.

Steffanie Scott's section commentary discusses governance in relation to food studies and relates the chapters to her own research on local food systems in China. She explains that, despite the application of stricter regulations and enforcement in China, the analysis of these formal rules of government would be more relevant and powerful if they incorporated a broader consideration of the more complicated governance of food systems through the state, civil society, and market. Scott suggests that many of the governance challenges in today's food systems will require an approach that works the boundaries between approaches and draws insights from governance in different nations and places.

The third section of the book, "'Un-doing' Food Studies: A Case for Flexible Fencing," includes chapters that trouble the taken-for-granted assumptions that structure or inform much food studies work. These chapters particularly demonstrate how using the tools developed through existing disciplines can be an important starting place to disrupt disciplinary thinking and develop new approaches, ideas, and solutions to current challenges. Through an examination of the "un-doing boundaries," the chapters provide new insights into how to transform the structures that buttress the power of the dominant food system. In Chapter 8, Sprague and Huddart Kennedy problematize the prevailing focus on the marketplace as the most common strategy promoted for changing the food system. While making decisions about what to consume (or not) is important, alternative food networks when framed as market-based governance tend to obscure and externalize issues related to social justice and reproduce the logics and practices of neoliberal food economies. In Chapter 9, Bomford and Brock provide an interdisciplinary analysis of the concept of a sustainable diet. They examine the divergent definitions holding a common belief that widespread dietary changes will accomplish desirable environmental, social, or economic outcomes despite considerable variation in what outcomes are identified as desirable and how they are defined, measured, and compared.

In Chapter 10, Lee and Soma examine the phenomena of food waste. Bringing together their different disciplinary perspectives, their chapter challenges the assumption that food waste in the global South is primarily a problem related to wasteful agricultural production and demonstrates that understanding household food consumption practices is equally important. In Chapter 11, Trenouth, Polyakov, Gupta, and Zougris use latent semantic analysis—a statistical method for the analysis of textual data—to trace the development of scholarship on alternative food networks (AFN). By bringing this quantitative method to an area dominated by qualitative research, they contribute to ongoing debates surrounding AFNs and offer inspiration for unexplored topics in food studies.

Josée Johnston's section commentary echoes the book's purpose by questioning simplistic calls for boundaries to be undone. She argues that it is essential to consider both the way that disciplinary boundaries are constructed and deconstructed and the values they might serve as part of a process of knowledge creation in food studies and beyond.

The final section, "Scaling Learning in Agri-food Systems," includes two substantive contributions to the growing literature on food pedagogy. The chapters provide insights on the role of transformative learning as a vital part of individual and collective food system change. They address learning and critical pedagogy related to food in and across formal and informal learning settings and within expanding communities of food practice. In Chapter 12, Braun and Bogdan provide a cross-case analysis that examines the extent to which social practices of traditional food preparation and agricultural environmental stewardship play a role in the transformation of normative ideologies around food, people, and the environment. While transformative learning theory is often framed as an individualizing process of self-transformation, this chapter locates learning within the context of social practices and examines the importance of engaging in communities of practice for processes of self-transformation. In this way, the authors blur the division between transformation as either an individual or a collective process. This chapter suggests that the nexus between individual and collective processes of transformative learning are a key area to explore as a pathway to stronger, healthier, and more resilient food systems.

In Chapter 13, Sumner and Wever link what they refer to as "critical food pedagogy" with transformative learning through an examination of different pedagogical encounters with food in educational institutions and in community initiatives and organizations. They argue that, while many pedagogical encounters around food can actually reinforce the status quo, critical food pedagogy can pave the way for the personal and social changes necessary for the creation of more sustainable alternatives.

Mary Beckie's section commentary synthesizes how boundary processes are fundamental to scaling-up the learning and creativity necessary for a more sustainable food system. She argues that learning is most effective through engagement between diverse actors (e.g., between university and community researchers) and is essential for addressing complex challenges in food systems and for both personal and collective transformation.

Challenges and Opportunities for the Future of Food Studies

This volume, and especially the collaborative process that led to its creation, worked at the boundaries of different disciplines, knowledge producers, and substantive research areas that both divide and define food studies. The process of working the boundaries that underpinned this volume forces us to engage more explicitly with the edges of food studies to imagine and shape what food studies could become. This is not a straightforward or simple process, and it involves straying from well-worn and safer paths into experimental and unproven territory. While working the boundaries of food studies can produce insightful and long-lasting results, the road itself can be bumpy and fraught with challenges with no guarantee of achieving positive outcomes.

Throughout the process of putting this book together, there were a number of chapters that did not materialize, in part relating to the challenges of collaborations between teams of authors that attempted to work and reconcile the boundaries that divided them. A lesson we learned is that new collaborations can be well planned and have the commitment of all individuals, yet may not always result in successful outcomes—at least not those originally anticipated. Successfully working the boundaries requires critical reflexivity that carefully examines our own biases and assumptions in the process of working with others. Knowing when boundaries should be maintained and when they should be undone is a challenging and demanding question. While avoiding any uncritical acceptance of interdisciplinarity as dogma is important, what is less clear is whether and when boundaries should be raised, defended, blurred, bent, broken, or moved.

Overcoming the Cultural Boundaries of Food Studies

Throughout this project, we were committed to working the boundaries, which revealed four key emergent challenges that suggest further opportunities to develop the field of food studies. First, while the chapters each represent an interdisciplinary approach, the overall scope of interdisciplinary work in the book is relatively narrow. Most of the chapters focus primarily on social science and humanities analyses of food and food systems. As discussed above, the collaborations in this book came primarily from a call for proposals distributed through CAFS/ACÉA, an association that largely represents critical social scientist and humanities scholars. We recognize that the identity of food studies as a field of scholarship in Canada is defined by those who self-identify and actively participate in the organizations, journals, books, and other arena that make up the identity of the communities of practice. There is a notable absence of economists, agriculture scientists, cultural theorists, historians, and philosophers, to name only a few. Thus, despite aspirations for a wider interdisciplinary field in Canada, the collective identity of this community of practice reproduces its own boundaries (Brady, Levkoe, and Szanto 2015). There is much work to be done to engage with and to draw in other perspectives to develop a more interdisciplinary and transdisciplinary field food studies.

Crossing Boundaries between Different Epistemologies

A second challenge is the need to explore the possibilities for inter-epistemological inquiry within the field of food studies. Many of the chapters in this book are collaborative efforts among authors hailing from different disciplinary traditions but from similar epistemological ones. Indeed, it would seem that interdisciplinarity is far more straightforward when researchers are located within similar epistemological positions and that collaboration, for example between an economist from a positivist paradigm and a sociologist from a constructivist paradigm, may be far more difficult to reconcile. While interdisciplinary collaborations enrich bodies of knowledge, they do not necessarily push researchers to challenge or innovate in the ways that knowledge is defined and produced.

It can be even more challenging to engage in research that brings together different knowledge systems—for example, between academics and community-based practitioners. The engagement of food studies scholars in these kinds of work has been quite prominent at the CAFS/ACÉA conferences. For example, in 2012, CAFS/ACÉA was used as a platform for the development of a major Pan-Canadian research project using community-based and participatory action methodologies to explore new approaches to community-campus research partnerships that put community first (Andrée et al. 2014). However, whether this work is valued to the same extent as traditional social and natural science research has yet to be seen. Further, this transdisciplinary work valorizes different knowledge systems (e.g., of farmers and Indigenous peoples) and often mobilizes more political and practical knowledge in projects to transform society. This knowledge and academic labour is often considered irrelevant or even non-academic by many scholars trained to value elite scientific knowledge over other knowledge systems. For example, this tension boiled over when a disgruntled member of CAFS/ACÉA publicly opted out of the organization's listserv criticizing it for being dominated by activist-oriented interests. This exemplifies the divide between those from a "transformative research" world view (e.g., those who understand scholarship as political and knowledge as situated and contested) and those from a positivist world view (e.g., those who view scientific knowledge as neutral and separate from the social world) (Creswell 2013). The struggles between these research world views go far beyond food studies but are an important boundary to work for a more effective and vibrant food studies.

Engaging with Critical Theory and Social Justice

A third challenge is the need to foster more critical and supportive engagement with the struggles of historically marginalized and racialized groups, including Indigenous peoples, Francophone communities in Canada, youth, refugees, and migrants and food workers, to name only a few. To avoid erecting the hyphens that Fine (1998) warns of, food studies scholars must do more to engage communities who are thinking and working on these issues. As a first step, food studies scholars must examine their own privileges, biases, and complicities in reproducing power inequities and silencing certain kinds of scholarship. Examining these absences must be accompanied by a concomitant examination of power and privilege. It is not enough to simply research the "other." We must also examine the processes, one of which is research itself that contributes to marginalization and that constructs dominant and marginalized groups.

While most of the chapters are critically oriented to questioning the dominant logics of food systems, there is not always direct engagement with critical theory, social justice, and other more politicized frameworks. For example, there is a clear boundary in chapters that use the language of political economy (e.g., food systems, sustainability, agro-ecology, distribution) and those that use the language of socio-cultural and constructivist approaches (e.g., performative, discursive, representation). This division in language is also reflected in food studies more widely. Further, it raises the questions: Is it possible that food studies is too timid? Might food studies marginalize or implicitly exclude scholars pursuing more radical and critical agendas who themselves feel marginal in these spaces?

Overcoming the Institutionalization of Disciplinary Boundaries

As we reflected on this process of working the boundaries, it became clear that there are many barriers to interdisciplinary collaborations that are deeply entrenched in the norms, institutions, and subjectivities of the academy. While interdisciplinarity is often lauded by funders and public figures in research, the reward and incentive structures of the academy highly favour and encourage disciplinary approaches. For example, a scholar's identity within a specific discipline typically carries far more weight in tenure and promotion and other evaluative frameworks. Further, the atomizing conventions of an increasingly neoliberal academy often constrain effective collaboration. Early stage academics are particularly constrained by the pressures of a tight job market and the need to conform to conventional academic norms to be more widely marketable. Early career researchers and graduate students who pursue collaborative work through interdisciplinary or transdisciplinary research require much more support for this work in order to create working environments that enable these boundary-crossing career trajectories.

Throughout this book project we discussed with the authors ways to create more room to foster collaboration, especially across disciplines. We are fortunate to work within a community of practice and with mentors and peers that are helping to manoeuvre associations like CAFS/ACÉA so as to provide spaces where we can explore and support these kinds of initiatives. The interdisciplinary workshops and panels held at annual CAFS/ACÉA assemblies and the active supportive role of the senior scholars for these boundary-crossing projects are evidence of these important spaces being opened through CAFS/ACÉA that will enable new forms of collaboration. Yet, as much as these projects create the possibility for new agencies, these spaces are located a great distance from, and do little to challenge, the institutional framework that limits the pursuit of more integrated (and possibly institutionalized) collaboration and research. It is vital that we work together to challenge these institutional constraints within post-secondary institutions that will change the reward and incentive structures and foster new subjectivities where working the boundaries becomes a valued part of doing food studies in a relevant and meaningful way.

Conclusion: Critical Reflexivity and Learning

Working across disciplines, epistemologies, world views, and political orientations is challenging, and, over the course of this book project, a number of chapters were withdrawn, largely reflecting challenges that arose from working these boundaries. One writing team cited challenges in crossing disciplinary and epistemological boundaries and especially finding a common voice, eventually withdrawing their chapter from the book project. Other chapters where authors were from different disciplinary backgrounds were supported and shaped by peer reviewers and by the editors over the course of multiple iterations to encourage integration and consistency in voice. Some of the early versions of chapters were difficult to follow and clearly reflected the difficulties in reconciling the different positionings of the authors—perhaps similar to an awkward first date where conversations might seem forced, but with substantial effort (and maybe a little bit of luck), improves with time and thoughtful attempts to find common interests and modes of interaction.

In many of the chapters it seemed the greatest challenges arose with authors' attempts to engage in collaboration at a later stage of the research process (e.g., bringing projects together only at the writing stage) rather than projects that emerged from earlier or longer-term engagement. Inter-epistemological and transdisciplinary research requires what Murphy (2011) calls an "upstream" approach that involves collaboration at the initial stages rather than the more common "downstream" approach of interpretation and dissemination of results. Another chapter that involved collaboration between university-based researchers and their community partners was ultimately withdrawn, largely because the different goals and approaches of the academics, the community partners, and the parameters of our book (i.e., the editorial requests) were difficult to reconcile in the relatively short time period of preparing the final manuscript.

While this book makes a significant contribution to collaborative, inter-disciplinary food studies scholarship, it reflects the broader tenor of the field in that it points to future, more radical possibilities for working the bound-aries. If critical learning for social transformation are core goals of food stud-ies, then it is essential that food studies scholars engage more deeply with some of the more transgressive and provocative areas of theory and research emerging from areas such as queer theory, fat studies, critical race theory, and gender studies. Moreover, if transdisciplinary research is to become effective in drawing from and blurring the boundaries between scientific, professional, and community knowledge systems, more work is needed to build mutual understanding and to curb the disproportionate power of elite science in society. This could result in the food studies community further developing its own critical stance and better positioning the field to address the complex issues of power, marginalization, and injustice that are often less prevalent or even perpetuated in existing food studies scholarship. One direction for this work would be for food studies scholars to work some specific boundaries more effectively, including those among the humanities and social sciences. Similarly, food studies organizations, journals, and net-works in Canada and beyond would benefit immensely from drawing in and engaging with researchers in natural sciences, agricultural sciences, and eco-nomics as well as those positioned outside of universities, including farmers, Indigenous peoples, and citizen-scientists.

If food studies is to take its mission of building more socially just food systems seriously, it is vital that we engage with researchers from across seem-ingly disparate fields to debate and negotiate the meaning, politics, strategies, and theories of food system change. There are important differences in the meaning and vision of a socially just food system, which looks very different to different stakeholders. For example, what does social justice mean to a farmer, an Indigenous person, an economist, or an anthropologist? As editors of this book, for example, we are positioned quite differently in relation to the ways we address questions of social justice and food systems. It is unlikely that we could agree on a singular defining vision of a socially just food system. However, our own collaborations have proven fruitful in that we have each learned through debating and reworking the boundaries between us in ways that are only made possible through focused collaboration.

Working the boundaries demands a critical and reflexive interrogation of our own paradigms and practices as well as a collective reflexivity as a community of food studies researchers. The chapters in section 4 on "learning" foreshadow the applicability of transformative learning and critical pedagogy to the practice and development of food studies as a self-critical community of practice capable of dynamic transformation through working the boundaries. This volume has emerged from these individual and collaborative reflexive processes and explores how we can productively engage with boundaries by deconstructing them in some instances, while embracing them and justifying them in others. Part of what makes exploring food so exciting is the productive tensions between disciplines, the differently positioned actors, and the epistemological frameworks that have the potential to produce hybrid knowledges that can be brought to bear on efforts to (re)imagine and realize a more just and sustainable food future. This book exemplifies a deliberate process of working the boundaries as an imperfect, iterative, contested, and partial process at the heart of a vibrant, interdisciplinary, and critical future for food studies.

References

Alkon, Alison Hope, and Julian Agyeman. 2011. *Cultivating Food Justice: Race, Class, and Sustainability.* Boston, MA: MIT Press.

Anderson, C.R., and S.M. McLachlan. 2015. "Transformative Research as Knowledge Mobilization: Transmedia, Bridges and Layers." *Action Research* online. http://dx.doi.org/10.1177/1476750315616684.

Andrée, P., D. Chapman, L. Hawkins, C. Kneen, W. Martin, C. Muehlberger, C. Nelson et al. 2014. "Building Effective Relationships for Community-Engaged Scholarship in Canadian Food Studies." *Canadian Food Studies / La Revue canadienne des études sur l'alimentation* 1 (1): 27–53. http://dx.doi.org/10.153 53/cfs-rcea.v1i1.19.

Atkins, Peter, and Ian Bowler. 2001. *Food in Society.* New York: Oxford University Press.

Brady, J., C. Levkoe, and D. Szanto. 2015. "Borders, Boundaries, and Becoming Food Studies: Looking Back, Pushing Forward." *Canadian Food Studies / La Revue canadienne des études sur l'alimentation* 2 (1): 4–8. http://dx.doi. org/10.15353/cfs-rcea.v2i1.56.

Counihan, Carole, and Penny Van Esterik, eds. 2012. *Food and Culture: A Reader.* 3rd ed. New York: Routledge.

Creswell, J.W. 2013. *Research Design: Qualitative, Quantitative, and Mixed Methods Approaches.* Thousand Oaks: Sage.

Fine, Michelle. 1998. "Working the Hyphens: Reinventing Self and Other in Qualitative Research." In *The Landscape of Qualitative Research: Theories and Issues*, edited by Norman K. Denzin and Yvonna S. Lincoln, 130–55. Thousand Oaks: Sage.

Gieryn, Thomas F. 1983. "Boundary-Work and the Demarcation of Science from Non-Science: Strains and Interests in Professional Ideologies of Scientists." *American Sociological Review* 48 (6): 781–95. http://dx.doi.org/10.2307/2095325.

Goodman, M., and C. Sage. 2014. *Food Transgressions: Making Sense of Contemporary Food Politics*. Burlington, VT: Ashgate.

Gottlieb, Robert, and Anupama Joshi. 2010. *Food Justice*. Cambridge, MA: MIT Press.

Guptill, Amy E., Denise A. Copelton, and Betsy Lucal. 2013. *Food and Society: Principles and Paradoxes*. Malden, NY: John Wiley & Sons.

Koç, Mustafa, Anthony Winson, and Jennifer Sumner. 2012. *Critical Perspectives in Food Studies*. Don Mills, ON: Oxford University Press Canada.

Mintz, Sidney W. 1985. *Sweetness and Power*. New York: Penguin.

Murcott, Anne, Warren Belasco, and Peter Jackson. 2013. *The Handbook of Food Research*. London: Bloomsbury.

Murphy, Brenda L. 2011. "From Interdisciplinary to Inter-Epistemological Approaches: Confronting the Challenges of Integrated Climate Change Research." *Canadian Geographer* 55 (4): 490–509. http://dx.doi.org/10.1111/j.1541-0064.2011.00388.x.

Nestle, Marion. 2002. *Food Politics: How the Food Industry Influences Nutrition and Health*. Berkeley: University of California Press.

Norberg-Hodge, Helena, Todd Merrifield, and Steven Gorelick. 2002. *Bringing the Food Economy Home: Local Alternatives to Global Agribusiness*. West Hartford, CT: Kumarian Press.

Patel, Raj. 2007. *Stuffed and Starved: Markets, Power and the Hidden Battle for the World's Food System*. Toronto: Harper Collins.

Power, Elaine, and Mustafa Koç. 2008. "A Double-Double and a Maple-Glazed Doughnut." *Food, Culture, & Society* 11 (3): 263–7. http://dx.doi.org/10.2752/175174408X347838.

Sage, Colin. 2011. *Environment and Food*. Milton Park: Routledge.

Tansey, Geoff, and Rajotte, Tasmin. 2008. *The Future Control of Food: A Guide to International Negotiations and Rules on Intellectual Property, Biodiversity and Food Security*. London: Earthscan.

Weis, Tony. 2007. *The Global Food Economy: The Battle for the Future of Farming*. Halifax, NS: Fernwood.

Weis, Tony. 2014. *The Ecological Hoofprint: The Global Burden of Industrial Livestock*. New York: Zed Books.

PART I: RE-PRESENTING DISCIPLINARY PRAXIS

CHAPTER 1

Visual Methods for Collaborative Food System Work

*Kirsten Valentine Cadieux, Charles Z. Levkoe,
Phil Mount, and David Szanto*

Figure 1.1. Five "visual story" posters combine to create one 17.5' x 4' banner, developed for the Homegrown Minneapolis Food Council by Arlene Birt of Background Stories. Labels and images are nested together in the social, environmental, infrastructural, and conceptual context of the city.

As public and scholarly attention to food issues increases, there is a need for ongoing efforts to portray or to represent the complexities of food—those manifold crossings and re-crossings of stomachs and minds, markets and materials, power and privilege, nature and culture. Indeed, even this list falls short of the myriad influences, actors, and processes that constitute our food systems. This chapter explores visualization as a way to participate in and represent food-system complexity. While some portrayals of food aim to be "precise" or "definitive," our interest is in methods that value process and conversation as much as output and accuracy. Such exploratory and emergent visual methods can also address challenges related to reductivism, authority, and the centralization of knowledge that are problematic in scholarly habits of representing food issues.

Figure 1.2. This photo illustration connects ideas from this chapter to related work by David Szanto. Using maps, photographs, notes, drawings, and recording devices that suggest the maker's process, this illustration implicates the apparatuses that produce visualizations. Photo by David Szanto.

Figure 1.3. This sparkline ⟋⟍ shows the relative frequency over the past fifty years of the use of the terms "food system" (in grey) and "food systems" (in black). A sparkline, is "a small intense, simple, word-sized graphic with typographic resolution" (Tufte 2006) that portrays relational change, usually in line with text. Source: Generated from Google Books Ngram Viewer, http://books.google.com/ngrams.

At a basic level, the term food system invokes a web of activities that includes growing and harvesting, processing and distribution, marketing and selling, and the consumption, disposal, and recirculation of nutrients. Using the term encourages us to attend to the interactive and interdependent network of relationships in the food world (Tansey and Worsley 1995). Yet we must equally acknowledge that there are many food systems, at many different scales: global, municipal, familial. Equally, a single human body can be considered a food system, as might the combined epistemologies of food studies. Beyond being a simple collection of components, food systems are dynamic and ever-changing assemblages of social, political, economic, and environmental elements. Some analysts have described them as "complex adaptive systems," self-organizing groupings of heterogeneous entities that interact with and affect other complex systems (Bawden 1991; Nelson and Stroink 2014; Homer-Dixon 2011; Vandermeer 2011). The recognition of this complexity has contributed to an emerging consensus on the need for collaboration across food-related disciplines and sectors, and for methods that produce meaningful knowledge.

We argue that visualizations based on collaborative methods can address some of the limitations imposed in text-only forms of representation or in forms that represent only one perspective—conditions that are relatively common and habitual in and beyond food studies scholarship. First, because of its efficacy in creating clarity, authoritative text tends to oversimplify the messy interactivity of food systems, reducing the very dynamics that make them important to study. As John Law (2004) has said, "Clear descriptions don't work if what they are describing is not itself very coherent" (2). Second, text is generally linear in structure, ocular-centric, and, even in collaborative work, often produced from a singular perspective. Food systems, by contrast, are cyclical, multisensory, and appear as different "constellations" of relationships (Massey 1999) depending on the positionality of the observer (on visuality and food, see Kirshenblatt-Gimblett 1999; Banes and Lepecki 2012; Howes and Classen 2013; Pauwels 2006).[1] And third, because of perceived authority and finality of meaning, the audiences of textual accounts may feel less privileged to creatively interpret such forms and/or participate in refiguring the knowledge they present. Again, because of the assembled nature of food systems, a more participative method is called for.

Clearly not all text-based accounts produce such problematics, yet a shift toward graphic visual methods—particularly in representing the diverse knowledge of multiple communities—appears to be generating a valuable space in food studies (Fraley 2011; Mount and Andrée 2013). Mitchell (1996) writes that "vision is as important as language in mediating social relations, and it is not reducible to language, to the 'sign,' or to discourse" (47). In food and other cultural contexts, the use of images to represent experience predates the written word, but as the medium has changed (e.g., the printing press, digital technology), so too have these visualizations (Berger 1972; Samuels and Samuels 1975). For food systems analysis and transformation, engaging with visual methods raises a series of important questions: How do we represent complex food systems in ways that are effective and meaningful, yet still express their complex entanglements? How do we acknowledge and represent the temporal and spatial fluidity of food systems? How do we support collaboration in making and reimagining knowledge, without reinforcing conventional power relations? In this chapter, we unpack these questions and propose a number of ways that visualization work addresses them.

Visualizations and Their Effects

The three images that open this chapter demonstrate a range of visualizations, constituting various food ideas, design techniques, and spheres of deployment. Rather than providing comprehensive explanations about the images, we present them as a sampler, to stimulate and encourage reader interpretations about how and why they were made, as well as how and what they communicate. Clearly, many other forms of visualization also exist, such as maps, charts, graphs, and figures—those images that typically accompany scholarly texts. For this discussion, however, we focus on visuals that are more open to viewer interpretation, and which incorporate complexity and collaboration both in their methods of production and in the ways they produce and reproduce knowledge.

Three additional visualizations—which we do unpack in detail below—serve as the backbone for this chapter. Drawn from the authors' first-hand experiences in the context of academic analysis, public conversations, and classroom teaching, they provide opportunities to exhibit and debate how visualizations can employ, translate between, and evaluate different processes in transformative food system work. While not a comprehensive examination, these cases provide a number of examples for transgressing certain epistemic boundaries within food studies. Together, they describe frameworks for polyvocal representation and participative interpretation, for questioning the privileging of text, including its role in creating unambiguous definitions, and for disrupting conventional power structures in authoring representational forms.[2] We further address some of the weaknesses of this approach, as well as the frequent need for visualization to be deployed alongside textual analysis. As a whole, this chapter also captures our own process in making a collaborative (though largely textual) representation of knowledge, including the futilities and happy accidents that arise.

Collaborative visualizations translate meaning across and through the different perspectives of those who produce and interpret them. They have the potential to resist takeover by the loudest voices, the best-funded public-relations campaigns, or the catchiest logo or story. In contrast to simply producing graphics of inputs and outputs common to many food system diagrams, collaborative visualization is a process for creating a collective space for communicating, exploring, and refining shared knowledge. This goes beyond merely describing; it is about transforming the people who make the descriptions, including those who would ordinarily be considered the "reader" or "audience." In this way, visualizations open a conversation—with multiple and potentially conflicting users—to discuss, interrogate, and propagate scholarship. We maintain that sharing knowledge-making in ways that are potentially awkward, slow, messy, and *out where people can see them* is what makes visualization a transgressive process.

Framing Concepts and Methods

Elliot Eisner (1997) challenged scholars to use alternative forms of data to expose "productive ambiguity," where "the material presented is more evocative than denotative, and in its evocation, it generates insight and invites attention to complexity" (8). In this chapter, we use the concept of visualization to describe a range of methods for visual representation that create meaning (Mirzoeff 2002; Sanders-Bustle 2003). Constructing visualizations that translate across boundaries of food disciplines, sectors, or perspectives involves processes of production, communication, and interpretation that require significant collaborative interaction (Cadieux 2013). Like any process that communicates simple representations of complex concepts, visual methods require careful attention to context and deployment.[3] The apparent simplicity of carrying out visual methods may elide the specifics of how those methods are employed, why they are important, and how they can be transformative in the study of food. In our teaching and publicly engaged research, for example, we find a significant mismatch between people's high expectations that they will be able to visually communicate their intentions and justifications for transformative food system work and their demonstrated capacity for such communication, presumably related to this apparent simplicity.

Within an academic or public-engagement context, the use of visualizations requires a systematic methodology for developing, sharing, and revising imagery to convey meaning (Prosser 1996).[4] Through the process of making them, visualizations have the potential to engage interdisciplinary groups in useful, collaborative, mediated conversations. Collaborative visualizations can also contest dominant power relations, not only by distributing knowledge across the group that collectively makes them, but by inviting participation and validating diverse forms of knowledge making in the acts of perceiving and interpreting the visualization. However, organizing principles are required, if collaborators are to be successfully oriented and empowered to assume an authorial voice in the visualization process.

In order to analyze the three case studies presented below, we introduce four themes that illustrate a range of issues in making food-system visualizations: modes and meanings of *representation*; codes and tools of *communication*; rules and products of *translation*; and *transformation* of elements and actors. These are not comprehensive categories, and we do not suggest that all four themes must be present to make an effective food system visualization. Nonetheless, these four notions repeatedly arose while we explored what makes visualization an important component in our case studies, and more generally in critical food studies.

Representation

The capacity for representing one thing by using another is often portrayed as a central characteristic of being human. Academic work is often situated within the realm of abstract representation such that highly specific tools and approaches are often taken for granted (Novak and Gowin 1984). To address this, many of the transgressive lineages we draw on here have turned specific attention to the question of representation, and particularly to issues of universalism, relativism, and power. Examples include anti-colonial and feminist work, especially in performance and cultural studies that have explored the cultural, practice-based, and non-representational turns in recent scholarship (Howett 1997; Thrift 2007). The insights of this critical examination remind us that representations are always partial, situated, and linked to the assemblages of experience, emotion, affect, materials, and relationships from which they emerge.

Keeping in mind these social processes, representation can be interpreted in a number of ways: something that *stands in for* another thing (e.g., a semiotic signifier); something that *acts on behalf of* the system (e.g., an individual speaking on behalf of a constituency); or something that *shows again* the system, in different space and time (e.g., a performance of a script). Critically, such diverse interpretations of representation also suggest that a visualization may carry greater fidelity (representativeness) if it incorporates greater polyvocality. Given that food systems are complex, increasing the number of "voices," or channels, through which a visualization communicates may express systemic complexity more faithfully.

Humanistic disciplines such as history, rhetoric, semiotics, epistemology, and science studies can be very helpful in developing appropriate and usable analytic tools for understanding and addressing the complex issues of food system representation.[5] In interesting contrast to the wordy debates over the adequacy of various modes of representation (Thrift 2007), the rise of graphic novels to illustrate contentious politics suggests the power of visual representation to include both the gestural and the didactic—aspects of the task of representing that have been salient since cave painting.

Communication

The type of communication demanded of a visualization reflects its purpose as a tool for research, pedagogy, or sense-making (Zepel 2013). While the primary aspect of communication is to encode the meaning of a system through representational symbols, it is equally important to attend to other elements and processes. These include the perceiver's role in decoding the meaning, and the need to create opportunities for perception as well as an invitation to participate. Both representation and communication are shaped by the objectives of the analyses brought to them, and framed by relevance and perspective, and are therefore less likely to be comprehensible, acceptable, or navigable to those whose knowledge or practice is absent, excluded, or challenged (Santos 2001).

To communicate through visualizations is to create an oddly delicate role as curator of expectations and perspectives that not only unsettle the viewer, but also suggest reflection and provide reassurance, as well as familiar tools of navigation (Bantock 1999). It is also crucial to enable multiple meanings to coexist as legitimate, despite differences and contradictions. For example, food systems transitions demand political engagement at local and regional scales using a flexible, open language that speaks to diverse communities—from agroecological producers to state managers (Gonzalez de Molina 2013). Successful communicative work recognizes that diverse practices, goals, and meanings may be different and even contradictory, and provides tools for navigating difference without closing down communication.

The strength of visualizations in portraying food systems is the ability to communicate complexity using the language of systems—otherwise known as multidimensionality (Meadows 2008). This can be expressed simply—such as in the sparkline in Figure 1.3—or can communicate layers of information through interactive online tools that move the visualization through space and time.[6] This latter example differs not only in visual complexity, but also in its emphasis on process as an integral element of visualization, and in its encouragement of interactions—between creator, representation and spectator—that challenge "the parameters that define authorship, intelligibility and purposefulness" (Santos 2001, 276). That is, with the power to communicate complexity comes the responsibility to do so in a manner that invites other voices, interpretations, and authors to the visualization-creation process.

Translation

As implied in our discussion of representation and communication above, the acts involved in expressing a complex food system via visual methods necessarily introduce differences in meaning. For this reason it is critical to attend to the diverse processes of making and perceiving visualizations, as well as the knowledge production and transformations that are induced. As documentarian Liz Miller (2011) has stated, translating from one medium to another (or from lived experience to visualization) always means that something is added and something is taken away. Even within the relatively simpler process of translating text from one language to another, the risk of altering its meaning is always present, given the translator's need to understand the universe within which the original text was situated (Nord 2005). Translations, though often considered transparent or equal to the original, might better be thought of in terms of *diffraction*, that is, a production of difference through the "heterogeneous history" of their making (Haraway 1997, 273).

A secondary interpretation of translation refers to the spatial and temporal displacements that take place when making visualizations. Because they are highly mobile (unlike most parts of the food systems they represent), visualizations can become disassociated from the actors they portray and the actors that make them. Furthermore, as they move into new spaces and times, they become associated with new elements of their contexts, as—in moving from one medium to another—meaning may be added or removed. In this way, a visualization is always newly iterated with each moment of perception—a communicative performance unto itself because of the translations away from the time and space of its initial production. In Latour's (2005) rendering, translation is not a *transportation* of impulse or meaning from one object to another, but a *transformation*—a change that takes place during the translational interaction, and one that speaks of the nature of the things that interact. In the context of our discussion here, those "things" transformed may include the elements of a food system, the visualizers of that system, and the people who come into perceptual contact with the visualization.

Transformation

Building on the three themes discussed above, visualizations have the potential to open new spaces for resistance when they engage their producers, viewers, and broader systems in a dialectic of creativity and subversive inquiry. Transformative visualizations are distinguished from repressive uses that are centrally controlled, encourage passive consumer behaviour, and are depoliticizing—all qualities that challenge transformative food work and shift energy and potential away from food system transformation. In general, we understand transformative visualizations as decentralized, interactive, and part of a broader political co-learning process,[7] incorporating three parallel and interconnected aspects that can generate emancipatory change.

First, visualizations can transform their producers through critical and creative engagement with the tools and methods of meaning-making, but these processes are not automatic. For visualizations to be transformative, they must provoke critical reflection on the systems being represented as well as the methods and context of the production process itself, for example including authors' and viewers' food system understandings in ways that allow others to engage. In this way, learning and experimenting with creative processes to produce and interpret visualizations can serve as scaffolding that makes connections between intellectual and activist pursuits (Sanders-Bustle 2004).

Second, transformation refers to changes in those perceiving and interpreting the visualization. Sanders-Bustle (2003) writes that engagement with visual representations can encourage viewers to be "creative and critical at the same time, to challenge the status quo, and to create possible worlds. In doing so, learners transform understanding and ultimately reconstruct their lives" (14). For example, participatory video has been used to encourage change in attitudes and social behaviour in order to engage and empower groups of people to be involved in development and policy decisions (White 2003). Such engagement may be assisted by transparent and accessible processes for maintaining relationships between diverse users of a visualization.

Third, visualizations can be transformative by challenging dominant power relations and systems of representation. There is a long tradition of using visualizations as counter-hegemonic tools for systemic transformation (Cockcroft and Weber 1977; Arnold and Burke 1983; Freire [1970] 2005;

Marino 1997; Barndt 2011). For example, maps have historically been used as instruments of state propaganda—by manipulating images, emphasizing particular supporting features, and suppressing contradictory information (Monmonier 1991). However, counter-maps have also been used as departure points for broader political engagement and activism, by revealing new understandings of the world as prerequisites for change (Bhagat and Mogel 2008; Fraley 2011). In addition, like the comics noted above, film has also been used as an intellectual tool in struggles against capitalism, imperialism, and colonialism. Gaines (1999, 88) argues that film is part of "revolutionary aesthetics" that go beyond text to circumvent the intellect and appeal to the senses (see also Eisenstein 1988). More recently, and especially with the rise of social media, there has been a resurgence in using visualizations as part of resistance to the commodified culture of global capitalism (Starr 2002; Barndt 2006; Nadus 2009).

Clear and credible methods of assessing and communicating the value of transgressive and productive visualization processes can increase their transformative power. Representations negotiate tension between salience, navigability, and enough richness to support credibility and legitimacy (Cash et al. 2003). Evaluation should capture the extent to which collaborative visualization processes engage an adequate range of perspectives and types of knowledge, address conflicts between perspectives, and translate productively between diverse perspectives.

In the next section, we present three examples of visual methods. Each is written from the perspective of the author involved (Charles, Phil, and David, sequentially), while the four themes discussed above are used as a framework for our collective analysis. Our discussion also pays close attention to how the visualizations navigate tensions between and within the elements of these themes, for example between comprehensibility and fidelity as components of representation, and between polyvocality and transformation in the process of exploring and communicating via visual methods.

Visualization Case Studies

The case studies presented in this section demonstrate the utility of critical visual methods in research, outreach, public exploration, analysis, and teaching. They also demonstrate how visualizations can transgress problematic boundaries in the study of food. Through the analysis of these case studies, we demonstrate the benefits of collaborative visual methods for critical food scholarship. Problem-opening methods such as those shared in these case studies can be hard to evaluate because they do not necessarily arrive at single-authored discrete contributions. Positive evaluations of useful, productive, and transgressive visualization processes help people resist the dominance of the kind of familiar, overly simplified representations of food that tend to close those problem-opening spaces that visual methods might reveal.

Case #1 (Charles): Canadian Food Movement Map

> The rhizome is reducible neither to One nor the multiple… it is composed not of units but of dimensions, or rather directions in motion. It has neither beginning nor end but always a middle (milieu) from which it grows and overspills.
>
> —Deleuze and Guattari (1987, 21)

From 2009 to 2013, I (Charles) was involved in a collaborative, action-based research project exploring the diversity of alternative food initiatives (AFIs) that have emerged amidst concerns about the corporate-led industrial food system. Specifically, our team was interested in exploring the history, structure, and processes of collaboration among the AFIs through provincial networks in Canada along with the evolution and structures of Canada's "food movement." Through this research I worked closely with provincial networking organizations in British Columbia (the BC Food Systems Network), Manitoba (Food Matters Manitoba), Ontario (Sustain Ontario: The Alliance for Healthy Food and Farming), and Nova Scotia (The Nova Scotia Food Security Network), along with over forty organizational representatives and hundreds of individuals across the provinces engaged in food systems transformation efforts. The research included a social network analysis, a provincial survey, in-depth interviews, site visits, and popular education workshops conducted in partnership with provincial network gatherings. The partners were involved from the outset through ongoing discussions, interpreting the data and analyzing and sharing the results at various points throughout the project. A central purpose of the research was to engage in a dialogue about how the networks function in order to make them work better as well as to expand the possibilities for food system solutions.

The initial findings of the research confirmed a number of assumptions and produced new revelations about the Canadian food movement. I observed that the organizations active in the provincial networks were involved in extremely diverse types of work, developed various kinds of relationships with each other, were building cross-sectoral and multi-scale relationships, and were extremely decentralized with few actors holding substantial power

(Levkoe and Wakefield 2014). I characterized the provincial food networks as assemblages constituted by the self-organization of diverse actors through non-hierarchical, bottom-up processes with multiple and overlapping points of contact. Because the research was intended to be community-based, it was important to communicate these findings in a way that did not require sifting through extensive data and hundreds of pages of text, but instead, to represent the food networks as the basis for interactive dialogue.

With the goal of moving beyond textual representations, I worked closely with Claudia Dávila, a Toronto-based graphic designer and illustrator, to develop a visualization that could communicate these ideas to a broad-based audience. We held multiple discussions about the research process, the findings, and the ways we wanted to communicate with the diverse participants. From these conversations, we developed a visualization that attempted to represent the fluid and complex network processes of organizations involved in the Canadian food movement. We discussed the idea of a visualization taking the form of a map-like illustration. The metaphor of a rhizome was used to depict horizontal, underground plant stems with the ability to create complex root systems. Rhizomes can expand relentlessly underground, often lying dormant for years, and re-emerge as healthy plants in different locations when the internal and external conditions are right. Each new plant is connected to the parent but exists as its own independent, flourishing entity. Using this metaphor, we described the food movement as a decentralized network of diverse, self-organizing, interconnected initiatives with no identifiable beginning or end. The metaphor was intended to reflect on the work of transforming the food system by suggesting a different way to think about engaging with resistance. Specifically, most critiques of AFIs have been overly focused on isolated food initiatives and have not adequately considered the actual and existing collaborations (Levkoe 2014). The rhizome highlights the way that relationships between organizations are constantly shifting and transforming knowledge and experience.

The visualization took a number of different forms, including slides used in my teaching at the University of Toronto and in public presentations to describe the way that, like a rhizome, the food movement in Canada has the power to extend its reach, forge growth in new territories, and make connections that may not be visible but are vital and life-supporting. The visualization was also displayed in an article in a popular magazine, a web and print version in *Food: An Atlas* (Levkoe and Dávila 2012), and a version distributed through a major report, and a newsletter (see Figure 1.4).

The visualization was well received by the partners and participants and was used as the basis for further strategic discussions. I observed that

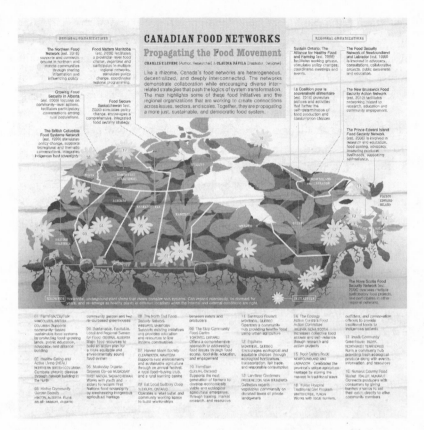

Figure 1.4. Canada food networks map, produced through a collaborative process, by Charles Z. Levkoe (text and research) and Claudia Dávila (illustration and design).

discussions using the visualization helped to recognize and privilege new forms of social empowerment often located on the margins of capitalist society. It also became a part of conversations about developing a diversity of strategies and tactics where incremental projects that take us in the right direction are as important as large-scale public events and protest. As a representation not only of the metaphorically rhizomatic potentials but also of the process of critical analysis of this network, the Food Networks Map provided a check-in for people involved in propagating alternative food initiatives in Canada to compare their understanding of their work on a micro-level with the macro picture suggested in Figure 1.4—and then to re-engage in the accompanying social process to revise or reproduce their efforts. The rhizomatic map—as metaphor of metaphor, and a translation between contemporary social theory trends and popular social organizing—captures in broad strokes the interconnected network of networks that underlie the nascent Canadian food movement. In this way, it functions as an entry point into a discussion about the power of interconnections and growth from below, including the power of that most ubiquitous of rhizomes, the grass-root. The strength of this visualization is not in attention to historical or developmental detail, or in an explicit challenge to power, but rather in its depiction of network as rhizome that is understandable, whether in a class-room or in conversation with those very networks. In addition to helping us perceive social networks less as pre-given structures and more as emergent tracings that result from a series of interactions, the rhizome as a visual metaphor also suggests its own limits. To follow the tracings of relationships, we would need to imagine rootlets or mycelia challenging to represent at this scale. Such a reflexive representation then invites further conceptualization efforts—it paves the way for more visualizations.

Case #2 (Phil): Web-Based Tools for Mapping Civil Society Organizational Impacts

> Actually, of course, a social calamity is primarily a cultural not an economic phenomenon that can be measured by income figures or population statistics.
>
> —Polanyi ([1944] 2001, 164)

One consequence of the austere retreat of the state (across all levels of government) is the rise of non-profit, charity, cooperative, social enterprise, and community-based groups, delivering multiple services and addressing a variety of needs and neglects in our communities—and often stepping in where public funds and programs have been withdrawn. As part of the social economy, these initiatives tend to prioritize community or ecological objectives over profit maximization (Sonnino and Griggs-Trevarthen 2013). Because food is both essential to survival and woven throughout the fabric and relationships of communities, it is a natural starting point for many social and community-based enterprises. According to Connelly et al. (2011), among the most numerous, active, and complex social economy initiatives are those involved in the production, processing, and/or distribution of food, particularly in communities where access to healthy food is a challenge. This rise of the social economy opens the door to a potential post-neoliberal reality where members of each community identify and address their own social program priorities, leading to targeted, useful, community-based solutions.

However, the tenuous nature of grassroots program development means that valuable and poorly acknowledged time is spent chasing funds from a complex mix of individual donors, government departments, and private, charitable, and public foundations and trusts. As a result, one of the critical concerns of community-based food initiatives—as with social economy groups more broadly—is the ability to secure and ensure consistent access to core program funding (Mount et al. 2013).

Aside from stiff competition for a limited pool of resources, a second significant challenge is the ability to effectively communicate the value of the services delivered by these social economy programs. The interconnectedness and complexity of these initiatives, as well as diverse goals that can stretch across the food production/consumption chain, create a challenge for the measurement of social impact. Often the qualities and synergies that make such programs effective and efficient—those that spur innovations in social service delivery—are the most difficult to capture through widely accepted economic and performance measurements (Abi-Nader et al. 2009). As a result, the ability to measure social impact is increasingly prioritized—as a means of both reassuring participants that the goals of their community organizations and initiatives are being adhered to, and demonstrating (to participants and funders) that key objectives are being met. One clear challenge for organizations in the social economy is to devise measures of social impact and effective reporting tools that capture outcomes that are difficult to quantify and yet central to their mission. Corollary challenges involve not losing more ambiguous outcomes in this process, and not allowing clear, mission-oriented impacts of particular funders to efface more complex and systemic community goals, achievements, and even identity constructions (Hetherington 2011).

With the help of program leaders and coordinators at FoodShare—one of Canada's leading community-based urban food organizations—I (Phil) was part of a team that worked to co-create an effective and simple social asset and impact measurement tool, using an open-source concept mapping software and an intentional, reflective process. This exercise was part of a project that mapped networks and resources with leaders from twenty community-based food hubs from across Ontario (Mount and Andrée 2013). One of the challenges in creating an effective visualization for an organization like FoodShare is the sheer scale, diversity, and complexity of its operations. Figure 1.5 shows the visualization that was created through an in-depth case study intended to capture the growth and complexity of FoodShare's programs across the food spectrum, from school nutrition and education to food access. The image represents the various community and

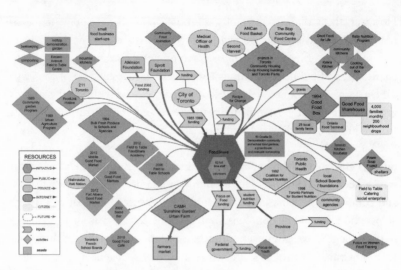

Figure 1.5. FoodShare's organizational map, created through a process of collaborative cartography. Produced by Phil Mount.

public partners, funding sources, and programs using the systematic application of colour, shapes, and flows. Different layers are used to communicate historical development, transporting the user to different spatial planes that capture shifting relationships and funding, or the impact and reach of Food-Share's many programs. An effective visualization of these interconnections demands a multidimensional approach, allowing the user to interact and pursue programmatic detail through layers of representation, including links to organizational web-based resources. As Figure 1.5 demonstrates, a simple two-dimensional image cannot capture the complexity of the organization's reach and effectiveness, and barely manages to accommodate the volume of programs on offer.

With the assistance of the coordinators of FoodShare's School Grown social enterprises, our research team is in the process of mapping the diverse network, initiatives, assets, and outcomes as a means of capturing and sharing innovative practices. The intent is to develop a collaborative mapping process that will help other initiatives within the social economy to identify community assets that exist because of the group's efforts; evaluate the social impact of their various programs; reflect on under-used resources and potential; and develop visually powerful reporting tools that effectively communicate the group's ability to generate social impact, value, and innovations in community development.

In this context, dynamic electronic and web-based tools have the potential to deliver layers of complexity that capture the synergistic value produced through these mutually beneficial relationships, as well as the more direct value produced for each organization. The two-dimensional map allows the organization's members to reflect on relationships and resources, as well as their priorities in program development. However, a web-based visualization could encourage interactive exploration and wiki-development— allowing the users to not only discover but also add to the full complexity of the picture through layers of collaborative creation.

Critical to this effort is the creation of a visual library: an archive and catalogue of cues that help to explain the details and complexity of the system without adding to that complexity, and without simply resorting to text-based explanations.[8] One of the key roles of that library catalogue is to clarify the complexity of program delivery by civil society organizations which, like FoodShare, create collaborative and multi-scalar partnerships between various layers of government, funding agencies, and other civil society organizations in pursuit of their goals, while simultaneously developing innovative social enterprise solutions to supplement their funding.

In the way this concept diagram presents a potential solution to a specific problem, it not only enables participants in complex social networks like FoodShare to orient themselves to others with whom they may share goals, practices, and solidarity, but it may also lead to solving bigger challenges in the NGO sector, food systems work, and the field of food studies. Showing programs, audiences, and support networks, along with other salient social assemblages, this project is exemplary of a trend toward using concept diagramming for documenting and tracking public engagement efforts and accomplishments in food systems work (see Cadieux et al. 2013). For civil society organization initiatives, rich conceptual diagrams can help collaborators develop and share their understandings of their place in food system work. Collaboration between researchers and the public is often heavy in the research set up and conceptualization, but projects also tend to rely on central teams for populating and organizing diagrams.

Food producers, people from NGOs, and academics may be linked in part through overlapping networks, working together on many different projects to try to improve the food system. Understanding what is already being done, who has been involved, and what they have accomplished is a central need that is often articulated. At the same time, although participants often call for the convenience of a unified source of information, they may also be sceptical of centralized control, since there are considerable tensions between different sectors of mainstream and alternative food initiatives, reflecting group identity and differing goals in relation to food and food system improvement. This project suggests how open-source software and transparent processes—for developing representations of the impacts of social organizing around food—can help address these challenges and assist in the development and maintenance of web-based tools as data commons, a popular response to the challenges posed by "big data."

Part of what seems most important about this kind of work (whether it happens electronically or with post-it notes or conversation around a chalkboard) is the ability of many different users to engage in exploring how a system might be understood. This functionality is currently absent from almost all online tools, with interactivity largely limited to preset functions and participation relegated to "comments" sections. Synchronous collaborative document platforms such as Google docs (or wikis) may be transcending such boundaries, but these rarely incorporate significant visual components. Invitations to participate in exploratory visual assemblages appear to need significant scaffolding to make users comfortable with their capacity (and authority) to modify a site. Group norms may also be crucial to establish early and reinforce often. Curatorial functions may be another necessity, although these could be carried out in part by sharing the authority over knowledge with advisory and participant communities to help address concerns about the centralization of power over knowledge by motivated interest groups.

Case #3 (David): Food Ecologies and Their Framings

> Transparency is not necessarily a good thing...sometimes it is good to leave students puzzled, uncertain about what is being said. Even confused.
>
> —Law and Hassard (1999, 9)

At the University of Gastronomic Sciences (UNISG) in Pollenzo, Italy, I (David) have taught a course that deals with methods for doing and representing interdisciplinary food research. Like a small number of other academic institutions, UNISG has remobilized the term *gastronomy*, interpreting it as a union of knowledge-making through both discursive and embodied/experiential modes. Biochemistry, photography, and cured meat tasting classes sit side-by-side, and so students require "methodologies" that are hybrid rather than disciplinary. My methods course dealt with intersubjectivity, multimodal techniques, and making food-system representations (as well as digesting those of others).

Building on critical perspectives gathered during earlier coursework, the students' first assignment is to explore how methodologies are not transparent in producing knowledge. They are asked to produce two material visualizations: (1) a *frame* that shows how material-discursive structures mediate research; and (2) a *personal ecology* that depicts themselves, their food, and other relevant actors. They may use any materials and are encouraged to acknowledge personal bias. Both exercises allow the students to reconceive the concept of "food system": as a self-food network; as a set of discourse and research practices; even as a classroom exercise involving words, pictures, paper, scissors, and pedagogy.

The work of students Charlotte Myer and Ashley Hunka in 2013 illustrates how visualization can be used in pedagogy. As described below (and used with their permission), these visualizations represented and communicated and translated, but also transformed (the students, the teacher, his colleagues, and the assignment itself). They may also operate across time and space, which you, the reader, can judge for yourself. Try the following experiment: Look at the photos below and—before reading the captions or commentaries—let your own perceptions run free. Then come back to the text and read my "authorial" interpretations of the visualizations, but consider how you are equally a participant in making knowledge with them.

Charlotte Myer's frame was originally a rectangle of fresh-baked focaccia with a small circular bite taken out of the centre of it. As more was eaten, the hole grew and the frame revealed a larger landscape behind it, even as the focaccia itself eventually disappeared. In Charlotte's own words:

> I first chose my focaccia frame because it represents one of my favourite foods, one that I eat at least once a week here in Italy, and that to me feels essentially Italian. After all, I'm here for this year in order to study the world through the lens of food, so it only seemed appropriate that I "frame" my world view in that way. However, the more I thought about the focaccia frame in the context of this [course], another thought occurred to me. When I first came to [UNISG], I was hungry. For focaccia, yes, always, but also for learning and knowledge, for expertise in this field that I feel so passionate about. And, as with this frame, the more knowledge and information I consumed, the broader my view became, and the more I was able to see.

The material engagement that this visualization involved enabled Charlotte to reflect on herself and her experience as a student, and it produced an

Figure 1.6. Charlotte Myer and (some of) her focaccia frame, after mid-morning hunger had set in. Photo by David Szanto.

understanding about the temporal variability of frameworks of understanding. Just as food changes in time, so, perhaps should the methods that are used to study it. This example also elegantly represents what happens to many UNISG students. Deeply embedded in their educational process, they *incorporate their subject* during guided tasting lectures and they *are incorporated into their subject* during study trips: their subject-object perceptions dissolve over time. This interpenetration, and the reflexivity it generates, requires a mutability between the framer and the framed. In Charlotte's case, the frame was transubstantiated into the framer; the effect is demonstrated by her own words.

Charlotte's "personal ecology" is shown in Figure 1.7. Flat, folded up, and in action, it demonstrates another type of visualization that, because of its design, becomes an invitation for both material and discursive manipulation.

As a visualization, the giant paper fortune teller demands engagement; it does not fully enact itself if it is not picked up and manipulated. These photos elicit a near-visceral response for me, a frustration born out of wanting to grab the thing and play with it, but not being able to. It recalls childhood and the unknown, a sense of possibility and even magic. By its shape and the shared history of many adults, the fortune teller presents evident affordances—those design-based cues that indicate how a thing should be used.

Charlotte's second visualization suggests the impermanence of food ecologies, of their necessarily interactive nature, of a series of preinscribed potentials, and yet of the power that imagination plays in the way those potentials eventually realize themselves. Through her leveraging of a shared

Figure 1.7. Charlotte Myer's "fortune-teller" food ecology. Photo by David Szanto.

history of play, and because of the permutations of the device, many possible interpretations become available.

In contrast to Charlotte's pleasure in making and reflecting on her food ecology, Ashley Hunka found the process revealing about her own discomfort with text. Her visualization was a response to that discovery, producing value out of the tension between textual stability and food-system impermanence (see Figure 1.8). Ashley wrote:

> I'm going to be honest. In terms of writing, I'm the type of person who gets stuck writing very easily—I'm a perfectionist, I get really anxious about my pieces. And so I made a point to not do that this time. I was cavalier with [it] and just said, Okay, let's go...and then it was just a chronological word association.... [I thought about] Ukrainianism, which is an extremely important aspect of my life, [and being] Canadian, which I'd also say is a huge part of my cultural identity, and living in Germany, and beer, and pretzels.... I wrote on both sides of the page and wrapped everything because it's chronological but it's [also] messy, and it's all connected in a way. So when I did the 3-D snowflake and was wrapping things around and whatnot, that meant something to me because it's all kind of entangled. And in terms of snowflakes, it's a form of Canadian identity and snow and whatever... and also snowflakes are supposed to be meek, and each one is unique, blah blah blah, and so just to show that, yeah, someone else might do ecologies but only I made this particular snowflake.

After bringing it to class, Ashley wanted to get rid of her visualization immediately—she wanted me to take possession of it and not have to see it or deal with it again. Her explanation of how much she hates feeling committed to words demonstrates the tension between language, its symbolic meaning, and the stabilization that writing entails. While clearly useful in representing identities and histories, text can also be too specific, making its creator responsible to its finality. Ashley partially resolved this tension by dutifully going through the text-making process, and then cutting and folding and stapling her page back together to demonstrate the complex, interconnected, and non-chronological nature of her writing—to undermine its textual power over her. The words and their linearity become almost irrelevant in terms of conventional semiotic representation. Much more evident is the shape that ultimately results: the entangled Germanpretzel-Canadiansnowflake-UkrainianChristmasdecoration form.

Figure 1.8. Ashley Hunka's frame-and-ecology. Photo by David Szanto.

The two students' narratives speak to the utility of visualizations as a pedagogical tool, helping to make sense of and communicate a system's complexity that might otherwise overwhelm or seem impenetrable. They also show that visualizations can require discursive explanation to untangle motivation, process, and output, particularly when the makers are embedded in the system that is depicted. Even the odd physical manipulation may be necessary. While this may require additional effort for those on both sides of the visualization process, it is a process that invites intuition and unexpected sense-making, including the inscription of embodied knowledge. Such collaborations remind us of Donella Meadows's (2008) recipe for reclaiming intuition about whole systems: "At a time when the world is more messy, more crowded, more interconnected, more interdependent, and more rapidly changing than ever before, the more ways of seeing, the better" (6).

Conclusion: Synthesizing Collaborative Meaning and Problematizing Food Representation

Examining these cases, we suggest that collaborative visual methods present an opportunity to transgress traditional boundaries by challenging the ways that academic approaches to food studies tend to privilege text, and by challenging the largely unproblematized nature of mainstream food representations. The analysis of these three examples of visualizations add communicative functions that transcend many traditional methods of communication. Although they may slow projects down and add considerable challenges, we have found collaborative visual methods to be invaluable for reflecting our understandings to each other in ways that could be incorporated, critiqued, and revised. Each of our case studies—and the practices we adopted in common from them—enables meaning to be conveyed across a number of accessible channels (via proximity, colour, shape, material, etc.) and offers additional communicative potentials, especially for conveying food system complexity in a more manageable way. These visualizations are examples of how the "author(s)" are decentred as the sole site of knowledge and new sites of knowledge-making are created to include the perceivers/interpreters of visualizations. Arguably, these critical visual methods destabilize common hegemonies in academic and popular text and images and make the representation of knowledge less objective and rational. Beyond the visualization itself, the *processes* of exploring how to make collaborative visual representations explained in each case study have achieved transformative goals in the large collaboration processes in which the representation tasks were embedded: they have fostered effective methods for representation and communication; presented different perspectives; built good entry points and sustained frameworks for collaborative polyvocality; and contested dominant power relations through the transformative food efforts they represent.

Acknowledgments

We thank our many collaborators for working through messy learning processes with us, and the editors, other authors, and reviewers of this collection for engaging in collaboration so wholeheartedly. We also extend ongoing appreciation to those who keep sharing their collaboration and visual tools with us in sessions at the Canadian Association for Food Studies and

Agriculture, Food, and Human Values Society/Association for the Study of Food and Society meetings—and beyond! These have contributed significantly to the development of our shared ideas and practices and can be explored here: http://nourishingontario.ca/magical-mystery-museum-tour/.

Charles Levkoe acknowledges funding support from the Social Science and Humanities Council of Canada. David Szanto acknowledges funding support from the Vanier Canada Graduate Scholarship (SSHRC).

Notes

1 While visualizations are necessarily also visual-centric, making them, especially collaboratively, generally involves greater material, embodied engagement than text-only productions.

2 This is particularly problematic in the commercial food sector, often dominated by graphic communications produced by research and development infrastructures that do not justify or share their methods publicly. (See Mirzoeff 2002, 295, for a discussion of mainstream visual culture in terms of spectacle, display, and surveillance.)

3 Visual representations are never neutral and need to be understood within a specific context. Leppert (1996) writes, "When we look at images, whether photographs, films, videos, or paintings, what we see is the product of human consciousness, itself part and parcel of culture and history. That is, images are not mined like ore: they are constructed for the purpose of performing some function within a given sociocultural mix" (3).

4 By *systematic*, we mean reproducible, attentive, and intentional, yet not necessarily predetermined or prescripted. In many ways, this captures the tension and transgressiveness that exists in visualization work—between academic rigour (knowledge through order) and co-learning (knowledge through participation, engagement, sharing, collaboration) (Jordan et al. 2014).

5 Although reviewing representational theory is beyond the scope of this work, we have been influenced by trends within the social sciences that combine attention to the communicative functions of representations (Nørretranders 1998; Vygotsky 1978), particularly within the realm of public negotiation and collaborative and pedagogical work (White 1995; Novak and Gowin 1984), where scholarly attention to issues of power and knowledge has been informed by postcolonial scholarship (Mitchell 2005).

6 An example is the Gapminder project popularized by Hans Rosling.

7 For more on this distinction, see Hans Enzensberger (1974).

8 This process tests the balance between utility, fidelity, and adequacy in visualizations. Sizes, shapes, and colours cannot be selected at random by users; each must be deliberately chosen to reflect useful information that is either intuitive to the next viewer (for example, the size of the shapes reflects the scale of the initiative that they represent), or easily "explained" by a legend within the visualization. As the scale of the visualization project increases, either the complexity of the legend must increase, or the detail of specific case descriptions must be sacrificed—in order to ensure that those providing feedback and reflections on an initiative are talking about the same things, and so that other initiatives can understand and apply such lessons to their own context. (For more on the ongoing development of the legend used in this set of case studies, and in Figure 1.5, see Mount and Andrée 2013.)

48 CONVERSATIONS IN FOOD STUDIES

References

Abi-Nader, Jeanette, Adrian Ayson, Keecha Harris, Hank Herrera, Darcel Eddins, Deb Habib, Jim Hanna, Chris Patterson, Karl Sutton, and Lydia Villanueva. 2009. *Whole Measures for Community Food Systems: Values-Based Planning and Evaluation.* Fayston, VT: Center for Whole Communities; http://www.wholecommunities.org/practice/whole-measures/.

Arnold, Rick, and Bev Burke. 1983. *A Popular Education Handbook.* Toronto: Ontario Institute for Studies in Education.

Banes, Sally, and André Lepecki. 2012. *The Senses in Performance.* Routledge.

Bantock, Nick. 1999. *The Museum at Purgatory.* New York: HarperCollins.

Barndt, Deborah, ed. 2011. *Viva! Community Arts and Popular Education in the Americas.* Toronto: Between the Lines.

Barndt, Deborah, ed. 2006. *Wild Fire: Art as Activism.* Toronto: Sumach Press.

Bawden, Richard J. 1991. "Systems Thinking and Practice in Agriculture." *Journal of Dairy Science* 74 (7): 2362–73. http://dx.doi.org/10.3168/jds.S0022-0302 (91)78410-5.

Berger, John. 1972. *Ways of Seeing.* London: Penguin Books.

Bhagat, Alexis, and Lize Mogel, eds. 2008. *An Atlas of Radical Cartography.* N.p.: Journal of Aesthetics and Protest Press.

Cadieux, Kirsten Valentine. 2013. A Field Guide to Making Food Good: An Interactive Tool for Participatory Research Supporting Difficult Conversations. Public 1:1. http://public.imaginingamerica.org/blog/article/a-field-guide-to-making-food-good-an-interactive-tool-for-participatory-research-supporting-difficult-conversations/.

Cadieux, Kirsten Valentine, Charles Z. Levkoe, Phil Mount, Matthew Potteiger, Deborah Barndt, Katerie Gladdys, Kathleen Brandt, and Brian Lonsway. 2013. Workshop on Collaborative Public Art and Science Efforts to Visualize Food System Improvement Efforts. Agriculture, Food, and Human Values Society meeting, East Lansing, Michigan.

Cash, David W., William C. Clark, Frank Alcock, Nancy M. Dickson, Noelle Eckley, David H. Guston, Jill Jäger, and Ronald B. Mitchell. 2003. "Knowledge Systems for Sustainable Development." *Proceedings of the National Academy of Sciences of the United States of America* 100 (14): 8086–91. http://dx.doi.org/10.1073/pnas.1231332100. Medline:12777623

Cockcroft, Eva S., and John Pitman Weber. 1977. *Towards a People's Art.* New York: E.P. Dutton.

Connelly, Sean, Sean Markey, and Mark Roseland. 2011. "Bridging Sustainability and the Social Economy: Achieving Community Transformation through Local Food Initiatives." *Critical Social Policy* 31 (2): 308–24. http://dx.doi.org/10.1177/0261018310396040.

Deleuze, Gilles, and Felix Guattari. 1987. *A Thousand Plateaus.* Minneapolis: University of Minnesota Press.

Eisenstein, Sergei. 1988. *Selected Works.* Vol. 1. Edited and translated by Richard Taylor. Bloomington: Indiana University Press.

Eisner, Elliot W. 1997. "The Promise and the Perils of Alternative Forms of Data Representation." *Educational Researcher* 26 (6): 4–10. http://dx.doi.org/10.3102/0013189X026006004.

Enzensberger, Hans Magnus. 1974. *The Consciousness Industry: On Literature, Politics and the Media*. New York: Continuum Books/ Seabury Press.

Fraley, Jill M. 2011. "Images of Force: The Power of Maps In Community Development." *Community Development Journal: An International Forum* 46 (4): 421–35. http://dx.doi.org/10.1093/cdj/bsq011.

Freire, Paulo. [1970] 2005. *Pedagogy of the Oppressed*. New York: Continuum International Publishing Group.

Gaines, Jane M. 1999. "Political mimesis." In *Collecting Visible Evidence*, edited by Jane Gaines and Michael Renov, 84–102. Minneapolis: University of Minnesota Press.

Gonzalez de Molina, Manuel. 2013. "Agroecology and Politics. How to Get Sustainability? About the Necessity for a Political Agroecology." *Agroecology and Sustainable Food Systems* 37 (1): 45–59.

Haraway, Donna J. 1997. *Modest–Witness@Second–Millennium.FemaleMan–Meets–OncoMouse*. New York: Routledge.

Hetherington, Kregg. 2011. *Guerrilla Auditors: The Politics of Transparency in Neoliberal Paraguay*. Durham, NC: Duke University Press. http://dx.doi.org/10.1215/9780822394266.

Homer-Dixon, T. 2011. "Complexity Science." *Oxford Leadership Journal* 2 (1): 1–15.

Howes, David, and Constance Classen. 2013. *Ways of Sensing: Understanding the Senses in Society*. New York: Routledge.

Howett, Catherine M. 1997. "Where the One-Eyed Man Is King: The Tyranny of Visual and Formalist Values in Evaluating Landscapes." In *Understanding Ordinary Landscapes*, edited by Paul Groth and Todd Bressi, 85–98. New Haven, CT: Yale University Press.

Jordan, N., J. Grossman, P. Lawrence, A. Harmon, W. Dyer, B. Maxwell, K.V. Cadieux, R. Galt, A. Rojas, C. Byker, et al. 2014. "New Curricula for Undergraduate Food-Systems Education: A Sustainable Agriculture Education Perspective." *NACTA Journal* 58 (4): 302–10.

Kirshenblatt-Gimblett, Barbara. 1999. "Playing to the Senses: Food as a Performance Medium." *Performance Research* 4 (1): 1–30. http://dx.doi.org/10.1080/13528165.1999.10871639.

Latour, Bruno. 2005. *Reassembling the Social: An Introduction to Actor-Network-Theory*. Oxford: Oxford University Press.

Law, John. 2004. *After Method: Mess in Social Science Research*. New York: Routledge.

Law, John, and John Hassard. 1999. *Actor Network Theory and After*. New York: Wiley-Blackwell.

Leppert, Richard. 1996. *Art and the Committed Eye: The Cultural Functions of Imagery*. Boulder: Westview.

Levkoe, Charles Z. 2014. "The Food Movement in Canada: A Social Movement Network Perspective." *Journal of Peasant Studies* 41 (3): 385–403. http://dx.doi.org/10.1080/03066150.2014.910766.

Levkoe, Charles Z., and Claudia Davila. 2012. "Canadian Food Networks: Propagating the Food Movement." In *Food: An Atlas*, edited by Darin Jensen and Molly Roy, 83. Oakland: Guerrilla Cartography.

Levkoe, Charles Z., and Sarah Wakefield. 2014. "Understanding Contemporary Networks of Environmental and Social Change: Complex Assemblages within Canada's "Food Movement." *Environmental Politics* 23 (2): 302–20. http://dx.doi.org/10.1080/09644016.2013.818302.

Marino, Dian. 1997. *Wild Garden: Art, Education and the Culture of Resistance.* Toronto: Between the Lines.

Massey, Doreen. 1999. "A Global Sense of Place." In *Reading Human Geography: The Poetics and Politics of Inquiry,* edited by Trevor Barnes and Derek Gregory, 315–323. London: Arnold.

Meadows, Donella H. 2008. *Thinking in Systems: A Primer.* White River Junction, VT: Chelsea Green Publishing.

Miller, Elizabeth L. 2011. "Mapping Memories." Guest lecture presented at Encultured Eating: Introduction to Food Studies, October 5, Concordia University, Montreal, QC.

Mirzoeff, Nicholas, ed. 2002. *The Visual Culture Reader.* London: Routledge.

Mitchell, W.J.T. 2005. *What Do Pictures Want? The Lives and Loves of Images.* Chicago: University of Chicago Press.

Mitchell, W.J.T. 1996. "What Do Pictures Really Want?" *October* 77: 71–82. http://dx.doi.org/10.2307/778960.

Monmonier, Mark S. 1991. *How to Lie with Maps.* Chicago: University of Chicago Press.

Mount, Phil, and Peter Andrée. 2013. "Visualising Community-based Food Projects in Ontario." *Local Environment: The International Journal of Justice and Sustainability* 18 (5): 578–91. http://dx.doi.org/10.1080/13549839.2013.788491.

Mount, Phil, Shelley Hazen, Shawna Holmes, Evan Fraser, Anthony Winson, Irena Knezevic, Erin Nelson, Lisa Ohberg, Peter Andrée, and Karen Landman. 2013. "Barriers to the Local Food Movement: Ontario's Community Food Projects and the Capacity for Convergence." *Local Environment* 18 (5): 592–605. http://dx.doi.org/10.1080/13549839.2013.788492.

Nadus, B. 2009. *Arts for Change: Teaching outside the Frame.* Oakland: New Village Press.

Nelson, Connie H., and Mirella L. Stroink. 2014. "Accessibility and Viability: A Complex Adaptive Systems Theory Approach to a Wicked Problem for the Local Food Movement." *Journal of Agriculture, Food Systems and Community Development* 4 (4): 191–206. http://dx.doi.org/10.5304/jafscd.2014.044.016.

Nord, Christiane. 2005. *Text Analysis in Translation: Theory, Methodology, and Didactic Application of a Model for Translation-Oriented Text Analysis.* New York: Rodopi.

Nørretranders, Tor. 1998. *The User Illusion: Cutting Consciousness Down to Size.* New York: Viking Penguin.

Novak, Joseph D., and Bob D. Gowin. 1984. *Learning How to Learn.* Cambridge: Cambridge University Press. http://dx.doi.org/10.1017/CBO9781139173469.

Pauwels, Luc, ed. 2006. *Visual Cultures of Science: Rethinking Representational Practices in Knowledge Building and Science Communication.* Lebanon, NH: Dartmouth College Press.

Polanyi, Karl. [1944] 2001. *The Great Transformation: The Political and Economic Origins of Our Time.* Boston: Beacon Press.

Prosser, Jon. 1996. "What Constitutes an Image-based Qualitative Methodology?" *Visual Sociology* 11 (2):25–34.http://dx.doi.org/10.1080/14725869608583763.

Samuels, Mike, and Nancy Samuels. 1975. *Seeing with the Mind's Eye: The History, Techniques and Uses of Visualization.* New York: Random House.

Sanders-Bustle, Lynn. 2004. "The Role of Visual Representation in the Assessment of Learning." *Journal of Adolescent & Adult Literacy* 47 (5): 416–23.

Sanders-Bustle, Lynn, ed. 2003. *Image, Inquiry, and Transformative Practice: Engaging Learners in Creative and Critical Inquiry through Visual Representation.* New York: Peter Lang.

Santos, Boaventura de Sousa. 2001. "Toward an Epistemology of Blindness: Why the New Forms of 'Ceremonial Adequacy' neither Regulate nor Emancipate." *European Journal of Social Theory* 4 (3): 251–79. http://dx.doi.org/10.1177/13684310122225109.

Sonnino, Roberta, and Christopher Griggs-Trevarthen. 2013. "A Resilient Social Economy? Insights from the Community Food Sector in the UK." *Entrepreneurship and Regional Development* 25 (3-4): 272–92.

Starr, Amory. 2002. "Art and Revolution: Revitalizing Political Protest." In *Global Uprising Confronting the Tyrannies of the 21st Century,* edited by W. Elton and L. Wolf, 33–37. Gabriola Island, BC: New Society Publishers.

Tansey, Geoff, and Anthony Worsley. 1995. *The Food System: A Guide.* New York: Routledge.

Thrift, Nigel. 2007. *Non-Representational Theory: Space, Politics, Affect.* New York: Routledge.

Tufte, Edward R. 2006. *Beautiful Evidence.* Cheshire, CT: Graphics Press.

Vandermeer, John H. 2011. *The Ecology of Agroecosystems.* Mississauga: Jones & Bartlett Learning.

Vygotsky, Lev. 1978. *Mind in Society: The Development of Higher Psychological Processes,* edited by Michael Cole, Vera John-Steiner, Sylvia Scribner, and Ellen Souberman. Cambridge, MA: Harvard University Press.

White, Shirley A. 2003. *Participatory Video: Images that Transform and Empower.* Thousand Oaks: Sage Publications.

White, Stephen K., ed. 1995. *The Cambridge Companion to Habermas.* Cambridge: Cambridge University Press.

Zepel, T. 2013. Visualization as a Digital Humanities ____? Paper presented at HASTAC Conference, 2 May, Toronto, ON. https://www.hastac.org/blogs/tzepel/2013/05/02/visualization-digital-humanities.

CHAPTER 2

Stirring the Pot: The Performativities of Making Food Texts

David Szanto, Carmen Wong, and Jennifer Brady

> Performance studies, to my mind, is less "a thing done" than a set of questions asked, and the more performance studies keeps on the slip, remains diffuse, and resists congealing within delimited boundaries, the greater service it provides to our collective inquiries in the academy.
>
> —Rebecca Schneider (2006, 253)

Food[1] is a performance. Definitions of the term "performance" vary widely—from theatrical presentation to the way materials behave under certain conditions to any act of doing or making. Yet all of these imply a coming together of meaning, matter, and movement, and the effects that such a convergence can produce. Theatre scholar Richard Schechner (1985) has described performance as a "twice-behaved behavior" (35–6), which Marvin Carlson (2004) clarifies as "any behavior consciously separated from the person doing it" (3). In a less anthropocentric framing, Erving Goffman's (1973) position is that performance is "all the activity of a given participant on a given occasion which serves to influence in any way any of the other participants" (25). In a broad reading of "participant," non-human and inanimate things might also be considered to be performers: organisms (Emmel 1973), non-living matter (Barad 2007; Bennett 2009; Ingold 2011), and even text (Callon 2006; Law and Singleton 2000). More recently, and as the epigraph above expresses, theorist Rebecca Schneider (2006) has proposed that performance is a way to keep scholarship "on the slip" (253)—that is, imprecise and perpetually in a state of questioning. Similarly, Jill Dolan (1996) names performance as a strategy for being *transgressive*, in that it requires making manifest the presence, position, and power of the people and processes that "make knowledge."

Given these interpretations, performance is a useful framework that allows us to attend to the ways that material and semiotic actors come together within a given food system. Actors in the material realm may include humans, food and non-food substances, and structures in the human-made and natural environments. The semiotic realm may comprise language, images, symbols and meaning, and interpretation. Their interactions—gestures, processes, movements, interpretations, expressions of ideas—activate the performance. Performance can thus be interpreted as what happens when we "do with food," or perhaps more simply, just when we "do food." For food studies, performance is a framework with which we may holistically theorize and examine the dynamics of food systems and the interactions and effects they comprise.

In other fields, performance is coming to be seen as a way to cross various practices, including in the social sciences and humanities, art and design, physical and biological sciences, activism and politics, community and participative projects, and such already-transdisciplinary realms as complexity and systems theory, feminist technoscience, and ecology. Because of this breadth of exposure, linking food with performance may offer opportunities for building connections within and beyond what is customarily understood as *food studies*. For this and other reasons that we detail below, a turn toward performance is both transgressive and integrative, a destabilizing move that nonetheless can also help balance divergent concerns within research processes.

In contemplating the social, physical, and cultural ecologies that food inhabits, we begin with these questions: How might a performance-based approach enable an understanding of the complexity inherent to food scholarship? How might performance enable research methods that explicitly acknowledge and engage the body and the senses within food-related work? How do we *write* about performance-based research effectively? To explore some possible responses to these questions, we present the insights gained when three individuals, differently positioned as food scholars, educators, students, artists, activists, and professionals, engage in a reflexive food performance. In addition to exploring responses to the questions we pose above, our aim in producing this performance is to express the blurriness of the boundaries between "head work" and "hand work" (Antoniou 2004;

Brady 2011; Heldke 1992), between self and other, between production and consumption, and between other common dualities within scholarship. Our research performance and resulting text therefore transgresses some of the epistemological, disciplinary, spatial, and temporal boundaries that typically shape academic work. We also demonstrate some of the challenges of translating lived experience into text, including the temporal stabilization that is created.

Performance, Performativity, and Food Studies

In the most straightforward sense, food is a performance in that something must be done to plant or animal tissue for it to be considered *food*. These include the chemical and physical transformations of cuisine (e.g., pounding and soaking manioc roots to make them safe to eat), the symbolic gestures that "give" food meaning (e.g., touching a *kirpan* to the collectively made food within the Sikh *langar*), and even the naming processes of food things (e.g., calling a farinaceous mixture of minced edibles stuffed into a container a "pudding"). At the wider scale of food systems, we enact policies that produce laws that in turn regulate production and distribution of grain crops; or we bundle petrochemical commodities with paper-based pork futures, such that military conflicts in one part of the world induce food-market collapses in another.

In a more complex and abstracted sense, food is a performance in that it alters and constitutes our realities. Through acts of growing, procuring, making, and eating food, as well as feeding others, we transform the ecologies around us. Through the same processes, we enact our gender, sexuality, race, and class, we construct our national identity, we code personal and familial memory and cultural tradition, we reinforce cycles of poverty and racism. In this way, performance with food converges with ideas about performativity[2]— that is, that material or social change occurs in the world when words are uttered and gestures are made within certain conditions (Austin 1978; Butler 1988; Derrida 1982). Certainly a number of food scholars have shown that, within the webs of food production and consumption, words can have transformative effects on the material nature of things (Mansfield 2003; Von Hoffmann 2012). Similarly, performativity interprets identity as being produced through everyday acts. Cooking and feeding, for example, can be understood as highly gendered activities; rather than simply being done differently by men and women, they are activities that in part *produce* one's manhood or womanhood (Beoku-Betts 2002; Bugge and Almas 2006; Cairns et al. 2010; Hollows 2003; Smith and Wilson 2004).

As Dolan (1996) suggests, issues of positionality[3] and power arise in performances (including the making of academic texts). We have therefore drawn on Massey's (2013) theorization of place—as a "constellation," "meeting place," or "intersection" of relationships—to allow the responses to and interpretations of performance that we three authors have each had to coexist. We take these perspectives to be true *together*; different translations of experience are not contradictory, but meaningful—that is, defined by distinct intersections of social, cultural, historical, physical, and political relations, Carmen, David, and Jennifer (the authors) relate to food, performance, and scholarly/artistic inquiry in a variety of ways. Nonetheless, we are also connected through our common relationships with the discourses that shape and inform these things. As Schneider expresses, performance is a process and a trajectory, rather than an end point or product. For this chapter, we have chosen to consider performance both as *that which happens* with food (i.e., a research subject), as well as a way to *understand and represent* that which happens with food (i.e., a research process).

Process

Our research process began with the assemblage of the writing team. As the people who eventually performed the research and who are performing this text, we are a part of this project's physical and theoretical apparatus. Our bodies, our academic histories, our social and political trajectories—all are implicated. So too are our kitchens, the tools and appliances therein, our computers, the internet, the Post-It notes we have gathered, and so on. Whereas a "complete" inventory of this apparatus might become silly, the very subject and mode of our investigation compels an acknowledgment that myriad elements—including but not limited to three human beings— performed this work.

The initial team consisted of David and Carmen, a doctoral student in Montreal and a performance maker in Washington, DC, respectively. Following the initial meeting to discuss the book project, Jennifer (another doctoral student, based in Kingston) joined us, and Carmen re-entered academia as a master student (in Coventry, UK, and later Belgrade, Serbia). Our scholarly foci include gastronomy and performativity (David), consuming food in performance (Carmen), and feminist and embodied perspectives of food and food studies scholarship (Jennifer). While Jennifer and David have met a number of times in person, the relationships with Carmen were exclusively long-distance.

Our research process unfolded in three kitchen-based online interviews, following a round-robin structure. Each of us took turns in one of three roles: provocateur, cook, and reflexive interviewer. The provocateur was responsible for emailing the cook and the reflexive interviewer a "provocation," which consisted of an ingredient or theme that was to serve as inspiration for what the cook and interviewer would prepare and then discuss during the interview. During each interview, only the cook and reflexive interviewer participated, although the provocateur had already emailed them her or his "provocation."

Each interview proceeded with a similar process. Upon receiving the provocation, the cook and interviewer arranged a time to meet online, via Skype. In advance of the interview, the interviewer prepared a food item or dish in response to the provocation, and then saved it to eat with the cook. During the interview, the cook also made food that incorporated the theme or ingredient, while the interviewer posed questions. In all cases, the interviewer and cook made different dishes. The interviews were unstructured, and raised various questions about the demonstrative aspects of performance (What are you doing now?), the symbolic aspects (Why did you choose that recipe? How is that ingredient significant to you?), and the transformative and destabilizing aspects (Are you performing for me right now? What are you trying to show/say/do?). At the end of each interview, the cook and the reflexive interviewer ate the food item or dish, continuing the discussion. Following each interview, the cook and the interviewer wrote a reflexive piece about their experience.

Selected excerpts from this work and from the interviews are given below. Upon completion of the cycle, the authors met via Skype to discuss the process, the analysis of the interviews, and additional questions about performance. The production of this text took place individually on our local personal computers, and more collaboratively on Google Drive, with one person taking the lead on various sections, followed by feedback and editing.

Food Performance Interviews

I

Jennifer provokes:

Pick an ingredient that is attached to memories that are both bad and good, positive and negative, happy and sad. The memories that the ingredient is attached to can be from different points in your life.

Carmen cooks:

David stumped me when, without much Skype small talk as I began cooking, he asked if I was performing. I could have reached for Josette Féral's (1982) tripartite definition of manipulation of body, manipulation of space, and how the performer relates to the spectator (171), but the question raised a perplexing self-reflexivity: Which part of this Skype-cooking now was more performative, and which less? The act of responding to Jennifer's provocation, preparing it, and feeding myself was itself effortless. Under the purview of interrogation, self-examination, and evaluation, the cooking actions I enacted while being watched took on a complex, pleasure-wary self-consciousness: Would I provide a tasty-enough performance (or a filling-enough explanation, at the very least) for David's spectating consumption?

I had selected frozen roti-prata (an Indian fried flatbread) to prepare as my ingredient response to Jennifer's food assignment. While manufactured in Singapore, where I grew up, it could not have been farther away from the real stuff. The raw roti-prata I had in front of me was a convenient and problematic store-bought placebo in my reach for nostalgia, reflecting my tenuous definition of home and current state of displacement. Under the lens of Svetlana Boym's (2007) incisive unpiecing of nostalgia, the roti-prata became a holder of both *restorative* and *reflective* nostalgia (13). My performance of cooking it attempted to reconstruct (restore) a taste of "home": all I had to do was remove it from its two protective film layers and plonk it on a heated frying pan, flipping it till golden brown. And yet, I was melancholically (reflectively) aware of the devilish differences in the details: the materiality of the plastic packaging displaced the lined brown paper package it would usually be folded into; the round frozen discs were nothing like the jiggly mounds of white dough that the prata vendor would usually (performatively) stretch thin and fold into layers, into imperfect squares to fry on a ghee-laced griddle.

Despite, or perhaps because of David's digitalized presence—with me, yet not there—the awareness of everyday private acts of hedonism around my food-making was made more keen. I noticed how, in directing this performance of the food and myself, my actions became stretched into a certain awkward elegance, a comfortable floundering into clumsiness, the way one would try to hold a "natural" pose for the camera. In this usually un-spectator-ed act of sprucing up a convenience-nostalgic food, my visual and sensory pleasure in my foods' performance for me was heightened: my taking tactile pleasure in fluffing up the layers of the cooked roti-prata by cradling its oily edges with cupped hands, dipping my forefinger into the small pile of sugar, savouring each granular crunch.

Examining pleasure in meal-making with a distant co-diner brought on other post-prandial reflections on my performative presence in that particular time, space, and circumstance. It became clear that after nine years of cooking to feed others (primarily a partner I recently separated from), I was finally free to cook to please only myself, a welcome albeit strangely lonesome reality. Because I need only cater to my own gustatory desires, I could be capricious and associative in my bricolage of pairing foods and flavours and enjoy my own pleasure of invention, even if the foods I prepared evoked melancholic notions of faraway homes (my estranged Singapore, my rootlessness). My experience falls squarely into Carolyn Korsmeyer's (2008) consideration of how perception becomes worked into the aesthetic experience of food: "Once we notice the extent and character of cognitive experience in eating, what looked to be merely sensuous enjoyment seamlessly extends through discriminatory savouring to recognizing symbol, representation, and a panoply of cultural artifactual properties, leading the tongue and the mind from flavour and sensuous satisfaction to meanings both local and global" (140).

David reflects:

Jennifer's Proustian provocation confounded me. Trying to imagine a memory-laden ingredient, I kept coming up with eating *moments* instead: eating cottage cheese with tomato, carrot, and black pepper after a bad day at kindergarten; getting sick in a train on orange soda from a can; tickling the roasted-mustard crust off a *gigot d'agneau* and onto my fork. Rather than "raw" food matter, *doing* with food—that is, performing—seemed to be the site of good/bad memories.

Eventually, I chose margarine, layered with bad associations (the taste, texture, and disease correlations), neutral ones (my immigrant grandparents' fondness for its "modernity" and kosherness), and, surprisingly, many positive recollections as well. The strongest happy memory is about making *liptauer* with my grandfather, one of his many contributions to the culinary household. When I visited my grandparents, he and I would make it together. Equal parts cream cheese and margarine, cut into slices and alternated on the plate for eventual amalgamation with a big fork. (When my grandfather turned away, I would sneak a yellow-and-white fingerload and eat it, fast and pig-like, loving the melty-salty-milky mixture.) Some tinned anchovies, pressed with a finger onto the same plate and scraped rapidly with a sharp knife to *shred*—not chop—them. Minced white onion, a few tablespoons. All of this mashed, folded, mashed some more; rotate the plate, scrape up the unmixed parts, fold it again, mash it some more. When it was mostly homogeneous, then (very carefully!) a sprinkling of cayenne, always before the paprika so you could see how much you had added. A little more, sometimes, because even then I liked things hot. After: the paprika—lots and lots of it (enacting my pseudo-Hungarian heritage?). More folding and mashing, and when it was all orange and smooth and wonderful, we put it into the brown-glazed crock, sprinkled on a little more paprika, closed it up with the pressure hinge that fit into the little notch on the top of the lid, and put it in the fridge to solidify and mature.

Carmen's own "madeleine," like my margarine, plunged her quickly into the past:

DS: What ingredient did you choose?

CW: Prata—for me, I grew up in Singapore—in the morning you go down to the different stalls, and what's usually open is this Indian place where they make pratas, but by hand. Usually they serve it with a curry; vegetable curry or meat curry. When my partner came with me to Singapore, he would constantly reach for pratas.... I'm going to make two—one savoury and one sweet. Well, one plain, with sugar. In Singapore, they made these prata with an egg inside, or mutton. And now it's all Nutella! and ice cream! like a crêpe, basically.

Pratas are closely connected to the histories of Carmen's relationship with her now ex-partner. Yet because they had also been articulated into our research exercise, the performance I witnessed wefted between Carmen-as-food-scholar and Carmen-as-ex-girlfriend. As Fischer-Lichte (2008) might describe it, I perceived Carmen both "being a body" and "having a body," a character and an actor at once (76). Rather than creating some sort of dichotomy, however, this double state formed a whole.

As Carmen cooked and we talked further, I found that her interpretation of performance tends more toward the theatrical—a representation of an idea, a context of spectacle and spectators, an intentionality—rather than my own more general notion of doing/making.

DS: Do you think about performance when you're not being "a performance person"? That is, what's happening in your head right now?

CW: It's just…dinner. Last night, though, I came back thinking about this. Being a barista at a coffee shop is far more performative, so much so that I break stuff. Trying to have flair, and instead I break a dish, and that's really embarrassing. Far more than what I'm doing in this kitchen.

Carmen also noted that as I was watching her, her webcam watched the kitchen, and her roommates were watching me (on her computer screen). The "perceptual multistability"[4] of this food performance was playing itself out (Fischer-Lichte 2008, 88). The difference between Carmen's and my experience of the "same" situation points to the variable agency of positionality in perception: one performance, yet multiple constellations of performers. So although she was engaged in what might have otherwise been a rather normative cooking experience—a "social drama" (Turner 1982) of sorts—it acquired a greater theatricality, including the effects of the multiple envelopes of spectatorship. The cooking might have been mundane presentation, but the apparatus around it transformed it into it a representation of the mundane, an "exceptional mundane."

DS: What is performing in your space right now? What isn't?

CW: [*looks around*] Maybe I am being performative for you right now. Let me think about that, that's pretty hard. Let's see, there's no one here right now. I think as long as there's an audience, then it's a performance. [*adds onions and chile to pan and shakes*] Okay, I'm performing now. [*bobs her head*] There's so much pleasure in just doing that. The onions and the pan give me pleasure. The food is doing the performing. It's performing for—with—me. The chile is starting to make me cough. [*adds egg to pan, sneezes, laughs*] Ha, chile at work. I'm having trouble getting my chapati off the plate. I had refrigerated it a bit. [*puts it in pan with egg and flips it over*] Sanitation is a performance. Everybody washes their hands more when they are being watched. Usually you stretch it really thin and slap it on the griddle, and then put the egg on it and the onions, if they use onions. But I don't have the space for that now.

Perhaps because she was being observed by me, a relative stranger, Carmen became more attentive to her movements, the built environment around her, and the histories between her and her ingredients. She seemed compelled to make discursive clarifications (about her interpretation of performance and peformativity, about what she was doing, including how and why); she became aware of her cooking and eating gestures (the "elegance" of sautéing onions, the frugality and pleasure in licking up motes of sugar); she justified her culinary liberties ("Beef with chapati—that would never happen. Nutella, or salmon paste on the prata…"). The process of the interview—as I discovered later in my own experience cooking on Skype for Jennifer—shifts attention around, from discourse to action to matter. In performance, both "performer" and "spectator" are made more mindful of the ecology around them, a meeting place of agencies that performatively "create the self, the context, and new rules or laws" (Miller 2007, 231).

II

David provokes:

Here's your ingredient: canned fish (any variety). Have fun!

Jennifer cooks:

I felt relieved upon reading David's food provocation. It was something easy and within reach, both in the sense of having access to the ingredient, and in the sense that making something with canned fish was easily doable. I was acutely aware of my co-participants' expertise in the areas of food, art, performance, and cooking, and I was worried about how my engagement with food would compare with theirs. Although I am not wholly new to this area of inquiry—cooking as a method of knowledge-making is something that I had explored previously (Brady 2011)—the process we had developed felt intimate, and I am not that familiar with either David or Carmen. Having the same ingredient directive alleviated any of my fears about the differences between Carmen and I.

In reflecting on the salience of this experience, I think my apprehension and sense of relief underscores the relationality of corporeality and subjectivity that are performed through interaction with others (Burns 2003; Davies and Gannon 2006). It is through the collaborative planning process with David and Carmen, and later, the cooking and eating interactions with Carmen, that the collaborative knowledge-making process illuminated relationships as sites of intercorporeality and intersubjectivity. Cooking while being interviewed drew my attention to the corporeality of knowledge-making. Lisa Heldke (1992) writes, "I *know* things literally with my body, that I, 'as' my hands, know when the bread dough is sufficiently kneaded, and I 'as' my nose know when the pie is done" (218). The potential for intimacy that emerges from cooking together—as cooking is a sensual act that draws on our embodied knowledge and desires—heightens the potential for danger and vulnerability, but also for a deeper understanding of how difference, and attendant power inequities, are produced (Sharma et al. 2009).

The interviewing process also brought to mind Maria Antoniou's (2004) work, in which she uses cooking to bring to light the complexities of negotiating her Cypriot and lesbian identities that are often difficult and too painful to "work loose" through more academic, cognitive performances (130). She writes that cooking as a form of inquiry "challenges the mind/body binary. And redefines cooking as 'mentally-manual,' 'theoretically practical,' a 'thoughtful practice.' As both 'hand work' and 'mind work' [that] helps me to grasp and articulate my experiential complexity. Writing often traps me in my head, but cooking acknowledges the holism of my body. Recognizes my body as agent" (130). In challenging the mind/body binary, Antoniou feels free to explore and imagine alternate possibilities because her cooking is not subject to scrutiny in the same way as her academic work. Similarly, as I was being interviewed by Carmen, I was able to work through aspects of my identity that sometimes feel incoherent as they compete for my attention and physical and emotional resources. Provoking this exploration with a call to cooking allowed me, like Antoniou, to understand my struggles in the context of my everyday life and not via the lens of theory, even though our conversation evoked important issues that may provide the matter for later theorization.

Still, being interviewed while cooking was awkward and vulnerable, but also enlightening. Being interviewed made me aware of the taken-for-granted things that I do in the kitchen, the way that I do them, and why. Also, I wished that I had something really meaningful to cook. I would have liked to prepare something that would make for a juicier performance, something that had a bit more flair. I make tuna sandwiches every week, mostly for my daughter who loves them. The tuna sandwich very much represents my relationship with cooking, feeding, caring (for myself and others) right now; a mother, a partner, a grad student, the family cook. Cooking used to be something I spent a lot of time doing: building skills, picking apart and assembling recipes, inventing new dishes, and spending all day in the kitchen to make something indulgent and fabulous for dinner. My cooking life now is considerably stripped back in comparison. I felt like a bit of a fraud talking about food and performance when, although of course my making the tuna sandwich is performative on many levels, it felt like it made for a bit of a dull performance. I felt myself trying to almost justify that I used to make "fancy" tuna sandwiches with curry powder and bits of finely chopped up green apple, toasted almond slices, and green onion on homemade bread. I used to cook. Now I just glop mayonnaise into the tuna and slap it on bread. This isn't to say that I wish my reality were permanently different, but that my relationship with cooking is so very changed. It is less about pleasure and artfulness, and more about feeding and caretaking— tasks that are sometimes less joyful than the way that I used to "do" cooking. This change in the way that cooking features in my life speaks to a broader shift in my social, cultural, and economic positioning and thereby, my every- day performance of self, such as the way that I "do" my gender, race, and class subjectivities (West and Zimmerman 1987).

I am also reminded of Gloria Anzaldua's (1999) writing on "invoked art," a concept that blends together the cognitive and emotional, the prac- tical and the theoretical, performance and dialogue. She contrasts invoked art, familiar from her Mexican-American childhood to the art cultures of Western European society in which is art is "dedicated to the validation of itself" and lacks performative and ritualistic power. In describing invoked art, she writes, "My people did not split the artistic from the functional, the sacred from the secular, art from everyday life" (88). Rather, for Anzaldua, invoked art is a living thing, an emerging process, and a part of everyday life and survival that is not focused on the outcome or the finished product. Art can change and maintain its integrity, and in fact part of its expression is its consumption and subsequent evolution. Anzaldua's writing reminds me that my sense of vulnerability and "survival cooking," as I might call it, is an art form, a form of creative expression that is emotional, relational, embodied, colourful, and performative.

Carmen reflects:

Jennifer apologized for the simplicity of her performance: fixing a tuna salad sandwich for a quick lunch after a busy week. I for one appreciated the sheer un-fussiness of her choice, which conjured artist Alison Knowles' *Identical Lunch* project (1967–73). Knowles' regular midday meal of "a tuna fish sand- wich on wheat toast with lettuce and butter, no mayo, and a cup of soup or a glass of buttermilk" (0:00:29) developed into a performance series that included getting other Fluxus artists to eat the same lunch. Her reperformances of it in different countries used local variations that simulated the stock ingredients; in another performance, the contents of the lunch were blended to a soup, rendering truly identical portions of the meal.

Cecilia Novero's (2010) food-focused description of the Fluxus movement in her chapter on neo-avant-garde artists is a particularly colourful one; this politically engaged art movement from the 1960s "declared that everything is art or deserving to be called art, and its members organized numerous eclectic activities, festivals, music and theatrical events. Through simple performative acts of language—declarations—they created new fields and ideas 'for' the experience of art" (240). Artists from the Fluxus movement created or "scored" simple performative acts "out of the experience of the everyday" (240). Jennifer's tuna-sandwich performance however, may seem to stand apart from Knowles' focus on everyday repetition as part of art, but it reflected her personal tastes, peculiarities, socio-economic standing, and hyper-awareness of her layered role of mother-academic-partner. During our Skype conversation, when Jennifer mused on her performing with food becoming intrinsically stitched to mothering, Elsbeth Probyn's (2000) connection of eating with identities became particularly resonant: "As eating reactivates the force of identities, it also may enable modes of cultural analysis that are attentive to the categories with which we are now perhaps overly familiar: sex, ethnicity, wealth, poverty, geopolitical location, class and gender" (9).

To forge a closer connection between the two different performances of tuna fish sandwiches conducted and eaten, I have chosen to record, frame, textualize, and lyrically translate the content of this lunch interview with Jennifer as an composition of event scores modelled after (and in homage to) the notated Fluxus performance events worksheets (Friedman et al. 2002). The Lefebvrean (1987) construct of everydayness as a "common denominator" that "reveal[s] the extraordinary in the ordinary" (9) is something the scores attempt to capture from our interview, and a way to weave in how performativity operates in the everyday. Informed by the signifying details Jennifer discusses extensively (doing food as mothering), or infers but doesn't highlight (eating with her fellow academics at work), this series of notated, orchestrated directions become an interpreted distillation of the roles Jennifer plays in her performances with food. The use of scoring accentuates the performances with food that are prevalent within our research methodology (of Skype-cooking), and simultaneously implicates the repetitive and repeatable nature of Jennifer's performance, as it invites whoever is so inclined to read and enact these actions as a re-performance.

Each score denotes the year the performance was first performed, usually in the performer's home unless otherwise noted.

Composition for a Lunch

1 female performer, engaged in some kind of academic occupation, joined by lunching colleagues at their common place of work.

Pour water into a glass.

Open a new browser page on your computer.

Visit www.ravelry.com. Eat lunch while browsing website.

At 2:00 p.m., boil some water for tea.

Retrieve good dark chocolate (or homemade cookies) from desk drawer.

Savor tea with chocolate.

(Date unknown)

Variation No. 1 for Composition for a Lunch: Tuna Sandwich

This performance variation must take place with an audience over Skype videochat. Venue should include as invisible scenography, a learning tower, a copy of "Tin Fish Gourmet," and a sink full of dirty dishes. The responsibility of the spectator is to ask questions about whether this is a performance throughout the performance.

Performer makes a tuna-fish sandwich with bread chosen to signify the performer's socio-economic status and taste preferences, in the following manner:

Open can of tuna, drain it *well*, scrape contents of can into a soup bowl with a fork.

Add two heaping tablespoons of cold mayonnaise to tuna. Mix. It is imperative that the mayonnaise is cold, and that other ingredients that could be added to the tuna are considered and discussed.

Butter the bread. Spread tuna salad on bread.

Eat the tuna sandwich with a glass of water.

Extract energy from this meal to accomplish tasks for the day.

2013

Dream of a Sourdough Mother

Engage in the following morning ritual with your young daughter:

Take care to attend and be mindful of the food in this daily performance of breakfast.

You might ask: What would you like to eat? How does this taste? Is the texture pleasing? Are you feeling full? What else is your body feeling?

Raise curiosity, mimesis, body-awareness.

2012–ongoing

Delegated Performance (for Derek)

Andante

Do scramble eggs.
Do cook French onion soup.
Do not make coffee.

(Date unknown)

Meal with Unbroken Chairs

Instructions may be revised by invited guests, whose wishes must be honoured.

Invite guests to have a meal as part of this performance.
Prepare for this meal first by shopping for fresh ingredients.
Use a tasty, tried-and-true recipe. Cook this dish from scratch.
Serve this to guests who should be seated on unbroken chairs.

(Date unknown)

III

Carmen provokes:

Cook with something you have pilfered. Yep. Stolen. Shoplifted. Something you could have but did not pay for, whether in cash or barter. I will let you manage the risk factor. Have fun not getting caught!

David cooks:

Carmen's invitation to steal was so transgressive! I was delighted. The very evening before, I *had* stolen some food—a couple of handfuls of pralinized almonds—from a dinner reception following a food-and-art colloquium. The caterer was a friend, and the context permitted a certain degree of bad-boy behaviour. Later, however, when faced with stealing from a shop, I was torn. I love breaking rules, but to steal from a food store felt deceitful and unfair. I ended up going next door to Frères Sakaris and popping a sprig of cilantro into the plastic bag that held the flat-leaf parsley I was going to buy anyway. It was literally one stalk with five floppy leaves on it, and I still felt I had betrayed a neighbourhood relationship.

I came to realize that I figure theft as a reaction against the domination of power structures—whether abstract or concrete, in the form of individuals or organizations. Because I wield both the economic and social privilege that keeps me feeling pretty empowered, there are few occasions in which I would want to steal as an act of disruption. Sakaris, as a medium-sized food shop, roughly parallels my own socio-economic status. To steal from them made no sense.

By contrast, the evening of my eager praline poaching *was* a context in which I felt disruptive. The scene: the house of a wealthy real estate mogul, lots of great art on the walls, a community of international food academics, and piles of luxurious foodstuffs. My quasi-lefty genes, acting in concert with the scenography (plus a few glasses of The Hegemony's wine), drew me to the kitchen and to the bounteous leftovers. I nicked the almonds and ran out the door, cackling silently.

Afterwards, and in talking with Jennifer, I felt that I had gotten away with two relatively justifiable thefts. Neither the caterer nor Sakaris felt a loss either materially or symbolically. Trust was not lost (unless perhaps they read this text) and I had not betrayed my own self. I did what Carmen required, without serious compromise. Yet in a slowly creeping way, I started to view Carmen differently—very slightly. My more reactive response was: How *dare* she require me to steal! Does she think I would *do that*? She clearly doesn't know me, and I'm not sure I want to know *her*. My more reasoned response (at which I quickly arrived, Carmen) was that, in proposing an act outside of my nominal behaviour, Carmen temporarily displaced her own self from my personal ecology. Her simple provocation, meeting the resistances of my reiterated identity, became a "performative utterance" (Austin 1978). It acted—if only briefly—to situate her outside my moral frameworks.

During the Skype interview, I found it difficult to talk and cook at once. I had to keep stopping "making" in order to start "thinking" about Jennifer's questions. The "mentally manual practices" of cooking (Heldke 1992) were intensive enough that I couldn't seem to process abstract notions simultaneously. Similarly, in daily experience, I don't like cooking with someone else or chatting while I'm making food. Cooking occupies my whole self, rather than being a sideline to "more important" social interactions. The angles of my kitchen support this. At the cutting board and sink I can remain "off-stage," away from the gaze of my guests; at the stove, my back is to the living room. But with Jennifer, the point was to *demonstrate* what I was doing: the space of my kitchen became a "stage," and my actions became showier. The gaze of my laptop's webcam performed as well, keeping me in a self/other mode of sequential *doing-and-representing* (Hacking 1987), rather than a more integrated self/self mode of *being*. I wasn't trying to be theatrical, yet I became more conscious of my movements, of my agency in framing the images on both Jennifer's computer screen and my own, of the responses I was getting from Jennifer, and of my choreography around the kitchen and with my food.

In kitchens other than my own, I often feel a strong sense of theatrical improvisation or "*bricolage*" (Callon 2006) with the socio-technical environment around me. In my partner's loft, the open kitchen features a central island at which guests generally assemble. While Jean entertains verbally, I entertain gesturally behind him, my back to his. He faces the guests; I face the counter and stove. I am nonetheless highly aware of my manipulation of tools and food, of my occasional interjections into conversation, and of the ways that this series of performances are being perceived. When dinner finally arrives on the table, I am almost not interested in our guests' responses to my food. They eat it, but it is a residue of the performance, rather than the performance itself.

Jennifer reflects:

I was at first intrigued by Carmen's ingredient statement; I thought it was brilliant and provocative, until I actually had to consider *stealing* something. The prospect of stealing food, rather than some other item, made stealing even more fraught. Getting caught stealing food would be humiliating in many ways, and I think it challenged my middle-class sense of privilege (entitlement?) not only to food, but to a dignified way of gaining access to food. Lucy Long (2002) notes that the "physical presence and pervasiveness" of food can "ground" theory but also "illuminate" it (81). The impending humiliation and my pride and sense of entitlement about how I gain access to food through the marketplace are salient examples of the ways in which I perform my subjectivity, particularly my middle-class positionality, through food. In the end, I decided I could not steal something from a store or a shop. I finally decided to pilfer Halloween candy from my daughter's stash, which she had worked hard to gather a few nights before.

As the interviewer, I was struck by how intimate it felt to be in David's kitchen. Geographers, particularly feminist geographers, have drawn attention to the importance of space, specifically kitchen space, in the performance of identity and power (Christie 2006; Robson 2006). The kitchen space was important in enlivening embodied knowledges that would not be present had we met in a more academic space (i.e., office, library). Being immersed in the kitchen space, in which performances of identity and power take place through food, heightens the corporeality of the experience and makes more available embodied knowledge. Cooking together in the kitchen space brings to the fore knowledges that are significant to the performativity of identity and are often otherwise left out of academic inquiry.

Discussion and Summary

Rather than simply telling the reader how and why we envision performance as an important future approach to food scholarship, our goal with this chapter has also been to activate performance in both the construction and interpretation of a text. Performance, and related theoretical concepts such as performativity, show how food and food scholarship can be understood as boundary objects: differently enacted and differently perceived by each individual, yet linked through multiple commonalities. In this way, performance both transgresses and transects traditional academic disciplines, methods, and epistemologies. Our cyclical interview process and reflexive responses demonstrate that performance requires different means of being attentive to the multiplicities of food, as well as to the ways in which these multiplicities are implicated in the "doing" or performativity of complex identities and relationships (West and Fenstermaker 1995).

In each of the interviews, we found ourselves becoming sensitized to the built and social environment around us, to our own actions, and to the sense of our words. That the interviews took place over Skype, but within the intimate space of our kitchens, produced a voyeuristic effect in some of us, both for the "watcher" and the "watched." Carmen's attention was drawn to her roommates' presence, as well as her roommates' attention to what she was engaged in. Jennifer became pre-emptively self-conscious about her concomitant identities and the ways they revealed themselves (to herself, to Carmen, and now to the reader) through her cooking choices and actions, as well as the histories that came before. David, too, was made aware of the doing-showing connections inherent to thieving, cooking, talking, and movement. Even as we performed various acts and made utterances in response to each other's questions, we performed ourselves, simultaneously becoming present to those processes of self-making. Performance can thus be seen as a *discursive framework*, a way to characterize food and foodways as complex systems; yet performance can also be an *enacted method*, a tool with which to examine food's complexity.

In both senses, performance requires that we view space and process, ingredients and actions, relationships and power, and bodies and minds as elements of an extensive assemblage—a material-discursive ecology of food. It also brings attention to the ways that such a system can present different profiles, coming into focus through action and text. As food scholars, our actions and our texts parse these profiles differently, yet these distinctions also elide the co-production of food knowledge. As humans who make and eat and theorize about food, and who are differently positioned in relation to such knowledge and to the academy, we must learn to dance with these performative contradictions. Somewhere in this dance—in the *between space* bounded by separation and holism, by lived experience and representations about lived experience—our so-called food realities start to emerge.

Five key themes emerge from the literature on performance theory, themes that also showed themselves to be relevant during the process of producing this chapter: representation, production, transformation, destabilization, and complexification. Our interview process demonstrated that in representing a given performance with food, we produced different framings of its significance, sometimes overlapping, sometimes divergent. We translated and transformed our lived experience through the production of texts about it. In the perceptual space between these texts, another, more complexified rendering starts to emerge. Performance as a method therefore seems to require both polyvocality and ongoing reflexivity, in order to make sense of the complex and emerging realities of performance as a subject. This process also decentralizes knowledge, situating it in the bodies of each actor. Neither Jennifer nor Carmen nor David singly "own" the knowledge produced here, nor can they purport to be experts in this method. Indeed, *through the performative participation of those who then read this text*, what has been learned or known continues to be diffused across multiple bodies.

Our final performance-related theme—destabilization—is particularly significant in the context of this collection. Performance disrupts the epistemological formations that have traditionally structured authority, teaching, and learning, bringing to the fore the relationality and inter-corporeality that have frequently been silenced as sites of knowledge production in the academy (Burns 2003; Ellingson 2006; Lupton 1996; Sandelowski 2002; Sharma et al. 2009). Moreover, performance implicates that materiality and bodily action are already present in the making of conventional academic "outputs"—that is, text. This is in contrast to the historic views structured by androcentric, Cartesian systems of knowing, which privilege cognition, reason, objectivity, and deduction. Curtin and Heldke (1992) point to this paradigm of knowledge production as being at the root of the long-standing disdain for food scholarship, something that has recently, and fortunately, shifted. Yet, by treating food not only as something to be thought *about*, but also as a practice to be thought *with*, that paradigm can be remade.

Ultimately, performance as a method in food scholarship can transgress the boundaries that unproductively insulate communities. While scholars, activists, professionals, and artists have started to chip away at these divides, they often remain doggedly intact. We believe that food performances of the sort made and discussed here can bridge the public, productive spaces of academia with the private, reproductive space of the home, as well as other hybrid spaces that food necessarily embraces. Rather than upholding the notion that private, commercial, and "non-scholarly" public spaces are separate from and irrelevant to knowledge-producing activities, our performance-interview cycles demonstrate that all spaces and their everyday undertakings are potential— and performative—sites of valuable food knowledge.

Acknowledgements

David Szanto gratefully acknowledges the support of the Vanier Canada Graduate Scholarship (SSHRC) and the Fonds québécois de recherche— Société et culture.

Jennifer Brady would like to thank the Social Sciences and Humanities Research Council for its generous support.

Notes

1 In this chapter, we use the word "food" to express both edible substances and their symbolic representations, food-making and consumption processes, as well as food systems, regimes, milieus, webs, etc.

2 Initially conceived in relation to linguistic philosophy, performativity has come to be adopted by theorists in political science, gender studies, queer theory, art and design, economics, biogeophysical and human ecology, science and technology studies, and many other fields. In addition to the references provided, see: Butler 1990 and Miller 2007. On the related concept of "doing" identity, see West and Fenstermaker 1995.

3 Positionality is a theoretical concept developed by feminist thinker Linda Alcoff (1988) and is widely used as a concept to understand the ways in which one's position in the world, relative to systems of privilege and oppression, impact one's world view. Positionality refers to the aspects of one's identity that, together, influence one's perspective of the world, including what one values as knowledge.

4 Perceptual multistability suggests that in any context, a state of simultaneous, different realities coexist, and that each individual within that moment activates her own reality through perception. This notion further implicates perception as

an active role, and the perceiver as a participant-performer in the situation, rather than a passive "audience" or "spectator" of it.

References

Alcoff, Linda. 1988. "Cultural Feminism versus Post-Structuralism: The Identity Crisis in Feminist Theory." *Signs* 13 (3): 405–36.

Antoniou, Maria. 2004. "My Cypriot Cookbook: Re-imagining My Ethnicity." *Auto/Biography* 12 (2): 126–46. http://dx.doi.org/10.1191/0967550704ab009oa.

Anzaldua, Gloria. 1999. "The Path of Red and Black Ink." In *Borderlands/La Frontera: The New Metiza*, 00–00. San Francisco: Aunt Lute Books.

Austin, John Langshaw. 1978. *How to Do Things with Words*. Cambridge, MA: Harvard University Press.

Barad, Karen. 2007. *Meeting the Universe Halfway*. Durham, NC: Duke University Press. http://dx.doi.org/10.1215/9780822388128.

Bennett, Jane. 2009. *Vibrant Matter: A Political Ecology of Things*. Durham, NC: Duke University Press. http://dx.doi.org/10.1215/9780822391623.

Beoku-Betts, Josephine A. 2002. "'We Got our Way of Cooking Things': Women, Food, and Preservation of Cultural Identity Among the Gullah." In *Food in the USA: A Reader*, edited by Carole Counihan, 277–94. New York: Routledge.

Boym, Svetlana. 2007. "Nostalgia and its Discontents." *Hedgehog Review* 9 (2): 7–18.

Brady, Jennifer. 2011. "Cooking as Inquiry: A Method to Stir Up Prevailing Ways of Knowing Food, Body, and Identity." *International Journal of Qualitative Methods* 10: 321–34.

Bugge, Annechen B., and Reidar Almas. 2006. "Domestic Dinner: Representations and Practices of a Proper Meal among Young Suburban Mothers." *Journal of Consumer Culture* 6 (2): 203–28. http://dx.doi.org/10.1177/1469540506064744.

Burns, Maree. 2003. "Interviewing: Embodied Communication." *Feminism & Psychology* 13 (2): 229–36. http://dx.doi.org/10.1177/0959353503013002006.

Butler, Judith. 1988. "Performative Acts and Gender Constitution: An Essay in Phenomenology and Feminist Theory." *Theatre Journal* 40 (4): 519–31. http://dx.doi.org/10.2307/3207893.

Butler, Judith. 1990. *Gender Trouble: Feminism and the Subversion of Identity*. New York: Routledge.

Cairns, Kate, Josée Johnston, and Shyon Baumann. 2010. "Caring about Food: Doing Gender in a Foodie Kitchen." *Gender & Society* 24 (5): 591–615. http://dx.doi.org/10.1177/0891243210383419.

Callon, Michel. 2006. "What Does It Mean to Say That Economics Is Performative?" In *Do Economists Make Markets? On the Performativity of Economics*, edited by Donald MacKenzie, Fabian Muniesa, and Lucia Siu, 311–57. Princeton, NJ: Princeton University Press.

Carlson, Marvin. 2004. *Performance: A Critical Introduction*. 2nd ed. New York: Routledge.

Christie, Maria Elisa. 2006. "Kitchenspace: Gendered Territory in Central Mexico." *Gender, Place and Culture* 13 (6): 653–61. http://dx.doi.org/10.1080/09663690601019828.

Curtin, Deane W., and Lisa M. Heldke. 1992. "Introduction." In *Cooking, Eating, Thinking: Transformative Philosophies of Food*, edited by Lisa Maree Heldke and Deane W. Curtin, xiii–xviii. Bloomington: Indiana University Press.

Davies, Bronwyn, and Susanne Gannon. 2006. "The Practices of Collective Biography." In *Doing Collective Biography*, edited by Bronwyn Davies and Susanne Gannon, 1–15. Berkshire, UK: Open University Press.

Derrida, Jacques. 1982. *Margins of Philosophy*. Translated by Alan Bass. Chicago: University of Chicago Press.

Dolan, Jill. 1996. "Producing Knowledges That Matter: Practicing Performance Studies Through Theatre Studies." *TDR* 40 (4): 9–19. http://dx.doi.org/10.23 07/1146587.

Ellingson, Laura L. 2006. "Embodied Knowledge: Writing Researchers' Bodies into Qualitative Health Research." *Qualitative Health Research* 16 (2): 298–310. http://dx.doi.org/10.1177/1049732305281944.

Emmel, Thomas C. 1973. *An Introduction to Ecology and Population Biology*. New York: Norton.

Féral, Josette. 1982. "Performance and Theatricality: The Subject Demystified. Translated by Teresa Lyon." *Modern Drama* 25 (1): 170–81. http://dx.doi.org/10.1353/mdr.1982.0036.

Fischer-Lichte, Erika. 2008. *The Transformative Power of Performance: A New Aesthetics*. New York: Routledge.

Friedman, Ken, Owen Smith, and Lauren Sawchyn, eds. 2002. *The Fluxus Performance Workbook*. Performance Research e-publication. http://monosko.org/File:Friedman_Smith_Sawchyn_eds_The_Fluxus_Performance_Workbook.pdf.

Goffman, Erving. 1973. *The Presentation of Self in Everyday Life. Woodstock*. Woodstock, NY: Overlook Press.

Hacking, Ian. 1987. *Representing and Intervening : Introductory Topics in the Philosophy of Natural Science*. Cambridge: Cambridge University Press.

Heldke, Lisa M. 1992. "Foodmaking as a Thoughtful Practice." In *Cooking, Eating, Thinking: Transformative Philosophies of Food*, edited by Lisa Maree Heldke and Deane W. Curtin, 203–29. Bloomington: Indiana University Press.

Hollows, Joanne. 2003. "Oliver's Twist: Leisure, Labour and Domestic Masculinity in the Naked Chef." *International Journal of Cultural Studies* 6 (2): 229–48. http://dx.doi.org/10.1177/13678779030062005.

Ingold, Tim. 2011. *Being Alive: Essays on Movement, Knowledge and Description*. London: Routledge.

Knowles, Alison. 1967–73. *Identical Lunch*. Accessed 2 Jan 2014 from http://vimeo.com/36770058.

Korsmeyer, Carolyn. 2008. "Taste, Food and the Limits of Pleasure." In *Aesthetic Experience*, edited by Richard Shusterman and Adele Tomlin, 127–42. London: Routledge.

Law, John, and Vicky Singleton. 2000. "Performing Technology's Stories: On Social Constructivism, Performance, and Performativity." *Technology and Culture* 41 (4): 765–75. http://dx.doi.org/10.1353/tech.2000.0167.

Lefebvre, Henri. 1987. "The Everyday and Everydayness. Translated by Christine Levich." *Yale French Studies* 73 (73): 7–11. http://dx.doi.org/10.2307/2930193.

Long, Lucy. 2002. "Food Studies: Interdisciplinary Buffet and Main Course." *Appetite* 38 (1):81–82.

Lupton, Deborah. 1996. *Food, the Body and the Self.* London: Sage.

Mansfield, Becky. 2003. "Fish, Factory Trawlers, and Imitation Crab: The Nature of Quality in the Seafood Industry." *Journal of Rural Studies* 19 (1): 9–21. http://dx.doi.org/10.1016/S0743-0167(02)00036-0.

Massey, Doreen. 2013. *Space, Place and Gender.* New York: John Wiley and Sons.

Miller, Hillis J. 2007. "Performativity as Performance/Performativity as Speech Act: Derrida's Special Theory of Performativity." *South Atlantic Quarterly* 106 (2): 219–35. http://dx.doi.org/10.1215/00382876-2006-022.

Novero, Cecilia. 2010. *Antidiets of the Avant-Garde: From Futurist Cooking to Eat Art.* Minneapolis: University of Minnesota Press.

Probyn, Elspeth. 2000. *Carnal Appetites: FoodSexIdentities.* London: Routledge.

Robson, Elsbeth. 2006. "The 'Kitchen' as Women's Space in Rural Hausaland, Northern Nigeria." *Gender, Place and Culture* 13 (6): 669–76. http://dx.doi.org/10.1080/09663690601019869.

Sandelowski, M. 2002. "Reembodying Qualitative Inquiry." *Qualitative Health Research* 12 (1): 104–15. http://dx.doi.org/10.1177/1049732302012001008.

Schechner, Richard. 1985. *Between Theater and Anthropology.* Philadelphia: University of Pennsylvania Press. http://dx.doi.org/10.9783/9780812200928.

Schneider, Rebecca. 2006. "Intermediality, Infelicity, and Scholarship on the Slip." *Theatre Survey* 47 (2): 253–60. http://dx.doi.org/10.1017/S0040557406000238.

Sharma, Sonya, Sheryl Reimer-Kirkham, and Marie Cochrane. 2009. "Practicing the Awareness of Embodiment in Qualitative Health Research." *Qualitative Health Research* 19 (11): 1642–50. http://dx.doi.org/10.1177/1049732309350684.

Smith, Greg M., and Pamela Wilson. 2004. "Country Cookin' and Cross-dressin': Television, Southern White Masculinities, and Hierarchies of Cultural Taste." *Television & New Media* 5 (3): 175–95. http://dx.doi.org/10.1177/1527476403260644.

Turner, Victor. 1982. *From Ritual to Theatre.* New York: Performing Arts Journal Publications.

Von Hoffmann, Viktoria. 2012. "The Rise of Taste and the Rhetoric of Celebration." In *Celebration: Proceedings of the Oxford Symposium on Food and Cookery 2011,* edited by Mark McWilliams, 356–63. Totnes, UK: Prospect Books.

West, Candace, and Don H. Zimmerman. 1987. "Doing Gender." *Gender & Society* 1 (2): 125–51. http://dx.doi.org/10.1177/0891243287001002002.

West, Candace, and Sarah Fenstermaker. 1995. "Doing Difference." *Gender & Society* 9 (1): 8–37. http://dx.doi.org/10.1177/089124395009001002.

CHAPTER 3

Problematizing Milk: Considering Production beyond the Food System

Jennifer Brady, Victoria Millious, and Matt Ventresca

Walk down the dairy aisle of your nearest grocery store and notice the plurality of milk. Available for purchase is a range of cow and goat milks; soy and nut milks; milks that have been fortified with vitamins D and A; lactose-free milk; milk with 1-percent, 2-percent, or 3.5-percent fat content; milk sold in quantities of 1 litre, 2 litres, and 4 litres; milk packaged in plastic, cardboard, and glass; milk that is organic; milk emblazoned with pictures of farms, with mountains, or milk sold in packaging devoid of pastoral iconography. Each milk product carries with it a genealogy, an inheritance comprising decades of agricultural practices and organized labour, of scientific studies, dietetic trends, and marketing savvy. According to Barthes (1972), milk's mythic density, its soothing, enveloping purity, renders it an everlasting exotic substance and national opiate (60–1). Regardless of positionality, we as food scholars, citizens, and eaters have to engage with milk, even if only to ignore it. The enduring centrality of milk as a foodstuff and natural resource suggests that today, when it comes to milk, we have no choice but to choose.

Citing such radically diverse iterations of milk, Greta Gaard (2013) writes that "food history is a history of ideas, and milk—a commodity that the American dairy industry has marketed as 'natural' and 'wholesome'—is not a homogeneous entity but one that has various meanings and compositions in different historical and cultural contexts" (596). Subsequently, Gaard (2013) identifies a need to develop a critical, intersectional framework that is sufficiently inclusive of a wide range of disciplinary approaches to describe the socio-cultural significance of milk across nations, genders, races, species, and environments. Milk has long featured in work hailing from the applied bio-physical (Pereira 2014) and social sciences (Gulliver and Horwath 2001; Kim and Douthitt 2004), health promotion (Erasmus and Webb 2013), and industry, agricultural, and food systems research (Mikkola and Risku-Norja 2014). Unlike Gaard's work, however, scholarly writing on food and con-sumption has less often considered how a consumable, such as milk, and the practices by which it is produced, marketed, sold, purchased, and consumed are wrought with meanings that emerge through those very practices.

Food and food systems are commonly conceptualized as being influ-enced by social and historical forces as they pertain to changes in food pol-icies, technologies, labour practices and consumption patterns within the food studies literature. However, in our view, food is not a static substance which is acted upon by these social and historical forces. Rather, the mean-ing and very materiality of food is brought into being through these social forces. The distinction is made even clearer when we consider the alternative meanings of the word "produced." Milk is typically produced for purchase via various technologies: milking machines, pasteurization processes, bot-tling equipment, distribution channels, and grocery store cooling systems. Social and cultural contexts may impact these processes—for example, the modern interest in raw, unpasteurized milk. Conversely, milk may also be produced—that is, given meaning as a material substance—via various com-peting discursive practices. Our focus is not on the many different contexts of foodstuffs so much as how different discursive practices *produce* very dif-ferent materially meaningful iterations of the same foodstuff.

Gaard also appeals for interdisciplinary scholarship, and calls on schol-ars to foster interdisciplinarity from within the food studies community (Johnston 2008; Power and Koç 2008). Deutsch and Miller (2007) note that food studies tends toward multidisciplinarity, with scholars from var-ious disciplinary positions contributing to its body of work, but not neces-sarily working collaboratively across disciplinary silos. To answer that call, this chapter has been produced by scholars hailing from diverse disciplinary traditions. In bringing together our diverse experiences in critical nutrition studies and critical dietetics (http://www.criticaldietetics.org; Brady), the sociology of sport (Ventresca), and film and cultural studies (Millious), our aim is to undertake scholarly inquiry of food that engages with the poten-tials and limits of this type of collaborative interdisciplinarity.

Moreover, we hope that our approach to theorizing the multiple and shifting meanings of food through a case study of milk will inform inter-epistemological collaboration across the epistemic divides that typically shore up disciplinary boundaries. Epistemology refers to a branch of philosophy that considers what knowledge is and how it is created. Epistemology seeks to answer questions such as, How do we know what we know and what is truth? To illustrate, positivism and constructivism are two epistemological positions that are often contrasted as informing very different responses to these questions. Positivism holds that truths can be known through objective, systematic study, such as through the scientific method. In contrast, constructivism opposes objectivity and maintains that knowledge is a human construct created through inter-subjective interactions among humans, non-human beings, material objects, and the world. Reaching across these boundaries serves to disrupt the "epistemic authority" of particular knowledge systems in relation to various problems, concerns, or interests (Murphy 2011, 492). While food studies aims to be inclusive of diverse perspectives and approaches to knowing food and its meanings from the social and natural sciences and humanities, in practice, research within the field often relies heavily on social science approaches that take the ontological status and meanings of food for granted. Our chapter, however, is situated in a critical, constructionist approach to knowledge that we assert serves as a contrast to these dominant ways of knowing.

Thus, we call upon food studies scholars to acknowledge and embrace diverse ways of knowing, studying, and representing food. We echo Murphy's (2011) emphasis on epistemological considerations in interdisciplinary research. Murphy urges interdisciplinary researchers to employ "upstream" practices—methodology and development of the research questions that are concerned with "how it is known" that must take place early on in the development of research projects—and contrasts these to the more commonly used, yet sometimes superficial "downstream" approaches—data collection and knowledge dissemination that focus on "what is known" that are typically carried out in the final stages of a project (492). She advocates that researchers interested in interdisciplinary work begin their collaborative efforts at the upstream stage of a project, to an explicit consideration of the "epistemological underpinnings of the knowledge systems" at play, which she says is not typical of interdisciplinary work (492).

To this end, we adopt a cultural studies approach to craft three analyses that trouble milk as a mundane and known object, and that seek to understand how milk is *produced* as a socially and culturally symbolic substance through three different frames: critical dietetics, sports drink marketing, and pro-breastfeeding activism (i.e., lactivism). Grossberg (2010) describes cultural studies as "necessarily interdisciplinary" and writes that "cultural studies can be seen as a contextual analysis of how contexts are (or even better, of how a specific context is) made, challenged, unmade, changed, remade, etc., as structures of power and domination" (23). Hence, in adopting a cultural studies perspective, we seek to explore our subject matter—milk—as an object that is produced through a complex web of interconnecting historically, temporally, culturally, and socially dependent cultural practices that give rise to multiple materialities and lived realities.

In the tradition of cultural studies, we use contextual analysis (Grossberg 2010; King 2005) in constructing our three analyses. Contextual analysis comprises discourse analysis (Foucault 1972; Mills 2004), visual methods (Rose 2012), genealogy (Saukko 2005), and theory of articulation (Slack 1996). Contextual analysis is not a structured method that is driven by a step-wise process, but is a methodological sensibility, or practice, with which scholars "reconstruct or fabricate the network of social, political, economic, and cultural articulations, or linkages, that produce any particular cultural phenomenon and trace, in turn, how the phenomenon (re)shapes the formation of which it is a part" (King 2005, 27). Given the enormity of fully exploring the productive network of any particular cultural phenomenon, contextual analyses are necessarily partial and unfinished (King 2005), as is the case with the analyses that follow. The respective contributions to this chapter also draw from larger research projects. However, in each of the proceeding three analyses we aim to shed light on various aspects of the web of articulations that produce milk as a cultural phenomenon with very different material expressions and consequences. Our analyses are thus highly contextual and consider the production of milk through a contemporary, North American viewpoint and from three divergent, though necessarily partial, perspectives. Together our analyses illustrate milk as a substance with multiple materialities that are continuously defined and redefined by their historical, social, and cultural contexts.

Nutrition Science and the "Production" of Milk

This section considers the cultural production of milk as a nutritious dietary staple from the perspective of critical dietetics (www.criticaldietetics.org). Critical dietetics is an emerging field of research that draws on the humanities and the physical and social sciences to guide and inform critical perspectives of social and environmental issues as they pertain to health, food, eating, the body, dietetic practice, and nutrition (Aphramor et al. 2009). Specifically, this section queries how nutrition recommendations, which are undergirded by biomedical understandings of health, food, and eating, have produced a cultural meaning and materiality of milk.

In her book on the rise of milk as "America's Drink," Dupuis (2002) argues that throughout the mid-nineteenth and mid-twentieth centuries, new ways of understanding food and eating led to a redefinition of milk as "the perfect food" (113). Prior to this time, milk was wrought via discourses of motherhood and pastoralism, but with the upsurge of nutrition science, milk took on a new social and cultural relevance as a health-promoting substance. Scrinis (2013) describes this time as the "era of quantifying nutritionism which is marked by its focus on quantifying the processes and needs of the body as well as the nutrient content of foods themselves (51). One particularly important development was the discovery of vitamins A and B in 1914 and 1911, respectively, and then vitamins C, D, E, K, and riboflavin (B2), folic-acid (B6), and beta-carotene throughout the 1920s and 1930s (Ostrowski 1986). Deficiency typified many North Americans' diets at this time, and foods that were found to contain these were heralded as protective foods and promoted for consumption via nutrition guidelines. This was particularly true for milk, which was described by Elmer McCollum, a Yale researcher who was instrumental in the discovery of vitamin A, as "the greatest of all protective foods because it is so constituted as to correct the deficiencies of whatever else we are likely to eat" (quoted in Scrinis 2013, 66). Whereas milk previously had symbolized nourishment, nurturance, and care, as the first superfood, it came to stand for nutriment and the reasoned use of modern scientific principles to service one's dietary needs.

While nutrition guidelines entrenched milk in ideas about what constituted the scientifically deduced, quantified diet, it also imbued milk with meaning beyond its nutrient content or "protective" capacities. Milk became a substance that demarcated white, Anglo-European Canadian consumers and the marginalized, poor, and racialized other. Ian Mosby notes that with the 1942 publication of Canada's Official Food Rules, an early iteration of what is now more widely known as Canada's Food Guide, dietary recommendations for milk consumption increased from one-half to one pint (one to two 8-ounce cups) for adults and one and a half pints to one quart (three to four 8-ounce cups), an amount financially out of reach for a large majority of Canadians (Mosby 2014). With these milk consumption guidelines in place, the standards were set by which experts could measure and assess not just optimal or even adequate diets, but acceptable people. Dupuis notes that the cultural production of milk linked "the perfect whiteness of this food and the white body genetically capable of digesting it" (11). Along those lines, nutrition guidelines became a means of measuring, assessing, and comparing Canada's white, Anglo-European population and other marginalized groups (Biltekoff 2013). Milk, as the ultimate protective food, was loaded with cultural meaning that had the power to constitute and distinguish the healthy, rational consumer, and the uneducated, often racialized and poor, non-consumer.

Krista Walters's (2012) analysis of Canada's first national nutrition survey in 1964, which collected data on the dietary intakes of both Indigenous and non-Indigenous Canadians, provides an example of the cultural meanings of milk as a nutritional substance being deployed for political ends. Walters notes that rather than being a simple enumeration of Canadians' dietary intake, for Aboriginal populations the survey was an "inherently disciplinary practice" that was informed by racialized, classed, and gendered discourses, and was ultimately part of a wider agenda to colonize Aboriginal bodies (443). With this survey and others that followed, milk was entrenched as a marker of right eating, and as Biltekoff argues, right eating is more about delimiting right people from "unhealthy other[s]" than promoting scientific, evidence-based dietary advice (44). These surveys rationalized and idealized Western foodways, which were inaccessible to Aboriginal communities due to poverty, remote location, and commonly a genetic inability to digest lactose, the main carbohydrate in milk. Milk and milk products became the normative food choices among an array of others that have a similar nutrient profile, but that were more typical of Aboriginal and other non-Anglo-European diets.

Today, the ways in which nutrition discourse produces the cultural value of milk is evident in the ongoing work by McIntyre and colleagues. McIntyre and colleagues have conducted quantitative and qualitative studies of the milk consumption practices of "milk insecure," lone mothers (McIntyre, Williams, and Glanville 2007; Glanville and McIntyre 2009; Williams, McIntyre, and Glanville 2010). The authors identify "milk insecurity" as a phenomenon related to food insecurity, but distinct in that milk is particularly difficult for their participants to secure, is associated with specific serious health concerns related to nutritional deficiencies, and, more so than other foods, has cultural meanings that make it particularly symbolically significant for these women. McIntyre, Williams, and Glanville (2007) contend that beyond simply describing their struggles to secure enough milk for their families, these women use milk and its nutritive benefit metaphorically to convey the potent experiences and emotions associated with being milk insecure. For these women, milk is "a social marker, an aesthetic experience, a source of meaning and metaphor" (275). The metaphoric value of milk is, in part, tied to these women's roles as the sole providers for their children.

However, the way in which milk is produced by nutrition science as an especially nutritious food intensified the women's experiences of milk insecurity and the ways in which they drew on the cultural significance of milk to express their hardships.

While this analysis of the production of milk is necessarily partial, it underscores that even when "produced" via nutrition science with its appeals to expertise and objectivity, milk is nevertheless imbued with cultural meaning. Unlike the marketing of milk as a sport drink or in breastfeeding activism, as the following analyses consider, nutrition science is often viewed as apolitical, consisting merely of facts about a food—in this case, milk. Yet, as this brief look at the historical and contemporary implications of the production of milk via nutrition science suggests, it is the very reduction of milk to a set of facts and figures that is instrumental in the production of its cultural meaning and political uses.

Media, Sport, and the "Production" of Milk

Since the late 1990s, the dairy industries in both Canada and the United States have launched advertising campaigns that, supported by scientific studies and testimony from celebrity athletes, promote the perceived benefits of milk consumption for high-performance and recreational athletes (Cole and Cate 2007; Ventresca and Brady 2015). This rebranding effort has carved a substantial niche for milk and other dairy-based products within the billion-dollar sports beverage industry. This section considers the implications of this rebranding process for how milk is produced, sold, and understood in contemporary marketplaces: How do these promotional campaigns shape understandings of milk, its nutritional composition, and its benefits? How do advertisements enact the multiple meanings and compositions of milk and situate milk within different historical and cultural contexts?

These questions emerge from a conception of popular culture as a site of power, resistance, and struggles over meaning. Media representations are not simply reflections of society, but are entangled with issues of identity politics, social structures, and the workings of consumer capitalism (Fiske 2005; Hall 2005; hooks 1992; McRobbie 1990). Cultural domains like advertising, then, are important sites through which commodities are woven into everyday practices and activities; yet the meanings attributed to these consumer products are malleable and context-specific. In this way, the longstanding status of milk as a natural and wholesome "miracle food" is as much a product of carefully constructed promotional messaging as it is a reflection of milk's inherent "goodness" (Dupuis 2002; Gaard 2013; Valenze

2011). A series of iconic advertising campaigns have shaped our perceptions of both the benefits of milk consumption and to whom these benefits are most available and useful. Indeed, the contemporary marketing of milk as a sports drink illustrates how understandings of a particular commodity can change over time. But diverse or conflicting messages within popular advertising campaigns also demonstrate the fluctuating ontological status of a commodity like milk.

Scholars have mapped how shifts in advertising campaigns and health promotion strategies have contributed to changes regarding the historical meanings of milk (Dupuis 2002; Valenze 2011). In the previous section, we outlined how understandings of milk throughout the twentieth century have been structured around shifting narratives of health, nutrition, and "progress." The pervasiveness of nutritionism as a means for conceptualizing milk became firmly entrenched through the iconic milk moustache ads launched by the dairy industries in the late 1980s. This wildly popular campaign comprised one of the large-scale efforts to maintain milk's prominence in both nutritional programs and consumer routines alike. Accompanied by catchy slogans like "Milk: It Does a Body Good" and "Got Milk?," these advertisements typically featured a compelling visual image of a well-known celebrity sporting a "milk moustache," a visible white residue located above the upper lip, presumably left over from drinking some quantity of milk. These images rapidly became a pop culture phenomenon and, for a time, the opportunity to appear in a milk moustache ad was a measure of one's celebrity status (Cuneen and Spencer 2003).

As the milk moustache ads gained popularity, athletes were also commonly employed as the dairy industries' celebrity endorsers. Thus, the ways in which milk has been actively rebranded as a sports drink effectively build upon past promotional messaging associated with the product. Yet this repackaging of milk as a locker room technology to be consumed by athletes to improve performance and recovery alters how milk is imagined in the popular consciousness. Cole and Cate (2007) highlight how the claims made in a great number of contemporary milk advertisements mirror those made about illicit performance-enhancing substances like anabolic steroids. Sport-specific advertising and promotional websites assert that consuming milk after exercise will aid in rehydration and muscle recovery, while replenishing vital vitamins and nutrients that will improve future workouts ("Workout Recovery" 2013). These claims are supported through reference to scientific studies funded by the dairy industry that position milk as offering athletes more comprehensive nutrition compared to other sports supplements and drinks (Cole and Cate 2007; "Compare It" 2014). The superiority of milk as a post-workout beverage is shown to emerge from its potent combination of protein, electrolytes, and carbohydrates. While still drawing on discourses of nutrition and naturalness, these types of promotional campaigns have reframed the consumption of milk as a practice that produces healthy, well-nourished, and *athletic* bodies (Ventresca and Brady 2015).

Yet the movement of milk into sporting contexts also resituates milk-related advertising within the constellation of meanings and practices through which we conceptualize athletes and their bodies. Indeed, the representations of athletes in milk ads are shaped by and contribute to histories of sports marketing that trade on longstanding gender, race, and class stereotypes. Cuneen and Spencer (2003), for example, examined representations of gender in a series of milk moustache advertisements from the 1990s that featured celebrity athletes. The authors' study followed an extensive body of sociological literature that describes how sports ads are particularly culpable in reproducing and naturalizing common gender stereotypes (Duncan and Messner 2005; Kane, LaVoi, and Fink 2013; Messner, Duncan and Jensen 1993). The imagery employed in the sport-related milk moustache ads analyzed by Cuneen and Spencer relied heavily on common misconceptions about sport and gender, and placed women in passive, non-athletic, and sexualized roles. By contrast, men were portrayed in poses and scenarios that implied athleticism and active behaviours. Cuneen and Spencer point to some implicit contradictions stemming from the campaign's use of gender stereotypes in ads that primarily targeted women and promoted the value of health and nutrition. They argue that the sexualized and trivialized representations of women in advertisements for a "wholesome" commodity like milk could adversely shape gender norms and influence sport participation patterns for girls and young women. But how do these representations influence understandings of the material constitution of *milk itself*? Can the stereotypes perpetuated through these campaigns produce multiple and competing perceptions of the benefits of milk consumption? We have outlined how the branding of milk as a sports drink involved repurposing the discourses of nutritionism through which milk is most commonly understood and how these meanings transplanted milk into new social milieus. But even within these promotional contexts, can the benefits and potentials attributed to milk change depending on who is shown to be consuming it?

A substance like milk that is primarily known through its physical, chemical, and nutritional properties is also discursively constituted by the promotional discourse surrounding food commodities. The co-constitutive relationship between the product and its marketing materials emerges through the pervasiveness and cultural reach of food advertising. The media discourses through which food is represented are shaped by intersecting notions of gender, sexuality, race, and class that impact how food is known, produced, and consumed (Williams-Forson and Counihan 2012). As many of the trends observed by Cuneen and Spencer persist in more contemporary milk advertising, it is crucial to consider how a socially constructed category such as gender influences how milk is understood as "healthy" or useful for particular types of consumers.

These gendered distinctions are evident when comparing the visuals of milk moustache ads from the past decade featuring race car driver Danica Patrick, tennis player Ana Ivanovic, and skater Sasha Cohen to those representing male athletes like basketball players Dwight Howard and Steve Nash, or football player Reggie Bush. Patrick is portrayed, for example, holding a helmet against her thigh while wearing an (impeccably-styled) jacket and black leather pants that look noticeably more fashionable than the suits typically worn behind the wheel of a racecar. Similar to Cuneen and Spencer's findings, Patrick's clothing, stylized makeup, blow-dried hair, and sexualized stance emphasize her appearance rather than her athletic prowess. Ivanovic and Cohen are shown in standard sporting attire, but following the gendered conventions of their respective sports, their uniforms are revealing and visibly hyper-feminine. Ivanovic and Cohen are also portrayed in passive and sexualized poses, rather than in positions that demonstrate strength or athletic competence. The sexualized representations of Patrick, Ivanovic, and Cohen contrast greatly with the ways in which Howard, Nash, and Bush are depicted. Nash is shown jumping to perform a difficult basketball manoeuvre, while Howard and Bush stand in ways that accentuate their muscular and athletic bodies. These men are shown to embody the characteristics of hyper-masculinity; they are portrayed in full uniform and appear active, strong, and confident.

Yet what is especially important about the representation of athletes in milk ads is how the text accompanying these powerful visuals does not explicitly make reference to gender. While mostly being crafted around witty puns related to the sport associated with the athlete being portrayed, the written messages about nutrition, building muscle, and "refueling" are relatively consistent and almost interchangeable between advertisements. Indeed, a reference to milk helping an athlete "look their best" in the text supplementing the image of Sasha Cohen is the only reflection of the visual emphasis on appearance and outward femininity in ads featuring women athletes.

The contradiction between the written text and visual image in these milk moustache advertisements illustrates the multiplicities of milk. Although milk is commonly described through scientific discourses of nutrition and biology, the benefits of milk consumption can be constructed differently depending on the particular context. The physical properties of milk remain the same, but the meanings attributed to the substance continuously vary. In this case, the visual imagery accompanying the consistent promotional rhetoric about milk's nutritional value frames these benefits according to conventional gender performances. These images promote a powerful and significant message that shapes how milk is understood and consumed: men who drink milk will be strong, active, and muscular, while women can employ milk's benefits to be ultra-feminine, beautiful, and, indeed, look their best.

This analysis does not represent a comprehensive or exhaustive survey of sport-related milk advertisements, nor is it meant to point to a rigid gender dichotomy portrayed through these promotional materials. Rather, as illustrated in broader examinations of the gendered representations of athletes, these depictions are context-specific and enact complex and fluid notions of identity (McDonald and Birrell 2000). Certainly, some milk moustache ads portray female athletes as muscular or in uniform, actively participating in their sport.[1] But the purpose of this analysis is to interrogate how the consumption of milk is implicated as part of distinct gender performances that influence how food substances are understood as "fueling" different types of bodies.

It is important to note, however, that the cultural processes through which food-related meanings and practices are shaped by identities are not limited to notions of gender. Advertising campaigns are sites through which multiple identities are simultaneously produced, performed, and connected. In a milk ad from 2010, for example, black basketball player Chris Bosh is pictured in a milk ad standing beside a giraffe to visually emphasize his height (Bosh stands at a towering 6 feet, 11 inches). While the ad's text underscores the role of milk in helping teenagers grow, the comparison that equates Bosh with an African mammal (albeit not a particularly ferocious one) reproduces the longstanding histories of black athletes being racialized as animalistic, savage, and biologically superior "natural athletes" (Carrington 2010; Hoberman 1997). It is impossible to separate the portrayal of "height" in this ad from the connotations that milk is a vector for the production of black masculine bodies understood through social constructions of race. The depictions of Howard and Bush as hyper-masculine and hyper-muscular are similarly informed by understandings of the "natural" black athlete, and the consumption (and whiteness) of milk takes on new meanings in and through these racialized discourses. Thus, milk is understood according to the cultural contexts, from farming to sport to breastfeeding, within which its consumption is situated by marketing campaigns. Spheres of advertising and representation are not separate from those of food production. Advertising campaigns and the identities they enact are crucial in determining how food items like milk are produced, sold, and consumed.

Breastfeeding and the "Production" of Human Milk

Similar to animal- and plant-based milks, how we think about and understand human breast milk evolves in relation to the ideologies, politics, and scientific advancements of a particular cultural context. Today, contemporary Canadian and American maternal culture grapples with an emerging milk myth: the myth of medicinal breast milk. Advances in the scientific testing of breast milk are ushering in a new era of pro-breastfeeding culture (also known as lactivism) that rejects infant formula as a preferred feeding method and champions breastfeeding, and more specifically, breast milk. As with many parenting and dieting philosophies, lactivism can be divided into factions of varying intensity and politics. The contemporary lactivist movement is grounded in a nutritionist understanding of breast milk as a quantifiably superior foodstuff. La Leche League International (LLLI), the largest and oldest mother-to-mother breastfeeding education and support organization, now routinely draws from biomedical testimony to substantiate their longstanding position that "breast is best." For example, the February 2014 issue of *Breastfeeding Today*, LLLI's online magazine, concludes with an article titled, "Breastfeeding is a Shared Gift." Here LLLI reminds mothers that breastfeeding is the right choice as it provides optimal nutrition and long-term health benefits. After reminding readers that "[babies' needs] *will* come first," the article discusses how breastfeeding mutually benefits mothers by protecting them from a number of terrifying diseases including diabetes, obesity, rheumatoid arthritis, and breast cancer (Issue 22, available online at http://breastfeedingtoday-llli.org). This framing of breast milk as "the gift of health" to babies that includes additional health benefits for mothers coincides with the majority of lactivist literature in conjuring an unequivocal medical opinion on the inherent superiority of breastfeeding that does not exist (Colen and Ramey 2014).

The simple story anchoring contemporary lactivism is that recent observational studies indicate that breastfed babies have improved health outcomes including fewer ear infections and stomach viruses when compared to formula-fed babies. Consequently, a range of authority figures including government bodies, medical professionals, and research scientists now instruct mothers to exclusively breastfeed their babies for a minimum of six months and continue partial breastfeeding for up to two years. A considered and comprehensive analysis of contemporary lactivist texts including books, websites, and newsletters reveals how not only scientific studies, but also complex and seemingly disparate social forces, underscore the belief that breast is best. A neoliberal health care climate that places all responsibility for a child's health at the level of the individual caregiver(s) and a trending parenting culture referred to as "total motherhood" that lauds intensive mothering practices, such as co-sleeping, baby-wearing, and exclusive, on-demand breastfeeding, collude with breast milk's cure-all status within popular medical literature, aligning both breastfeeding and breast milk with good mothering.

Our intent here is not to debate the health benefits of breast milk but to illustrate how such a seemingly natural food substance is deeply, socially constructed. While lactation is physiological, breastfeeding is simultaneously a biological process and a cultural practice. How breastfeeding is practised, who breastfeeds, and the signification of both the act and milk itself alters dramatically across histories and geographies. With the stakes so high—the health and wellness of both mothers and babies—a critique of the biomedicalization of breast milk might read as unsavoury. But while the materiality of breast milk raises many important questions about the concrete possibilities for optimizing infant health, it also silences others, and these silences are worth listening to. Scientific breastfeeding recommendations and lactivist campaigns pressure mothers to breastfeed while rarely acknowledging that exclusive breastfeeding requires a significant amount of time and other resources. Feminist and critical public health scholars have examined how breastfeeding advocacy can increase feelings of anxiety, frustration, stress, guilt, and failure among mothers and articulate why these consequences are not negligible (Crossley 2009; Knaak 2006; Wolf 2011). The remainder of this section draws from a textual analysis of the vanguard lactivist organization Best for Babes and its "Beat the Booby Traps™" campaign to illustrate what the biomedicalization of breast milk looks like and why it might be problematic. By shifting focus from breastfeeding as a lauded *mothering practice* to breast milk as desirous *product*, we examine how this materially focused lactivist campaign draws from a nutritional standpoint to position breast milk as an elite and coveted, if not vital, infant food and preventative health commodity.

We can see the clash of social forces pressuring mothers to breastfeed within the American not-for-profit lactivist organization Best for Babes (hereafter BFB) and its Beat the Booby Traps™ poster campaign. Launched online in 2009, BFB can be understood as a response to and revitalization of the types of images of breastfeeding mothers made popular by LLLI. BFB strives to rebrand breastfeeding as chic, urban, and sexy, a sort of luxury infant feeding method as opposed to a traditional one. BFB's trademarked mission is to "give breastfeeding a makeover," a slogan that perhaps best encapsulates the post–Demi Moore, celebrity "body-back" culture that has magnified heteronormative beauty expectations of pregnant and postpartum bodies, subjecting mothers to high levels of scrutiny and surveillance. The result is a maternal culture that pressures mothers to embody intensive mothering practices, chiefly exclusive and sustained breastfeeding, while nonetheless conforming to stringent beauty standards, and all without compromising their careers and identities outside the domestic environment.[2] In essence, BFB promotes breastfeeding using the utopic "have it all" magazine idiom that has long antagonized contemporary womanhood by confusing individual determination with social privilege.

BFB's hot pink website (www.bestforbabes.org) offers a wealth of material ripe for a feminist textual analysis, much of which is synthesized within the organization's Beat the Booby Traps™ public service awareness (PSA) poster campaign that debuted in Fit Pregnancy magazine in May of 2009. The campaign has since appeared in *Mom & Baby* magazine and *USA Today*, as well as on numerous lactivist websites, mommy blogs, and across social media networking platforms such as Twitter and Facebook. The Booby Traps campaign features three near-identical posters of a white, silhouetted, playboy-bunny female torso against a hot pink background. A unique slogan is written across the cartoon breasts and is further explained at the bottom of each poster in small grey font. The three slogans are: "Economic Stimulus Packages," "Life-saving Devices," and "The Miracle Isn't the Bra." The "Economic Stimulus Packages" slogan ties into contemporary American economic woes and reveals the socio-economic status of BFB's intended audience. The descriptor at the bottom of the poster reads as follows:

> Breastfeeding boosts your bank account and your baby's immune system, saving you on hospital visits, doctor's bills, medicine

and missed days of work. It could also save billions on health care costs. Is your hospital, physician, employer and insurer doing their part to help you succeed? Let us help you find out at bestforbabes.org.

The Beat Booby Traps campaign provides a framework for how BFB globally frames breast milk as a coveted biocommodity. The campaign mobilizes support for a neoliberal healthcare system whereby individual mothers are tasked with supplying "life saving" and "miraculous" breast milk for the health of their babies and the well-being of the nation. Despite BFB's claims to champion and support all mothers, regardless of how long or whether they breast-feed, a fulsome textual analysis of BFB reveals that the organization enforces rather than challenges mainstream conceptions of the superiority of breast milk for infant health. That infant formula might be the best feeding option for the well-being of the overall family, the co-parent's relationship to the baby, the mother's career, her lifestyle, or her physical and mental well-being goes unmentioned. Moreover, BFB encourages women who are physiologically incapable of producing (sufficient) breast milk to source breast milk donations or to purchase breast milk via online platforms such as Only the Breast, where buyers and sellers create profiles and organize private breast milk purchases (www.onlythebreast.com). While much not-for-profit human milk sharing and banking efforts are organized to assist premature babies or babies with various health complications, sites such as Only the Breast reveal that human breast milk is subject to price-point variations and demarcations that are not dissimilar to meat and non-human dairy products. Sellers post profile pictures and pitch their diets (i.e., vegan or organic), daily health behaviours (exercise routines and pharmaceutical use), and environmental influences (urban versus rural lifestyle) to potential buyers, and price their breast milk accordingly. The rise of internet breast milk markets cues scholars to revisit what we know so far about global tissue economies, the valuation of biological labour, and the relationships between national visibility, profitability, and public health policies, and to reflect as to whether or not—and how—the salability of mothers' milk via the internet indicates revolutionary infant feeding practices (see, respectively, Boyer 2010; Jones 2013; Smith 2015). Of chief concern here is that not only does the current fever for breast milk reflected within BFB and made accessible through sites such as Only the Breast recreate historic wet nursing practices and their often unequal power relations, but the increasing focus on breast milk *as a product* redefines women's bodies and women's relationships to their bodies in potentially problematic ways.

We should begin asking how breast milk has become so valuable and where the rhetoric of medicinal breast milk is heading. Observational studies that attribute higher IQ scores and improved overall health to breastfed babies are likely only part of the story. Sites such as Only the Breast indicate that men and women purchase breast milk as a performance-enhancing drink, a phenomenon no doubt informed by the recent rebranding of cow's milk as a performance-enhancing sports beverage (Ventresca and Brady 2015). If breast milk continues to be treated as a natural resource and commodity, as illustrated in BFB's Beat the Booby Traps campaign, then we need to carefully reexamine the social systems and structures that organize its availability *for all*, not just the upwardly mobile. At present, breast milk's superiority is mobilized in ways that wilfully disregard the physical and economic realities of modern American life, in particular the gross socio-economic stratification across families and the enduring patriarchal structures, such as a lack of guaranteed maternal leave and free childcare, that make it difficult for women to work and parent. In this way, breastfeeding becomes an oppressive discourse. By asking women to compromise their individual identity as women in order to satisfy an imagined maternal imperative—to become the organic vessels of money-saving, life-saving, and miraculous breast milk—the concept of breastfeeding used in this case draws stark lines between what in women's experiences should be considered good mothering and what should not.

The treatment of breast milk in lactivist campaigns indicates the need for food studies researchers to engage with the materialities and articulations of milk. Milk is not only multiple but also simultaneous—it is many things and also many things *at one time*. We can understand BFB's lactivist campaign not as a utopian symbol of what our society would like to become, but as a misunderstood sign of where we are now, and thus we can begin addressing the very real consequences that such articulations have for mothers and children. Whether or not scientific breast milk studies show to what extent "breast is best" is no longer the most important question; we should be asking instead how certain framings of milk capitalize on the concepts of health, purity, and normality with far-reaching sociocultural implications traceable from domestic practices to large-scale economies such as the dairy industry.

Conclusion

While contemporary health food fads might point to a culture obsessed with scientific exactness, our analysis reveals how even the most basic facts about nutrition are co-constituted alongside changing social, cultural, political, and economic contexts. The rise of nutritionism in the early twentieth century saw the quantification of milk, the nutrients it contains, and its consumption by different groups. Yet, while the nutritional and "protective" properties of milk were at the fore of public discussion about food and health, this discussion served to produce milk through a number of intersecting discursive formations. Milk has garnered and continues to garner symbolic and cultural meaning that lends it significance as a consumable substance. This discursive process is not simply a matter of what milk "means," but involves the production of knowledge about what milk "is" as a material object.

The mobilization of celebrity athletes in milk advertising and the shift to marketing milk as a post-workout sports drink are some of the ways in which the nutritional properties of milk are shaped and given meaning. Yet these nutritional components and their benefits are constructed as functioning differently depending on the perceived consumer. Milk advertising, such as the iconic milk moustache campaigns, work to construct images of the product's ideal consumers, but also actively construct understandings of the commodity itself. Similarly, even a cogent and salutary cultural conceptualization of breastfeeding must deal with some of the most unruly and most culturally disruptive of natural forces: female sexuality, child sexuality, women's, children's, and mothers' rights, the body in public spaces, and, perhaps most troubling of all, the treatment of the maternal body as the producer of a commodity—the fetishized substance of breast milk. And while the hyper-stylized celebrity images and cartoon posters associated with BFB's brand of lactivism—along with past and present cow's milk celebrity advertisements—may simply speak to the conservative demands of the glamour industry, when organized within careful discursive research these representations provide insights into the meanings and understandings of food that are linked to policy, economics, and health. We argue that this complex constellation of meanings complicates a supposedly mundane substance like milk and requires attention to multiple and diverse ways of knowing that stretch across disciplinary boundaries.

Food scholars have a responsibility to produce critical scholarship that traverses and interrogates the boundaries through which food studies is defined and practised. Yet, such work often languishes when compared to food production or food systems research. However, the very usefulness of scholarship that seeks to change the food system is partly dependent on a successful and complicated engagement with critical perspectives of food. This is where interdisciplinary food scholarship may intervene to make sense of the competing forces acting upon our ability to judge what counts as positive change in regards to feeding, eating, and living. As Johnston (2008) similarly asserts, interdisciplinary scholarship is central to the future vitality and "public relevance" of food studies (271). We seek, however, to build upon this position and argue that the practice of food studies may be advanced by not only traversing disciplinary boundaries, but by aiming to traverse epistemological ones.

We undertook this analysis of the multiple and shifting meanings of food in the hope that such work may inform interepistemological collaboration in the future. Our paper demonstrates how an everyday substance like milk is not "known" in static and concrete ways, but is continually constituted and reconstituted by scientific, promotional, and institutional discourses that are always contested and in flux. We argue that, together, our diverse disciplinary backgrounds greatly enhanced our capacity to demonstrate the multiplicities of milk. We also acknowledge, however, that each of the three analyses above are rooted in a constructivist approach that interrogates the historical and social specificities of knowledge without necessarily traversing or stretching epistemological boundaries. Moreover, our shared commitment to cultural studies methodologies limits the extent to which our collaboration can fulfill the potentials of interepistemological practice. Yet, by making explicit the ways in which milk is produced through various intermingling discursive practices, our investigation reveals how a greater sensitivity to different ways of knowing might inform critical perspectives on food and food systems and greater interepistemological practice in the future. In Murphy's (2011) words, we have sought to bring to light "how it is known," which she argues is an essential first step in designing the kind of "upstream" research questions and methods that may ultimately lead toward more definitively interdisciplinary work (492).

How might food studies scholars proceed toward greater interepistemological exchange? A first step might include a greater awareness and public discussion about the underpinning epistemological paradigms that inform our work and how these shape our decisions about the hows and whys of research design and the process. For example, such discussions should attend to the ways in which an epistemological paradigm is connected to the data collection methods chosen as well as the benefits, but also limitations, of that paradigm, and the choices that it guides us to make. This connection between epistemology and method is too often overlooked as if to be self-evident and not in need of interrogation (Darlaston-Jones 2007). Moreover, in keeping with Johnston's argument to embrace public intellectualism, such discussions must take place via scholarly fora such as journals and conferences, but also via those that are more readily accessed and accessible to the non-academic community, such as popular media outlets.

Acknowledgements

The authors would like to thank the Social Sciences and Humanities Research Council for funding that has supported their work on this paper.

Notes

1. For example, a milk moustache ad from 1999 shows tennis players Venus and Serena Williams holding tennis racquets and appearing strong, muscular, and in control. Similarly, a recent video from the Canadian "Recharge with Milk" website depicts Olympic gold medalist Ashleigh McIvor in active sport-settings while focusing on her athletic training regimens.

2. Owing to celebrity post-partum bodies and the pressure to be a "yummy mummy," body-back culture refers to the healthiest body maintenance practices such as dieting and exercise that new mothers are expected to perform. Dworkin and Wachs (2004) refer to this phenomenon as the "new third shift for mothers," following their work outside the home and their domestic duties.

References

Aphramor, Lucy, Yuka Asada, Jennifer Atkins, Shawna Berenbaum, Jenna Brady, Shauna Clarke, John Coveney, Marjorie DeVault, Lisa Forster-Coull, Ann Fox, et al. 2009. "Critical dietetics: A declaration." *Practice* 48: 2.

Barthes, R. [1957] 1972. *Mythologies*, translated by Annette Lavers. New York: Farrar, Straus and Giroux.

Biltekoff, Charlotte. 2013. *Eating Right in America: The Cultural Politics of Food and Health*. Durham, NC: Duke University Press. http://dx.doi.org/10.1215/9780822377276.

Boyer, Karen. 2010. "Of Care and Commodities: Breast Milk and the New Politics of Mobile Biosubstances." *Progress in Human Geography* 34 (1): 5–20. http://dx.doi.org/10.1177/0309132509105003.

Carrington, Ben. 2010. *Race, Sport, Politics: The Sporting Black Diaspora*. Thousand Oaks, CA: Sage.

Cole, C.L., and S.L. Cate. 2007. "Testing Barry Bonds' Mustache." *Journal of Sport and Social Issues* 31 (4): 313–4. http://dx.doi.org/10.1177/0193723507310104.

Colen, Cynthia G., and David M. Ramey. 2014. "Is Breast Truly Best? Estimating the Effects of Breastfeeding on Long-Term Child Health and Wellbeing in the United States Using Sibling Comparisons." *Social Science & Medicine* 109: 55–65. http://dx.doi.org/10.1016/j.socscimed.2014.01.027.

"Compare It." 2014. *Rechargewithmilk.ca*. Last Modified 29 January 2014. http://www.rechargewithmilk.ca/compare_it.

Crossley, Michelle. 2009. "Breastfeeding as Moral Imperative: An Autoethnographic Study." *Feminism & Psychology* 19 (1): 71–87. http://dx.doi.org/10.1177/0959353508098620.

Cuneen, Jacquelyn, and Nancy Spencer. 2003. "Gender Representations Related to Sports Celebrity Portrayals in the Milk Mustache Advertising Campaign." *Sport Marketing Quarterly* 12 (3): 140–50.

Darlaston-Jones, Dawn. 2007. "Making Connections: The Relationship between Epistemology and Research Methods." *Australian Community Psychologist* 19 (1): 19–27.

Deutsch, Jonathan, and Jeffery Miller. 2007. "Food Studies: A Multidisciplinary Guide to the Literature." *Choice* 45 (3): 393–401. http://dx.doi.org/10.5860/CHOICE.45.03.393.

Duncan, Margaret C., and Michael Messner. 2005. Gender in Televised Sports: News and Highlights Shows, 1989–2004. Los Angeles: Amateur Athletic Foundation. http://library.la84.org/9arr/ResearchReports/tv2004.pdf.

Dupuis, E. Melanie. 2002. *Nature's Perfect Food: How Milk Became America's Drink*. New York: NYU Press.

Dworkin, Shari L., and Faye Linda Wachs. 2004. "'Getting Your Body Back': Post-Industrial Fit Motherhood in Shape Fit Pregnancy Magazine." *Gender & Society* 18 (5): 610–24. http://dx.doi.org/10.1177/0891243204266817.

Erasmus, Lourens Jacobus, and Edward Cottington Webb. 2013. "The Effect of Production System and Management Practices on the Environmental Impact, Quality and Safety of Milk and Dairy Products." *South African Journal of Animal Science* 43 (3): 424–35. http://dx.doi.org/10.4314/sajas.v43i3.13.

Fiske, John. 2005. "Popular Discrimination." In *Popular Culture: A Reader*, edited by Raiford Guins and Omayra Zaragoza Cruz, 215–22. Thousand Oaks, CA: Sage.

Foucault, Michel. 1972. *The Archeology of Knowledge and Discourse in Language*. New York: Pantheon Books.

Gaard, Greta. 2013. "Toward a Feminist Postcolonial Milk Studies." *American Quarterly* 65 (3): 595–618. http://dx.doi.org/10.1353/aq.2013.0040.

Glanville, Theresa N., and Lynn McIntyre. 2009. "Beverage Consumption in Low-Income, 'Milk-Friendly' Families." *Canadian Journal of Dietetic Practice and Research* 70 (2): 95–8. http://dx.doi.org/10.3148/70.2.2009.95.

Gulliver, Pauline, and Caroline C. Horwath. 2001. "Assessing Women's Perceived Benefits, Barriers, and Stages of Change for Meeting Milk Product Consumption Recommendations." *Journal of the American Dietetic Association* 101 (11): 1354–7. http://dx.doi.org/10.1016/S0002-8223(01)00324-8.

Grossberg, Lawrence. 2010. *Cultural Studies in the Future Tense*. Durham, NC: Duke University Press. http://dx.doi.org/10.1215/9780822393313.

Hall, Stuart. 2005. "Notes on Deconstructing the Popular." In *Popular Culture: A Reader*, edited by Raiford Guins and Omayra Zaragoza Cruz, 64–71. Thousand Oaks, CA: Sage.

Hoberman, John. 1997. *Darwin's Athletes: How Sport has Damaged Black America and Preserved the Myth of Race*. Boston: Houghton-Mifflin.

hooks, bell. 1992. *Black Looks: Race and Representation*. Boston: South End Press.

Johnston, Josée. 2008. "Struggles for the 'Up and Coming': Challenges Facing New Food Scholars and Food Scholarship." *Food, Culture, & Society* 11 (3): 269–74. http://dx.doi.org/10.2752/175174408X347847.

Jones, Frances. 2013. "Milk Sharing: How It Undermines Breastfeeding." *Breastfeeding Review* 21 (3): 21–5.

Kane, Mary Jo, N.M. LaVoi, and J.S. Fink. 2013. "Exploring Elite Female Athletes Interpretations of Sport Media Images: A Window into the Construction of Social Identity and 'Selling Sex' in Women's Sport." *Communication and Sport* 1 (3): 269–98. http://dx.doi.org/10.1177/2167479512473585.

Kim, Sora, and Robin A. Douthitt. 2004. "The Role of Dietary Information in Women's Whole Milk and Low-Fat Milk Intakes." *International Journal of Consumer Studies* 28 (3): 245–54. http://dx.doi.org/10.1111/j.1470-6431.2003.00347.x.

King, Samantha. 2005. "Methodological Contingencies in Sports Studies." In *Qualitative Methods in Sports Studies*, edited by David L. Andrews, Daniel S. Mason, and Michael Silk, 21-38. New York: Berg.

Knaak, Stephanie J. 2006. "The Problem with Breastfeeding Discourse." *Canadian Journal of Public Health Revue* 97 (5): 412–4.

McDonald, Mary, and Susan Birrell, eds. 2000. *Reading Sport Critically: Essays on Power and Representation*. Boston: Northeastern University Press.

McIntyre, Lynn, Patricia Williams, and Theresa N. Glanville. 2007. "Milk as Metaphor: Low-Income Lone Mothers' Characterization of Their Challenges Acquiring Milk for Their Families." *Ecology of Food and Nutrition* 46 (3-4): 263–79. http://dx.doi.org/10.1080/03670240701407640.

McRobbie, Angela. 1990. *Feminism and Youth Culture: From Jackie to Just Seventeen*. New York: Routledge.

Messner, Michael, Margaret C. Duncan, and Kerry Jensen. 1993. "Separating the Men from the Girls: The Gendered Language of Televised Sports." *Gender & Society* 7 (1): 121–37. http://dx.doi.org/10.1177/089124393007001007.

Mikkola, Minna, and Helmi Risku-Norja. 2014. "Discursive Transformations within the Food System Toward Sustainability: Climate Change and Diary." *International Journal of Sustainable Development* 17 (1): 62–77. http://dx.doi.org/10.1504/IJSD.2014.058437.

Mills, Sarah. 2004. *Discourse*. New York: Routledge.

Mosby, Ian. 2014. *Food Will Win the War: The Politics, Culture, and Science of Food on Canada's Home Front*. Vancouver: UBC Press.

Murphy, Brenda L. 2011. "From Interdisciplinary to Inter-epistemological Approaches: Confronting the Challenges of Integrated Climate Change Research." *Canadian Geographer* 55 (4): 490–509. http://dx.doi.org/10.1111/j.1541-0064.2011.00388.x.

Ostrowski, Paul. 1986. "Who Discovered Vitamins?" *Polish Review* 31 (2–3): 171–83.

Pereira, Paula C. 2014. "Milk Nutritional Composition and its Role in Human Health." *Nutrition* 30 (6): 619–27. http://dx.doi.org/10.1016/j.nut.2013.10.011.

Power, Elaine, and Mustafa Koç. 2008. "A Double-Double and a Maple-Glazed Doughnut." *Food, Culture, & Society* 11 (3): 263–7. http://dx.doi.org/10.2752/175174408X347838.

Rose, Gillian. 2012. *Visual Methodologies*. 3rd ed. London: Sage.

Saukko, Paula. 2005. *Doing Research in Cultural Studies: An Introduction to Classical and New Methodological Approaches*. Thousand Oaks, CA: Sage.

Scrinis, Gyorgy. 2013. *Nutritionism: The Science and Politics of Dietary Advice*. New York: Columbia University Press.

Slack, Jennifer D. 1996. "The Theory and Method of Articulation in Cultural Studies." In *Stuart Hall: Critical Dialogues in Cultural Studies*, edited by David Morley and Kuan-Hsing Chen, 113-129. New York: Routledge.

Smith, Julie. 2015. "Markets, Breastfeeding and Trade in Mothers' Milk." *International Breastfeeding Journal* 10 (9): 1–7.

Valenze, Deborah. 2011. *Milk: A Local and Global History*. New Haven, USA: Yale University Press.

Ventresca, Matt, and Jennifer Brady. 2015. "Food for Thought Notes on Food, Performance, and the Athletic Body." *Journal of Sport and Social Issues* 39 (5): 412–26. http://dx.doi.org/10.1177/0193723514561548.

Walters, Krista. 2012. "'A National Priority' Nutrition Canada's *Survey* and the Disciplining of Aboriginal Bodies, 1964–1975." In *Edible Histories, Cultural Politics: Towards a Canadian Food History*, edited by Franca Iacovetta, Valerie J. Korinek, and Marlene Epp, 433–52. Toronto: University of Toronto Press.

Williams, Patricia, Lynn McIntyre, and Theresa N. Glanville. 2010. "Milk Insecurity: Accounts of a Food Insecurity Phenomenon in Canada and Its Relation to Public Policy." *Journal of Hunger & Environmental Nutrition* 5 (2): 142–57. http://dx.doi.org/10.1080/19320248.2010.489369.

Williams-Forson, Pysche, and Carole Counihan. 2012. *Taking Food Public: Redefining Foodways in a Changing World*. New York: Routledge.

Wolf, Joan B. 2011. *Is Breast Best? Taking on the Breastfeeding Experts and the New High Stakes of Motherhood*. New York: New York University Press.

"Workout Recovery." 2013. *Rechargewithmilk.ca*. Last modified 17 December 2013. http://www.rechargewithmilk.ca/workout_recovery.

CHAPTER 4

Food Talk: Composing the Agricultural Land Reserve

Arthur Green and Robyn Bunn

Agricultural land is a scarce resource in British Columbia (BC), Canada. Only 5 percent of the provincial land base is considered suitable for agriculture, 2.7 percent capable of growing a reasonable range of crops, and 1.1 percent as prime agricultural land (Smith 2012).[1] Since the 1970s, debates over these limited agricultural lands have been a permanent part of BC's political landscape. The focal point of these debates is the Agricultural Land Reserve (ALR), a provincial land-use zone created in 1973 to permanently preserve approximately 4.7 million hectares of the province's best agricultural lands. The desire to support agriculture and food security drove the creation of the ALR in the early 1970s when urban sprawl near Vancouver consumed up to 6,000 hectares of farmland annually (Smith 1974, 2012; PALC 1983).

Debates over the ALR amalgamate competing discourses that influence public perceptions of the nature of and solutions to problems confronting agricultural lands. These debates over agricultural lands involve disputes over values, ideologies, and material interests (Demeritt 1995; Bunce 1998; Dixon and Hapke 2003). Food studies scholars are ideally placed to these complex debates and to develop integrated, critical understandings of how discourse, rhetoric, and performativity interact in ways that impact food system change (Knezevic et al. 2014). In this chapter, we analyze the discourses used within these debates to better understand how rhetorical strategies influence how agriculture is ideologically situated, regionally governed, and locally practiced. The rhetorical strategies deployed in debates over BC's

ALR, and North America's agricultural lands, have important impacts on broader food system dynamics.

In this chapter, we use critical discourse analysis to examine how a specific rights-based rhetorical strategy is used to both justify and challenge agricultural land-use policies in the Okanagan Valley, one of Canada's most productive agricultural regions and an important case study of wider debates over agricultural lands in BC and beyond. Debates over BC's agricultural lands increasingly invoke a rights-based rhetorical strategy that uses the language of food (Condon et al. 2010; Wittman and Barbolet 2011). Terms such as "food security" (the right of access to food), "food sovereignty" (the right of people to play a role in shaping their food systems), and "locavorism" (a consumer right to local food) are rights that are claimed in debates at all political scales by both proponents and opponents of food system change (Riches 1999; Van Esterik 1999; Patel 2009; Wittman 2011; Claeys 2012; Allen 2013). Such rights claims are core to the evolution of the modern food movement and outline food justice in policy and practice (Patel 2009; Claeys 2012; Allen 2013). These rights claims are central to the discourses employed by advocates of different policy regimes (Holt-Giménez and Shattuck 2011). Invoking this rights-based rhetorical strategy influences not only the outcomes of debate, but also how participants in debates represent themselves, their landscapes, and the ALR. We argue that this rights-based strategy of talking about food system change can be referred to as "food talk" and that how food talk is used in debates over agricultural land is an important area for analysis by academics, policy makers, and activists.

We define food talk as a rhetorical strategy that uses rights claims to justify food system change. The rhetoric of food talk reflects the current proliferation of food-related discourses and is imbued with sets of meanings, embodiments of identity, and socio-political positioning that require investigation and conscious, contextual deployment (Frye and Bruner 2012). While Thompson (2012) proposes that food talk has similarities to rights talk, we argue that food talk is actually an extension of the rhetorical strategy of rights talk into debates over food system change. Rights talk is a persuasive approach to legitimizing political claims within nation-states as it frames all political currency as entitlements and all legitimate political arguments as only those that can be articulated as rights-based claims (Glendon 1991). Critiques of food talk parallel critiques of rights talk. Critics find that this rhetorical strategy of making rights claims is innately linked to liberal individualism and risks being a strategy of individuals making divisive claims against each other rather than collective claims for food system change (Kneen 2009; Thompson 2012). Yet, in practice, food talk is deployed by individuals, organizations, and social movements to negotiate power at all political levels (Patel 2009; Wittman 2011). In fact, food talk draws on the authority of the nation-state and international institutions to create new types of rights claims, representing the evolution of rights talk in a context of increasing politicization of food systems debates (Claeys 2012).

While food talk can be used as a tool to change food systems, there are potential negative outcomes of deploying food talk to empower marginalized peoples. Foremost, the use of food talk risks institutionalizing subversion—that is, those that use food talk to articulate political positions may alter how they approach social change and how they represent themselves (Claeys 2012). Moreover, like rights talk, food talk fails to address the instability and performativity of rights in social contexts wherein conflicting understanding of rights as well as conflicts between different rights must be negotiated (Tushnet 1984, 1989). For example, the meaning of many of the terms used in food talk can only be substantiated through empirical investigation of the contexts in which the terms are produced, distributed, and consumed (Allen 2013; Desmarais and Wittman 2014). Terms such as "food security" and "food sovereignty" have been reinterpreted over time (Patel 2009), change through action and implementation by regional and local actors (Hinrichs 2013; Allen 2013; Brunori, Malandrin, and Rossi 2013), and are sometimes used by conflicting actors for radically different referents and intended outcomes (Lee 2013; Maye and Kirwan 2013). Despite this ambiguity, food talk is extensively used in public debates and defines the policy context for making food system change. By validating specific political positions, actors, and discourses, the rhetorical strategy of food talk affects policy decisions and changes how agriculture is practised on the ground. Food talk influences how BC's ALR has become embodied in law, policy, and practice.

Although BC's ALR is often cited as an exemplary provincial initiative toward food security and agricultural land preservation (Campbell 2006; Condon et al. 2010), it is not the only legislation of its type in Canada. In southern Ontario, the Foodland Guidelines legislation of 1978 was created to preserve agricultural land for local food production and environmental protection, and has evolved into the Greenbelt Protection Act of 2005 (Beesley 2010). Similarly, with the Act Respecting the Preservation of Agricultural Land and Agricultural Activities (originally passed in 1978 and revised in 1997), Quebec established an agricultural zone across the province to protect fertile farmlands (CPTAQ 1999; Caldwell and Dodds-Weir 2009).

These Canadian policies often result in unique legislation and bylaws that suit local conditions, yet stem from similar concerns about how to respond to the threat of urban sprawl to agricultural production and lands (Beesley 2010). The debates over modifications to, and the continuation of, these other land policies invoke food talk. Understanding how this rhetorical strategy has been deployed in BC may provide insights into the ways that discourses in these other regions influence policy outcomes.

Most of the research related to the public debates over BC's ALR over the last forty years has focussed on the potential impact of different policy models (Stobbe, Cotteleer, and van Kooten 2009; Wittman and Barbolet 2011; Connell et al. 2013) or on the categorization of discourses and policy negotiations (Demeritt 1995; Garrish 2002). In this chapter, we argue that a more nuanced understanding of the ways in which rhetorical strategies such as food talk are used is essential to inform debates and decision making regarding the governance of agricultural land.

The Okanagan's Agricultural Landscapes and the Agricultural Land Reserve

The Okanagan Valley is a 200-kilometre-long, 20-kilometre-wide valley that follows the Okanagan Lake basin within the traditional territory of the Syilx (Okanagan) Nation in BC's interior—over 400 kilometres to the east of Vancouver and the Lower Mainland. It is home to over 7.5 percent (346,000) of British Columbians, making it the highest-density population in the interior. Despite recent rapid population growth, a diverse agricultural sector continues to be a major contributor to the economy and modern identity of the Okanagan. Vegetable production, ranching, dairy operations, haymaking, and various animal farms can be found throughout the valley. Irrigation and favourable growing conditions have also allowed the Okanagan to establish a commercial reputation as one of the top fruit and wine production regions in Canada (Statistics Canada 2011). The resulting mosaic of urban development within the working agricultural landscape renders the agricultural identity relevant to even rapidly urbanizing areas. The region's agrarian past and present are realized through the landscape and continue to play a significant role in shaping the Okanagan identity (Koroscil 2003; Wagner 2008; Hessing 2010). The agricultural lands in the ALR are an important part of this cultural landscape. At its inception, the ALR included 189,838 hectares of the Okanagan land base. Since 1974, the amount of ALR land in the Okanagan decreased about 5 percent to 180,183 hectares (PALC 2013).

While land has been lost and some high-quality farmland swapped out of the ALR with properties of lesser agricultural value, the ALR has prevented a complete loss of farmland in areas of urban sprawl. This is particularly evident around Kelowna, where, despite strong ALR support, up to 12.9 percent of the city's ALR has been converted out of agriculture (MAL and PALC 2008). As a result, for many local residents, proposed changes to ALR lands or the activities that can be undertaken on these lands imply changes to regional identity.

Conflicting visions of what activities should be allowed on agricultural lands and how agricultural lands should be governed focus on the ALR legislation. Supporters of the ALR legislation discursively position it and the lands it protects as one of the pillars of a sustainable food system. Detractors position the ALR as a dysfunctional set of policies that undermine innovation, property rights, and rural livelihoods. These conflicting positions and visions are negotiated through the processes of local policy creation and regulatory implementation. Food talk is deployed in these negotiations to discursively align local issues and arguments to larger ideological positions and aspects of provincial debates. In this sense, food talk mediates multi-scalar efforts to achieve what Allen (2010) describes as a socially just food system "in which power and material resources are shared equitably" (297). The rhetoric of food talk is especially powerful in these negotiations as there is relatively little publically available research about how the ALR functions or how it impacts the Okanagan landscape and local food justice. In a context wherein many arguments are based on relatively poor statistics or anecdotes, skillful political use of food talk can sway policy, policy makers, and public opinion.

Methods: Critical Discourse Analysis for Food Studies Research

The integrative field of food studies provides a powerful window into the rhetorical strategies, discourses, and power relations that influence BC's ALR. Food studies scholars increasingly use and note the contemporary importance of conducting discourse analysis to examine food and food systems as "fundamental manifestations of issues, tensions, and conundrums related to political, economic, social, and health systems" (Knezevic et al. 2014, 3). For example, in Canada, the increasing momentum of communities of discourse gathered around terms like "food sovereignty" has been noted by several authors who call for a more nuanced examination of how this term is discursively produced and relates to policy advocacy (Desmarais and Wittman 2014). Discourse analysis provides tools to reveal how claims to certain power relations (e.g., right to be fed, right to food, and right to feed) are created and implemented through discursive practices (Van Esterik 1999; Lee 2013). Researchers have used different techniques of discourse analysis to examine rhetorical strategies and discourses that influence debates over agricultural legislation and land policy throughout North America (Demeritt 1995; Bunce 1998; Dixon and Hapke 2003). In this chapter, we engage specifically with critical discourse analysis (CDA).

CDA challenges assumptions that underpin different discourses thus providing a tool to critique the status quo, particularly the dominant neoliberal discourse that has dominated policy making since the 1970s (van Dijk 1993; Fairclough 2004; Knezevic et al. 2014). CDA allows strategic critique of the use of discourses in the "development, promotion and dissemination of the strategies for social change of particular groups of social agents, and in hegemonic struggle between strategies" (Fairclough 2004, 7). Following Fairclough (1995), we use a three-dimensional CDA framework that examines what Fairclough calls "text," "discourse practice," and "sociocultural practice" so that analyses of texts should not be isolated from analysis of institutional and discursive practices within which texts are embedded.

Our primary texts were public applications submitted to the Agricultural Advisory Committee (AAC) of Kelowna. AAC applications typically consist of the following: (1) maps generated by city staff regarding land capability, soil class, satellite images, parcel lines, and zoning; (2) maps generated by consultants (e.g., agrologists) that often indicate soil test locations and soil gradients; (3) ground-level photographs showing land-use patterns; (4) a highly structured report to the committee written by planning staff typically including sections on the purpose, background, site context, project description, and relation to current development policies; (5) the two-page application completed by a landowner; (6) a collection of supporting materials deemed relevant and supportive of the case; and (7) an Agricultural Impact Assessment, if a professional agrologist has prepared one. Applicants typically work with city staff and a professional agrologist to develop their application. They then present their application to the AAC in a public forum where recommendations are made to modify the applications before moving them on to the city council. After the council votes to recommend the application to the provincial Agricultural Land Commission (ALC), the ALC evaluates the application to make a final decision to approve, approve pending changes, or reject the application.

In analyzing the application texts, we examined the structure of the texts (what information was included), how food talk was used to represent arguments within the text, and how food talk was used to set up writer and reader identities and relations. These texts allow examination of discourse practices—the processes of producing, distributing, transforming, and consuming texts. In addition to looking for food talk terms, we examined intertextuality[2] to provide evidence of links to broader provincial, national, and global debates. In addition to the application texts, we used a purposive sampling strategy to gather materials for analysis of the broader "sociocultural practice." We included nine interviews with key decision makers in the Okanagan. We also gathered position statements by political groups and organizations concerned with food security in the Okanogan. Furthermore, we analyzed local media and online discussion forums where comments by individual community members yielded an illustrative range of the opinions held by citizens of the Okanagan.

Composing the ALR

Our analysis revealed that food talk discursively links arguments in application texts and in debates over specific agricultural lands with broader political debate themes and ideological stances. Public statements made by provincial politicians, municipal politicians, and Okanagan residents in debates over the ALR deploy food talk to make claims about what the government should or should not do in regard to agricultural land policy. For example, a right to "food security" is cited by Okanagan farmers and provincial politicians as a reason to support the ALR: "It is inconceivable that the [BC] Liberal government can even consider reducing protection for farmland in British Columbia when there is overwhelming evidence and concern at the global and national level about the looming food security crisis across the world and in our own backyards" (BC farmer Jenny Horn, Letter to Premier, April 2014); "The British Columbia Local Food Act is to improve and maximize food security, economic return and population health outcomes from our public land trust—the agricultural land reserve [sic].... Our province currently lacks a strategy that ensures we are fully capitalizing on our agricultural land base in a way that grows our economy, improves population health and food security. Instead, the government has a plan to undermine that, in the form of Bill 24" (Adrian Dix, NDP MLA and party leader, Hansard House Blues BC, April 2014).

When not explicitly using rights claims like "food security," public statements parallel the below quotes from an Okanagan resident and a provincial politician by suggesting a broader right to an undefined "food future" for unspecified "local" people that the government has a duty to support:

"As the planet heats, and we become less able to import produce from Mexico and South America, our ability to grow food locally will become vital. It is vital to preserve arable land for future generations" (Contributor to discussion forum, Stop the Swap, January 2014); "I know that farmers, local food lovers, and people concerned about the safety and sustainability of our food will continue to put wind in the sails of their elected representatives, pushing them to do the right thing and stand up for our food future" (Nicolas Simons, NDP MLA and agriculture critic, Official Press Release, February 2014).

Several of the application texts that we examined utilize food talk to discursively link text arguments to broader public debates and ideologies that support discourse-based visions of the ALR. Our analysis of texts and other materials suggests six key discourses are found in ALR debates: agrarianism, Arcadianism, agricultural landscape as Okanagan identity, neoliberal market productivism, progressive farming, and radical farming. The six discourses that we identified above have also been recognized by other researchers examining agricultural land policy in BC and throughout North America (for more information on these discourses, see Demeritt 1995; Dixon and Hapke 2003; and Holt-Giménez and Shattuck 2011). In our data, the use of particular discourses was associated with how people defined terms like "food security," "agriculture," "the public good," "producer rights," and "the local." In addition, the different discourses correlated with positions regarding the ALR. These positions simplify the complexities of the ALR by characterizing it as either an impediment to "rational" land use or as an effective policy fulfilling its purpose to preserve agricultural lands that are in productive use. Lacking better publically available data on land change and production in the ALR, these characterizations of the ALR often relay on old data, anecdotes, and ideology.

While the formal nature of ALR applications limits the ideological tenor of arguments as compared to media releases and internet forums, there was still evidence that applicants drew from the above discourses and deployed food talk as a rhetorical strategy. Applicants for changes to the ALR argue that the impacts on agricultural lands should be balanced with other, sometimes ambiguous benefits. Recurring arguments for making changes to ALR lands include saving the family farm, benefits to the public good, providing net benefits to agriculture, increasing cost efficiency, encouraging innovation, and the claim that there were mistakes in the original ALR boundaries. In the two cases we present below, we examine how debate participants and applicants use food talk in attempts to influence public understanding of the

ALR and to position themselves and their arguments regarding changes to the ALR. These deployments of food talk are used to neutralize and undermine counterarguments as an exercise of power. The first case demonstrates how an ALR application text incorporates food talk in an argument for subdivision of a family farm. The second examines food talk in a local debate over a proposed municipal application to make ALR boundary changes— revealing the political process of composing an ALR application text itself.

Subdividing the Small Farm

The Kowalczyks' sixteen-hectare family farm is located within the ALR and in an area of rapid population growth within the city boundaries of Kelowna. As protected agricultural land, any subdivision of the Kowalczyk farm requires a costly and time-consuming ALR application. In 2013, the Kowalczysks began working with contracted soil specialists and city staff to make an application that would go to the appointed members of the Kelowna AAC, municipal politicians on the city council, and ultimately the ALC, where a final decision would be rendered on the subdivision. They made a similar application in the 1990s that was rejected, but the Kowalczyks reasoned that this application to subdivide the farm into two smaller family farms should be approved, as their subdivision would provide a net benefit to agriculture. They argued that it would support "local" food security by increasing the number of small farmers, diversifying local agricultural production, improving productivity from the land parcel, and saving their own family farm business.

The applicants deployed agrarian, progressive, and radical farming discourses. They deployed food talk drawing on several media sources to link their proposed subdivision to large political debates. They used extensive quotes from international media (Ahmed 2013), regional media linking the ALR to food production (Steeves 2013), reports on food security and food sovereignty from national non-profit organizations (Rosset 1999; People's Food Policy Project 2011), and an academic article on food sovereignty (Wittman 2011). While these materials come to similar conclusions about the positive support that small farms offer for "local" food security, the concept of "local" is usually geographically ambiguous, or associated with the province or country rather than a municipality.

Two key interlinked arguments used in the text were related to providing a net benefit to agriculture and saving the family farm. Arguing for the net benefits to agriculture, the application text focusses on supporting food security by working against the limits that land speculation has caused for new farmer entry. The average age of farmers in BC is 55.7 and the high cost of land prevents young farmers from entering the sector because it often surpasses potential agricultural profit margins (Stobbe, Cotteleer, and van Kooten 2009; Tunnicliffe 2013). The application states the following:

> It will encourage farming on agricultural land…. Studies done as early as 1999 and into 2012 show that nothing ensures a community's food security as well as a variety of small multi-functional farms rather than the larger monoculture models…. The subdivision of this lot will generate two farms where there was only one. This acreage will be ideal in size and price range for the majority of farmers that are in the market for land today in BC…. The highest demand for agricultural land in BC is for two to five hectare sized farms in or close to urban areas…. Because large parcels (anything larger than five hectares) are either beyond the grasp of young farmers or would start them out with such a heavy debt load the likelihood of growing their business past it is very small.

The application also incorporates a narrative about the family farming history, linking their farm to local food security and arguing for the importance of small-scale agriculture. The applicants then discuss the incorporation of innovative value-added agricultural products into their business to demonstrate their efforts to profitably farm the land and to recount how a previous rejection of an ALR application to subdivide the land in the 1990s led to the family farm's current problematic financial situation. They write,

> The most successful way to benefit agriculture is to integrate it into the urban landscape; this is remarkably true in spaces like the Okanagan Valley and Kelowna in particular. As the studies and papers included with this application indicate, smaller farms are more likely to not only fit into said landscape, but also encourage more people to get into the business of farming/agriculture. The type of agriculture is also very important. A smaller acreage facilitates a more diverse agro-ecology which is not dependent on world commodity pricing. The farmers are in better control of their markets and revenues which in turn makes them more likely to continue farming and preserve the land for future farming….
>
> We apply for subdivision now in a much more dire situation, having barely come through the recession…. We entreat you to

> take the above into consideration as well as the information we
> have provided with the subdivision proposal information draw-
> ing from extensive review of reports and studies on the subject
> done by local, provincial, national and global stakeholders in
> food security and agriculture.

The applicants use food talk to position their proposed ALR variance as beneficial to agriculture and position themselves as dedicated farmers who are essential to the Okanagan's unique agricultural landscape. Their use of food talk aligns them with the visions of agricultural landscape articulated in discourses of agrarianism, Arcadianism, and progressive farming. To an extent, the application conflates food security and food sovereignty, not recognizing the more radical rights demands inherent in food sovereignty, which require much more fundamental and structural changes to the food system and the planning processes of the ALR (Holt-Giménez and Shattuck 2011). Yet, even without these more radical rights claims, the application's reliance on the progressive farming discourse's version of "food security" is problematic in a policy context dominated by the neoliberal policy discourse and in regard to the bureaucratic interpretation of the ALR legislation.

The progressive farming interpretation of food security directly conflicts with the dominant neoliberal market productivism (agribusiness) interpretation of food security. The progressive interpretation recognizes a global environmental crisis, and then argues for a definition of food security as culturally appropriate, nutritious, and locally sourced foods (though "local" remains geographically ambiguous). The progressive interpretation positions food security as a human right that the state is obligated to secure and the applicants cite this interpretation of food security as the original intent of the ALR legislation. The neoliberal approach to food security, in contrast, rejects that there is a food security crisis at all, and makes the underlying assumption that promoting a profitable international import-export trade structure will provide the general population access to cheap food. Rights claims deployed within the neoliberal market productivism discourse emphasize ideological aspects of neoliberalism. Fetishes with private property rights and idealized markets manifest as an emphasis on allowing lands to be put to "best uses" (i.e., open to international land markets) that would in turn increase the financial stability of current producers and contribute to economies of scale for the BC food supply. By emphasizing cheap agricultural commodities obtained by international trade and a model of agribusiness geared toward exports, the neoliberal version of food security contradicts a food security based on local farmers producing for local consumers. Wittman and Barbolet (2011) outline these contradictions as they analyze assets (such as the ALR) and structural constraints to implementing a food sovereignty policy model in BC, even while neoliberal provincial and federal policies actively undermine any sort of local food system.

The progressive farming perspective of food security also seems to contradict the provincial ALC staff's interpretation of their mandate to support agriculture by limiting the subdivision of ALR lands and even the language of legislative basis of the ALR, the Agricultural Land Commission Act of 2002. The ALC staff interprets the legislation as a mandate to support agriculture by limiting subdivisions regardless of who owns the land (ALC staff, personal interview, June 2014). So, consolidation of lands under any large-scale land owner is, in this interpretation of ALR legislation, more preferable than subdividing agricultural parcels that would facilitate the entry of small farmers into the current land market. In theory, the existing farming tax incentives enable large-scale landowners to pursue highly productive forms of agriculture. Yet, in practice, these incentives often result in the conversion of land to hay for fodder, which is more profitable than the production of food crops. As such, the legislation provides a disincentive for small-scale mixed farming and encourages farmers to pursue the most profitable farm output, which may not include foodstuffs that contribute to local food security. The realization of "agriculture" in the legislation reveals a fundamental disagreement in interpretation about the value of specific types of agricultural landscapes (one of small-scale farmers focused on regional markets or large scale farmers focused on export) and how to support agriculture in these landscapes. For progressive and radical farming discourses, the legislation seems to undermine the stated goal of supporting agriculture because the legislation has not adequately confronted one of the main challenges to making agriculture lands productive in BC—that is, getting dedicated farmers on the land.

In this case, the Kowalczyk family's application to subdivide the land was both grounded in and challenged by food talk—specifically, claims to support food security—but also a broader set of rights claims and debate themes that include defining agriculture, "the local," and a net benefit to agriculture. The reaction to this application (which is still under consideration at the time of this writing) by bureaucrats and politicians has been negative as the current policy context predominately interprets food talk terms within the neoliberal discourse. Whether or not the applicants are sincere, this application presents a powerful example of the deployment of food talk and how counterpoising deployments of food talk can lead to radically different outcomes.

Stop the Swap

The "Stop the Swap" campaign was organized by residents of the town of Summerland in opposition to their city council's proposal to remove agricultural land from the ALR, in exchange for (re)including another parcel of land that is significantly more marginal for agricultural production. Food talk within this campaign and during public hearings regarding the "swap" is illustrative of the themes that emerged from the analysis of the debates surrounding the ALR in the Okanagan.

Summerland has a population of 11,280 (Statistics Canada 2012), and like many other communities in the Okanagan, tourism and agriculture are important for the community's economy (District of Summerland 2015). Summerland city council is attempting to amend the Official Community Plan (OCP) by removing eighty hectares of class 1, 2, and 3 ALR land to enable residential development in an area north of the city centre. Some of this land slated for removal is currently in use for agriculture. Council has suggested a ninety-one-hectare area of undeveloped hillside for ALR inclusion as compensation for the intended exclusions. A portion of the area that council intends to include in the land reserve was previously removed from the ALR for development in 2005. This land has been assessed as class 5 and 6 when it was ALR land, and at the time it was removed from the ALR it was argued to be unsuitable for agriculture. None of the proposed area has been under agricultural production; in fact, much of it is forested (SSAL 2014). This area has been part of Summerland's urban growth strategy since 1995 as a potential site for residential or recreational development (District of Summerland 2015).

After council announced these amendments to the OCP in December 2013, many Summerland residents responded negatively to the planned exclusions of agricultural land for development (e.g., letters to the editor were written to several local periodicals). The community organized a forum called "Save Summerland's Agricultural Land" for the Stop the Swap campaign soon after the proposed removal was announced. Members of this group have been strong voices in opposition to the proposed land swap, organizing a rally, writing letters to local and provincial government representatives, speaking to the media, and gathering signatures against the amendment to the ALR in Summerland (Global News 2013). Local food, future food security, the importance of agriculture in Summerland's economy, and the atmosphere and aesthetics of their community in attracting tourists and new residents have been central to the arguments against moving forward with the land swap. A Summerland orchardist explained: "Agricultural land is important for local and provincial food security; it's beautiful, it's economically important, and should continue to be protected because, once developed, it will never grow food again" (Summerland farmer, personal interview, April 2014).

In support of the amendment to remove the land, Summerland's council and community members justify this proposal by claiming that developing the area will lower the residents' carbon footprint by creating new neighbourhoods within walking distance of downtown (public hearing transcript, March 2014). While council recognizes the economic benefits of agriculture for their community, the arguments made by opposition about the need to ensure productive land for the future was refuted in public statements made by Summerland's mayor (Graham 2014). Mayor Janice Perrino stated to a local journalist, "When I hear the fear mongering about food supply I think to myself 'My goodness!' There would have to be an incredible world crisis to actually need that particular land as a food source" (Graham 2014).

Opposition to proposed changes of the OCP amendment was evident when several hundred residents attended the second public hearing on 22 April 2014 (McIver 2014). Of the thirty-nine community members that addressed council, thirty-eight spoke out against council going forward with this proposal (District of Summerland 2014). Despite this substantial opposition, on 28 April 2014, Summerland's city council voted four to one in favour of amending the OCP, which would re-designate ALR as open for development, and forwarded the exclusion application on to the ALC, where at the time writing, it remains pending (SSAL 2014).

The use of food talk in these debates excludes voices in the community as discourses reinforce inequitable relationships in regards to food justice. Campaign organizers wrote that "the ALR's contribution to current and future food security is of critical importance. Uncertainties relating to climate change and international markets make it all the more important to maintain our food producing lands so that future generations will have the ability to produce food locally" (SSAL 2014). Texts that cite future food security, "the local," and locavorism make assumptions about the geographic spaces in which food security should be pursued and the relevant political levels at which particular policy changes are required. Debate participants that mention future food security are often ambiguous about the population for which food security policy is focused. In addition, as shown in the first case, they commonly invoke food talk rhetoric giving "food security" different operational definitions within opposing discourses. Research on household food insecurity in Canada indicates that those facing food insecurity are the most marginalized community members (Rideout et al. 2007). Race, gender, ability, and class are identified as major contributing factors, and marginalized members of rural communities are often more at risk because of reduced access to resources such as food banks.

As Kneen (2009) asserts, claiming a right to food, even in a community with a strong local agricultural base, does not translate to all community members having equal access. Left out of discussions about ALR and food access are voices from marginalized and excluded groups that have significant interests in land use and foodways, such as migrant agricultural workers that have no formal political voice (Tomic et al. 2010) and Aboriginal community members that have little say in, but may be impacted by, decisions made on agricultural lands that are in close proximity to reserves or traditional hunting, fishing, and foraging lands. In the Okanagan, all of the ALR-designated lands are on unceded Syilx territory. There was no mention of Aboriginal rights to land or traditional foodways during the public hearings or the online forum for the Stop the Swap campaign. In addition, the rights of migrant workers have been overlooked. Approximately 5,000 foreign workers (and more than 6,000 in 2016) came to BC each year through the federal Seasonal Agricultural Workers Program (SAWP) (Employment and Social Development Canada 2012). Of those workers, approximately 1,500 to 2,000 work on farms in the Okanagan. ALR policy has a direct impact on the well-being of foreign workers who live on-farm and whose housing is under the constraints of allowable building limitations. Yet these labourers have no voice in decision making around this issue and are isolated by food talk deployment in community discussions. Rights-based claims within food talk that assert a collective right to agricultural land reaffirm boundaries as to who is included in "we" and "ours" and reproduce social norms that exclude non-citizens, Aboriginal peoples, and others not able to participate fully because they are marginalized.

The Stop the Swap campaign argues for preserving ALR in Summerland as the duty of this generation of community members to ensure the rights of future generations of residents. The benefits of the ALR, then, are exclusive to Summerland residents. But not only are benefits limited to the defined community, they are also accessible only to those who can afford them. This is specific to property ownership and residency since anyone who can't afford the costs of living in Summerland will not be considered "eligible" to benefit from the ALR. The first theme involves the nebulous idea of "the local" mentioned above, an idea that connotes an often unspecified geographic community, sometimes associated with nostalgic and idealized versions of the rural. In this case, the local is constrained to the District of Summerland. The presence of ALR lands in Summerland is positioned as giving residents access to "local food." Yet the disconnection between locality and income is apparent in this situation. The latest census data (2012) for Summerland shows a predominantly white population, with less than 1 percent of residents identifying as belonging to a visible minority group. While Summerland has a high level of education and an average annual after-tax family income of over $80,000, the apparent affluence of community members hides a class division as Summerland's low-income status rate is 11.3 percent (Statistics Canada 2012). While many people in Summerland may have the capacity to access locally produced foods, a significant percentage may be excluded by the cost of local food that caters to tourists seeking the "local experience."

Another theme in this debate revolves around defining the public good or the relative weight of several public goods. Three prominent aspects of this theme were the framing of "agriculture versus development," the emphasis on short-term financial gains as a public good, and the emphasis on the cultural functions of agriculture. In the case of Summerland's proposed amendment that would entail removal of land from ALR specifically to be developed for housing, this debate captures the ongoing perceptions of a struggle between agricultural uses and urban or ex-urban "development" in the form of new residential spaces and thus allows non-agricultural economic development and sustainable urban design advocates (ironically) to argue that agriculture is a relatively non-productive land use. This is seen as a public good from a planning perspective, citing the desirability of higher-density urban spaces, the walkability of neighbourhoods that include housing and businesses, and the need to reduce sprawl that also could result in a lower carbon footprint. This perspective downplays the value of having agriculture or even green spaces within the city limits because that would run counter to the perceived value of using urban space to its "fullest potential." It would seem that the few to benefit from this "public good" would be those who can afford to buy new single-family homes in an area within walking distance to the city centre. Of course, increased home ownership provides an increase to the tax-base within the municipality; however, those in opposition do not view the gains to the community's public purse to outweigh the long-term consequences of the loss of prime agricultural land.

Advocates of preserving the ALR emphasize landscape aesthetic and the role of agricultural lands in collective identity. Summerland residents articulating this perspective identify strongly with agriculture as the regional identity and associate their community with both the Arcadian bucolic utopia and agrarian visions of working landscapes with associated "good farmer" and "strong local community" ideas. This idea was evident in one comment posted on Stop the Swap's website: "Removing agricultural land and modifying our community's character eliminates one of the only advantages Summerland has in attracting new residents and retirees to choose our town over other towns in the Okanagan. This is especially true given that the ALR land we are discussing is within easy viewing and walking distance from the downtown core" (SSAL 2014). Opposition to development also includes an element of identity loss. The language and tenor used suggest a sense of bereavement when community members speak about former agricultural lands transformed into housing developments or commercial spaces. The language of food becomes a language of stewardship and thus a community right to defend both a productive future and an identity grounded in a nostalgic, moral landscape.

The case of the proposed land swap in Summerland is an example of how food talk is used in rights-based claims to future food security, access to local food, and agricultural land preservation for the benefit of the community. Those speaking against the removal of land from ALR for development construct agricultural lands as spaces where these concepts come to fruition. However, in practice, the benefits of the ALR are not accessible to everyone in the community, and the claims associated with agricultural spaces are exclusive to particular community members. Though a decision from the ALC on Summerland city council's application is still pending at the time of the writing of this chapter, council members rejected the arguments made by the opposition, illustrating adherence to the neoliberal model in which "growth" is the priority, and that priority is interpreted as the need to "develop" in the form of housing and businesses at the cost of agriculture.

Conclusion

This chapter demonstrated how the deployment of food talk is used to influence public debates over governance of ALR lands. In so doing, the chapter shows how CDA can be used to help social scientists "illuminate and challenge the dominant epistemological frameworks that assign problem definitions and solutions" (Allen 2013, 136). CDA techniques allowed us to analyze the deployment of a specific rhetorical strategy (in this case food talk), identify communities of discourse, and analyze how doublespeak convolutes public understanding, influences public debates over agricultural lands, and impacts implementation of policy on the ground.

In conducting CDA, we examined ways in which food talk allows local residents to link arguments in ALR applications and local agricultural land debates to broader ideological frames and provincial, national, and global debates. We found that while food talk is used to change public understanding of the ALR, it also repositions applicants to the ALR and advocates of food system change as claimants for rights. This repositioning requires evidence of individual or group rights and can inadvertently exclude marginalized groups if not carefully deployed.

Food talk can be a double-edged sword for marginalized groups such as migrant workers, small farmers, and the economically underprivileged. The reproduction of different discourses involved in debates over agricultural lands creates communities of discourse that use different versions of food talk. In the case of the ALR, terms such as "food security" and "local food" take on different, often contradicting definitions within competing discourses. The power relations of different communities of discourse are revealed when more dominant discourses are able to redefine the referents of food talk and influence policy outcomes. As shown in the cases presented above, wherein productivist strategies for export-oriented markets lead to challenges to the ALR, and as recognized in literature on BC's policy climate (Wittman and Barbolet 2011), neoliberal market productivism has preponderant authority in BC's current policy context. The hegemonic status of this discourse relates to the circles of power that perpetuate the discourse through the creation and implementation of provincial and municipal policies. It is these circles that choose which food talk is legitimate and who will benefit from new policies and interpretations of existing legislation. For ALR applicants, a misunderstanding of how proponents of the dominant neoliberal discourse interpret their rights claims can lead to rejection of their attempts to support agriculture.

In summary, attention to how food talk is discursively deployed reveals pathways to influence policy models by changing terminology and rhetorical strategies. As we have shown above, linking rhetorical strategies to discourse and policy outcomes is critical to realizing policies that promote food justice.

Notes

1   The Canadian Land Inventory (CLI) classifies the agricultural potential for lands into seven classes (1–7) from highest to lowest. Prime agricultural lands include CLI class 1–3 lands. Class 1–4 lands include land capable of growing a range of crops. The constraints of class 5 allow only the production of perennial forage crops and specially adapted crops, class 6 lands typically can support some grazing, and class 7 lands are not capable of supporting grazing.

2 "Intertextuality" refers to the relation of the application texts to other texts—that is, how texts cite and draw from other texts to validate points regarding changes to ALR lands.

References

Ahmed, Nafeez. 2013. "Dramatic Decline in Industrial Agriculture Could Herald 'Peak Food.'" *The Guardian*, 19 December.

Allen, Patricia. 2013. "Facing Food Security." *Journal of Rural Studies* 29:135–8. http://dx.doi.org/10.1016/j.jrurstud.2012.12.002.

Allen, Patricia. 2010. "Realizing Justice in Local Food Systems." *Cambridge Journal of Regions, Economy and Society* 3 (2): 295–308. http://dx.doi.org/10.1093/cjres/rsq015.

Beesley, Kenneth B. 2010. *The Rural–Urban Fringe in Canada: Conflict and Controversy*. Brandon, MB: Rural Development Institute, Brandon University.

Brunori, Gianluca, Vanessa Malandrin, and Adanella Rossi. 2013. "Trade-Off or Convergence? The Role of Food Security in the Evolution of Food Discourse in Italy." *Journal of Rural Studies* 29: 19–29. http://dx.doi.org/10.1016/j.jrurstud.2012.01.013.

Bunce, Michael. 1998. "Thirty Years of Farmland Preservation in North America: Discourses and Ideologies of a Movement." *Journal of Rural Studies* 14 (2): 233–47. http://dx.doi.org/10.1016/S0743-0167(97)00035-1.

Caldwell, Wayne J., and Claire Dodds-Weir. 2009. Canadian Approaches to the Preservation of Farmland. *Plan*: 17–20.

Campbell, Charles. 2006. *Forever Farmland: Reshaping the Agricultural Land Reserve for the 21st Century*. Vancouver: David Suzuki Foundation.

Claeys, Patricia. 2012. "The Creation of New Rights by the Food Sovereignty Movement: The Challenge of Institutionalizing Subversion." *Sociology* 46 (5): 844–60. http://dx.doi.org/10.1177/0038038512451534.

Condon, Patrick M., Kent Mullinix, Arthur Fallick, and Mike Harcourt. 2010. "Agriculture on the Edge: Strategies to Abate Urban Encroachment onto Agricultural Lands by Promoting Viable Human-Scale Agriculture as an Integral Element of Urbanization." *International Journal of Agricultural Sustainability* 8 (1): 104–15. http://dx.doi.org/10.3763/ijas.2009.0465.

Connell, David J., Christopher R. Bryant, Wayne J. Caldwell, Arthur Churchyard, Greg Cameron, Tom Johnston, Matias E. Margulis, Doug Ramsey, and Claud Marois. 2013. "Food Sovereignty and Agricultural Land Use Planning: The Need to Integrate Public Priorities across Jurisdictions." *Journal of Agriculture, Food Systems, and Community Development* 3 (4): 1–8. http://dx.doi.org/10.5304/jafscd.2013.034.011.

CPTAQ. 1999. *Summary of the Act Respecting the Preservation of Agricultural Land and Agricultural Activities*. Quebec: Commission de protection du territoire agricole du Québec.

Demeritt, David. 1995. "Visions of Agriculture in British Columbia." *BC Studies* (108): 29–59.

Desmarais, Annette A., and Hannah Wittman. 2014. "Farmers, Foodies and First Nations: Getting to Food Sovereignty in Canada." *Journal of Peasant Studies* 41 (6): 1153–1173.

District of Summerland. 2014. *Public Hearing Minutes, April 22, 2014.* http://www.summerland.ca/departments/council/councilagendas_minutes.aspx (accessed 21 Feb. 2016).

District of Summerland. 2015. *Summerland Official Community Plan.* Summerland. http://www.summerland.ca/docs/default-source/default-document-library/2014-ocp---schedule-a-2015-10-15.pdf?sfvrsn=0 (accessed 21 February 2016).

Dixon, Deborah P., and Holly M. Hapke. 2003. "Cultivating Discourse: The Social Construction of Agricultural Legislation." *Annals of the Association of American Geographers* 93 (1): 142–64. http://dx.doi.org/10.1111/1467-8306.93110.

Employment and Social Development Canada. 2012. Number of temporary foreign worker positions on positive Labour Market Impact Assessments (LMIAs) under the Agricultural Occupations, by location of employment. *Labour Market Opinions - Annual Statistics.* Retrieved February 21, 2016, from http://www.edsc.gc.ca/eng/jobs/foreign_workers/lmo_statistics/annual-agriculture.shtml.

Fairclough, Norman. 2004. "Critical Discourse Analysis and Change in Management Discourse and Ideology: A Transdisciplinary Approach to Strategic Critique." *Studies in Organizational Discourse,* 1–16.

Fairclough, Norman. 1995. *Critical Discourse Analysis: The Critical Study of Language.* London: Longman.

Frye, Joshua, and Michael Bruner, eds. 2012. *The Rhetoric of Food: Discourse, Materiality, and Power.* New York: Routledge.

Garrish, Christopher. 2002. "Unscrambling the Omelette: Understanding British Columbia's Agricultural Land Reserve." *BC Studies* 136: 25–55.

Glendon, Mary Ann. 1991. *Rights Talk: The Impoverishment of Political Discourse.* New York: Free Press.

Global News. 2013. Background Information. *Global BC,* 12 December. http://globalnews.ca/news/1027802/watch-farm-land-for-development/.

Graham, Adam. 2014. Summerland Mayor Further Explains Decision to Delay Vote on Agricultural Land Swap. *EZ Local News,* 12 March.

Hessing, Melody. 2010. "After the Harvest: Towards a Sustainable Okanagan?" *BC Studies* 168: 121–34.

Hinrichs, Claire C. 2013. "Regionalizing Food Security? Imperatives, Intersections and Contestations in a Post-9/11 World." *Journal of Rural Studies* 29: 7–18. http://dx.doi.org/10.1016/j.jrurstud.2012.09.003.

Holt-Giménez, Eric, and Annie Shattuck. 2011. "Food crises, Food Regimes and Food Movements: Rumblings of Reform or Tides of Transformation?" *Journal of Peasant Studies* 38 (1): 109–44. http://dx.doi.org/10.1080/03066150.2010.538578.

Kneen, Brewster. 2009. *The Tyranny of Rights.* Ottawa: The Ram's Horn.

Knezevic, Irena, Heather Hunter, Cynthia Watt, Patricia Williams, and Barbara Anderson. 2014. "Food Insecurity and Participation." *Critical Discourse Studies* 11 (2): 230–45. http://dx.doi.org/10.1080/17405904.2013.866590.

Koroscil, Paul M. 2003. *The British Garden of Eden : Settlement History of the Okanagan Valley.* British Columbia: Published by Paul M. Koroscil.

Lee, Richard Phillip. 2013. "The Politics of International Agri-Food Policy: Discourses of Trade-Oriented Food Security and Food Sovereignty." *Environmental Politics* 22 (2): 216–34. http://dx.doi.org/10.1080/09644016.2012.730266.

MAL and PALC. 2008. *The Agricultural Land Reserve and its Influence on Agriculture in the City of Kelowna.* Victoria; Burnaby.

Maye, Damian, and James Kirwan. 2013. "Food Security: A Fractured Consensus." *Journal of Rural Studies* 29: 1–6. http://dx.doi.org/10.1016/j.jrurstud.2012.12.001.

McIver, Susan. 2014. "Summerland Approves Controversial Land Swap." *Kelowna Daily Courier*, 29 April.

PALC. 2013. *Provincial Agricultural Land Commission Annual Report 2012/2013.* Burnaby, BC: Provincial Agricultural Land Commission.

PALC. 1983. *Ten Years of Agricultural Land Preservation in British Columbia.* Burnaby, BC: Provincial Agricultural Land Commission.

Patel, Raj. 2009. "Food Sovereignty." *Journal of Peasant Studies* 36 (3): 663–706. http://dx.doi.org/10.1080/03066150903143079.

People's Food Policy Project. 2011. *Resetting the Table: A People's Food Policy for Canada.* Food Secure Canada, http://foodsecurecanada.org/sites/default/files/fsc-resetting2012-8half11-lowres-en.pdf.

Riches, Graham. 1999. "Advancing the Human Right to Food in Canada: Social Policy and the Politics of Hunger, Welfare, and Food Security." *Agriculture and Human Values* 16 (2): 203–11. http://dx.doi.org/10.1023/A:1007576706862.

Rideout, Karen, Graham Riches, Aleck Ostry, Don Buckingham, and Rod MacRae. 2007. "Bringing Home the Right to Food in Canada: Challenges and Possibilities for Achieving Food Security." *Public Health Nutrition* 10 (6): 566–73. http://dx.doi.org/10.1017/S1368980007246622.

Rosset, Peter M. 1999. *The Multiple Functions and Benefits of Small Farm Agriculture: Policy Brief 4.* Washington, D.C. http://citeseerx.ist.psu.edu/viewdoc/summary?doi=10.1.1.178.8840 (accessed 15 September 2014).

Smith, Barry E. 2012. *A Work in Progress—The British Columbia Farmland Preservation Program.* Burnaby, BC.

Smith, Barry E. 1974. "The British Columbia Land Commission Act 1973." MA thesis University of British Columbia.

SSAL (Save Summerland's Agricultural Land). 2014. Save Summerland's Agricultural Land, 1 October. http://savethesummerlandalr.com.

Statistics Canada. 2011. *2011 Census of Agriculture.* Ottawa: Government of Canada.

Statistics Canada. 2012. Focus on Geography Series, 2011 Census. Statistics Canada Catalogue no. 98-310-XWE2011004. *Analytical products, 2011 Census.*

Steeves, Judie. 2013. Changes Needed to Make Farming Economically Viable Again. *Capital News*, 28 November.

Stobbe, Tracy, Geerte Cotteleer, and Gerrit C. van Kooten. 2009. "Hobby Farms and Protection of Farmland in British Columbia." *Canadian Journal of Regional Science / Revue canadienne des sciences régionales* 3: 393–410.

Thompson, John R. 2012. "'Food Talk': Bridging Power in a Globalizing World." In *The Rhetoric of Food: Discourse, Materiality, and Power*, edited by Joshua J. Frye and Michael S. Bruner, 58–70. New York: Routledge.

Tomic, P., R. Trumper, and L. L. M. Aguiar. 2010. "Housing Regulations and Living Conditions of Mexican Migrant Workers in the Okanagan Valley, BC." *Canadian Issues / Thèmes canadiens*: 78–82.

Tunnicliffe, Robin. 2013. *Young Agrarians Land Access Guide 2.0.* Vancouver, BC: Young Agrarians; FarmFolk CityFolk; Real Estate Foundation of BC.

Tushnet, Mark. 1989. "Rights—An Essay in Informal Political Theory." *Politics & Society* 17 (4): 403–51. http://dx.doi.org/10.1177/003232928901700401.

Tushnet, Mark. 1984. "An Essay on Rights." *Texas Law Review* 62 (8): 1363–403.

van Dijk, Teun A. 1993. "Principles of Critical Discourse Analysis." *Discourse & Society* 4 (2): 249–83. http://dx.doi.org/10.1177/0957926593004002006.

Van Esterik, Penny. 1999. "Right to Food; Right to Feed; Right to Be Fed: The Intersection of Women's Rights and the Right to Food." *Agriculture and Human Values* 16 (2): 225–32. http://dx.doi.org/10.1023/A:1007524722792.

Wagner, John R. 2008. "Landscape Aesthetics, Water, and Settler Colonialism in the Okanagan Valley of British Columbia." *Journal of Ecological Anthropology* 12 (1): 22–38. http://dx.doi.org/10.5038/2162-4593.12.1.2.

Wittman, Hannah. 2011. "Food Sovereignty: A New Rights Framework for Food and Nature?" *Environment and Society: Advances in Research* 2 (1): 87–105.

Wittman, Hahhan, and Herb Barbolet. 2011. "'Super, Natural': The Potential of Food Sovereignty in British Columbia." In *Food Sovereignty in Canada: Creating Just and Sustainable Food Systems*, edited by Annette A. Desmarais, Nettie Wiebe, and Hannah Wittman, 190–211. Halifax, NS: Fernwood Publishing.

Commentary on Part I: Re-presenting Disciplinary Praxis

Penny Van Esterik

Visual methods in food studies, performance art, milk advertisements, and agricultural land policy in BC—these papers cover all phases of the food system, from production to consumption, and points in between. They consider how discourse, rhetoric, and performativity shape food systems, and influence food justice. According to the editors of this book, the theme of representing considers how stakeholders, as well as food itself, is represented and what this means for how we think about what it is we are seeking to understand and sometimes change as scholars, activists, and students.

How do these papers advance our understanding of how food represents? They all come from different disciplinary perspectives, some using multiple disciplines within a single paper. I imagine that two of the papers could be summarized briefly and given to food activists for their consideration, with the idea that the knowledge produced could be of practical use to them. The papers on media and performance make no claims about direct practical application, but rather help the reader think about and interpret food and eating in different, more complex ways. Yet all contribute to our understanding of how food represents. To explore this subject, I will consider how disciplines shape representation, how knowledge links to policy and practice, and the importance of considering intention and context in food studies research, linking the little and the large. As I am somewhat low-vision, I cannot skim the latest literature or even google the newest theoretical debates on food issues to sound more erudite. As a result, after

2010, I began to just cite myself as the ultimate authority. While not a very praiseworthy academic practice, it provides an imposed positionality.

Fortunately, Raymond Williams's *Keywords* was written in 1985 when I was at my peak, and I had highlighted the term "representation" in fluorescent pink, in anticipation of my dwindling visual abilities. According to Williams (1985, 266–9), the word "represent" appeared in the fourteenth century and acquired a range of meanings around making present, in the physical sense of presenting oneself to authority and making present in the mind or to the eye. Only later did it acquire the additional meaning—that is, to symbolize or stand for something that is not present. It acquired more political and legal meanings, as a state or condition represented by a particular institution, as in representing the people of your district, representing their opinions or speaking on their behalf. The complexity and ambiguity of the term continues in the domain of art and literature, where a representation is a symbol or image presented to the eye or mind, a visual embodiment of something. Szanto, Wong, and Brady evoke this meaning by reference to the performance frame as "twice-behaved behaviour"—behaviour re-presented, or presented again for an audience. These interconnected political and artistic meanings resonate in inner-city urban Black culture and rap music. The online slang dictionary[1] lists a phrase such as "You betta represent" to mean that people should be candid about or acknowledge their origin or roots, however humble; rather than trying to dissemble, people should take pride in their group or neighbourhood without shame.

Disciplining Food Studies

In order to start a conversation across disciplines, I begin from my own disciplinary base, anthropology, a field that has been poaching across disciplines for so many decades that the crossings go unremarked. The poachings are then absorbed into the discipline, justified on the basis of the claim that anthropology is concerned about the human condition across time and space. This is why the *Food and Culture* reader that I have edited over the years with Carole Counihan (1997, 2008, 2013) can focus primarily on the work of anthropologists and still cover substantial work in food studies.

Disciplines bring different logics to knowledge production—the lab logic of nutrition, the clinic logic of dietetics, the field logic of ethnography and geography, and the performance logic of theatre, for example. Disciplinary frames often supply methodological tools that can travel across disciplines. The authors of these papers use gender analysis and critical discourse analysis; these conceptual and methodological tools travel easily across disciplines. Clearly, different disciplines can use the same conceptual tools. The more food studies researchers share conceptual tools, the more the field will be able to develop sharable research questions.

Perhaps more important is knowing when and how to cross disciplines, or as Josée Johnston (this volume) phrased it in her commentary on "Undoing Food Studies," when to "bend the fences" (288). One technique is to develop hybrids such as biocultural, agro-industrial, or political ecology. But there is room in food studies to retain distinct disciplinary methods. A disciplinary base provides some standards for what constitutes evidence. Historical and ethnographic methods, for example, provide data that can inform policy making or activism or, ideally, both. Some things are best tackled within a discipline rather than across disciplines. I still want a toxicologist to check the chemicals and toxins in my food, even as I complain that their gaze might be too narrow when it comes to asking why and how those toxins got there in the first place.

Beyond food-specific frames such as meal formats, local and sustainable food, or slow food is the awareness that all food systems are embedded in social and cultural processes far removed from food and eating. This is the dilemma of context that consumes anthropologists, as they find every food-related practice is related to just about everything else (or as Geertz noted, turtles all the way down). For example, what is the relation between the natural environment—the material conditions of soil, geology, and climate—and the cultural traditions and local customs developed within that environment? How do both relate to the global food system, including structures such as advertising agencies, marketing boards, and other regulatory systems?

Policy and Praxis

The power of food studies is its ability to fit the appropriate disciplinary frame to the problem at hand. The way we represent makes some things possible and other things difficult or impossible. One challenge in food studies, then, is to consider the most suitable frame for accomplishing the author's intention.

Food studies researchers need to decide on their priorities. If their intention is to reduce hunger among inner-city homeless, issues around representation may not be the most appropriate frame.

Not all papers in this section link to policy or praxis—nor should they—but all should provide arguments that help us understand the food system. People whose priorities are food praxis, community development, or policy making should be able to use them to inform their work. From the perspective of food praxis, some disciplinary approaches matter more than the others. Cultural studies and performance theory does not draw the researcher into action the same way that political ecology or class analysis might. These latter frames almost demand action. Nor does critical discourse analysis inform policy in the same way that economic analysis does—unfortunately. In fact, some say that policy making is only informed by economic analysis, with little regard for history or cultural interpretation.

As a food activist, I find that cultural studies and performance studies too easily depoliticize food issues, taking them out of context and thus out of the purview of policy makers and activists. I have used these approaches for specific pieces of research: I analysed films and historical archives about the state banquets in *The King and I* (Van Esterik 2008) and feminist performance art at the lactation station bar (Van Esterik 2006). I felt some embarrassment lest my colleagues who knew my work on the political economy of baby food companies would view my papers as trivial and irrelevant to "the big picture." But I found the research experience very useful as a way to understand the historical depth of culinary colonialism in Thailand and the disparagement of human milk as a product, both parts of "the big picture." That is why I stress the need to link the little and the large.

The Little and the Large

Szanto, Wong, and Brady open their article with, "Food is a performance"; to many food activists who encounter hunger on a regular basis, food is also a material substance in short supply in many households (Van Esterik 2005). Food activists in particular take care to differentiate food as material substance and food as representation or performance. As a self-professed lactivist, I have been involved in a small part of the food sovereignty movement for over forty years. My definition of "lactivist" would differ from that of Brady, Millious, and Ventresca. Lactivists act on the assumption that breastfeeding is the normal way to feed a human infant, and they work to remove some of the obstacles mothers face, including promotional practices of infant formula companies and lack of support. While the cultural critique of milk advertising campaigns is important, placing it in the broader context of the power of dairy marketing boards, for example, would allow activists to build on media-based research. That larger frame requires different advocacy tactics.

It would be easy for lactivists and other food activists to get stuck in outmoded approaches to advocacy. Visual and performance modes offer new approaches to this work. In the advocacy work on breastfeeding, we thought that lobbying at UN meetings for improved maternity benefits and changes to baby milk marketing practices, as well as consumer boycotts, were effective means of influencing infant feeding policies. But since both the political climate and nutritional and biomedical evidence changes rapidly, advocacy strategies also need to change. In the age of social media and public-private partnerships with food companies, these techniques are not sufficient. Even media analysis changes when food companies provide nutritional education to the public, often disguised as advertising campaigns, blurring more boundaries.

Unlike the dilemmas of discourse faced in the debates around Agricultural Land Reserves, breastfeeding activism doesn't get caught in the trap of having to choose between the language of eating local or sustainable or just; breastfeeding is part of a local, sustainable, and just food system, simultaneously. The policy and community actions required concern not how breasts or milk is represented, but how new mothers are supported for their nurturing practices—a tall order. While acknowledging the power of representation, I would hate to see readers left with the impression that lactivists use knowledge about human milk only to coerce women to breastfeed against their will.

The editors call for a more nuanced approach to critiques of the industrial food system. Activists do not do grey well; as experts in the black and white, activists have much to learn about how to do grey. Current advocacy approaches create opponents, encouraging the backlash evident in the baby-food case. What theories could generate a non-oppositional praxis? Is a non-oppositional activism possible? Can we use these papers to imagine an advocacy style that does not re-present the saintly-sinful opposition?

New Directions

These papers are strong reminders of the need to link the little and the large. From the intimacy of breastfeeding to the Agricultural Land Reserve regulations, the dilemmas of representation take place within broader contexts. This book suggests some new directions for food studies. One way to change the underlying values governing our society and our food system is to begin with the way we nurture our children; nurture as a foundational concept includes feeding and caring for each other and sharing decent food. Can nurture provide a new language of progressive politics? Is it only market incentives that drive change or do nurturing practices also drive change? We cannot assess this in the real world unless we ask the questions raised in these papers. Even economists are hinting that income is not a good proxy for quality of life, and certainly not the only thing that matters. Since 2012, the UN has published a World Happiness Report; no doubt food has an important place in that scale. Of course, to be well-nourished is not the same as to be nurtured, but it is close enough. It will be a struggle to insert nurture into some of the structures of late capitalism. Differences in power cannot be erased by empathy, but representing food in powerful new ways gives us some useful new paths to follow.

Note

1 See "represent" in http://onlineslangdictionary.com/meaning-definition-of/rep resent. Accessed 11 December 2014.

References

Counihan, Carole, and Penny Van Esterik. 1997. *Food and Culture: A Reader.* New York: Routledge.

Counihan, Carole, and Penny Van Esterik. 2008. *Food and Culture: A Reader.* 2nd ed. New York: Routledge.

Counihan, Carole, and Penny Van Esterik. 2013. *Food and Culture: A Reader.* 3rd ed. New York: Routledge.

Van Esterik, Penny. 2008. "Vintage Breastmilk: Exploring the Discursive Limits of Feminine Fluids." *Canadian Theatre Review* 137 (Winter): 20–3.

Van Esterik, Penny. 2006. "Anna and the King: Digesting Difference." *Southeast Asia Research* 14 (2): 289–307. http://dx.doi.org/10.5367/000000006778008130.

Van Esterik, Penny. 2005. "No Free Lunch." *Agriculture and Human Values* 22 (2): 207–8. http://dx.doi.org/10.1007/s10460-004-8280-2.

Williams, Raymond. 1985. *Keywords: A Vocabulary of Culture and Society.* Rev. ed. Oxford: Oxford University Press.

PART II: WHO, WHAT, AND HOW: GOVERNING FOOD SYSTEMS

Governance Challenges for Local Food Systems: Emerging Lessons from Agriculture and Fisheries

Kristen Lowitt, Phil Mount, Ahmed Khan,
and Chantal Clément

Over the past three decades, the changing influence and perception of the state has led to increased awareness of the potential for civil society to play an active role in addressing issues around sustainability, food security, and community well-being through the rubric of governance. Conceptually, the idea of governance seeks to expand beyond the day-to-day workings of government by considering the results and processes of a wider series of political, economic, and social interactions—the processes of rules rather than the rules of institutions themselves (Walters 2004). Governance is not static, but instead is comprised of "a broad, dynamic, complex process of interactive decision-making that is constantly evolving and responding to changing circumstances" (Commission on Global Governance 1995). Perceived as a framework that is more inclusive of civil society actors and informal decision-making processes (Kjaer 2004), governance moves beyond a narrow focus on institutionalized, hierarchical, and formalized rules in government.

Governance literature grew out of a need to look beyond the traditional hierarchical government in the face of new processes for rule-making that arose as a result of globalization and its political and economic implications. As a response to a more globalized governance regime, citizens are perceived as being less likely to accept the norm of the state government as rule-maker and controller at both the local and global levels (Marsden et al. 2012). As such, governance literature is also more mindful of power struggles, whether in considering the relative power and influence of actors in a system, or in prescribing possible solutions for more participatory and inclusive decision-making processes. Scholarship around governance is extremely diverse (Kjaer 2004). It has been used to explore issues of "good governance" in the context of development and democratization in the developing world (Palmer et al. 2012), "global governance" in light of new political realities in a globalized world (Rosenau and Czempiel 1992), "multi-level governance" in understanding European Union dynamics (Jessop 2005) and global environmental change (Armitage 2007), or "corporate governance" in the context of private enterprise, among others. In this chapter, questions about governance—in local agriculture and fisheries initiatives—provide a theoretical nexus point that allows us to explore issues of scale, values, and power for sustainable outcomes. While drawing out these cross-cutting themes, our case studies also highlight the importance of place in shaping how particular local food systems (LFS) governance arrangements arise and the form they take. By so doing, we build further support for critical LFS scholarship calling for governance mechanisms that can support scale development and reflexivity in values.

Background: Governance in Local Agri-Food Systems and Small-Scale Fisheries

Governance mechanisms in the context of local or alternative food systems offer an alternative to the dominant, industrial, and increasingly problematic global food system. Academic and popular discourse emphasizes alternative production practices (e.g., agroecology and organic), alternative values (e.g., community food security and civic agriculture), and alternative markets (e.g., short food supply chains) that bring producers and consumers together in new relationships (e.g., alternative food networks). While approaches vary, most fit comfortably within the broader category of LFS, as they share an emphasis on the localization of food production and consumption relationships.

Local food systems are often described as sites for social justice, sustainability, and resistance to a disempowering global food system (Blay-Palmer 2010). As such, new forms of interaction, inclusion, and community-based social engagement common to LFS are also identified as alternative modes of governance, contrasting with the isolation, exclusion, and centralized decision-making of the dominant food system. Distributions of power in LFS are generally perceived as being more collaborative than traditional structures; they depend more significantly on democratic engagement, public conversation and contestation, and political will (DuPuis 2006). Thus, governance literature on LFS has also sought to re-engage with the concept of "embeddedness," the notion that markets have always been shaped by non-economic forces (Polanyi 1968), such as socio-cultural norms or policies, to help mitigate their negative consequences. Adapted into an LFS context, this could include new markets shaped by norms of reciprocity, social justice, or sustainability. Lastly, LFS also combine the use of traditional institutional actors with civil-society organizations, third-party certifiers, business and citizen lobby groups, and consumer groups (Humphrey and Schmitz 2001). Thus, governance within LFS appears to be based more on "socially-interactive rule-making around markets" than the dominant system (DuPuis 2006, 2).

However, some have suggested that this vision of LFS governance—based in more democratic and socially just governing principles—overstates the reality. As Allen (2010) pointed out, local food systems don't start on a blank slate, but begin from existing asymmetries in wealth and privilege in and across regions and may unintentionally perpetuate them. Although some LFS may be more civically engaged, DuPuis (2006) argued that this doesn't mean LFS are intrinsically "fair." Others have even challenged the extent to which LFS actually increase social equity and democracy (DuPuis and Goodman 2005).

At the same time, questions about how geographic scales are constituted and transformed have become a main focus of inquiry in collective decision-making around food systems. More than a simple relationship to size and level, scales are fundamentally relational—constructed and reproduced through social practices (Marston 2000). Some researchers have begun to challenge the normative idealization of the local in LFS, including the notions of shared values and reconnection that characterize much of the LFS discourse. For example, Mount (2012) argued that such "tenuous assumptions" about the values underlying LFS can overlook important evidence of hybridity, and thinking about LFS as hybrid and flexible makes it possible to imagine governance processes that allow for negotiation and scale development (110). DuPuis and Goodman (2005) likewise argued for a more open governance process for LFS in which actors are "reflexive" about their norms and values (2).

These critiques suggest that careful consideration of the relationship between scale, values, and power will be key to understanding the potential of alternative, localized forms of governance. To what extent do these models provide viable, legitimate, and lasting solutions that can create space for food system diversity and innovation, and challenge the narrative of the dominant food system? In this chapter, we offer new insights into these pressing questions for LFS governance by drawing on the rich body of fisheries governance literature, with its history of challenging access and ownership rights as well as critical perspectives on scale, values, and power (Berkes et al. 2006). Here, power can be understood according to Gaventa (2006) as "power over" (i.e., control of), "power to" (i.e., empowerment), and "power with" (i.e., the power sharing of co-management arrangements). Analyses of local governance structures must take care to assess how these various types of power interact to shape or alter *what is possible* for local initiatives. In localized fisheries resource-sharing arrangements, for example, the newly-claimed "power to" often encounters resistance from pre-existing power (Jentoft and Eide 2011), or sees local goals and values circumvented by power exerted in formal political and policy-making channels (May 2013). Power and powerlessness are two sides of the same coin, and often reflect the tensions and conflicts between stakeholders as they negotiate what is and what ought to be (Khan 2011). Each of these types of power can be manifested at various scales (from global to local), can take place in farmland, fishing docks, or boardrooms, and influence policy formulations on production and harvesting, processing requirements, or land tenure and access rights.

LFS research has focused almost exclusively on agriculture to the exclusion of other types of food production systems, including fisheries, and yet we argue there are considerable opportunities to further our understanding of LFS governance at the edge between farming and fisheries (Lowitt 2013). Fisheries make vital contributions to food systems from local to global scales (Smith et al. 2010). Like agriculture, they also face problems related to industrial-scale practices and top-down governance structures that often exclude local communities (Jentoft 2000). For these reasons, a growing number of fisheries researchers are arguing for alternative participatory and community-based governance approaches to rebuild fishing systems (Khan and Neis 2010). However, parallel to some cautions about idealization of the local scale in LFS research, Johnson (2006) argued that fisheries governance "should be directed foremost at social and ecological goals rather than the simple promotion of small-scale fisheries on the assumption that they embody social justice and ecological sustainability" (747).

To bring food and fisheries research into closer dialogue, we present a series of case studies from diverse geographic contexts spanning farming and fishing systems to critically interrogate questions about the scale(s) on which LFS are governed; the values that underpin LFS governance; and what structures of governance are best suited for addressing inequities in power and working toward goals of democracy and social inclusion.

Case Studies

For this chapter, we have selected four case studies that are representative of LFS in three different countries: Ireland (Europe), Nova Scotia and Newfoundland, Canada (North America), and China (Asia). The case studies entail diverse systems of food production, exchange, and governance, including land-based (livestock and agriculture) and aquatic (fisheries) systems. Each case study is based on research undertaken by the authors, brought together for the first time in this chapter. The evidence base for the case studies draws on a range of research methods and approaches, including key informant interviews, focus groups, and analysis of policy documents.

In each of the case studies that follow, we examine how issues of scale, values, and power were negotiated. These three themes have been identified in existing LFS research as having a key impact on governance outcomes and the potential for food systems innovation. These concepts provide an analytical framework for understanding the governance of LFS (both the structures and process) in our case studies, and allow us to draw some important considerations and potential ways forward for the future governance and long-term sustainability of LFS.

Glenbarrow Farms, Ireland

Bovine spongiform encephalopathy (BSE) is a disease that attacks the brain and central nervous system of adult cattle and eventually causes death. The first recorded cases in Ireland occurred in 1989, and while controls were put in place the following year, the number of cases continued to rise until 2002 (Irish Department of Agriculture, Food and the Marine 2013). Ireland experienced the second-highest number of recorded cases of BSE in the world, after the UK (Office International des Epizooties 2014). After the BSE crisis shook European consumer confidence in beef, the Department of Agriculture, Food and the Marine and Bord Bia (the Irish Food Board) demanded national changes, looking to re-establish Irish beef export markets through quality assurance schemes that would guarantee safe food production practices on all farms in Ireland.

Glenbarrow Farms, a large cooperative of beef producers in Co. Laois, created an innovative, locally developed value chain model with a guaranteed market and favourable prices, using a collaborative process that addressed many of the power and control issues that plague groups attempting to establish short food supply chains (Mount and Smithers 2014). Despite its large size, the cooperative also prioritized membership for small farms that were struggling to adapt to the high quality standards imposed at a national level, and the ongoing pressures to increase size and consolidate.

In Co. Laois, a primarily beef-farming region in the heart of the country, local economic development, municipal government and agricultural organization representatives worked together to find an appropriate outlet for a new EU funding agency (LEADER: Liaison Entre Actions de Développement de l'Économie Rurale) aimed at local, grassroots rural development projects. While initiatives that focused on alternative rural industries were considered—with the intent of diversifying the region away from beef production—consumer and producer surveys showed strong support (87 percent) for a locally-branded beef cooperative (Laois LEADER 1998).

The Glenbarrow cooperative was established with the intent of providing a value-added outlet to the county's struggling beef farmers, and in that sense, it was spectacularly successful. Over 250 farm members joined early in the project, and shipped significant volumes—over 1,000 head of cattle in their heaviest month. Decision making rested with the co-op board, headed by a farmer and comprising elected farm members, and representatives from Glanbia (a large agricultural cooperative which supported the group financially), Teagasc (the Irish Ministry of Agriculture), and LEADER. While operational decisions and workload naturally resided with a smaller and more active group of core leaders, the full board handled future strategies and the annual negotiations of the processor premium.

The co-op was self-sustaining and structured as a not-for-profit organization: each farmer paid a one-time membership fee (which established a reserve fund), and per-head payments, which paid for operations and the group coordinator. Farm members met rigorous quality and production standards, but benefited from the processor/distributor's guaranteed premium, which gave the co-op stability. The commitment of all members of the chain to constant improvement of both the product and the return to farmers increased throughout the life of the co-op.

In recognition of Glenbarrow's commitment to encouraging and facilitating the membership of small, struggling farms, the processor committed to improving overall herd quality on these farms, helping to reduce the number of cull animals. The processor also agreed to a transparent pricing mechanism where no favouritism was given to herds shipping larger numbers. This addressed common complaints about the commodity market, where prices fluctuate rapidly and individual farmers face a significant power deficit when negotiating prices on the day of sale.

The group was open to alternative, direct-marketing strategies but limited in its capacity to deliver "local food" from the outset by its scale. While the co-op attempted to break into the local retail and institutional markets through direct distribution, they found little demand for a premium local beef product. Developing this market—or a direct-to-consumer market—would have required a significant investment in time and at least one dedicated staff member. Although the processor fully supported the intent to develop a local market, they had little experience or market connections in the region, since market realities dictated that 90 percent of their beef was exported to Europe. Given that the returns would have been only marginally higher than their existing rate from the processor, the co-op decided to forego the local market. The group's reliance on their processor for marketing meant that the Glenbarrow brand remained largely outside of the group's control. In effect, the Glenbarrow brand delivered a high quality product for large-scale European consumers, and a model of production practices and independent verification, aimed primarily at other Irish producers. This was an interesting result, given that the cooperative was originally established to develop a local, county brand and market.

The Glenbarrow case study illustrates the interconnected roles of power, scale, and values in shaping the governance and outcomes of localization initiatives. Led by their priority of maximizing the benefit to struggling, small-scale beef farmers in the county, the cooperative board delivered results by focusing on recruitment and a guaranteed market through a collaborative relationship with a single processor. As a result, less focus was placed on the democratization of governance, leaving decisions in the hands of the board and a core group responsible for operational decisions. Success at farm recruitment meant that a more localized marketing strategy would only ever be a marginal outlet for their volumes, and the investments needed to diversify into local markets never gained traction. The historical regional dependence on export markets meant that the infrastructure to market locally did not exist, making that option more expensive and less attractive. While the efforts to promote the concept of local food from local farmers were unsuccessful, the cooperative achieved their goals of developing a substantial market with a premium price for a large number of the county's small-scale beef producers.

Alternative Seafood Distribution Models in Atlantic Canada

Fisheries have played a vital role in the development of coastal communities in Canada. The fish and seafood industry contributed nearly $4 billion to the Canadian economy in 2008 (Fisheries and Oceans Canada 2011b). Small enterprises operating in the inshore fishery accounted for over 90 percent of fishing vessels in 2008 (Fisheries and Oceans Canada 2011b). However, independent small-scale fish harvesters face substantial livelihood challenges. Similar to the agricultural industry, fish harvesters are increasingly operating in a political and economic climate that promotes the sale of high volumes of seafood at low costs—primarily for export. Fish harvesters usually have access to a limited number of buyers and rarely have reliable access to pricing information (Murray and Neis 2012). Since the Canadian seafood industry is tied to global markets, regional distribution systems are often lacking. Local chefs, retailers, and consumers often have sporadic access to high-quality, fresh seafood (Ecology Action Centre 2013; Murray and Neis 2012). Alongside marketing challenges, federal and provincial policies also act as major barriers for small-scale fish harvesters who often have to navigate complex quota rules or pay large regulatory fees to maintain their vessels and businesses (Khan 2012).

In this context, alternative approaches are beginning to emerge that seek to provide fish harvesters with more control over their livelihoods, a fairer price for their catch, and offer consumers access to fresh and local seafood. To illustrate, we turn to two case studies in Atlantic Canada: a community-supported fishery in Nova Scotia (NS), and emerging cross-sector collaboration between the fishing and tourism industries in Newfoundland and Labrador (NL).

"Off the Hook" Community-Supported Fishery, Nova Scotia

As Canada's second major exporter of seafood, NS exported 112,472 tons in 2010 (Fisheries and Oceans Canada 2011a); in contrast, only 22,000 tons were consumed in-province that same year (Nikoloyuk and Adler 2013). Distributors at New England auctions sell most of the province's seafood, where high volume and low costs are necessary to compete internationally. International auctioning rarely allows local fish harvesters to access adequate price information and prices rarely reflect their actual operating costs. To address the increasingly unsustainable seafood prices, the Ecology Action Centre (EAC) in Halifax, NS, partnered with local fishers in 2011 to create Off the Hook, a community-supported fishery (CSF), with the goal of moving away from commodity marketing toward local marketing.

Off the Hook is a cooperative of five small-scale fishermen out of Digby Neck and Islands in the Bay of Fundy, providing sustainably caught fish directly to local shareholders in and around the Halifax area. Off the Hook's fish harvesters cited the increasingly complex government policies, globalizing seafood markets that limit their control over prices, and worsening resource availability as the main reasons for shifting to direct marketing in the local area. The co-op recognized that small-scale fish harvesters lacked power, control, and opportunity on global commodity markets, especially in the context of provincial and federal policies that are oriented toward larger industrial fishing systems. As a response, the CSF is based on the vision of empowering local fish harvesters, whose livelihoods make up the backbone of many coastal communities.

The cooperative draws from the Community-Supported Agriculture (CSA) model, connecting consumers to local, sustainable, and fairly priced food for a predetermined amount paid at the beginning of the season. Consumers are typically willing to pay more for local, sustainably harvested seafood, particularly when they know that any price premium will benefit smaller-scale fisheries and their local marine environment (Beaton 2010). Off the Hook has assumed direct control of all distribution processes and decision making is firmly in the hands of the fish harvesters themselves, while the business's coordination and management are contracted to two EAC staff members. In its first year, the CFS attracted over 100 customers— a number they doubled by their second year.

As a small endeavour, Off the Hook's fishermen do not sell exclusively through the CSF and continue to sell a majority of their catch to buyers at the wharf. However, the majority of the fishermen stressed that the better price and higher value market gained through the CSF model has turned their work into a financially viable operation. In addition, while Off the Hook fisher harvesters benefit from a more reliable income, new market opportunities, and greater ownership and control over their livelihoods as a cooperative, the CSF is also well positioned to respond to the consumer movement demanding more local seafood, eco-certification, and traceability schemes. The cooperative highlights the more sustainable harvesting methods being carried out by many local smaller-scale owner-operated fleets, which are otherwise unadvertised or poorly reflected in conventional retail pricing. In particular, Off the Hook uses Thisfish, a seafood traceability system developed by Ecotrust Canada, which consumers can use by scanning the CSF's barcodes with their smartphone.

The CSF was founded on the belief in the interconnectedness between marine environments, society, and local economies. Off the Hook's coordinators found that the CFS model developed stronger interpersonal connections between consumers and producers, who meet when products are exchanged every week at a set location. One CSF fisher stressed his belief that the mutual, interconnected benefits of CSF "could save fisheries and revive coastal communities."

However, Off the Hook coordinators expressed difficulty in implementing some of the creative ways they are seeking to work with value chains. Both federal and provincial regulations continue to impede the ability to sell directly to restaurants, especially in regards to food safety standards and the need for costly inspections and permits. For example, although all of the chefs surveyed by the EAC expressed interest in buying local filleted fish through direct marketing, small-scale harvesters across the province expressed difficulty in navigating the complex and onerous permits and licences required to do business with restaurants (Beaton 2010). Beyond required fishing and boat licences, a federal Food Establishment Permit—generally required by any foodservice facility—is also mandatory for fish harvesters wanting to fillet their own catch for direct sale, even though these harvesters have no intention to act as foodservice providers. If this federal permit is acquired, harvesters then need to incur the additional cost of applying for a provincial permit. These real and opportunity costs are more easily absorbed into the operating budgets of larger businesses, although they are proportionally much more substantial for smaller scale operators.

Finally, fishers are limited by the relatively small consumer base in NS, the transaction cost of processing, as well as the higher upfront cost of a CSF share for consumers which constrains the quantity of fish that can be caught and sold directly and thus undermines the scaling-up of the CSF. However, since 2013, Off the Hook has been seeking to create a provincial seafood hub based on "producer empowerment" (Nikoloyuk and Adler 2013). The hub would involve creating a network of fishermen from different areas of NS based on a network of local distribution hubs. Until then, Off the Hook is hoping to bring in new producers and diversify product types (such as offering sustainable harvest clams or shrimp in future seasons) to gain access to greater local market shares.

Fisheries–Tourism Synergies, Newfoundland and Labrador

When ground fisheries collapsed in the early 1990s and small-scale fishers looked for ways to improve their livelihoods, one strategy that emerged was collaboration with other sectors. In the Bonne Bay region in Gros Morne National Park on the west coast of the island of NL, there has been growing awareness of the potential mutual benefits to be gained through closer collaboration among those in the fisheries and tourism sectors. While the provincial government manages the tourism industry and the federal government primarily manages the fisheries sector, there are many ways in which they depend on each other (Lowitt, 2011). The growing importance of local seafood as a culinary tourism attraction depends on a viable small-scale fishery; at the same time, some family fishing members combine fishing with seasonal work in tourism to make a living.

Restaurants in the Bonne Bay region currently buy most of their seafood from local fish processing plants where fish harvesters sell the majority of their catches. Harbour Seafoods is the largest fish processing plant in the region, buying from over 260 individual fish harvesters along the west coast of NL. While most restaurants are satisfied with the overall quality of the seafood from processing plants, some would like to tell a clearer story about the seafood they serve from ocean to plate. As one tourism operator said, "Each product you put on your menu has a story to tell behind it." Tourists expressed a similar interest in learning about local seafood. As one tourist said, "Cod, that's what we want. It's unique to you here."

For these reasons, some restaurant operators said they would prefer to source fish directly from harvesters rather than fish processing plants, so that they could know precisely who caught the fish, how, when, and in what waters. Some harvesters also believed there could be benefits in marketing directly, such as having more control over prices and capturing a higher price. As one harvester said, "If you're taking care, taking time to bring in a good product, you want to see a good price for it."

However, formalizing direct buying arrangements is a challenge in the current regulatory context. The provincial Fish Inspection Act does not allow fish harvesters to sell directly to anyone except a licensed buyer or processor, meaning they cannot sell directly to restaurants, retail stores, or individual customers (Murray and Neis 2012). At the same time, some fish harvesters expressed concern about pursuing new markets to avoid jeopardizing existing markets. Others commented on the potential mismatch between large volumes of seafood being caught and the relatively small capacity for sales in local markets. Further, eligibility for employment insurance—an important source of income for sustaining fishing livelihoods year-round—is based on harvesters selling their catches to a licensed buyer or fish processing plant. This illustrates the complex ways in which the welfare state and markets are also entangled in the governance of fisheries.

Nonetheless, other models of marketing seafood are emerging that are not direct per se, but instead are based on new arrangements among harvesters, fish processors, and buyers. For example, one processing plant keeps a small number of lobsters in salt-water pens after the lobster fishery has closed, allowing a restaurant to continue to access fresh lobsters for several weeks beyond the regular lobster season. Culinary tourism also presents new opportunities to develop niche and value-added products that may be harvested and processed in smaller quantities and sold to restaurants. Some restaurants already buy smoked fish and salt cod from one plant in the region that produces these items. While collaboration among the fishing and tourism sectors is emerging informally, it will be important to build enhanced organizational capacity and structures in the future to ensure that these collective efforts take place on a more sustained and coordinated basis.

Integrated Rice-Fish Farming, China

Rice-fish farming has played a significant role in sustainable local food systems for over a thousand years in China. Rice-fish systems use one habitat to produce both a grain and a protein source, based in the synergistic interactions between the rice and fish in these integrated farming systems (FAO 2010; Fuller and Min 2013). Sustaining these traditional mixed farming systems within a context of rapid urbanization and population growth has been a governance challenge, especially as rice is a staple for more than a billion people. Nonetheless, these traditional LFS continue to thrive largely because of the ecological resilience of these integrated agro-ecosystems and strong cultural values underpinning them (Xie et al. 2011). For these reasons, integrated rice-fish farming was recognized as one of twenty Globally Important Agricultural Heritage (GIAH) systems by the United Nations' Food and Agricultural Organization (FAO) in 2005 (DelaCruz and Koohafkan 2009).

In Qingtian County, Zhejiang Province in China, where one of the GIAH sites is located, the rice-fish culture production system is comprised of 461 hectares of rice paddies in which several indigenous species of common red carp are farmed (Jiao et al. 2009; FAO 2010). The county has a population of close to 472,000 inhabitants that are mostly rural and agrarian (Jiao et al. 2009). The main actors in these LFS are farmers and their households, consumers, local governors, government agencies, and the research and scientific community. The scale of production is relatively small, with a per-capita land acreage of about 0.44 ha per farmer (FAO 2010). Production ranges from 150 to 750 kg/ha and earnings can reach up to $6000

USD/ha (Jiao et al. 2009). Ownership within the rice-fish system is public with government support provided in the form of technical assistance from farm extension workers and research input from the Academy of Sciences (FAO 2010). These assistance programs complement the Household Contract Responsibility System established in 1978 to act as an incentive for increased agricultural productivity by reallocating communal and public lands to peasant households and encouraging intensive cultivation of small plots for subsistence and market exchange (Tilt 2008).

Some scientists have argued that, in comparison to mono-food production systems, rice-fish production systems are adaptive and ecologically sustainable due to better waste management and circular economy principles (UNEP 2011; Fuller and Min 2013). For example, this symbiotic farming system contains Azolla plants that minimize the need for external inputs since they fix nitrogen and provide a natural source of fertilizer for rice. The rice in turn provides a shaded habitat for the fish, which then benefit the rice by oxygenating the water and circulating nutrients (FAO 2010; Xie et al. 2011). Experimental results show that rice yields in rice-fish systems are equal to rice monocultures, more stable over time, and require less fertilizer and much less pesticides (Xie et al. 2011). This integrated system has proven "cost effective" in meeting the economic and food security needs of rural communities (UNEP 2011; Xie et al. 2011).

Despite the growing levels of mechanization and technological advancement in food production systems in China, there remains interest in this farming system due to its low ecological footprint and contribution to community well-being (Min 2009). As has been demonstrated in fisheries and other food production systems, shared values can simplify the decision-making process and guide collective choices (Mount and Smithers 2014). In Zhejiang Province, the values that continue to support integrated rice-fish farming reflect customary traditions and a cultural heritage that spans centuries. This stability and continuity in value systems derive in large part from the mutually reinforcing nature of the socio-cultural and environmental benefits of this holistic farming system, in which the value of community assets and a sense of belonging are intimately connected to stable and sustainable production practices, household employment, and livelihoods. However, as out-migration from agrarian communities intensifies because of new economic prospects in larger urban centres, continuity in these values is at risk.

Because there is a high local demand for fresh and live fish products, there remains a market for small-scale, local, traditional producers. However, an emerging challenge is that production is increasingly being influenced by buyers and other intermediaries that give preference to intensive rice mono-culture production with high fertilizer use and farm inputs. These buyers are interested in purchasing only from those who produce and market at a large scale, rather than dealing with small rice-fish producers who have much smaller harvests. Knowing this, the GIAH initiative has encouraged product quality and market standards by offering equally competitive farm gate prices, thereby augmenting household incomes (FAO 2010). Although rice-fish pro-duction, harvest, and marketing have traditionally taken place at the house-hold level, as incentives are provided for higher yield, there are opportunities for post-harvest enterprises in value-adding and co-management initiatives at the community level (Min 2009; FAO 2010). Further, as the other case studies have shown, by marketing collectively, these rice-fish farmers have the potential to extend beyond the local, fresh markets to reach other consumers who are increasingly interested in food produced with safe, sustainable, and traditional practices (Garnett and Wilkes 2014).

Discussion

This chapter has presented four case studies of LFS in the agricultural and fisheries sectors to examine how issues of scale, values, and power—including control/ownership structures—are navigated with a view to informing future directions for LFS governance (Table 5.1). Collectively, these case studies illustrate how "local" food systems arise out of particular political, social, economic, and historical contexts. In other words, these case studies of LFS help make clear the extent to which scale and place are mutually constituted within an evolving context of social practices. We argue this dynamic interaction shapes what is possible, and transforms how local food systems are organized and governed. Despite the growing awareness of the social construction of scale, the "considerable ambiguity" surrounding scale is still too often skimmed over in food scholarship (Johnson 2006, 747).

Our case studies demonstrate the importance of understanding scale and how it is constructed in relation to LFS governance. For example, Off the Hook sells fish from a small region of NS to a local customer base in an even smaller subregion. However, the CFS has increasingly adapted their marketing strategies to meet the global trend toward consumer reas-surance in the form of traceability schemes. One of the hallmarks of LFS to date has been the direct relationship between producers and consumers, through which consumers gain knowledge and trust in the food products

Table 5.1. *Case studies summary.*

	Scale	Values	Power (ownership/control)
Glenbarrow Farms Co-operative (Ireland)	Local and regional [EU]	Local control; cooperation; support for small scale, disadvantaged farms	Cooperative; regional multi-stakeholder board; value chain including processor / marketer (not retailers); formed through EU endogenous regional development program
Outcomes	Local brand/market unexploited – too labour and time intensive, low return vs. established regional market; favourable price for farms of all scales maintained through strong relationship with processor, education, continual improvement in value-added practices		
"Off the Hook" community supported fishery (NS, Canada)	Local and provincial	Revaluing consumer-producer relationships; controlled by local small producers; environmental sustainability	Cooperative; shorter value chain; formed through "alternative" market structure i.e., CSA model and direct marketing to consumers and restaurants
Outcomes	Stronger producer-consumer relationships; success in terms of income security for participating fishers; limitations due to provincial food safety regulations; limited capacity to scale up because of small local market and limited infrastructure for local distribution;		
Cross-sector fisheries-tourism collaborations (NL, Canada)	Global (tourists) linked to local (fisheries)	Mutual cross-sector benefits; collaboration; tell an "ocean to plate" story	Informal arrangements among processors, harvesters, and restaurant buyers

(Continued)

Table 5.1. (*Continued*)

	Scale	Values	Power (ownership/ control)
Outcomes	Difficult to formalize cross-sector arrangements in the current regulatory context; new collaborations are built on strong working relationships established through conventional supply chains; future potential for direct marketing to move small volumes of seafood into the tourism sector, alongside established supply chains.		
Integrated rice-fish farming (China)	Local, regional, and global (primarily Asia Pacific)	Local control, traditional heritage, based on traditional and scientific knowledge synthesis	Multi-scale formal and informal arrangements involving diverse stakeholders (public, private, community, academia, and multilaterals)
Outcomes	Traditional LFS continue to persist because of strong cultural values and ecological resilience of integrated rice-fish systems; future opportunities to add value and market beyond the local level with support of the GIAH initiative.		

they are eating. While Off the Hook still involves direct exchange between harvesters and consumers, the CSF's products also come with a tag so that the consumer can trace the fish online and continue to learn more about where it came from and who caught it. Off the Hook shows how the direct relationship between consumers and harvesters/producers in LFS is increasingly operating alongside, and being transformed by, dominant narratives of traceability and standardization, whose rules and regimes are often designed for more global food products.

The Ireland case study also shows how scales intersect in terms of LFS governance arrangements. In the Glenbarrow Cooperative, most of the farms would never have accessed an elite value-added market without an intermediary processor designed specifically to include small-scale producers. The case also challenges the assumption that local control should necessarily imply local consumption, instead showing that the financial sustainability of local enterprises can come in the form of providing high-quality produce for export markets (see Morgan, Marsden, and Murdoch 2006, 72–3). In this way, the rice-fish farming case study from China is similar. While rice-fish farming is recognized as a GIAH system on the basis of its ties to cultural heritage and locally based production, the GIAH designation is providing new opportunities to small and traditional producers to develop more rigorous market and quality assurance standards and potentially reach consumers beyond local markets.

Further, the historical dimensions of both place and scale have received less attention in LFS research (Allen 2010). Yet understanding the history that situates local initiatives may be crucial to their success. For example, while cooperatives hold the potential for increased producer control over revenues and decision making, in many regions of the world the model faces strong ideological opposition and producer scepticism because of past failures (Borgen 2001). In the Glenbarrow example, the presence (and support) of an established, successful, national agricultural cooperative (Glanbia) provided a reassuring model whose value should not be underestimated. In the case of integrated rice-fish farming in Zhejiang Province, over the span of centuries shared values and holistic management approaches have helped to define principles for various stakeholders, and have given this food production system the resilience and longevity required for its GIAH listing (DelaCruz and Koohafkan 2009). Similarly, the ongoing efforts to preserve the "local" behind small-scale fisheries in both NS and NL can be understood as an acknowledgment of their pivotal historical role in the development of coastal communities.

As the previous example shows, values often play a key role in the social construction of scale and place. However, the local scale is often conflated with progressive values and thus the role of values is often overstated. In LFS, values such as inclusion and community-based social engagement are often contrasted with the isolation and exclusion operating in the global food system. Our case studies provide further support that this distinction is over-simplified as it promotes a normative idealization of the local. For example, processors and fish harvesters in the Bonne Bay region are beginning to establish new ways of working together to meet demand for emerging local markets, such as restaurants. However, these collaborations are based on relationships that developed over many years of working together in the dominant fisheries production system. The example of Off the Hook brings nuance to the notion that LFS are intrinsically more fair and equitable. While aimed at improving the livelihoods of producers, the CSF generally targets medium- to higher-income consumers and inadvertently excludes lower-income customers.

Similarly, our case studies indicate that LFS, with their focus on values of democracy and social inclusion at the local level, can sometimes overlook how multi-scale power relations can shape LFS outcomes. While new forms of governance arrangements for LFS emphasize non-government actors (especially civil-society groups), our case studies indicate that government laws and regulations still have considerable influence over the success of LFS governance arrangements and the particular form that these take. For example, Off the Hook, despite strong relationships between consumers and harvesters, was limited in the types and forms of seafood they could sell because of existing provincial and federal regulations around food safety and fish processing. Similarly, seafood direct-marketing initiatives in NL are constrained by existing provincial rules that require fish be sold to only a licensed buyer or processor, and not at the dock as is commonly permitted in many other coastal communities.

In other cases, government regulations supported systems of property ownership that encourage local food production. For example, recognizing the dire status of over-exploited and depleted marine stocks, fish production within integrated rice and fish culture systems in China has increased from 25 percent of total fisheries production in the 1980s to about 50 percent in the mid-1990s (Zhong and Power 1997). Likewise, the total acreage in rice-fish production has doubled from about 800 ha in the mid-1990s to 1,500 ha in the early 2000s (Min 2009). This has been possible through national land reforms that support community food production and access rights, as well as government support in terms of technical inputs and services. The systems of property ownership and regulatory frameworks within which LFS operate are thus fundamentally important in the governance of LFS and reflect institutionalized forms of power relations that shape the extent to which LFS can contribute to progressive goals such as inclusion and democracy.

Conclusion

In this chapter, we cross-examined a series of case studies from agriculture and fisheries to explore the intersection of scale, values, and power in the governance of LFS. Our findings indicate that there is a need to consider the social construction of scale, and how this intersects with values, power relations, and place. This is important to developing LFS governance mechanisms that are more adaptable, hybrid, and can account for cross-scale development (Mount 2012). Our case studies reinforce earlier research (Allen and Kovach 2000; Goodman 2004; Sonnino and Marsden 2006), which suggests that the distinction between local and global—which typifies much LFS research—is often over-drawn, and consequently, opportunities for innovation in LFS governance at the intersections of these scales may be overlooked. However, while we caution against the normative idealization of the local scale, we also argue for being attentive to how place shapes the particular political, social, economic, and historical contexts out of which "local" food systems arise. Along these lines, while we argue for LFS governance mechanisms that can support scale development and reflexivity in values, we also note that explicit efforts must be made to ensure that LFS governance arrangements remain accountable to those most directly involved and impacted by LFS organizing, including small-scale producers and harvesters (Chuenpagdee 2011).

Building on our research in this chapter, we encourage scholars and practitioners of LFS to continue to engage more deeply with governance debates taking place in other fields. In particular, we stress the need for continued collaboration and dialogue among food and fisheries researchers. These sectors of the food system both make vital contributions to food security and further synergies can arise by working across the boundaries between agriculture and fisheries as actors in both systems face a similar set of governance challenges as they work toward broader goals of democracy, inclusion, and equity for long-term sustainability.

Acknowledgements

Ahmed Khan is funded by UNEP-IEMP under the Young International Scientist Fellowship Grant no. 2012 Y1ZA0010. Professor Min Qingwen provided useful materials on GIAHS and insights on resilience for local food systems.

Chantal Cleément's research draws from her work with the Policy Working Group of the ACT for the CFS Project based out of Mount Saint Vincent University in Nova Scotia. In particular, the Ecology Action Centre Marine Team provided valuable insights on the development of provincial fishery initiatives.

Phil Mount's research relied on interviews and insights from the management teams at Glenbarrow Cooperative and their processor, Slaney Foods.

Kristen Lowitt's research was undertaken as part of the Community-University Research for Recovery Alliance (CURRA) project at Memorial University.

References

Allen, Patricia, and Martin Kovach. 2000. "The Capitalist Composition of Organic: The Potential of Markets in Fulfilling the Promise of Organic Agriculture." *Agriculture and Human Values* 17 (3): 221–32. http://dx.doi.org/10.1023/A:1007640506965.

Allen, Patricia. 2010. "Realizing Justice in Local Food Systems." *Cambridge Journal of Regions, Economy and Society* 3 (2): 295–308. http://dx.doi.org/10.1093/cjres/rsq015.

Armitage, Derek. 2007. "Governance and the Commons in a Multi-Level World." *International Journal of the Commons* 2 (1): 7–32. http://dx.doi.org/10.18352/ijc.28.

Beaton, Sadie. 2010. Local Seafood Direct Marketing: Emerging Trends for Small-Scale Fishers in Nova Scotia. https://www.ecologyaction.ca/files/imagesdocuments/file/Marine/directmarketingNS.pdf.

Berkes, Fikret, T.P. Hughes, R.S. Steneck, James A. Wilson, D.R. Bellwood, B. Crona, C. Folke, L.H. Gunderson, H.M. Leslie, J. Norberg, et al. 17 Mar, 2006. "Globalization, Roving Bandits, and Marine Resources." *Science* 311 (5767): 1557–8. http://dx.doi.org/10.1126/science.1122804. Medline: 16543444

Blay-Palmer, Alison, ed. 2010. *Imagining Sustainable Food Systems: Theory and Practice*. Aldershot, UK: Ashgate Publishing.

Borgen, Svein Ole. 2001. "Identification as a Trust-Generating Mechanism in Cooperatives." *Annals of Public and Cooperative Economics* 72 (2): 209–28. http://dx.doi.org/10.1111/1467-8292.00165.

Chuenpagdee, Ratana, ed. 2011. *World Small-Scale Fisheries: Contemporary Visions*. Delft, The Netherlands: Eburon Academic Publishers.

Commission on Global Governance. 1995. Our Global Neighborhood: Report of the Commission on Global Governance. http://www.gdrc.org/u-gov/global-neighbourhood/index.htm.

DelaCruz, Marie Jane, and Parviz Koohafkan. 2009. "Globally Important Agricultural Heritage Systems (GIAHS): A Shared Vision of Agriculture, Ecological and Traditional Societal Sustainability." In *Dynamic Conservation and Adaptive Management of China's GIAHS: Theories and Practices (I)*, edited by Qingwen Min, 16–36. Beijing: China Environmental Press.

DuPuis, E. Melanie, and David Goodman. 2005. "Should We Go 'Home' to Eat? Toward a Reflexive Politics of Localism." *Journal of Rural Studies* 21 (3): 359–71. http://dx.doi.org/10.1016/j.jrurstud.2005.05.011.

DuPuis, E. Melanie. 2006. Civic Markets: Alternative Value Chain Governance as Civic Engagement. *Crop Management Online*. http://economics.ag.utk.edu/hbin/2006/Dupuis%20Crop%20Management.doc.

Ecology Action Centre. 2013. Social Impact Investing for Sustainable Fishing Communities. https://www.ecologyaction.ca/files/images-documents/file/Marine/EAC-Social%20Finance%20report.pdf.

FAO. 2010. *Globally Important Agricultural Heritage Systems (GIAHS): The Rice-Fish Culture System in China*. Rome: FAO.

Fisheries and Oceans Canada. 2011a. Provincial and Territorial Statistics on Canada's Fish and Seafood Exports in 2010. http://www.dfo-mpo.gc.ca/media/back-fiche/2011/hq-ac05a-eng.htm.

Fisheries and Oceans Canada. 2011b. Canadian Fisheries Statistics 2008. http://www.dfo-mpo.gc.ca/stats/commercial/commercial-pub-eng.htm.

Fuller, Tony, and Qingwen Min. 2013. "Understanding Agricultural Heritage Sites as Complex Adaptive Systems: The Challenge of Complexity." *Journal of Resources and Ecology* 4 (3): 195–201. http://dx.doi.org/10.5814/j.issn.1674-764x.2013.03.002.

Garnett, Tara, and Andreas Wilkes. 2014. *Appetite for Change: Social, Economic and Environmental Transformations in China's Food System. Food Climate Research Network.* Oxford: University of Oxford.

Gaventa, John. 2006. "Finding the Spaces for Change: A Power Analysis." *Institute of Development Studies* 37 (6): 23–33. http://dx.doi.org/10.1111/j.1759-5436.2006.tb00320.x.

Goodman, David. 2004. "Rural Europe Redux? Reflections on Alternative Agro-Food Networks and Paradigm Shange." *Sociologia Ruralis* 44 (1): 3–16. http://dx.doi.org/10.1111/j.1467-9523.2004.00258.x.

Humphrey, John, and Hubert Schmitz. 2001. "Governance in Global Value Chains." *IDS Bulletin* 32 (3): 19–29.

Irish Department of Agriculture, Food and the Marine. 2013. About BSE in Ireland. http://www.agriculture.gov.ie/animalhealthwelfare/diseasecontrol/bse/aboutbseinireland/.

Jentoft, Svein. 2000. "The Community: A Missing Link of Fisheries Management." *Marine Policy* 24 (1): 53–60. http://dx.doi.org/10.1016/S0308-597X(99)00009-3.

Jentoft, Svein, and Arne Eide. 2011. "A Better Future: Prospects for Small-Scale Fishing People." In *Poverty Mosaics: Realities and Prospects in Small-Scale Fisheries*, edited by S. Jentoft and A. Eide, 451–69. Dordrecht: Springer. http://dx.doi.org/10.1007/978-94-007-1582-0_20.

Jessop, Bob. 2005. "The Political Economy of Scale and European Governance." *Tijdschrift voor Economische en Sociale Geografie* 96 (2): 225–30. http://dx.doi.org/10.1111/j.1467-9663.2005.00453.x.

Jiao, Wen-Jun, Qingwen Min, Sheng-Kui Cheng, Dan Zhang, and Ye-Hong Sun. 2009. "Ecological Footprint Analysis on the Traditional Rice-Fish Agricultural Area: A Case Study of Qingtian County, Zhejiang Province, China." In *Dynamic Conservation and Adaptive Management of China's GIAHS: Theories and Practices (I)*, edited by Qingwen Min, 194–215. Beijing: China Environmental Press.

Johnson, Derek. 2006. "Category, Narrative, and Value in the Governance of Small-Scale Fisheries." *Marine Policy* 30 (6): 747–56. http://dx.doi.org/10.1016/j.marpol.2006.01.002.

Khan, Ahmed S., and Barb Neis. 2010. "The Rebuilding Imperative in Fisheries: Clumsy Solutions for Wicked Problems?" *Progress in Oceanography* 87 (1–4): 347–56. http://dx.doi.org/10.1016/j.pocean.2010.09.012.

Khan, Ahmed S. 2011. "Is Rebuilding Collapsed Fisheries a Wicked Problem? Lessons from a Fish Chain Analysis of Northern Gulf Cod Fisheries." PhD diss., Memorial University, St. John's, NL.

Khan, Ahmed S. 2012. "Understanding Global Supply Chains and Seafood Markets for the Rebuilding Prospects of Northern Gulf Cod Fisheries." *Sustainability* 4 (12): 2946–69. http://dx.doi.org/10.3390/su4112946.

Kjaer, Anne Mette. 2004. *Governance.* Cambridge: Polity Press.

Laois LEADER. 1998. "Proposal to Establish the O'Moore Co-operative and the Glenbarrow Brand." Prepared for the board of Laois LEADER rural development company.

Lowitt, Kristin. 2013. "Examining Fisheries Contributions to Community Food Security: Findings from a Household Seafood Consumption Survey on the

West Coast of Newfoundland." *Journal of Hunger & Environmental Nutrition* 8 (2): 221–41. http://dx.doi.org/10.1080/19320248.2013.786668.

Lowitt, Kristin. 2011. *Examining the Foundations for Fisheries-Tourism Synergies and Increased Local Seafood Consumption in the Bonne Bay Region of Newfoundland. Prepared for Community-University Research for Recovery Alliance.* Memorial University and Rural Secretariat.

Marsden, Terry, Stefan Sjöblom, Kjell Andersson, and Sarah Skerratt. 2012. "Exploring Short-Termism and Sustainability: Temporal Mechanisms in Spatial Policies." In *Sustainability and Short-Term Policies: Improving Governance Spatial Policy Interventions*, edited by Stefan Sjöblom, Kjell Andersson, Terry Marsden, and Sarah Skerratt, 1–16. Surrey, England: Ashgate Press.

Marston, Sallie A. 2000. "The Social Construction of Scale." *Progress in Human Geography* 24 (2): 219–42. http://dx.doi.org/10.1191/030913200674086272.

May, Candace K. 2013. "Power across Scales and Levels of Fisheries Governance: Explaining the Active Non-Participation of Fishers in Two Rivers, North Carolina." *Journal of Rural Studies* 32: 26–37. http://dx.doi.org/10.1016/j.jrurstud.2013.04.002.

Min, Qingwen, ed. 2009. *Dynamic Conservation and Adaptive Management of China's GIAHS: Theories and Practices (I)*. Beijing: China Environmental Science Press.

Morgan, Kevin, Terry Marsden, and Jonathan Murdoch. 2006. *Worlds of Food: Place, Power and Provenance in the Food Chain*. Oxford Geographical and Environmental studies. Oxford: Oxford University Press.

Mount, Phil. 2012. "Growing Local Food: Scale and Local Food Systems Governance." *Agriculture and Human Values* 29 (1): 107–21. http://dx.doi.org/10.1007/s10460-011-9331-0.

Mount, Phil, and John Smithers. 2014. "The Conventionalization of Local Food: Farm Reflections on Local, Alternative Beef Marketing Groups." *Journal of Agriculture, Food Systems, and Community Development* 4 (3): 101-119.

Murray, Ian, and Barb Neis. 2012. Navigating the Legislative Requirements for Fisheries-Tourism Initiatives in Newfoundland and Labrador. http://www.curra.ca/documents/TCR_Fisheries_Tourism_Regulations_Report.pdf.

Nikoloyuk, Jordan, and David Adler. 2013. Valuing Our Fisheries: Breaking Nova Scotia's Commodity Curse. Ecology Action Centre. January. https://www.ecologyaction.ca/files/images-documents/file/Marine/Valuing%20our%20Fisheries%20FINAL.pdf.

Office International des Epizooties. 2014. BSE Situation in the World and Annual Incidence Rate. http://www.oie.int/animal-health-in-the-world/bse-specific-data/number-of-reported-cases-worldwide-excluding-the-united-kingdom/.

Palmer, David, Anni Arial, Rebecca Metzner, Rolf Willmann, Eva Müller, Fred Kafeero, and Eve Crowley. 2012. "Improving the Governance of Tenure of Land, Fisheries and Forests." *Land Tenure Journal* 1: 39–62.

Polanyi, Karl. 1968. *Primitive, Archaic and Modern Economics: Essays of Karl Polanyi*. New York: Anchor Books/DoubleDay.

Rosenau, James N., and Ernst-Otto Czempiel, eds. 1992. *Governance without Government: Order and Change in World Politics*. Vol. 20. Cambridge: Cambridge University Press. http://dx.doi.org/10.1017/CBO9780511521775.

Smith, Martin D., Cathy A. Roheim, Larry B. Crowder, Benjamin S. Halpern, Mary Turnipseed, James L. Anderson, Frank Asche, et al. 2010. "Sustainability and Global Seafood." *Science* 327 (5967): 784–6. http://dx.doi.org/10.1126/science.1185345. Medline:20150469

Sonnino, Robertta, and Terry Marsden. 2006. "Beyond the Divide: Rethinking Relationships between Alternative and Conventional Food Networks in Europe." *Journal of Economic Geography* 6 (2): 181–99. http://dx.doi.org/10.1093/jeg/lbi006.

Tilt, Bryan. 2008. "Smallholders and the 'Household Responsibility System': Adapting to Institutional Change in Chinese Agriculture." *Human Ecology* 36 (2): 189–99. http://dx.doi.org/10.1007/s10745-007-9127-4.

UNEP. 2011. *Towards a Green Economy: Pathways to Sustainable Development and Poverty Eradication.* http://www.unep.org/greeneconomy/GreenEconomyReport.

Walters, William. 2004. "Some Critical Notes on Governance." *Studies in Political Economy* 73: 27–46.

Xie, Jian, Liangliang Hu, Jianjun Tang, Xue Wu, Nana Li, Yongge Yuan, Haishui Yang, et al. 2011. "Ecological Mechanisms Underlying the Sustainability of the Agricultural Heritage Rice-Fish Coculture System." *Proceedings of the National Academy of Sciences of the United States of America* 108 (50): E1381–7. http://dx.doi.org/10.1073/pnas.1111043108. Medline:22084110

Zhong, Yiguang, and Geoff Power. 1997. "Fisheries in China: Progress, Problems, and Prospects." *Canadian Journal of Fisheries and Aquatic Sciences* 54 (1): 224–38. http://dx.doi.org/10.1139/f96-265.

CHAPTER 6

The Bottle at the Centre of a Changing Foodscape: "Bring Your Own Wine" in the Plateau-Mont-Royal, Montreal

Anaïs Détolle, Robert Jennings, and Alan Nash

> I don't know where and when it all started. I do remember as a little kid walking up St. Denis on summer nights with my father—this was the late 70s or early 80s—and hearing people hissing from front stoops offering to sell us some hash, musicians playing in the streets, and a bunch of BYOB restaurants around the corner. So the scene was, early in my mind, associated with some sort of counter culture and with the Plateau. Later, this type of restaurant was associated with friends' birthdays, a way to save money and to avoid getting stuck with a limited and crappy wine list. Living on the Plateau, it was just a convenient choice among a host of options, part of the fabric of life.
>
> —*Sarah Musgrave, food journalist at the* Montreal Gazette, *2014, personal correspondence.*

In Canadian society, there have been longstanding tensions between public attitudes toward alcohol and regulation (Heron 2003). The public sphere in particular has posed challenges for governance as regulators, the public, and private businesses attempt to manage consumption. This chapter explores the growth and significance of one case study of a compromise between these actors: "Bring Your Own Wine" (BYOW) restaurants in Montreal. This phenomenon—known as "Bring Your Own Bottle" (BYOB) or, more colloquially, as "Bring Your Own Booze," in other parts of the world and elsewhere in Canada—is most commonly known as "*Apportez votre vin*" (AVV) in French-speaking Quebec. Whatever its exact name, the BYOW offers a fascinating window into the processes of the governance of consumption and within food studies more broadly. The case illustrates the effects of bringing a private or domestic drinking practice into the public sphere, and the transformative effects of the bottle of wine as the centre of a shifting commercial environment.

Our research into Montreal's BYOWs has been framed from its beginnings as a collaborative and interdisciplinary research process that builds upon the authors' different fields in anthropology, geography, and urban studies. In this we are deliberately responding to the call of many leading scholars that work conducted in the field of food studies should be interdisciplinary (Belasco 2008, 6; Koç, Sumner, and Winson 2012, xii)—the "conversation" around different perspectives that is one of this book's major themes. Our choice of BYOWs has been further prompted by the realization that the changing role of alcohol shows the often subversive part commodities can play in achieving change, and that this could be demonstrated through the use of new critical perspectives of analysis such as the *foodscape*. In these ways, our study of BYOWs addresses this book's two other major themes—those of "transgressing boundaries" and "critical inquiry"—since it illustrates how such insights can bridge traditional disciplinary or theoretical boundaries. Certainly, our study of BYOWs via the use of a foodscape optic resists any temptation to generalize food and community, but instead brings together work from a variety of social science disciplines to examine them from multiple angles.

This study takes place in the central Montreal borough of the Plateau-Mont-Royal, which according to our study was the birthplace of BYOW in Canada. "The Plateau" has experienced powerful forces of gentrification and social change since the 1970s when BYOWs first emerged on the iconic streets of Duluth and Prince Arthur. According to one account, this rapid gentrification has made the Plateau one of the "hippest places to live" in North America (Walljasper and Kraker 1997).

Our analysis will examine how this specific format of restaurant has interacted with wider processes of gentrification in the Plateau. Many restaurants enable their customers to purchase drinks with their meal from their wine list, but what makes the BYOW particularly worthy of study is that by permitting clients to bring their own wine (or beer)—purchased at a convenience or liquor store beforehand—the clients have a far greater opportunity to demonstrate their discriminating taste or sense of hospitality.

The BYOW restaurant, by amplifying these qualities, thus becomes a catalyst for social change. Montreal's BYOWs offer an additional incentive for study because the practice of "bringing your own wine" throughout the province of Quebec has, since the very beginnings of the phenomenon, been operated without the restaurant charging any money for opening the customer's bottle. Such "corkage" charges can sometimes be steep and thus their absence in Montreal removes one obvious source of profit for restaurateurs while creating an element of thrift for the customer. Such differences in the potential to generate revenue continue to be a feature of Montreal's BYOWs, since unlike those BYOWs recently established in British Columbia and Ontario, Quebec's BYOWs are not permitted to sell alcohol of their own.

The role of BYOW in Montreal's restaurant world is hard to pin down. It is perhaps read best through the changing lenses of a *foodscape*, an approach we outline below. Thus, one interpretation might be that the practice is simply a commercial strategy to attract more customers. On the other hand, BYOWs, with their ability to reduce customer costs may be seen as foci for an anti-consumerism critique of the conventional North American restaurant. However, their connection with areas that are undergoing urban regeneration places them squarely with the more market-driven processes of gentrification. Furthermore, building on the ability of the customer to choose their own wine, yet another view of BYOWs has emphasized how wine conveys a sense of distinction among those sometimes called "foodies."

Montreal's BYOWs challenge existing practices that surround the regulation of alcohol, the profitability of the restaurants, and the commodification of hospitality. Our aim is to explore how and to what extent BYOWs are situated in processes of social and economic change. Since our study also shows the extent to which Montreal's BYOWs have developed as a result of a grassroots, almost playful, disobedience of provincial liquor control legislation, we also wish to show the importance of transgressive practice in the creation of what we see as new spaces of consumption and new forms of governance.

Where a Bottle of Wine Interacts with Space, Class, and Urban Change

Our review of the literature has revealed an underlying confluence in recent scholarship in geography, urban studies, and anthropology. Discussions of commodities, space, place, and social relations have shifted to less rigid, less dualistic, and more fluid, more subjective models that are complex and nuanced. The framework employed in our discussion of BYOWs is that of the *foodscape*, which we use to integrate our discussion of three key phenomena: commodities and spaces of consumption; distinction; and gentrification. The notion of the foodscape builds upon the attempt of anthropologist Arjun Appadurai (1996) to evacuate causality and move beyond a fixed vision of cultural groups. As he has argued, "terms with the common suffix *-scape*... indicate that these are not objectively given relations that look the same from every angle of vision but deeply perspectival constructs, inflected by the historical, linguistic, and political situatedness of different sorts of actors" (33).

Commodities and Spaces of Consumption

In *The Social Life of Things*, Appadurai suggests a broad definition of commodities. They are "distinguishable from 'products,' 'objects,' 'artifacts,' and other sorts of things—but only in certain respects and from a certain point of view" (1986, 6). Commodities are not specific to one economic system or one class of objects; rather, they are a phase in the life of a thing. Thus, the idea of commodity is defined not in and of itself, but by the process of exchange. For Appadurai (1986), commodity exchange is never bereft of culture, and the status of the commodity can change based on time, place, and the actors involved. As the object passes through phases of commodification and decommodification, it takes on different symbolic meanings in different contexts and can also determine the value of the human actors. Commodities fluctuate between *paths*, where social norms regulate their status, and *diversions*, where objects move in or out of commodity status as a strategy of competition between different actors in society. Appadurai's discussion of commodities allows us to re-evaluate the transition of wine as an object and as a commodity in the BYOW restaurant.

While the bottle of wine isn't necessarily decommodified—high alcohol taxes make wine a luxury item in Quebec, (Van Praet 2013)—the relationship between the restaurateur and the restaurant customer is altered by the setting of BYOW. The restaurateurs, by choosing this format, have removed their interest in wine as a commodity, shifting the relationship between the various actors of BYOW: clients, proprietors, food, drink, and the environment itself. This chapter explores the motivations of entrepreneurs who adopt this format.

Our study of BYOW restaurants in Montreal also draws on a growing body of literature that discusses the significance of *public* and *private* *space* in the wider context of *spaces of consumption* and *spaces of hospitality*. Of particular significance here are distinctions between public space and private space—areas which are shaped by behaviours of the public market, where the conditions of production can comfortably take place, or the private home, where we find the conditions of reproduction. Don Mitchell and Lynn Staeheli have recently suggested that a public space is only fully definable in comparison with more private spaces: "The public space of a restaurant is different from the private space of its kitchen" (Mitchell and Staeheli 2009, 511).

Ideas of public and private space underpin Peter Jackson and Nigel Thrift's (1995) pioneering work "Geographies of Consumption." In essence, they argue that consumerism is antithetical to public space since it is founded on ideas of leisure more in keeping with the private arena, and that—to resolve this tension—a new type of hybrid or *liminal* space is formed. This new space of consumption shares the characteristics of both public and private space. It sanctions behaviours that allow the spending of considerable amounts of time and money that neither the frugality of the traditional private sphere or the economically rational public sphere would tolerate.

Two examples serve to show how the emergence of newer places and modes of eating away from home do more than merely create a new dining experience; they challenge existing social and economic relationships. Spang's (2001) *Invention of the Restaurant* has shown how the development of dining outside the home was to create new hybrid public/private spaces in late eighteenth-century Paris—ones in which the king's courtiers could dine as discreetly as if at home. Similarly, Hurley's (1997) work on the early-twentieth-century American diner has shown how once women began to attend diners in larger numbers, those places became domesticated and, in transitioning from a male-dominated public space to a more family-oriented one, became more widely popular in the process.

Claval (1990) described the explosion of the number of restaurants in major French and Quebec cities over the two preceding decades. He links this phenomenon to rising incomes and states that the proportion of people eating outside of the home increased faster than the population over this period. The reasons for eating outside of the home have also changed, according to Claval. Longer work schedules and commutes between different economic sectors of the city have made eating out a question of practicality for many people, and new fashions such as the business lunch have also emerged. Restaurants have also taken on a new role as spaces of entertainment, and recent work has pointed to the often contradictory position municipal governments find themselves as they, on the one hand, promote restaurant and bar development in downtown public spaces—often with enhanced late-night hours—while, at the same time, warning of the perils of alcoholism and increased health care costs (Jayne, Valentine, and Holloway 2008).

Bell (2007) describes the "drinkification" of specific areas of city centres as a bid to stimulate economic growth in those areas via the promotion of consumption. This "domestication by cappuccino" (quoted in Jayne, Valentine, and Holloway 2008, 461) is part of a broader critique of the role played by restaurants and bars as the advance guard of the forces of gentrification. Another view, found in Bell's "Hospitable City" (2007), is that bars and restaurants are central in creating "a convivial, hospitable ecology" (96), through which hospitality and commensality—the act of eating together—are woven into new patterns of urban living, an "ethic of conviviality" (8).

The most primal acts of consumption—eating and drinking—can have an important role in the creation of spaces, and we can therefore anticipate that BYOWs may well possess similar liminal qualities. Through the domestication of drinking in public and its incorporation into the foodscape, BYOWs offer the possibility of new hybrid spaces—ones in which the once-questionable act of drinking outside the home now becomes sanctioned by a more domestically oriented setting more reminiscent of the world of the home and of non-commodified exchange.

Distinction

Recent scholarship has pointed to a democratization of eating away from the home where eating out is no longer reserved for the wealthy (Claval 1990; Johnston and Baumann 2010). New forms of restaurant, such as fast food outlets, cater to a lower-income demographic, while social factors such as longer work schedules and two-income households have created greater demand for convenience and fast food options.

In *Foodies*, a study of North America's gourmet foodscape, Johnston and Baumann (2010) point to a shift in the tastes of restaurant enthusiasts. In the first half of the twentieth century, American restaurant culture was dominated by the prestige of European cuisine, in particular from France. In the past several decades, they suggest, this continent has become much more culturally omnivorous—that is to say, more generally interested in food cultures from all around the world, in the obscure, the ecologically responsible, and the authentic, rather than one particular vision of gastronomic excellence. This constitutes what they call a "rejection of overt snobbery" (3). The divide between highbrow and lowbrow has been, to some degree, replaced by more various distinctions between "good" and "bad" food, and an interest in variety itself.

They see this development as rife with more subtle strategies of social distinction. Indeed, their study draws heavily on the terminology of French sociologist Pierre Bourdieu (1979), whose seminal work, *Distinction: A Social Critique of Judgment and Taste*, describes taste as socially constructed. For Bourdieu, the symbolic power bestowed by cultural and social capital—for example, the knowledge of exotic cuisines, or perhaps ecological awareness—is every bit as important as economic capital or material wealth in determining and perpetuating class distinction.

Johnston and Baumann (2010) speak of "the contradiction between an overt democratic populism that seeks solidarity with others, and a more covert but perpetual drive to achieve social distance and distinction" (173). Carfagna et al. (2014) have identified contemporary high-capital consumers, especially prominent in the urban northeastern United States, who are concerned with the environmental impact of their purchases, prefer local businesses and products, and are interested in do-it-yourself alternatives.

Both Bourdieu (1979) and Appadurai (1986) give an active role to objects of consumption in their models: the former sees them as playing an active role in symbolizing, generating, and maintaining social hierarchies, while the latter sees them as actors in determining the value of the individual. It is useful to keep this in mind when considering the role of the wine in BYOWs. Demossier (2005), for instance, has studied the social role of wine consumption in France. Her study suggests that this commodity, so central to the French identity, has shifted from being the staple beverage of the family dinner table to an instrument of connoisseurs in some cases. What she calls the "national connoisseur"—the wine expert who studies, describes, and rates wine from across the country—has become more powerful in many ways than the producer. As wine has become a "noble drink" (133), a growing number of French people feel disoriented and intimidated by the ritualization of wine tastings and the knowledge required to participate.

While it is beyond the scope of our work to examine more deeply the role of wine in Quebec society (which is, we anticipate, likely to be quite different from the French context), wine remains central to the object of our study, BYOW restaurants. Demossier's work, and the broader literature on distinction, reminds us that the commodities central to any institution, the rituals that take place there, and the various actors involved are enmeshed in a complex network that is never divorced from economic disparities and perceptions of class and taste.

Gentrification

Restaurants are at the forefront of changes in attitude toward food, and are also an influential force in the changing tastes of gentrifiers. As such, they are liminal places of consumption where fashion and social convention are created and evolve, but this has political implications and must be considered critically. As Slater, Curran, and Lees (2004) suggest, "Academic inquiry into neighborhood change has looked at the role of urban policy in harnessing the aspirations of middle-class professionals at the expense of looking at the role of urban policy in causing immense hardship for people with nowhere else to go in booming property markets reshaped by neoliberal regulatory regimes" (1142).

The pedestrianization of Prince Arthur and Duluth Streets in 1979 and 1980, illustrated by the streets' unique cobblestone, is a physical manifestation of the gentrification process in the Plateau (Ville de Montréal, n.d.). In her profile of mid-1990s gentrifiers in Montreal, Damaris Rose (2004) emphasizes that many benefitted from city-run programs encouraging residential development in areas that had previously fallen out of favour. As inner cities become attractive, the same suburbanites who once avoided them or frequented them voyeuristically now purchase homes there.

Slater, Curran, and Lees (2004) contrast two prominent North American academic discourses on gentrification. The *revanchist city* describes the gentrification process as an influx of suburban wealth back into the inner city after years of abandonment, and a subsequent displacement and exclusion of working class and minority populations. The *emancipated city*, in contrast, describes the gentrification process as a critical response to the monotony of suburban life, as countercultural groups seek out inner-city spaces for their diversity, tolerance, and creativity. The authors suggest that studies of gentrification should keep both of these models in mind, rather than argue for one or the other. This vision also allows us to look beyond causality and understand gentrification as a complex and contradictory phenomenon, much in the same way the foodscape allows us to look at food.

This literature presented here has drawn on many disciplines. The common thread we see in the literature of anthropology, human geography, and urban studies is a willingness to engage with often tangled and messy relationship and contradictions without necessarily producing a definite, "untangled" description of them. In particular, Appadurai's (1986) understanding of commodities as being constantly in flux and moving through different phases allows us to examine the wine object as an active and dynamic element of BYOW, and introduces the foodscape as our principal framework for exploring the BYOW's overlapping interactions. Similarly, we look at domesticity, public life, and conventions of hospitality and commensality as being redefined along with restaurant culture. As this review has shown, this evolution has a strong relationship with new strategies of social distinction, the implications of which can be seen as emancipatory or exclusionary on the neighbourhood scale.

Sketching and Framing the Foodscape

It is tempting to see the foodscape as a fixed image. The difficulty of the "-scape" language is due to its shifting, plural, and overlapping qualities. In this study, we have therefore conceptualized the role of BYOW within the foodscape using metaphorical language from the world of visual art, *sketching* and *framing* a series of interactions in time and space. As academics, we invariably put boundaries around our subject of study, but this foodscape "frame" paradoxically implies that other perspectives exist outside of our own. What's more, the particular connections that we make between our interviews, our press review, and academic theory are more akin to preparatory studies or sketches than a finished landscape painting.

Our research involved two primary methods to examine our case study area of the Plateau, and to consider the location of BYOWs within that area. First, we systematically evaluated a range of documents including Canadian newspaper articles—mainly in the *Montreal Gazette*—for the last four decades and tourist guidebooks of the city. Second, we conducted fifteen interviews in English, French, and Arabic in eleven BYOW restaurants in the Plateau-Mont-Royal borough. These interviews were then analyzed through a careful examination of the themes and ideas that our interviewers reported—themes that were not always what we had expected but which enabled us to sharpen and occasionally rethink our own preconceptions as researchers. The conceptual framework outlined above framed and informed the line of questioning we used in our interview guide—a guide we adapted as we found links with the literature and our growing sense of the history of BYOW. Our interview contacts were developed by speaking to pioneers of BYOW in the Plateau and then by snowball sampling until we reached what Glaser and Strauss have called the "saturation point"—that is, the point when new interviews yield little additional information (Rubin and Rubin 2012).

The selected restaurants varied in price from economical to high-end, in cuisine from Greek and French to Afghan, and were founded between 1979 and 2009. Two final interviews were conducted by e-mail correspondence with prominent Montreal food journalists. To protect the identities of those in our survey, we have anonymized the names of those interviewed and the names of their restaurants—the only exception being cases of restaurants and individuals already named in newspaper accounts where we have retained names as published.

The Transformative Qualities of the Bottle of Wine

In the following discussion of our research, we begin with a brief history of BYOWs in Montreal. Building on this foundation, we then examine the role of BYOW in the foodscape of Montreal's Plateau using the three major themes developed from the literature. In what follows, our discussion of these important perspectives will allow us to consider the various interactions of BYOWs and to present them in the following order: (1) issues of domesticity, hospitality, and commensality; (2) the role of commodities, consumption, and distinction; and, (3) the part played by BYOWs in the processes of gentrification.

Our discussion revolves around the bottle of wine as the centre of experience and as an object whose value and role changes as we see it differently through the various positionings in the foodscape. But it is by no means the only player, and it is possible to argue that the role of commodities in general lays an emphasis on the part played by *actors*, while issues of hospitality stress the interaction of *spaces*, and gentrification highlights the involvement of BYOWs in the *processes* of change. However, as might be expected with a foodscape approach, such attempts at simple categorization can only be provisional.

A History of BYOW

Our history of BYOW begins with two accounts collected in our interviews. Both point to a single restaurant in the Plateau. The first claims that the practice began accidentally and states that an owner of this then-unlicensed establishment shared wine that he had himself brought into the restaurant with friends. That night led to a decision to allow customers to bring their own. The second account comes from an interviewee who worked at that time as a waiter in the same establishment. He said that the practice began in 1974, and was spread discreetly by word of mouth to the clients. The owner didn't know whether it was legal or not at the time, and was reluctant to approach the relevant authorities. As such, our interviewee was told to keep the bottles hidden, because they did not know what would happen if the police came. Shortly afterwards—and well before any formal legal framework for BYOWs developed—several neighbouring Greek and Vietnamese restaurants began the same practice.

These remarks emphasize the importance of wine as a subversive object. Analyzing the changes through a foodscape lens following Appadurai (1986), we could say that the bottle, which enters the space as a non-commodity, plays an active, transformative role, acting as a solvent that breaks down the administrative context. The casual extension of BYOW to clients can be seen as a diversion in the flow of commodities, where the established, socially regulated path of wine being sold by the restaurant to the client is called into question. But this, in turn, would gradually lead to a contested legitimization and officialization of BYOW in the law.

Press reports from this period point to a considerable resistance on the part of licensed establishments. Jacques Landurie, president of the Association des Restaurateurs du Québec, a group that represented some 2,000 restaurants and that wanted BYOWs banned, stated that BYOWs provided "unfair competition" to restaurants with liquor licences (*Montreal Gazette* 1985). He claimed that "it is unacceptable that people are allowed to bring wine into restaurants. It's becoming a plague." Public opinion was sharply divided between supporters of BYOWs who said they would "fight for their customers' right to wash down a meal with store-bought wine" and those who already viewed BYOWs with some concern. The former group included the president of the Hellenic Restaurant Association—whose 5,000 members were estimated to represent well over half the province's restaurants in 1985—who remarked, "I think it is a great service to the public." Interestingly, he added this opinion: "It's a kind of acquired right for those restaurants. I don't see how they can deprive them of that right" (Scott 1985).

Interviewed on 8 April 1986, the day after issuing its 284-page report into BYOWs in Quebec, Ghislain Laflamme, president of the Régie des alcools et des jeux, noted that "the public is...responsible for launching this phenomenon," and added that the high prices that restaurants charged their customers for wine were a big factor in the spread of BYOWs since 1982 (Delean 1986). The resulting Law 96, passed later in 1986 in response the Régie's report, banned consumption in licensed restaurants of alcohol purchased elsewhere, while permitting unlicensed establishments to pay for a permit to serve but not sell alcohol, creating the legal framework for BYOW (Laflamme et al. 1986). As such, the phenomenon has come full circle from a legal grey zone based on diversion of the wine commodity, to a new socially sanctioned path. We now turn to a more detailed exploration of the relationships between various actors and the specificity of BYOW as spaces.

Domesticity, Hospitality, and Commensality

A major theme to emerge from our interviews is the BYOW's ability to create its own type of ambiance. One BYOW owner believed his customers seek a more convivial atmosphere. Another added that the ambiance in his restaurant "is more relaxed, more fun." Interviewees claimed that as each client tends to arrive with a bottle of wine, they often drink more than in other restaurant settings. They also tend to stay longer after their meal to finish the bottles. One of the owners we interviewed even complained of large groups spending the whole night drinking, ordering only one or two appetizers between them. Two other interviewees similarly believed that the atmosphere of their BYOW is more informal and festive than conventional licensed restaurants.

Here, the wine object becomes the source of a non-commercial complicity between the thrift-seeker or wine connoisseur and the hospitality entrepreneur. Because it is not purchased on the premises, there is also the potential for exchanges between clients to take on new rituals of gift exchange and generosity. Each client arriving with his or her own bottle creates a different rapport than that of "the next round is on me."

Newspaper restaurant reviews have also suggested that BYOWs have a home-like ambiance, and hint that perhaps behaviours more appropriate to the private realm are sanctioned there. Thus, as early as 1985, the *Montreal Gazette*'s restaurant reviewer Ashok Chandwani described the experience of dining in the Modigliani in these terms: "The overall ambiance is that of being in someone's home. The fact that some parts of it are someone's home becomes obvious in the men's washroom, [where] there's toothpaste and other toiletries beside the washbasin" (Chandwani 1985). In a similar vein, Sylvain Desjardins describes the domestic-like informality of the Rites Berbères—a BYOW on De Bullion Street—which is "run by a husband and wife, who mingle easily with their guests and will even sit down if asked about the old country" (Desjardins 1997). The commensality of BYOW is a major selling point for clients, and the BYOW experience is in this way a commodity in and of itself.

If BYOWs are a hybrid of both public and private spaces, to what extent does the drinking of alcohol in such places actually recall drinking at home? Is it, in fact, a "domestication" of the public realm? Heron's study of drinking in Canada suggests that the long-term goals of government regulation have always located "problem drinking" in the public arena, while the family milieu is perceived as more likely to limit consumption (Heron 2003). This is consistent with Jayne, Valentine, and Holloway's (2008) finding in the British context. In this respect, the BYOW format may be seen as an unconventional approach to governance of public drinking since the customers are regulating their consumption in the same way as they would be in the home.

The extent to which Montreal's BYOWs are home-like settings can be judged again from Chandwani's experience in the Modigliani, where "you can bring your own bottle.... Or buy two—you'll want to linger if the piano player's on hand. It's a totally relaxed, unhurried restaurant" (Chandwani 1985). We are once more reminded of Appadurai's (1986) commodity diversion. The wine object is decommodified in order to allow a more home-like consumption unburdened by the social perception that public drinking is problematic. The casual qualities of BYOW are not unlike those of other informal restaurant settings; small family-run restaurants or hole-in-the-wall diners also blur the lines between domesticity and publicness. We feel, however, that it is the centrality of wine as an actor disrupting the usual exchange relationship found in the restaurant space that is specific to BYOW.

Commodities, Consumption, and Distinction

In our interviews with chefs and owners, we found that both groups were very sensitive to the perceived expectations and standards of their clients, and their responses are useful in exploring the relationship between clients and commodities. Two of the chefs we interviewed had worked in both licensed restaurants and BYOWs. They described to us in great detail the process of sourcing food in both types of restaurants and pointed to the specific challenges of BYOW. This comparative perspective suggested that in BYOW, wine, rather than food, is at the centre of the experience. The other restaurateurs we talked to were able to elaborate on the typical clientele of BYOW and the kinds of wine they choose to bring.

The general comments from our respondents on food sourcing in both types of restaurant indicated that, when the affluence of the clientele permits, expensive ingredients are brought in from small, specialized distributors and sold at low profit margins. Ingredients such as foie gras, scallops, lobster, or sushi-grade tuna are the mark of a high-end establishment. Their presence on the menu reassures the connoisseur of the quality of the restaurant, while the high profit margin plates that accompany these items, such as tartares and French fries, help to recuperate their expense. At one licensed establishment serving high-end Italian food, the chef stated, "We would buy expensive heirloom tomatoes and microgreens from small distributors at the Jean-Talon market, but we would get all our dry stock like flour and sugar from the cheapest industrial-scale distributors on the market."

Another strategy identified by actors in the restaurant industry is to recuperate food cost with alcohol sales—clearly not an option for BYOWs. Our interviewees indicated that more compromises were made in terms of food quality as a result in BYOW than in conventional restaurants. One sous-chef explains that if he wants to serve expensive ingredients, he has to reduce the portion because of the BYOW format. "Portions in restaurants are done by weight, and it's extremely precise. For example, for the same price as in a licensed restaurant, we might serve ten grams less foie gras. Generally, we try and serve more copious mains to make up for it, and the client doesn't mind because overall the bill is still lower." Another cook confirms this: "A classic restaurant can serve plates where 70 percent of the price is food cost. We can't go over 30 percent. We also encourage clients to purchase a fixed menu at $45, which helps us control costs." This illustrates the precision with which food costs are calculated in the menu-planning process.

The kitchen professionals we spoke to were more aware of the importance of certain foods as markers of social distinction than their clients. As one remarked, "I'd like us to order nice things but the regular clients don't want the menu to change—they'd rather have the old *carbonara* with the powdered cream sauce. They also would rather pay less than have higher quality ingredients." This remark speaks to the fact that wine, rather than food, is at the centre of the BYOW experience.

All of our sources indicated that thrift was one of the main reasons to patronize a BYOW restaurant. Much of the clientele has limited means. One chef described his clients as "students and artists who want to drink." Another mentioned "small families, first-daters, and couples." The cuisine of BYOW is often frugal because of the financial constraints of the business model and customer. One owner mentioned that she had chosen to operate this style of restaurant because she believed that the local clientele couldn't afford a more high-end restaurant. BYOW responds to the financial limitations of the customer and creates new opportunities for lower-income consumers to eat out of the house.

Most of our interviewees said that the kinds of wine that clients bring vary greatly. However the lower cost of the dining experience seems to have inspired certain clients to bring wines they could not have afforded to order on a licensed restaurant wine list because of the mark-up. While in the past, patrons would bring wines purchased at *depanneurs*—the local convenience store—and grocery stores, some clients now plan ahead, consulting the menu of the restaurant in advance to pair the wine with the meal, bringing more lavish bottles that are only available at SAQ outlets. The budding wine connoisseur of the Plateau uses the BYOW and the wine object to display sophistication in the way that Johnston and Baumann's (2010) "foodies" use food. BYOW can also be related to the broader "do-it-yourself" movement described by Carfagna et al. (2014), since individuals can take part in more steps of their wine purchase, and thus the selection process becomes a more highbrow process. This brings us back to seeing the BYOW experience as a commodity. The compromises made in the kitchen are acceptable to the client because the experience, whether motivated by the informal atmosphere, thrift, or displays of connoisseurship, is *worth it.*

BYOW and the Plateau

Rose (2004) posited that municipal policy has encouraged residential gentrification in Montreal; our interviews suggest it plays a similar role on the commercial side of things. Initial interventions by the city may have contributed to the development of BYOW. One restaurateur notes in this regard that Prince Arthur and Duluth became "special streets" after their redesign, and the nearby Saint Denis Street—a now very busy commercial avenue—developed as a secondary impact of their growth. The city's active involvement in street redesign in the areas where the BYOWs developed is consistent with how Bell's (2007) "city of hospitality" relates to the political commodification of urban experiences such as BYOW.

When asked about the evolution of BYOW over the last few decades, several themes emerged in the interviews. Most of the owners of older establishments expressed the feeling that BYOW had become less profitable. When asked about the financial benefits of the format, the owner of the oldest restaurant in our survey replied, "Well, lately nothing much"—a situation he attributed to the increasing municipal taxes charged to these businesses (over $35,000 per year), more scrutiny of restaurants' revenues—however small—and the difficulty of parking. By legalizing and institutionalizing BYOW, as well as encouraging urban regeneration in the Plateau, the city and province have actively participated in the gentrification process, monetizing the phenomenon as a source of tax revenue. One interviewee was sceptical of the intentions of the municipal government: "You could tell that the government just wants the money, nothing else."

The owners of more recently opened restaurants indicated that the clientele and fashion of the Plateau's BYOWs have changed significantly in the past decades. They remarked that there are fewer suburban clients and more local clients, and that the clientele tends to be more affluent than before, and more demanding in terms of the level of cuisine. Some also claimed that the food has improved in response to the change in clientele, which resonates with the foodies described by Johnston and Baumann (2010), as a group with an accrued interest in highbrow foods that symbolize social distinction and incarnate new wealth. The back-and-forth between suburban and urban lifestyles is an important aspect of the gentrification process, here typified in the words of one of our interviewees: "The older restaurants in the south of the Plateau have had difficulty with clients cancelling reservations because they couldn't find parking. Here—in the Mile End, more to the north of the Plateau borough—we don't have this problem, because our clientele is more local. There is more parking available here, but also, our clients know where to find parking, and often they don't drive to the restaurant."

It is clear that BYOW in Montreal was initially an attraction for a suburban clientele wishing to participate in an urban alternative to the conventional restaurant, and in this sense has emancipatory qualities for such customers (Slater, Curran, and Lees 2004). This same emancipatory process that brings suburban interest and wealth in central neighbourhoods can also push the cost of living higher than local residents and businesses can afford. The increase in the affluence of BYOW clientele and the displacement or marginalization of some of the older establishments seen in our interviews is consistent with the revanchist discourse on neighbourhood change, even while it may have allowed newer BYOWs to adapt to today's economic realities.

A concluding insight regarding BYOWs and gentrification comes from another restaurateur, who remarked, "It's 100 percent sure that these restaurants have changed the neighbourhood, but today it is the neighbourhood that is changing the restaurants." We see the evolution of BYOW and the Plateau not in linear relationships of cause and effect, but as a set of parameters working simultaneously for and against each other in the foodscape. The various lenses supplied to us by history, actors, spaces, and processes, when viewed through the kaleidoscope of the foodscape approach, present the BYOW as both a catalyst and a subject of change and emphasizes the transformative qualities of the bottle of wine.

Conclusion

Our case study provides some new directions for the study of consumption in Montreal and for the broader field of food studies in general. By building on recent theoretical developments in geography, urban studies, and anthropology that show concepts such as "space" and "things" are "socially constructed," we have not only shown the importance of engaging in an interdisciplinary "conversation" around food studies (a major theme of this volume), but also how that engagement enhances analysis with new insight. Thus, our examination of BYOWs has shown how subtle and almost subversive changes in the governance of alcohol sales in Montreal's restaurants are the catalyst for transformative changes such as the creation of new spaces of consumption. Our study of BYOWs has also highlighted the need to be very aware of "liminality," and we have come to see how new types of behaviour fashioned in such boundary areas can influence social changes as various as fashions in taste or the gentrification of a neighbourhood. These insights are, in keeping with this volume's second major theme, an outcome of having deliberately transgressed traditional disciplinary boundaries to discover that the phenomenon of real interest lie in the gaps between. Our BYOW study shows how the bottle (or at least the alcohol inside) is an important agent propelling change and concurs with other recent authors in suggesting that restaurant studies in particular, and food studies in general, needs to embrace such theoretical developments (Janeja 2010, 80–8; Murcott 2013, 16–17).

New, and more critical methods of inquiry are, of course, the focus of this book's third main theme—a direction we have sought to follow through our use of ethnographic methods and the theoretical insights of the "foodscape." In particular, we suggest that the foodscape optic has allowed us to combine work from a variety of social sciences disciplines to examine food and community from multiple angles. Far from drawing a definite portrait of the phenomenon, it has assembled and framed a series of sketches or impressions that suggest further lines of inquiry. A particularly exciting direction for further research on food governance may be a broader analysis of the relationship between alcohol policy in Canada and the culture of drinking that policy makers seek to regulate. It may also be worthwhile to pursue the views and opinions of customers of BYOW themselves—an aspect that time and resources have prevented us investigating here.

BYOWs are simultaneously an example of commercial ingenuity, as restaurateurs find new ways to turn a profit without relying on alcohol sales, and of collective resistance to the substantial regulation and cost of alcohol in Canadian society. They have challenged existing social norms of behaviour in public spaces by providing an environment for more relaxed, informal, and commensal ways of eating and drinking in restaurants. BYOWs have, in this way, produced new spaces of consumption, a stepping-stone between eating in the home and eating out, and a transition between domestic and public drinking.

Our study has provided some provisional and interesting answers to our main objectives regarding the growth and significance of BYOWs in the Plateau. We have suggested that BYOWS can be considered as commodified spaces and experiences that have a social life of their own, as liminal public spaces charged with more private concepts of domesticity, and as victims of, but also participants in, a rapid gentrification process. The study of BYOW shows us that this particular governance model results from *interactions* between commodities, spaces, and broader social forces, *processes* of transgression, legitimization, and legalization, and *motivations* like commercial ingenuity, thrift, and distinction. All of these forces are mobilized by the bottle of wine and visible through the foodscape approach.

Acknowledgements

The authors would like to thank the following: all of our informants for sharing their time and information with us; reviewers Martha and Matthew Koch, Christine Jourdan, Nathalie Cooke, and the co-authors and editors of the present volume for their precious comments; journalists Sarah Musgrave and Barry Lazar for their comments; and Nour Ghadanfar and Matthew Leddy for their help with the interview process.

References

Appadurai, Arjun, ed. 1986. *The Social Life of Things: Commodities in Cultural Perspective*. Cambridge: Cambridge University Press. http://dx.doi.org/10.1017/CBO9780511819582.

Appadurai, Arjun, ed. 1996. *Modernity at Large: Cultural Dimensions of Globalization*. Minneapolis: Minnesota University Press.

Belasco, Warren. 2008. *Food: The Key Concepts*. Oxford: Berg.

Bell, David. 2007. "The Hospitable City: Social Relations in Commercial Spaces." *Progress in Human Geography* 31 (1): 7–22. http://dx.doi.org/10.1177/0309132507073526.

Bourdieu, Pierre. 1979. *La distinction, critique sociale du jugement*. Paris: Les Éditions de Minuit.

Carfagna, Lindsey B., Emilie A. Dubois, Connor Fitzmaurice, Monique Y. Ouimette, Juliet B. Schor, Margaret Willis, and Thomas Laidley. 2014. "An

Emerging Eco-Habitus: The Reconfiguration of High Cultural Capital Practices among Ethical Consumers." *Journal of Consumer Culture* 14 (2): 158–78. http://dx.doi.org/10.1177/1469540514526227.

Chandwani, Ashok. 1985. "Modigliani Place to Go for that Touch of Home." *Montreal Gazette*, 20 September, C9.

Claval, Paul. 1990. "Introduction." In *Les restaurants dans le monde et à travers les âges*, edited by Alain Huetz de Lemps and Jean-Robert Pitte, 15–16. Grenoble: Les Éditions Glénat.

Delean, Paul. 1986. "Don't Ban Bring-Your-Own-Wine Restaurants: Liquor Watchdog." *Montreal Gazette*, 8 April, A1.

Demossier, Marion. 2005. "Consuming Wine in France: The 'Wandering' Drinker and the Vin-anomie." In *Drinking Cultures: Alcohol and Identity*, edited by Thomas M. Wilson, 129–54. Oxford: Berg.

Desjardins, Sylvain. 1997. "In Search of BYOW Restaurants: There's No Cellar but the Wine List Is Endless." *Globe and Mail*, 1 October, D2.

Heron, Craig. 2003. *Booze: A Distilled History*. Toronto: Between the Lines.

Hurley, Andrew. 1997. "From Hash House to Family Restaurant: The Transformation of the Diner and Post-World War II Consumer Culture." *Journal of American History* 83 (4): 1282–308. http://dx.doi.org/10.2307/2952903.

Jackson, Peter, and Nigel Thrift. 1995. "Geographies of Consumption." In *Acknowledging Consumption: A Review of New Studies*, edited by Daniel Miller, 202–35. London: Routledge.

Janeja, Manpreet K. 2010. *Transactions in Taste: The Collaborative Lives of Everyday Bengali Food*. London: Routledge.

Jayne, Mark, Gill Valentine, and Sarah L. Holloway. 2008. "Fluid Boundaries—British Binge Drinking and European Civility: Alcohol and the Production and Consumption of Public Space." *Space and Polity* 12 (1): 81–100. http://dx.doi.org/10.1080/13562570801969473.

Johnston, Josée, and Shyon Baumann. 2010. *Foodies: Democracy and Distinction in the Gourmet Foodscape*. New York: Routledge.

Koç, Mustafa, Jennifer Sumner, and Anthony Winson. 2012. "Introduction: The Significance of Food and Food Studies." In *Critical Perspectives in Food Studies*, edited by Mustafa Koç, Jennifer Sumner, and Anthony Winson, 11–14. Don Mills, ON: Oxford University Press.

Laflamme, Ghislain K., Raymond Boulet, André Laurence, and Régie des permis d'alcool du Qc. 1986. Rapport sur le phénomène dit du "vin libre." Edited by Régie des permis d'alcools du Qc. Quebec: Quebec Provincial Government.

Mitchell, Don, and Lynn A. Staeheli. 2009. "Public Space." In *International Encyclopedia of Human Geography*, edited by Nigel Thrift and Rob Kitchin, 511–16. Oxford: Elsevier. http://dx.doi.org/10.1016/B978-008044910-4.00990-1.

Montreal Gazette. 1985. "Don't Cork Competition." B2.

Murcott, Anne. 2013. "A Burgeoning Field." In *The Handbook of Food Research*, edited by Anne Murcott, Warren Belasco, and Peter Jackson, 1–25. London: Bloomsbury.

Rose, Damaris. 2004. "Discourses and Experiences of Social Mix in Gentrifying Neighbourhoods: A Montreal Case Study." *Canadian Journal of Urban Research* 13 (2): 278–316.

Rubin, Herbert J., and Irene S. Rubin. 2012. *Qualitative Interviewing: The Art of Hearing the Data.* Thousand Oaks, CA: Sage.

Scott, Marion. 1985. "Bring-Your-Own Eateries Fight Curbs." *Montreal Gazette,* 6 April, A3.

Slater, Tom, Winifred Curran, and Loretta Lees. 2004. "Gentrification Research: New Directions and Critical Scholarship." *Environment & Planning A* 36:1141–50. http://dx.doi.org/10.1068/a3718.

Spang, Rebecca L. 2001. *The Invention of the Restaurant. Paris and Modern Gastronomic Culture.* Harvard Historical Studies 135. Cambridge, MA: Harvard University Press.

Van Praet, Nicolas. 2013. "Quebec's High Taxes Make Cheap Wine Hard to Find." *Financial Post,* 11 January. http://business.financialpost.com/2013/01/11/quebecs-high-taxes-make-cheap-wine-hard-to-find/.

Ville de Montréal. n.d. "Les grandes rues de Montréal: La rue Prince Arthur et ses intersections." Accessed 4 December 2014. http://ville.montreal.qc.ca/portal/page?_pageid=5677,57651598&_dad=portal&_schema=PORTAL.

Walljasper, Jay, and Daniel Kraker. 1997. "The 15 Hippest Places to Live. The Coolest Neighborhoods in America and Canada." *Utne.com.* Accessed 1 December 2014. http://www.utne.com/arts/hip-hot-spots.aspx.

CHAPTER 7

Finding Balance: Food Safety, Food Security, and Public Health

Wanda Martin, Erika Mundel, and Karen Rideout

Over the past decade in Canada and elsewhere, there has been a rise in what some commentators have loosely identified as a "food movement" seeking to critique the food system with an eye toward improved health and sustainability (Pollan 2010; Wakefield 2007). This movement—really a collection of groups with multiple origins, priorities, and approaches, all of which have a stated interest in improving some aspect(s) of the food system—has increased public and political awareness of food issues. However, some food movement actors have at times found themselves at odds with established political and regulatory regimes within the dominant food system.

This chapter focuses on tensions that have emerged between two groups of food system actors: public health professionals responsible for *food safety* and *community food security* advocates working within public health (e.g., community nutritionists) or the at the community level (e.g., farmers and food activists). While both groups are concerned about a high-quality food supply, food safety legislation and policy focuses primarily on controlling microbial and other contamination of food. Community food security actors are more closely aligned with the food movement through their focus on a community food security framework, considering food safety alongside factors such as nutrition, sustainability, and support for local communities. This framework works toward increased access to quality food for all community residents through a food system that is just, healthful, and sustainable (Rideout et al. 2006).

Differences in world view between food movement actors and the dominant food safety regime have contributed to challenges in addressing complex food system problems. These challenges are illustrative of tensions arising within the public health system as health agencies slowly start moving toward a more holistic approach to protecting and promoting health. Guiding principles are shifting in an effort to address inequality throughout the health system, integrate chronic disease prevention into existing health protection agencies, and recognize the influence of systems and environments on individual behaviours (BC Ministry of Health 2013). This "whole of society" approach emerges from a different understanding of health than the biomedical underpinnings of Western healthcare systems, creating opportunities and challenges for public health professionals and the communities they serve (Mundel 2013). In this chapter, we shed light on the challenges of integrating new ways of thinking into the established health system. We also suggest that increasing mutual understanding between food safety and food security proponents can support the food movement and the broader goal of healthier food systems.

We use a case example to explore the tensions between food security and food safety and their implications for the food movement. In the early 2000s, British Columbia (BC) engaged in a process of public health renewal that created twenty-one core public health programs to be delivered by the regional health authorities. Food safety had long been a core program, but food security was new. In fact, BC was the first province in Canada explicitly to address food security through the public health system. These two seemingly interrelated programs were not closely aligned, leading to challenges for initiatives that fell under the purview of both programs. The Food Safety Core Program had a clearly defined mandate, a pre-existing workforce and responsible agencies, and an established regulatory framework. The new Food Security Core Program was a framework for action with suggested programs and policies but no consistent requirements for action and little direct oversight or enforceability. While the ministry implemented both programs with the intention of improving the quality of food available to British Columbians, the food safety program had pre-existing infrastructure and a legislated mandate for specific actions.

Through analysis of the BC experience, this chapter shows that different public health actors understand and address food system challenges and health problems in different and sometimes conflicting ways. Our analysis points to the importance of considering local variations within the context of province-wide public health policies and regulations. Reflecting on successful examples of collaboration, we suggest there is a need for clearly defined roles, responsibilities, and policy structures in order for proponents of food safety and food security to work together effectively. This requires consistency in underlying values and priorities, flexible operations, and clear communication.

Methods

This chapter weaves together the previous research and professional experience of the three authors. Martin (2014) asked how the intersections between food safety and food security are negotiated and what facilitates and constrains collaboration between the two sectors. Using surveys and semi-structured interviews with food system activists and professionals working in health protection or health promotion in BC, she identified some of the major challenges and points of intersection between proponents of food safety and food security. Mundel (2013) conducted a qualitative study on BC's Food Security Core Program and one of its key initiatives, the Community Food Action Initiative, to examine the relationship between public health and the food movement in BC. Using textual analysis, participant observation, and semi-structured interviews with community food leaders and public health staff, she explored how the public health system has both supported and constrained the food movement. Rideout (2012) used semi-structured interviews with alternative food system activists and food policy makers in BC (and India) to explore ways in which connections and relationships influence food choices and decision making about healthy eating. She is also an environmental public health policy analyst who facilitates collaboration between those working within the Food Safety and Food Security Core Public Health Programs in BC.

This chapter crosses both disciplinary boundaries and the so-called academic-community divide to offer a unique understanding of food system challenges and solutions in BC. Collectively, we drew on our own individual strengths and specialized knowledge to contribute to this collaborative work. This approach, based on three studies of similar populations and practical experience, offers a level of validity and reliability that can be challenging to obtain in qualitative research (Morse et al. 2008).

Tensions between Community Food Security and Food Safety

At their core, food security and food safety are both concerned with ensuring access to quality food. However, as we will show, they operate from different historical contexts, institutional frameworks, and operational paradigms.

These differences introduce challenges to collaboration between community food security advocates and those with a legislated mandate to protect the public from foodborne illness.

Community Food Security

The global industrial food system moves a huge volume of food, much of which is produced at large scales and traded globally (Clapp 2012). As this dominant food system has developed, there has been an increasing concentration of control over food by a small number of corporations (Clapp 2012; Heffernan 2000; Qualman 2001; Stuckler and Nestle 2012). The concentration of power has marginalized producers and eaters of food, with large corporations mediating most of the decisions that affect food policy and food choice. As such, profit is prioritized over the health of the (eating) public (Dixon and Banwell 2004; Lang, Barling, and Caraher 2009; Nestle 2002; Stuckler and Nestle 2012), the well-being of food producers (Allen 2010; Brown and Getz 2011), and the health of communities and ecosystems (Blay-Palmer 2008). Food policy analysts, activists, and health professionals have argued that the dominant food system must be reoriented toward the health of individuals, communities, and ecosystems (Community Nutritionists Council of BC 2004; Lang 2009; Desjardins et al. 2002; Welsh and MacRae 1998).

Recent food movement activity in Canada has focused on building community food security, "a situation in which all community residents obtain a safe, culturally acceptable and nutritionally adequate diet through a sustainable food system that maximizes community self-reliance and social justice" (Hamm and Bellows 2003, 37). The community nutritionists, anti-poverty activists, and academics that initially developed the concept of community food security were critical of approaches to addressing hunger through charity and a focus on individual responsibility (Riches 2002; Gottlieb 2001; Winne et al. 1997; Poppendieck 1999). Community food security aimed to shift the locus for change from individuals to the community, and emphasized a need to address the root causes of hunger by changing the food system (Allen 2004; Winne et al. 1997). This approach has expanded to include an emphasis on local and sustainable food production that benefits growers, eaters, and the environment by increasing individuals' and communities' skills and capacities to produce their own food, promoting access to healthful foods, and encouraging greater citizen participation in the food system. The emphasis on local and sustainable food has led some to criticize the community food security movement as elitist or exclusionary (e.g.,

DuPuis and Goodman 2005; Guthman 2003, 2007; also see Sprague and Kennedy, Chapter 8 of this volume). At its heart, however, the community food security movement thus seeks to address social justice, health, and ecological concerns (Allen 2004; Hamm and Bellows 2003; Johnston and Baker 2005; Wekerle 2004; Welsh and MacRae 1998; Winne et al. 1997).

Public health agencies, and community nutritionists in particular, have begun recognizing food security as a key determinant of health and have participated actively in efforts to build community food security in Canada (Community Nutritionists Council of BC 2004; Dietitians of Canada 2007; Desjardins et al. 2002; Rideout and Kosatsky 2014). The focus of our case study—the integration of food security into the BC public health system—set the stage for even greater involvement of the health sector in the growing community food security movement.

Food Safety

Food safety regulations aim to prevent foodborne illness by preventing the consumption of microbial or chemical contaminants (Serapiglia et al. 2007). Foodborne illness is the largest class of emerging infectious diseases in Canada (Weatherill 2009). Pathogens cause an estimated 400,000 episodes of foodborne illness, over 55,000 hospitalizations, and 1,351 deaths in the United States each year (Scallan et al. 2011). Foodborne illness also has economic implications for affected individuals, for establishments linked to contaminated food, and for society through lost productivity and healthcare costs (Copeland and Wilcott 2006).

Food safety oversight in Canada occurs at the federal, provincial, and regional levels. Health Canada sets national standards for food safety and nutrition quality and administers the Food and Drugs Act as it relates to public health, safety, and nutrition (Health Canada 2007). The Canadian Food Inspection Agency (CFIA) enforces food safety regulations for meat and dairy products transported between provinces and for foods imported from other countries. Provincial regulatory policies are set by the BC Ministries of Health and Agriculture and Lands, with enforcement, licensing, and education support from the BC Centre for Disease Control (BCCDC) and the regional health authorities. Environmental health officers[1] within the regional health authorities inspect food premises, such as restaurants and markets, that process or prepare food for retail sale. They also assist provincial and federal authorities with local foodborne illness outbreak investigations. BCCDC assists with laboratory testing for contaminants, assessment of novel processing techniques, and food safety education and training.

A regulatory apparatus to manage food safety risks is warranted given the potential hazards from foodborne illness, but pre-existing structures may not always be the best fit in current contexts. Some scholars have suggested that the established food safety mandate, which emerged from a historical place of managing adulterated and otherwise unsafe food, is less relevant to the modern context (Nestle 2003; Kerber 2013; Ostry et al. 2003). Many regulations are oriented toward large-scale production and its large-scale risk profile (McMahon 2013). However, as widespread outbreaks in the North American meat and vegetable industries illustrate (e.g., *E. coli* O157:H7 in XL Foods beef, *Listeria* at Maple Leaf Meats, and *E. coli* O157:H7 in bagged California spinach), highly structured regulatory systems do not always protect the public from foodborne illness. DeLind and Howard (2008) have criticized such systems as too onerous for small and mid-sized operations. McMahon (2013) suggests that addressing the root causes of foodborne illness would be more effective than trying to create safe food in an unsafe system, effectively questioning how we define food safety. From a public health perspective, this parallels a shift away from a focus on hazard protection and individual behaviour change toward chronic disease prevention and health-supporting environments.

Roots of the Tension between Food Safety and Food Security

How do the tensions between food security and food safety relate to different understandings of health, evidence, and risk? All food activities have inherent food safety risk, and the traditional health protection framework prioritizes mitigating those risks. Some food security advocates see food safety regulations as threats to community food security, particularly where they impact activities such as community kitchens, food gleaning, and on-farm animal slaughter, which have broader goals and public benefits. For example, licensing regulations for abattoirs can limit the viability of small slaughter operations, which can also limit availability of locally produced meat in rural or remote areas (Martin 2014; McMahon 2013; Miewald et al. 2013; Seed et al. 2013). Public health professionals promote all of these practices, challenging the public health system to support complementary yet potentially contradictory goals (Seed et al. 2013).

The organization of the public health system reflects these contradictions. The healthcare systems in Canada and most Western nations originated from a biomedical model that treats the biological causes of disease (Mishler 1981). Public health rhetoric increasingly recognizes the value of promoting health through supportive environments (BC Ministry of

Health 2013). Many public health professionals work from a health promotion framework that originated in the 1970s and 1980s (WHO 1978,
1986). This holistic approach envisions healthy environments that facilitate
healthy lifestyles and healthy communities for all people, an achievement
that requires social interventions (Raphael 2008). Food safety frameworks
that focus more on controlling agents of disease than on creating safer food
systems reflect the biomedical approach to health (McMahon 2013), while
community food security advocates are more closely aligned with holistic
health promotion or healthy environments frameworks.

The biomedical and holistic approaches are fundamentally and epistemo-
logically different. Proponents of one do not always recognize the legitimacy of the other. For example, practitioners who strive for evidence-based
decision making in healthcare often value scientific data (which is ostensibly neutral and generalizable) over socially-based knowledge (which is
context-specific and difficult to replicate) (Davison and Blackman 2005;
Newton 2012). A reliance solely on "neutral" or generalizable evidence
may delegitimize those who criticize accepted practices. We have observed
such criticisms from positions of authority as reactions to community food
security advocates who encourage alternatives to the mainstream system of
large-scale commodity production.

An additional challenge is the complexity involved in balancing multiple perceptions of risk. Regardless of the information available about the
risks of foodborne illness, people's tolerance for different types of risk varies
(Giddens 1999). People perceive risks to be higher when they are involun-
tary, unfamiliar, and inequitably distributed (Nestle 2003; Sandman 1993).
In the industrial food system, people can experience exaggerated food safety
fears because people know little about from where their food has come
(Blay-Palmer 2008). Prescriptive regulation becomes a necessary substitute
for first-hand knowledge when production and distribution of food happens
on a large scale, but the same regulations may not be the best way to manage
smaller, locally based operations that have different risks. Put simply, context
matters.

Along with different ideas about how best to ensure health and control
risk, there are different political views on the pathways to prosperity and
quality of life. One pathway privileges the national economy with a focus on
interprovincial and international trade, while the other advocates for strong
local economies where citizens support local business. A top-down prescriptive regulatory approach to ensuring food safety in large-scale industrial
food processing plants is reasonable and appreciated, given the relative ano-
nymity of the workforce in an industrial setting, the large distribution range

of the food product, and the dominance of the profit motive in corporations. Some supporters of community-based food systems consider the personal connections and moral basis of such systems as adequate insurance of food safety for consumers of direct-marketed food (McMahon 2011; Rideout 2012). Others, however, desire external oversight over hidden aspects of the food system or aspects they may not fully understand. While it is easier to be fully informed and develop relationships of mutual trust within smaller more connected food systems, it remains a challenge to be fully informed about one's food supply. Moreover, there is a societal expectation that government will protect the public from hazards such as foodborne illness (Rideout 2012). The challenge of public health is to strike a balance between protecting the public from health hazards and enabling access to foods that people consider desirable and healthy, while supporting healthy communities and a healthy ecosystem.

We argue that a key problem between food safety and community food security is reconciling these different philosophical and epistemological perspectives. A focus on giving individual farmers and consumers a choice of "opting out" of the food safety system is an individualistic approach that limits the scale and potential of achieving community food security (Guthman 2008). We suggest that it is not a question of more or less regulation, but rather a need to create space for multiple interpretations within policy or regulatory structures, interpretations that recognize different perspectives on the nature of health, understanding of evidence, and interpretations of risk. The challenge is bringing these multiple perspectives together in ways that reduce the risks of foodborne illness while addressing the broader goals of community food security. Accepting the need for everyone to understand and negotiate multiple perspectives may be the first step toward greater harmony between those working within a biomedical food safety paradigm and those with a holistic community food security paradigm. In the remainder of this chapter, we turn to our case study to explore how the different perspectives played out in BC. We examine the potential for shared action toward shared goals between two programs—one from a biomedical and one from a holistic paradigm—operating in a system dominated by the biomedical approach.

Food Safety and Food Security Tensions in Context: Public Health Innovation in British Columbia

In BC, the introduction of the Core Public Health Programs (BC Ministry of Health 2005) brought some of the underlying tensions in the food system to the fore. The Food Safety Core Program is an environmental health program based on established inspection, investigation, education, and surveillance activities (Table 7.1). The main objectives of the Food Safety Core Program are to prevent foodborne illness, minimize negative impacts of outbreaks, increase knowledge, and provide surveillance of food safety (Food Safety Working Group 2006). Environmental health officers are responsible for inspecting food premises, but there is a great deal of variability in how they interpret the regulatory framework. For example, retail (off-farm) sale of ungraded eggs, which is banned province-wide, is permitted in some regions where environmental health officers assessed the risk to be low and benefits high (Martin 2014). Although such local assessments are lauded, decisions about whether to assess and how to interpret risk leads to inconsistencies across local, regional, and provincial jurisdictions.

The Food Security Core Program is a health improvement program based on development of a comprehensive food policy framework and an array of programs, services, public awareness initiatives, and monitoring of food security programs (BC Ministry of Health 2005; Food Security Working Group 2014). Food security was a new public health program for BC in 2006, and BC remains the only province with a dedicated public health focus on food security. With no pre-existing structures, the Ministry of Health tasked each regional health authority with coordinating the program within the region and sharing experiences and best practice through the Provincial Health Services Authority. The program aims to create healthy food policy,[2] strengthen community action, create supportive food environments, increase food knowledge and skills, facilitate access, and provide surveillance and evaluation of food security programs (Food Security Working Group 2014) (see Table 7.1). In addition to being a new focus for public health action, the Food Security Core Program objectives are closely linked to the holistic approach to health discussed previously. As such, they require social interventions outside the usual purview of the health system.

Both food programs require intersectoral coordination and collaboration with community partners for success. Collaborative approaches between environmental health officers and those who undergo inspection are key elements for smooth and efficient operation of the food safety program (Food Safety Working Group 2006). The original vision of the food security program included integration of food security principles into primary care and hospital services, as well as other core programs including food safety (Food Security Working Group 2014).

Table 7.1. *Comparison of food safety and food security core programs.*

Program	Food Safety Core Program*	Food Security Core Program**
Goals	• Minimize the incidence of foodborne illnesses and outbreaks	• Increase food security for the population of British Columbia
Objectives	• Prevent foodborne illness by providing a food inspection program • Minimize negative impacts of any foodborne illness outbreak by conduct investigations; seize contaminated products • Increase knowledge and improve food safety practices among the food industry and the public • Provide surveillance and ongoing evaluation	• Create healthy food policy • Strengthen community action • Create supportive environments • Increase knowledge and skills • Facilitate services and resources for increasing accessibility, availability, and affordability of healthy foods • Provide surveillance, monitoring and evaluation of food security programs
Main components	• Food premises inspection • Local foodborne illness outbreak • investigations and assistance • Food safety education • Surveillance and evaluation	• A comprehensive food policy framework that supports strategic planning • Appropriate array of programs and services • Promotion and awareness initiatives (staff and public) • Surveillance, monitoring, and evaluation of programs
Ministries	• Ministry of Health • Ministry of Agriculture and Lands	• Ministry of Health
Operational jurisdiction	• BC Centre for Disease Control • Regional health authorities	• Regional health authorities
Professionals involved	• Environmental health officers (EHOs)	• Community nutritionists • Community developers • Public health policy analysts

(Continued)

Table 7.1. (*Continued*)

Program	Food Safety Core Program*	Food Security Core Program**
Legislation	• Health Act • Food Safety Act • Food Premises Regulation • Fish Inspection Act • Meat Inspection Regulation • Milk Industry Act • Sanitary Regulations • Municipal health bylaws	• Health Act

* Food Safety Working Group 2006
** Food Security Working Group 2014

Table 7.1 highlights key features of the two core programs, and illustrates the differences in paradigms between the two. Food Safety has concrete objectives and specific activities, some of which are mandated. Food Security works toward broader goals to facilitate, rather than enact, change via a general array of promotion and awareness efforts.

Sources of Tension between Food Safety and Food Security in British Columbia

During the implementation of Food Safety and Food Security Core Programs, areas of intersection between the two programs highlighted points of tension and opportunities for collaboration (Martin 2014). Early discussions on how to organize the core functions considered a single program to address all issues related to food. In the end, program architects maintained separate programs for Food Safety and Food Security, and incorporated healthy eating into a separate Healthy Living Program (Martin 2014). They felt that the new Food Security Program would have a greater opportunity to thrive as a separate entity rather than as part of a larger program covering all aspects of food. In addition to their place within the broader public health system, Food Security and Food Safety intersected in several ways that had implications for interactions between the two.

Tension arose in part from the new range of community food security activities, such as community kitchens and temporary markets, which added more and novel venues for food safety inspections by environmental health officers. Many new or temporary food premises do not have access to infrastructure that can facilitate compliance with food safety regulations. Moreover, environmental health officer involvement often occurs too late in the planning process to identify and address potential problems. Without careful planning and clear communication about new community food security activities, environmental health officers may be unprepared to face unusual foodservice, production, or processing situations and unable to help operators address food safety requirements. This causes undue strain on relationships between these health professionals and community food security advocates.

The difference in regulatory structure described earlier also played a key role in creating tension between the two core programs. As noted earlier, the Food Safety Core Program is highly regulated under provincial legislation (see Table 7.1), including basic standards for acceptable food production and processing procedures. The program is rooted in a well-established policy and regulatory framework with clearly mandated roles and responsibilities, and with a dedicated workforce. The Food Security Core Program, in contrast, provides community-level support through resources, advocacy, and leadership (Vancouver Coastal Health 2008). Programming varies by region in response to the needs of community members. It lacks a clear structure or departmental home and has few dedicated staff. Rather than legislation and specific programs such as food safety inspection, food security work consists of a series of discrete initiatives that differ across the province. The food programs both aim to create a safe and healthy food supply, but finding the right balance between access and safety remains a challenge.

These places of intersection between the Food Safety and Food Security Programs have seen underlying tensions play out on several issues. The challenge of inspecting novel food premises has occurred in regions across the province. Many new initiatives have focused on providing food in schools or daycares as part of educational, local food access, or cultural programs. For example, a preschool program for Aboriginal children has struggled with introducing traditional foods. Food provided in schools and daycares must come from pre-approved sources and be prepared in inspected kitchens. Although not the intention, these rules favour provision of packaged pastries over freshly prepared foods, particularly in settings that do not have access to full kitchen facilities (personal communication, K. Beverlander, BC Aboriginal Child Care Society, 6 July 2013). Other sites wishing to provide fresh fruits and vegetables for children's snacks have faced similar challenges.

Access to local foods is often a component of community food security goals. This has led to tensions in many communities, particularly with respect to meat and milk in rural or remote regions. Coincidentally, the introduction of the Food Security Core Program occurred at the same time as a major overhaul of meat inspection regulations that restricted sales of meat slaughtered on farms (Miewald et al. 2013). The new BC Meat Inspection Regulation was intended to standardize meat inspection in the province, protect public health, and foster confidence in the BC food supply (McMahon 2011). However, the changes led to higher slaughter costs, lost revenues, loss of farm status, and reduced livestock production (Johnson 2008). From a food security perspective, the streamlined regulations cut out a key source of locally produced meat for many communities, lowered producers' incomes, and eliminated a means of connection between producers and local consumers. This led to outcry from community food security advocates and fuelled distrust of food safety regulations (Seed 2011). This tension between small farmers and the Ministry of Health spread within the public health system where community nutritionists and food security coordinators were sympathetic to community members who were resisting the Meat Inspection Regulation (Seed et al. 2013).

Similar tensions have risen in remote communities with limited or sporadic access to imported foods. Distribution of local (unpasteurized) milk is prohibited because of the risk of contamination. In some remote communities that are too small to support licensed processing facilities, this can leave residents without a key source of nutrients when foods cannot reach the community from outside due to weather or other events. Such examples clearly illustrate the challenge of balancing food safety with community food security when other factors influence access to food. No one should have to choose between safe and fresh or nutritious food.

Approaches to Easing the Tension

There have been instances of successful collaboration between food safety and food security advocates in BC. Using several examples where tensions have been successfully addressed, we draw out key features for an approach that could facilitate collaboration on a larger scale.

We have discussed how novel food premises, often aimed at increasing access to healthy, local, or traditional foods, often meet regulatory roadblocks that create tensions for food safety and food security proponents. Local, and sometimes provincial, efforts have identified ways to facilitate new initiatives in ways that minimize food safety risks. The BC Centre for Disease Control produced a guideline for temporary markets, including farmers' markets, which streamlined requirements with a focus on high-risk foods (BC Centre for Disease Control 2014; Martin 2014). In addition, environmental health officers in northern BC teamed up with a community kitchens program to revise a manual on canning and small-scale food processing (Martin 2014). Environmental health officers in some regions allow off-farm sales of ungraded eggs, recognizing the low risk and high importance to the local community.

The Ministry of Health revised the contentious overhaul of the BC Meat Inspection Regulation following political efforts by farmers and community food security advocates. Dialogue with the Ministry of Health ultimately resulted in changes to the new regulations in an effort to better support the needs of small-scale farmers (Miewald et al. 2013). The parties worked together to develop an approach to meat safety that better fit the needs of diverse communities.

As with any change in program delivery, the potential impact of one program on another is challenging to anticipate. Opportunities for collaboration between the Food Safety and Food Security Programs presented themselves during the first years of implementation. Several health authorities now have an environmental health officer actively engaged with a food security working group. Ministry of Health staff involved in the two programs have begun working more closely to identify common ground, to address contradictions between these programs, and to explore how to align more closely yet remain as separate programs (personal communication, C. MacDonald, 1 October 2009; M. Day, BC Ministry of Health, 9 September 2010).

The examples presented here share an outcomes-based approach that recognizes the value of creative problem solving and the importance of relationship building across sectors. They also demonstrate how tensions between food safety and food security emerge from differences in underlying perspectives. We, too, recognize the link between these tensions and greater problems with the food system (Martin 2014; Mundel 2013; Rideout 2012). There is a need to change structural conditions to promote health, as well as a moral obligation to reduce health inequities and power imbalances through an improved public health regulatory system and a holistic approach to population health promotion (Martin 2014). Such structural changes are important to ease tensions in the food system over the long term. Here, we draw on learning from existing tensions and solutions to offer three more immediate approaches to the problem that are feasible within the current political and regulatory context: (1) focussing on outcomes when interpreting regulations; (2) interpreting food safety regulations consistently, yet allowing multiple interpretations; and (3) improving communications between people working in food safety and community food security.

First, food safety inspections that focus on systematic assessment and control of risk are essential in order to consider context and complexity in decision making. The Ministry of Health adopted such an outcomes-based approach in revising the BC Meat Inspection Regulation (Miewald et al. 2013). The flexible regulations enable environmental health officers to work with the intention of the law (i.e., minimizing risk of foodborne illness) without rigid, one-size-fits-all rules. Resources are targeted toward the greater risks in a systematic, evidence-based way (Black and Baldwin 2010). This kind of outcomes-based risk prioritization is better suited to address aggregate and cumulative risks, risk to susceptible populations, and a holistic approach to health and ecology (Hoffmann and Taylor 2005).

Second, while we acknowledge the need for flexibility when applying food safety regulations, there needs to be a consistent underlying vision shared among policy makers, inspectors, food premise operators, and food security advocates. Public health professionals can apply this clear vision with flexibility to fit the specific context. Innovative approaches to ensuring food safety while facilitating food security have been effective in some regions, but different areas of the province have not used such approaches consistently. For example, one environmental health officer worked with organizers of a local food event to implement an effective alternative to the usual hand-washing facilities required by food service premises. A similar event was almost cancelled elsewhere, until health staff from the two regions communicated and shared the innovative alternative. The flexible yet consistent approach requires mechanisms to share solutions and processes that could be borrowed, or adapted, for use elsewhere. Sharing such solutions on a province-wide basis is a challenge, but could provide a basis for guiding principles for what is considered appropriate when enforcing food safety regulations. It is a delicate yet important task to recognize that rules and regulations exist for good reasons but that regulators will apply them somewhat differently in different contexts. A standard equation for mitigating risk in all situations is not realistic, but a framework that shows how and why discretion is used could support context-specific risk assessments. Flexibility and consistency can coexist if there are clear decision-making processes and a consistent understanding of the intent of the law.

Finally, early, frequent, and open communication between environmental health officers and food security advocates or staff is extremely important. All parties need to communicate early when planning a new initiative or program, communicate often to avoid forging ahead on assumptions, and remain open to new information. The previous example of finding alternative hand washing facilities at a temporary food event illustrates good understanding of the intentions of the regulation, the risks involved, and a way to move forward that works for everyone. Such intersectoral collaboration is a challenge when actors are not versed in the diverse risks and benefits associated with a given activity (Benson 2008), or where they lack the training or authority to seek and enact creative solutions. This further highlights the importance of open communication and mutual education, not just between the food safety and food security sectors, but also between different layers of the regulatory system from the front lines to the highest ministerial level.

Trusting and positive relationships are essential to collaboration and information sharing. People need to trust in fair and equitable application of regulations, trust that people will practise safe food handling, and trust that reason will prevail over rules. Mutual understanding of goals and perspectives among all key actors will facilitate this trust. Martin (2014) used data from food safety and food security actors to describe how partnerships, communication, and education can begin to bridge the philosophical and practical divide. Opportunities for collaboration are few, in the BC context at least, and there needs to be greater emphasis within health authorities to make room for conversations to happen and relationships to be forged. Mundel (2013) highlighted a number of relationship building examples within the Food Security Core Program, such as between grassroots actors and health authority staff through the Community Food Action Initiative. The provincial Ministry of Health, home to the core programs, can play a leadership role in brokering these relationships. Leadership from provincial agencies is necessary to address tensions and to promote the value in improving population health.

We have suggested tools for easing tensions in the short term. Lasting change will require dissolving borders, and moving away from a reductionist paradigm toward a systems approach that recognizes interconnecting elements and reorients to focus on healthier food environments. Nationally, Health Canada (2007) has called for a more efficient and responsive food safety regulatory framework that addresses the contribution of food to chronic diseases and promotes an integrated system for food safety and nutrition.

Realizing such a vision would require collaboration between Health Canada, the Canadian Food Inspection Agency, the Public Health Agency of Canada, and provincial/territorial food safety authorities (Health Canada 2007), as well as involvement of food producers, all levels of the food industry, community-based organizations, and consumers. In other words, it requires top-down support for front-line change as well as bottom-up pressure and increased local authority. However, the complexity and opacity inherent in the current mainstream food system constrains individuals' (and, by extension, communities' and organizations') ability to fully participate (Blay-Palmer 2008; Jaffe and Gertler 2006; Lang, Barling, and Caraher 2009; Welsh and MacRae 1998). The lack of trust created by the current food system creates exaggerated fears (Blay-Palmer 2008) and encourages backlash against the food safety system by those who see it as overreaching (Rideout 2012). A system based on trust would not remove the need for a food safety system, but would promote the perception of the food safety system as a resource to support health. Partnerships, joined-up policies, and supportive environments are thus needed to ease tensions and change the food and health systems—systems that straddle the boundaries between almost every sector of society through production and processing, community, cultural, and environmental issues.

Conclusion: Toward a Safer, Healthier Food System

The tensions between public health professionals working in food safety and food security have received little scholarly attention. In the broader public health literature, Macdonald (2004) described how public health tensions between molecular and social epidemiology—another case of empirical versus theoretical or technical versus social—could be resolved by recognizing the interconnections between the two (Krieger 2001). As we have demonstrated in this chapter, recognition of the shared goals of food safety and food security programs can help resolve some of the tensions between them.

Despite many challenges, BC has seen successful collaborations between community food security and food safety proponents. These successes are characterized by a focus on healthy outcomes and operational contexts that facilitate creativity, collaboration, and communication. Building on these successes, we suggest moving forward with clearly defined roles, responsibilities, and policy structures in order for frontline actors to work effectively with a new approach. This requires shared principles and values, flexible decision making, and clear communication. More fundamentally, embracing holistic systems thinking at all levels of the health system hierarchy and putting corresponding institutional and policy mechanisms in place are essential. This longer-term approach can start with frontline workers, with support from their managers, while the slower process of organizational change takes place.

We have shown here that the Food Safety and Food Security Core Programs share the primary goal of ensuring access to a healthy food supply for the public. However, each program approaches that goal from a different paradigm, with different views on the meaning of health and different ideas on how it should be achieved. Focusing on the shared goal of a healthy food supply can be a starting point to articulating common values and developing frameworks for collaboration. The underlying goals of public health—to prevent disease and support health for all—remind us that food safety and food security are tools to protect against disease and promote good health. Safe food protects against foodborne illness. Community food security aims to protect against hunger, malnutrition, and noncommunicable diseases and promotes social and ecological well-being (Hamm and Bellows 2003; Rideout et al. 2006; Seligman et al. 2010; Vozoris and Tarasuk 2003). Open communication and careful consideration of context, along with recognition of common goals, can contribute to the creation a food system that protects health, prevents disease, and supports healthy and sustainable communities and ecosystems.

Notes

1 Environmental health officers are also known as public health inspectors.
2 A "healthy food policy" is one "that supports food security initiatives on all levels, thereby enhancing access to affordable, high-quality foods (using environmentally sustainable production and distribution methods)" (BC Ministry of Health 2005, 9).

References

Allen, Patricia. 2004. *Together at the Table: Sustainability and Sustenance in the American Agrifood System.* University Park: Pennsylvania State University Press.

Allen, Patricia. 2010. "Realizing Justice in Local Food Systems." *Cambridge Journal of Regions, Economy and Society* 3 (2): 295–308. http://dx.doi.org/10.1093/cjres/rsq015.

Benson, Todd. 2008. "Cross-Sectoral Coordination in the Public Sector: A Challenge to Leveraging Agriculture for Improving Nutrition and Health." In *Improving Nutrition as a Development Priority: Addressing Undernutrition within National Policy Processes in Sub-Saharan Africa,* ed. Shenggen Fan and Rajul Pandya-Lorch. Washington, DC: International Food Policy Research Institute.

BC Centre for Disease Control. 2014. *Guidelines for the Sale of Foods at Temporary Food Markets.* Vancouver, BC: BC Centre for Disease Control. https://www.vch.ca/media/Guidelines_Sale_Of_Foods_At_Temporary_Food_Markets_April_2014.pdf.

BC Ministry of Health. 2005. *Public Health Renewal in British Columbia: An Overview of Core Functions in Public Health.* Victoria, BC: Ministry of Health. http://www.health.gov.bc.ca/library/publications/year/2005/phrenewal.pdf.

BC Ministry of Health. 2013. *Promote, Protect, Prevent: Our Health Begins Here. BC's Guiding Framework for Public Health.* Victoria: BC Ministry of Health. http://www.health.gov.bc.ca/library/publications/year/2013/BC-guiding-framework-for-public-health.pdf.

Black, Julia, and Robert Baldwin. 2010. "Really Responsive Risk-Based Regulation." *Law & Policy* 32 (2): 181–213. http://dx.doi.org/10.1111/j.1467-9930.2010.00318.x.

Blay-Palmer, Alison. 2008. *Food Fears: From Industrial to Sustainable Food Systems.* Burlington, VT: Ashgate Publishing.

Brown, Sandy, and Christy Getz. 2011. "Farmworker Food Insecurity and the Production of Hunger in California." In *Cultivating Food Justice: Race, Class and Sustainability,* ed. Alison Hope Alkon and Julian Agyeman. Boston: MIT Press.

Clapp, Jennifer. 2012. *Food.* Cambridge: Polity Press.

Community Nutritionists Council of BC. 2004. *Making the Connection: Food Security and Public Health.* Community Nutritionists Council of BC. http://foodsecurecanada.org/sites/default/files/Making_the_Connection.pdf.

Copeland, Larry, and Lynn Wilcott. 2006. *Evidence Review: Food Safety.* Victoria, BC: Population Health and Wellness, B.C. Ministry of Health. https://www.vch.ca/media/Evidence_Review_Food_Safety.pdf.

Davison, Graydon, and Deborah Blackman. 2005. "The Role of Mental Models in Innovative Teams." *European Journal of Innovation Management* 8 (4): 409–23. http://dx.doi.org/10.1108/14601060510627795.

Desjardins, Ellen, Wayne Roberts, Kim McGibbon, Lynn Garrison, Debbie Field, Rebecca Davids, Vida Stevens, Gale Elliott, and Kayla Glynn. 2002. *A Systemic Approach to Community Food Security: A Role for Public Health.* Ontario Public Health Association. http://opha.on.ca/getmedia/a9c83f65-a5ef-4146-b4c1-ae69a015c579/2002-01_pp.pdf.aspx?ext=.pdf.

DeLind, Laura B., and Philip H. Howard. 2008. "Safe at Any Scale? Food Scares, Food Regulation, and Scaled Alternatives." *Agriculture and Human Values* 25 (3): 301–17. http://dx.doi.org/10.1007/s10460-007-9112-y.

Dietitians of Canada. 2007. *Community Food Security: Position of the Dietitians of Canada.* Dietitians of Canada. http://www.dieticians.ca/Dieticians_Views/Food-Security/Community-Food-Security.aspx.

Dixon, Jane, and Cathy Banwell. 2004. "Re-embedding Trust: Unravelling the Construction of Modern Diets." *Critical Public Health* 14 (2): 117–31. http://dx.doi.org/10.1080/09581590410001725364.

DuPuis, E. Melanie, and David Goodman. 2005. "Should We Go 'Home' to Eat? Toward a Reflexive Politics of Localism." *Journal of Rural Studies* 21 (3): 359–71. http://dx.doi.org/10.1016/j.jrurstud.2005.05.011.

Food Safety Working Group. 2006. *Model Core Program Paper: Food Safety.* Victoria, BC: Population Health and Wellness, BC Ministry of Health. http://www2.gov.bc.ca/assets/gov/health/about-bc-s-health-care-system/public-health/environmental-health/food_safety_model_core_program_paper.pdf.

Food Security Working Group. 2014. *Model Core Program Paper: Food Security.* Victoria, BC: Population Health and Wellness, BC Ministry of Health.

http://www2.gov.bc.ca/assets/gov/health/about-bc-s-health-care-system/public-health/healthy-living-and-healthy-communities/food_security_model_core_program_paper.pdf.

Giddens, Anthony. 1999. "Risk and Responsibility." *Modern Law Review* 62 (1): 1–10. http://dx.doi.org/10.1111/1468-2230.00188.

Gottlieb, Robert. 2001. *Environmentalism Unbound: Exploring New Pathways for Change*. Cambridge, MA: MIT Press.

Guthman, Julie. 2003. "Fast Food/Organic Food: Reflexive Tastes and the Making of 'Yuppie Chow.'" *Social & Cultural Geography* 4 (1): 45–58. http://dx.doi.org/10.1080/1464936032000049306.

Guthman, Julie. 2007. "Commentary on Teaching Food: Why I Am Fed Up with Michael Pollan et al." *Agriculture and Human Values* 24 (2): 261–4. http://dx.doi.org/10.1007/s10460-006-9053-x.

Guthman, Julie. 2008. "Neoliberalism and the Making of Food Politics in California." *Geoforum* 39 (3): 1171–83. http://dx.doi.org/10.1016/j.geoforum.2006.09.002.

Hamm, Michael W., and Anne C. Bellows. 2003. "Community Food Security and Nutrition Educators." *Journal of Nutrition Education and Behavior* 35 (1): 37–43. http://dx.doi.org/10.1016/S1499-4046(06)60325-4. Medline:12588679.

Health Canada. 2007. *Blueprint for Renewal II: Modernizing Canada's Regulatory System for Health Products and Food*. Ottawa: Health Canada. http://publications.gc.ca/collections/collection_2008/hc-sc/H164-43-2007E.pdf.

Heffernan, William D. 2000. "Concentration of Ownership and Control in Agriculture." In *Hungry for Profit: The Agribusiness Threat to Farmers, Food and the Environment*, ed. F. Magdoff, J. Bellamy Foster, and F.H. Buttel. New York: Monthly Review Press.

Hoffmann, Sandra Ann, and Michael R. Taylor. 2005. *Toward Safer Food: Perspectives on Risk and Priority Setting*. Washington, DC: Resources for the Future.

Jaffe, JoAnn, and Michael Gertler. 2006. "Victual Vicissitudes: Consumer Deskilling and the (Gendered) Transformation of Food Systems." *Agriculture and Human Values* 23 (2): 143–62. http://dx.doi.org/10.1007/s10460-005-6098-1.

Johnson, Brigitt. 2008. *Impact of the Meat Inspection Regulation on Slaughter Capacity in the North Okanagan Regional district (RDNO)*. Community Futures North Okanogan. http://www.socialplanning.ca/pdf/food_security/meat_inspection_summary_report.pdf.

Johnston, Josée, and Lauren Baker. 2005. "Eating Outside the Box: FoodShare's Good Food Box and the Challenge of Scale." *Agriculture and Human Values* 22 (3): 313–25. http://dx.doi.org/10.1007/s10460-005-6048-y.

Kerber, Eve. 2013. "Securing Food Justice, Sovereignty & Sustainability in the Face of the Food Safety Modernization Act (FSMA)." *Seattle Journal for Social Justice* 11 (3): 1271–314.

Krieger, Nancy. 2001. "A Glossary for Social Epidemiology." *Journal of Epidemiology and Community Health* 55 (10): 693–700. http://dx.doi.org/10.1136/jech.55.10.693. Medline:11553651.

Lang, Tim, David Barling, and Martin Caraher. 2009. *Food Policy: Integrating Health, Environment and Society*. Oxford: Oxford University Press. http://dx.doi.org/10.1093/acprof:oso/9780198567882.001.0001.

Lang, Tim. 2009. "Reshaping the Food System for Ecological Public Health." *Journal of Hunger & Environmental Nutrition* 4 (3–4): 315–35. http://dx.doi.org/10.1080/19320240903321227. Medline:23144673.

Macdonald, Marjorie A. 2004. "From Miasma to Fractals: The Epidemiology Revolution and Public Health Nursing." *Public Health Nursing* 21 (4): 380–91. http://dx.doi.org/10.1111/j.0737-1209.2004.21412.x.

Martin, Wanda. 2014. "Food Gone Foul? Food Safety and Security Tensions." PhD Thesis. Victoria: University of Victoria.

McMahon, Martha. 2011. "Standard Fare or Fairer Standards: Feminist Reflections on Agri-Food Governance." *Agriculture and Human Values* 28 (3): 401–12. http://dx.doi.org/10.1007/s10460-009-9249-y.

McMahon, Martha. 2013. "What Food Is to be Kept Safe and for Whom? Food-Safety Governance in an Unsafe Food System." *Laws* 2 (4): 401–27. http://dx.doi.org/10.3390/laws2040401.

Miewald, Christiana, Aleck Ostry, and Sally Hodgson. 2013. "Food Safety at the Small Scale: The Case of Meat Inspection Regulations in British Columbia's Rural and Remote Communities." *Journal of Rural Studies* 32: 93–102. http://dx.doi.org/10.1016/j.jrurstud.2013.04.010.

Mishler, Elliot G. 1981. "Viewpoint: Critical Perspectives on the Biomedical Model." In *Social Contexts of Health, Illness, and Patient Care*, ed. Elliot G. Mishler, Lorna R. Amarasingham, Stuart T. Haus, Ramsay Liem, and Samuel D. Osherson. Cambridge: Cambridge University Press.

Morse, Janice M., Michael Barrett, Maria Mayan, Karin Olson, and Jude Spiers. 2008. "Verification Strategies for Establishing Reliability and Validity in Qualitative Research." *International Journal of Qualitative Methods* 1:13–22.

Mundel, Erika. 2013. "Working the System to Change the System? Analyzing Intersections between the Food Movement and Health Establishment in British Columbia." PhD diss., University of British Columbia.

Nestle, Marion. 2002. *Food Politics: How the Food Industry Influences Nutrition and Health*. Berkeley: University of California Press.

Nestle, Marion. 2003. *Safe Food: Bacteria, Biotechnology, and Bioterrorism*. Berkeley: University of California Press.

Newton, Lorelei J. 2012. "It's Not (Just) About the Evidence: The Discourse of Knowledge Translation and Nursing Practice." PhD diss., University of Victoria, British Columbia.

Ostry, Aleck, Tara Shannon, Lise Dubois, and Tasnim Nathoo. 2003. "The Interplay of Public Health and Economics in the Early Development of Nutrition Policy in Canada." *Critical Public Health* 13 (2): 171–85. http://dx.doi.org/10.1080/0958159031000097643.

Pollan, Michael. 2010. "The Food Movement, Rising." *New York Review of Books*, 10 June: 31–3. http://www.nybooks.com/articles/2010/06/10/food-movement-rising/. Medline:21755647

Poppendieck, Janet. 1999. *Sweet Charity? Emergency Food and the End of Entitlement*. New York: Penguin.

Qualman, Darrin. 2001. *The Farm Crisis and Corporate Power*. Ottawa: Canadian Center for Policy Alternatives; https://www.policyalternatives.ca/newsroom/news-releases/farm-crisis-and-corporate-power.

Raphael, Dennis. 2008. "Getting Serious about the Social Determinants of Health: New Directions for Public Health Workers." *Global Health Promotion* 15 (3): 15–20. http://dx.doi.org/10.1177/1025382308095650. Medline:18784048.

Riches, Graham. 2002. "Food Banks and Food Security: Welfare Reform, Human Rights and Social Policy. Lessons from Canada?" *Social Policy and Administration* 36 (6): 648–63. http://dx.doi.org/10.1111/1467-9515.00309.

Rideout, Karen L. 2012. "From Corporate to Connected: Resisting Food System Distancing in India and Canada." PhD diss., University of British Columbia.

Rideout, Karen L., Barbara Seed, and Aleck Ostry. 2006. "Putting Food on the Public Health Table: Making Food Security Relevant to Regional Health Authorities." *Canadian Journal of Public Health* 97 (3): 233–6. Medline:16827415.

Rideout, Karen, and Tom Kosatsky. 2014. "Food Insecurity: A Public Health Issue for BC." *British Columbia Medical Journal* 56 (1): 29, 46.

Sandman, Peter M. 1993. *Responding to Community Outrage: Strategies for Effective Risk Communication*. Fairfax, VA: American Industrial Hygiene Association (AIHA).

Scallan, Elaine, Patricia M. Griffin, Frederick J. Angulo, Robert V. Tauxe, and Robert M. Hoekstra. 2011. "Foodborne Illness Acquired in the United States—Unspecified Agents." *Emerging Infectious Diseases* 17 (1): 16–22. http://dx.doi.org/10.3201/eid1701.P21101. Medline:21192849.

Seed, Barbara. 2011. "Food Security in Public Health and Other Government Programs in British Columbia, Canada: A Policy Analysis." PhD diss., City University, London.

Seed, Barbara, Tim Lang, Martin Caraher, and Aleck Ostry. 2013. "Integrating Food Security into Public Health and Provincial Government Departments in British Columbia, Canada." *Agriculture and Human Values* 30 (3): 457–70. http://dx.doi.org/10.1007/s10460-013-9426-x.

Seligman, Hilary K., Barbara A. Laraia, and Margot B. Kushel. 2010. "Food Insecurity Is Associated with Chronic Disease among Low-Income NHANES Participants." *Journal of Nutrition* 140 (2): 304–10. http://dx.doi.org/10.3945/jn.109.112573. Medline:20032485.

Serapiglia, Tino, Erin Kennedy, Sylvanus Thompson, and Ron de Burger. 2007. "Association of Food Premises Inspection and Disclosure Program with Retail-Acquired Foodborne Illness and Operator Noncompliance in Toronto." *Journal of Environmental Health* 70 (1): 54–9. Medline:17802819.

Stuckler, David, and Marion Nestle. 2012. "Big Food, Food Systems, and Global Health." *PLoS Medicine* 9 (6): e1001242. http://dx.doi.org/10.1371/journal.pmed.1001242. Medline:22723746.

Vancouver Coastal Health. 2008. *Food Security: A Framework for Action*. Vancouver, BC: Vancouver Coastal Health. http://www.vch.ca/media/Food_Security_Action_Framework_July2008.pdf.

Vozoris, Nicholas T., and Valerie S. Tarasuk. 2003. "Household Food Insufficiency is Associated with Poorer Health." *Journal of Nutrition* 133 (1): 120–6. Medline:12514278.

Wakefield, Sarah E. 2007. "Reflective Action in the Academy: Exploring Praxis in Critical Geography using a 'Food Movement' Case Study." *Antipode* 39 (2): 331–354. http://dx.doi.org/10.1111/j.1467-8330.2007.00524.x.

Weatherill, Sheila. 2009. *Listeriosis Investigative Review. Report of the Independent Investigator into the 2008 Listeriosis Outbreak.* Ottawa: Agriculture and Agrifood Canada. http://www.cpha.ca/uploads/history/achievements/09-lirs-rpt_e.pdf.

Wekerle, Gerda R. 2004. "Food Justice Movements: Policy, Planning, and Networks." *Journal of Planning Education and Research* 23 (4): 378–86. http://dx.doi.org/10.1177/0739456X04264886.

Welsh, Jennifer, and Rod MacRae. 1998. "Food Citizenship and Community Food Security: Lessons from Toronto, Canada." *Canadian Journal of Development Studies* 19 (4): 237–55. http://dx.doi.org/10.1080/02255189.1998.966 9786.

Winne, Mark, Hugh Joseph, and Andy Fisher. 1997. *Community Food Security: A Guide to Concept, Design and Implementation.* Medford, MA: Community Food Security Coalition; http://foodsecurecanada.org/sites/default/files/CFSguidebook1997.PDF.

WHO. 1978. *Declaration of Alma-Ata: International Conference on Primary Health Care, Alma-Ata,* USSR, 6–12 September 1978. Geneva: World Health Organization. http://www1.paho.org/English/DD/PIN/alma-ata_declaration.htm.

WHO. 1986. *Ottawa Charter for Health Promotion: First International Conference on Health Promotion,* Ottawa, 21 November 1986. Geneva: World Health Organization. http://www.who.int/healthpromotion/conferences/previous/ottawa/en/.

Commentary on Part II: Who, What, and How: Governing Food Systems

Steffanie Scott

Food safety, food security, terrestrial and aquatic food systems, and food-drink dynamics wrapped up with gentrification—this is indeed quite a range of angles from which to approach the "governing" theme in this section of the book. Governing is a central theme in food systems as it ties together the "who" (which actors) with the "what" (which strategies or initiatives) and the "how" (which forms of engagement or coordination) in building more resilient and sustainable socio-ecological systems. I am grateful to Lowitt, Mount, Khan, and Clément (Chapter 5) for their detailed review of the concept of governance. They helpfully point out the evolving nature of governance processes, and the shift in attention and dynamics from the narrower notion of rules of *government* to processes of *governance* that can involve civil society, along with the private sector, in addition to the state.

While much attention on the governance of food is typically focussed on global-level agricultural trade agreements or food aid or on certification systems, the three chapters in this section set their sights on more local- and regional-level governance dynamics. The chapter by Lowitt, Mount, Khan, and Clément demonstrates how governance mechanisms shape local and alternative food systems—systems that have been explicitly set up to counter many of the problems plaguing the industrialized food system. The case studies in their chapter critically analyze food systems that are "alternative" in terms of production practices, values, and marketing channels. Governance of alternative food networks relates to the redistribution of power and sharing of risk and resources. This may take the form, for example, of a community supported agriculture (CSA) farm model that spreads the economic risk of farming across a base of members. Or it may involve power being renegotiated in other ways to benefit the livelihoods of producers/providers/feeders, and share value more equitably across the food chain.

For Lowitt, Mount, Khan, and Clément, "questions about governance—in local agriculture and fisheries initiatives—provide a theoretical nexus point that allows us to explore issues of scale, values, and power for sustainable outcomes." Their analysis highlights the dynamic nature of local food system (LFS) governance, and how their evolution can reformulate the scale, values, and power relations of these networks. What attracts so many people to the food "movement" are the opportunities to "make a difference" and participate in initiatives—more specifically, localized forms of governance—that lead to positive change. The cases featured in Chapter 5 illustrate how the values of transparency and reflexivity, and spaces for negotiation, are enacted in the governance of LFS. Such new forms of market governance, which redistribute power, are a key characteristic of alternative food networks (Whatmore et al. 2003). Research on the governance dimensions of these sorts of models—on the logistics of direct marketing, certification, traceability, and building trust—can help to determine whether they will be economically viable and resilient in providing constructive alternatives to the ills of the conventional food system.

Different from the other two chapters in this section, Chapter 6 did not examine the goals of food security proponents. Instead, Détolle, Jennings, and Nash examine themes of commodities, consumption, and distinction in terms of the governing of alcohol consumption in bring-your-own-bottle (BYOB) restaurants in Montreal. Their analysis illuminates the intersections of changing cultural dynamics associated with gentrification in one neighbourhood of Montreal in the regulatory context of bringing domestic practices of wine consumption into the public sphere of restaurants. One of the threads connecting the three chapters in this section is the theme of local control. While Détolle, Jennings, and Nash do not explicitly deal with LFS, these authors do identify a connection between the popularity of the BYOB practice in restaurants and some conscientious consumers who choose to support local businesses and products, and are interested in do-it-yourself alternatives. BYOB appeals to consumers across a spectrum from thrift to distinction, and governance of this practice has been affected by the interplay of resistance toward provincial liquor control legislation and market-driven processes of gentrification. The nexus of actors—local government departments, restauranteurs, and the public—is an intriguing feature of this story.

This chapter points to the need for further research on food governance in terms of the economic and health connections embedded in alcohol policy and the culture of drinking that policy makers seek to regulate.

The timely chapter from Martin, Mundel and Rideout calls for a more nuanced appreciation of the connections between food safety and food security. The three authors—a "nurse educator," a farmer/food activist, and a food and health policy researcher—are in themselves an intriguing constellation of thinkers to be reflecting on connections between the "food movement" and regimes and regulatory structures within the food system.

As an insider to one of a growing number of food policy councils and food system roundtables in Canada, I have certainly heard complaints about contradictions between public health regulations for food safety and broader goals of food production/food security (and farm viability). What has captivated me since I began to get involved in food system work and research is the need for, and challenge of realizing, holistic systems thinking that bridges considerations of safe and healthy food, environmental health, food production/farm viability, and food access (among other dimensions). The chapter by Martin, Mundel, and Rideout squarely tackles a number of these tensions, as they "shed light on the challenges of integrating new ways of thinking into the established health system…[and posit] that increasing mutual understanding between food safety and food security proponents can support the food movement and the broader goal of healthier food systems." I am keen to promote this kind of analysis to rethink the food safety issues plaguing China (the geographical focus of my recent research), wherein small farmers and small-scale food processors are seen as the culprits in a dysfunctional system of food governance, and where feeders and eaters have been progressively alienated from, and do not trust, one another. The solutions of stricter regulations and enforcement have not solved the problems, and too few analysts seem to be seeking solutions that meet the combined goals of food safety and community food security.

I came to food studies from an interest in rural development and social justice (internationally, and later in my own backyard), and over time I came to see how these goals could not be realized in isolation from considerations of ecology and human health. The work of some pioneering public health units in Canada (in Waterloo, Toronto, and BC), along with visionaries who founded Food Secure Canada and people like Tim Lang, opened my eyes to these crucial synergies, and to how creative and innovative governance structures can institutionalize these multiple goals—and agendas of community food security and food sovereignty.

Chapter 7 concludes by noting that "recognition of the shared goals of food safety and food security programs can help resolve some of the tensions between them." Indeed, one of the most rewarding outcomes I have experienced as part of a food system roundtable in Waterloo, Ontario, is the recognition of shared goals and common agendas among diverse food system stakeholders, from university foodservice operators, food retailers, and distributors, to emergency food agencies, to public health planners, farmer organizations, and organic farming advocates. These goals range from farm viability, local food production, and protection of agricultural land, to ecosystem integrity and access to healthy foods. Facilitating dialogue—through a range of possible fora—is such a key step to identifying improved institutional and policy mechanisms (governance structures).

I will interject here to mention a few dynamics of food system governance in China where I have been involved in research on the organic food sector and alternative food networks (Scott et al. 2014; Si, Schumilas, and Scott 2015). I have observed a number of characteristics that strike me as potentially (or in part) positive structures for building more sustainable and resilient food systems: (1) short food supply chains and peri-urban food production; (2) the prevalence of many small but vertically integrated producers, including through contract farming and institutional procurement (farm to institution) arrangements (a topic attracting considerable interest in North America and Europe of late); (3) agriculture as a policy priority (e.g., the extensive supports for rural development associated with the New Socialist Countryside program); (4) resource protection measures including an agricultural land reserve and a policy of no net loss of farmland (though facing challenges of implementation in practice); (5) degrees of support for organic and other sorts of "ecological" food production practices; and (6) relatively strong political will for low-carbon planning. These emerging governance structures in China are worthy of further study, and could offer interesting insights for other parts of the world. They go a long way toward addressing the triple-bottom line of food system sustainability, though in a very different food system context from what we are familiar with in North America, and are likely not perceived in the way that food system "actionists" (Roberts 2014) elsewhere might look at them. I am excited about the prospects for cross-fertilization of ideas from diverse settings such as China, to encourage us to think in new ways about how food systems are, and can be, governed.

The three chapters in this section, and the perspectives put forth within this book overall, provide convincing arguments that governance structures within both conventional and local/alternative food systems (and the connections between the two), are subjects ripe for analysis, given how varied and dynamics the contexts are. I appreciated the reflections of Lowitt, Mount, Khan, and Clément on the intersections of multiple scales of governance in LFS, and I concur that this is a gap in the literature. These chapters provided a valuable reminder of the need to recognize common goals and promote dialogue and collaboration—be it between food and fisheries researchers, or between community food security and food safety proponents. Indeed, the authors in this section provide evidence of the synergies to be gained through the transgression of these boundaries.

References

Roberts, Wayne. 2014. *Food for City Building: A Field Guide for Planners, Actionists & Entrepreneurs.* Toronto: Hypenotic.

Scott, Steffanie, Zhenzhong Si, Theresa Schumilas, and Aijuan Chen. 2014. "Contradictions in State- and Civil Society-Driven Developments in China's Ecological Agriculture Sector." *Food Policy* 45: 158–66. http://dx.doi.org/10.1016/j.foodpol.2013.08.002.

Si, Zhenzhong, Theresa Schumilas, and Steffanie Scott. 2015. "Characterizing Alternative Food Networks in China." *Agriculture and Human Values* 32 (2): 299–313. http://dx.doi.org/10.1007/s10460-014-9530-6.

Whatmore, S., P. Stassart, and H. Renting. 2003. "What's Alternative about Alternative Food Networks?" *Environment and Planning A* 35 (3): 389–91. http://dx.doi.org/10.1068/a3621.

PART III: "UN-DOING" FOOD STUDIES: A CASE FOR FLEXIBLE FENCING

Evaluating the Cultural Politics of Alternative Food Movements: The Limitations of Cultivating Awareness

Cathryn Sprague and Emily Huddart Kennedy

Given concerns over the uneven social, environmental, and economic impacts of food and agriculture, the potential for citizen engagement in food politics to transform the food system has become a significant topic of discussion among citizens and academics. A number of scholars suggest that alternative food networks (AFNs) in Canada could transform such inequities, despite the market-based, neoliberal orientation of much of the food movement (Levkoe 2011; Wakefield 2007).[1] AFNs are ubiquitous across all components of the food system, from growing to processing, distribution, access, consumption, waste, and recycling. These initiatives provide opportunities for producers and consumers to interact and organize in pursuit of a range of goals, including increasing the accessibility of local, organic, or fair trade food, improving community health and nutrition, revitalizing the local economy, enhancing food security, offering alternatives to the dominant market paradigm, and reducing the environmental impacts of the food system (Goodman, DuPuis, and Goodman 2011). Evaluating the progress made toward such goals, a number of researchers conclude that AFNs have formed a movement that directly resists the "dominant corporate-industrial food system" (Wakefield 2007, 331) and that these networks form "one of the most important social movements of the early twenty-first century in the global north" (Morgan 2009, 343).

While these accounts emphasize the successes of AFNs, positive accounts often fail to critically examine the ways that food politics can reproduce existing power relations or to what extent they address institutional barriers to food system change (Lynch and Giles 2013). In an attempt to bring a critical awareness to how inequality and food politics are related, some scholars have called for more rigorous analyses of power relations, with an emphasis on scrutinizing race, class, and gender (Alkon 2008, 2013; Gibb and Wittman 2013; Guthman 2008; Lockie 2013; Sbicca 2012).[2] While survey data from more than ten countries in Europe and North America does not support the idea that organic food consumption is class or race based (Hughner et al. 2007), a number of qualitative studies point to the fact that political participation in alternative food initiatives tends to be higher among elite social classes (Guthman 2008; Alkon 2013). Further, civil associations tend to be relatively socially homogeneous, and non-elite members tend to speak out less than elites within these groups (Eliasoph 2013, 139).[3] While DuPuis and Goodman (2005) and Levkoe (2011) argue that reflexive localism can reduce the social inequalities associated with local food initiatives, Lockie (2013) argues that racial inequality is often "embedded in existing institutions, social practices, and geographies" and thereby reproduced, even if localism is not practised defensively (410). That is, if there are race- and class-based barriers to entry into food politics, then even the practice of reflexive localism may be limited in its transformative potential. Thus, Lockie (2013) calls for further empirical examination of how and why some people are mobilized while others may be excluded from AFNs.

A small but growing number of critical food scholars have taken on this task, examining the cultural politics of AFNs. Jackson (1991, 200) defined cultural politics as "the domain in which meanings are constructed and negotiated, where relations of dominance and subordination are defined and contested." For example, Guthman's (2008) work speaks to the cultural politics of local food initiatives in California by drawing attention to the ways in which everyday speech and action (discourses and practices) reproduce inequality structured by race and class. A focus on cultural politics helps to explain how practices with the capacity for significant transformation may fail to fundamentally reform the food system and instead continue to foster an ever-greater number of alternative options that do not challenge the dominant social order. Here, Guthman (2008) shows how AFNs in California are universalizing and exclusionary. Inadvertently, by ignoring the unique experiences that many people of colour have with food and agriculture and the food work done by minorities and other marginalized social groups, discourse and practice are narrowly focussed on the collective histories of white, middle-class actors.

Drawing on critical environmental and political sociology, we use the cultural politics lens to situate a Canadian case study amid discussions of the transformative potential of AFNs. We work across disciplinary boundaries by using food as a means of studying civic engagement, drawing on a range of literature to discuss transformative social change. To date, the majority of critical food studies literature has been based out of the western United States (e.g., Guthman 2008; Allen et al. 2003; Alkon and McCullen 2011), while more positive accounts of local food movements are common in studies of central Canada (Levkoe 2011; Wakefield 2007; Koç et al. 2008). A few notable exceptions in Canada include Gibb and Wittman's (2013) study of parallel AFNs among Chinese Canadians in Metro Vancouver, Lynch and Giles's (2013) analysis of discourse in sustainable food initiatives, and McClintock's (2014) exploration of how community gardens can be simultaneously radical and neoliberal. Overall, few studies have drawn on data from smaller urban centres or included data from both rural and urban areas. In this chapter, we draw on an empirical case study of eat local initiatives in Edmonton, Alberta, in order to identify the cultural politics of this case. To do so, we remain open to not only arguments of the exclusionary nature of AFNs but also evidence of transformative success. Considering our data vis-à-vis these diverse views provides the basis for a conversation about the cultural politics of AFNs. Specifically, we pose the following research question: How and to what extent do Edmonton AFNs transform the food system?

To answer this question, we use data from in-depth interviews and participant observation with farmers, entrepreneurs, government employees, educators, and community organizers, exploring the discourses and practices of actors in AFNs in order to understand the cultural politics of local food initiatives in Edmonton. This sets the stage for further discussion of how discourses and civic practices shape a cultural politics that focuses on taste, encourages consumer-driven change to the food system, and has the potential to reproduce neoliberal ideology.

Conceptual Framework, Case Study, and Methods

Drawing on Johnston's (2008) discursive methodological approach, we analyze the discourses and civic practices of actors in an empirical case study to explore the cultural politics of AFNs. Recognizing that discourse can foster political engagement, we focus our analysis on "how discursive activities create, sustain, and legitimate relationships of power and privilege" (Johnston 2008, 233–4). Civic practices are the speech and actions that, through the production and reproduction of etiquette that defines public engagement, create opportunities to talk about politics and public life. Eliasoph (1996, 2011, 2013) explores the physical and conceptual contexts (places and situations) that make conversations about new political imaginaries possible. The physical spaces where public issues are discussed, as well as the etiquette that makes this discussion possible, are important. Looking at discourses and civic practices in tandem aids our understanding of how systems of thought can define and limit the food and agriculture issues that dominate the public sphere. Many scholars suggest that civic practices are shaped by the issues identified as important in the public sphere (Johnston and Baumann 2010; Johnston, Szabo, and Rodney 2011). Thus, which issues a community prioritizes and how these issues are discussed in public shape the actions that citizens do (or do not) take to address them.

The driving force behind discourse and civic practices is ideology (Johnston 2008), a system of beliefs and ideas about the social world that shapes how we speak and act (Oliver and Johnston 2000). These systems of thought are rooted in norms and values about social life. Ideology shapes discourses, which refers to the "broad systems of communication that link concepts together in a web of relationships" (Ferree and Merrill 2000, 455). Discourses can be laden with controversy and conflict, as actors are constantly debating the meaning of words and ideas (455). Examining discourses and civic practices can provide a picture of which issues are prevalent in public life and how power, ideology, and discourses are related (Fairclough 2013). Both ideologies and discourses shape civic practices, which together can be used to explore the cultural politics of AFNs.

Using interviews and observation, we analyze how everyday speech and action define which food and agricultural issues dominate the public sphere. Ultimately, the way in which topics are defined and discussed influences the types of civic practices that emerge—ranging from practices that create transformative social change to those that reinforce current structures of power and inequality. Thus, the way that issues are discussed in public discourse and the civic practices that occur in public life are related to underlying ideologies (Johnston and Szabo 2011. We use this conceptual framework to demonstrate how ideologies, discourses, and civic practices comprise the cultural politics of AFNs.

Our case study from Edmonton, Alberta, uses twenty-two in-depth, semi-structured interviews and six participant observation events to compare the discourses and civic practices used by actors to foster food system change. Throughout the chapter, we use "Edmonton" as shorthand to include the surrounding region, which comprises both urban and rural settings up to 150 kilometers outside city limits. Edmonton was chosen for this study because of recent developments in municipal food policy as well as its proximity to farmland, which provided the opportunity to interview producers, consumers, and other food system actors. This setting also provides an example of AFN activities in a medium-sized city, offering an important contrast to other studies, which examine larger urban centres in Canada (e.g., Levkoe 2011; Gibb and Wittman 2013; Lynch and Giles 2013; Wakefield 2007) and the western United States (e.g., Guthman 2008; Allen et al. 2003; Alkon and McCullen 2011).

Prior to the study, controversy over the annexation of over 600 hectares of farmland northeast of the city mobilized hundreds of Edmontonians, and the city was beginning to develop its first food and agriculture strategy and food council (Beckie, Hanson, and Schrader 2013). As in many other cities in North America, food was becoming a prominent issue in municipal politics, providing a rich opportunity for exploratory inquiry into citizen engagement. In the months before the interviews, a number of local organizations had worked to mobilize citizens to attend the municipal food and agriculture hearings, where Edmonton's city council listened to input from citizens' panels and deliberated on a new city-wide strategy for food and agriculture. During data collection, the members of Edmonton's Food Council were announced.[4] The Edmonton Community Foundation (2013) reports that three out of ten Edmontonians are from a visible minority and that the city has the second-largest urban Aboriginal population in Canada (De Schutter 2012). The Food Council's terms of reference state that the council was intended to represent "cultural groups...demographic groups, youth, seniors, minority groups, newcomers...[and]...serve the public interest." Yet the council appeared to be demographically homogeneous: the fourteen members were all white, aged approximately thirty to fifty-five years, and were well-educated members of the middle or upper class.

These events shaped our approach to data collection, leading us to focus on how and why citizens promoted change to the food system, with a particular emphasis on how both environmental degradation and social equity were discussed by participants. During the hearings, over 500 Edmonton residents engaged directly with government by attending hearings, providing feedback on the strategy, and speaking to their councillors (Beckie, Hanson, and Schrader 2013). However, after the hearings, many residents began to shift their focus to alternative food projects, such as food hubs, educational programming, and community gardens. We observed how many of these projects operated primarily between civic and market spheres, without directly challenging or seeking support from the state. Further, many of these projects, whether conducted by farmers, community organizers, educators, or government employees, focussed primarily on getting consumers to buy, grow, and cook more local food. Noting the heavy emphasis on consumers as the intended audience rather than large corporations or the state, we turned our attention toward exploring the cultural politics of local food activities by focussing on discourse and civic practices. With this, we aim to provide a more nuanced understanding of the contextual characteristics that surround contemporary citizen engagement.

To understand how change through individual consumption is maintained as the pre-eminent strategy for social change, we constructed a sample that extended beyond the civil society organizations typically studied in scholarship on engagement. We recruited leaders from three sectors involved with AFNs: civil society (e.g., community organizers, educators, and volunteers), the state (e.g., federal and provincial policy makers and city planners), and the market (e.g., entrepreneurs and farmers' market managers) (see Table 8.1 for a description of this sample).

As we compare the political consciousness of a broad range of actors who are involved in both the production and consumption of food, we move beyond the urban–rural, producer–consumer divide that is common in food studies (Goodman, DuPuis, and Goodman 2011). During each interview, we discussed the projects, activities, and ideas that participants were implementing and why; what their ideal food system would look like; the ways they acted on a daily basis to achieve this goal; what changes they thought

Table 8.1. *Sampling by sector of involvement.*

Sector of involvement	Number of participants	Details
State	4	Municipal, provincial, federal government employees
Market	8	Farmers (cattle, goats, dairy, chickens, grain, vegetables, and fruit), farmers' market managers, entrepreneurs
Civil	10	Community organizers and leaders of food advocacy organizations focussed on gleaning, workshops, community gardens, and alternative agriculture demonstration sites

were needed to make their definition of sustainable food an obvious choice, like "falling off a log";[5] whether or not they felt their approach was political; and what challenges they had faced. We also observed and recorded field notes after six food-focussed events and meetings, detailed in Table 8.2.

Table 8.2. *Participant observation events.*

Event	Participants' sector of involvement	Details
Food hub discussion	Civil society	Various stakeholders in an inner-city neighbourhood met to discuss the potential for a food hub to be developed nearby.
Community garden work bee	Farmers; civil society	Inner-city residents, farmers, volunteers, and inner-city service agencies got together to harvest produce for the inner-city service agencies.
University consultation for urban agriculture	Civil society; state; market	The university led a discussion with staff, faculty, and students, as well as community members about the future of the campus farm.
Foodie networking event	Civil society; market	Local foodies, business owners, and farmers met over drinks to discuss local food.
Launch for a food security initiative	Civil society	An open event detailing a new source of funding for food security initiatives in Edmonton.
Citizens advisory panel	Civil society; state	Members of civil society (including representatives from agriculture, industry, non-profits, and government) met to discuss how government could create and implement policy and programs to promote food and agriculture.

At each event, we used a template for participant observation derived from Blee (2012) to record who was speaking, what was discussed, what civic practices were discussed and enacted, and who was in the audience. The field notes created after these events were analyzed along with interview transcripts, using a team-based, grounded theory approach and NVivo 10 software.

Motivations, Discourses, and Civic Practices of Edmonton's Local Food Initiatives

Given the significant implications that food and agriculture have for environmental and social justice issues, we aim to explore how and why people engaged in their community to promote food systems that are healthy for both people and the planet. This section summarizes the motivations, discourses, and civic practices of a range of actors in Edmonton's local food initiatives, providing insight into the political consciousness of key actors. Our findings demonstrate that while AFNs have the potential to transform the food system, they also reproduce dominant neoliberal ideologies in two key ways: first, through potentially universalizing discourses that fail to account for or encourage diverse participation. Second, through civic practices that fetishize consumer-driven change, relying on consumer-focussed initiatives such as education and awareness campaigns. In this section, we focus on two key findings related to the environmental and social justice impacts of the food system. The first is that actors tend to focus on the beneficial aspects of food projects, avoiding discussions of potentially controversial issues such as equity. The second is that farmers discuss the environment much more frequently and with more detail than other groups. We go on to consider the implications of these findings, exploring how the cultural politics of AFNs constrain their ability to transform dominant social systems.

Transformation through Taste: The ABC Model

Throughout the interviews and during participant observation, participants argued that if people were aware of where their food came from and experienced the superior taste of locally grown food, they would buy, grow, and eat more local food. This strategy assumes that education will lead to social change. Although participants offered some evidence that consumers can change their eating practices as a result of education, they tended to overlook the role that power and privilege play in shaping who has access to knowledge in the first place, and who can seamlessly act on newfound knowledge to change their practices. This position is exemplified in Betty, a community developer who works with a number of regional and national nutrition and food security organizations. She sums up what she sees as an effective approach to social change: "Knowledge, attitude, and behaviour. You have to work on the knowledge part, it's out there, but it's the attitude toward the value of being connected to your food. We don't have it." Adam, a farmer and entrepreneur, puts Betty's approach into practice in his efforts to transform the food system. When we asked about how he first began to change the way he ate, he responded: "[I changed my eating habits] as soon as I went to a [conventional] farm and saw what I didn't want to eat. It's as simple as that. Lots of people will go to Costco and buy pork chops. If you saw how those pigs are raised, you'd never buy that product again in your life. It's as simple as that. As long as you don't know about that experience or you don't have to face that reality, you'll buy it because it's cheap. So that was it for me, visiting farms."

The danger of the attitude, behaviour, change (ABC) model, as evidenced here, is its assumption that all actors begin with the same degree of power and privilege. Although our participants certainly understood the challenges around social justice, the ABC model creates little space for reflexive consideration of power and inequality. The most obvious barrier to increasing local food consumption is not awareness or connection, but cost. Lack of time, access, knowledge, and support from peer groups play a role as well—material barriers that are unlikely to be overcome simply by people visiting conventional farms and being disturbed by what they see.

During a community garden harvest, the issue of the cost of sustainable food came up in a group conversation. A woman who was picking organic tomatoes mentioned, "This is why tomatoes cost so much at the farmers market, because of all the hard work to pick them." As we sampled the fruit, those working around us commented that the taste was much better, and someone remarked that it was "weird how cheap tomatoes [were] in the grocery store." The woman who had brought up the price of tomatoes also mentioned that while growing up she had picked raspberries with her grandmother and therefore appreciated why they cost six dollars a pint: because of the time-consuming fight through thorny bushes to pick them. The consensus among those who spoke up seemed to be that alternative food was worth the cost, and that if people knew how much work it was and how much better it tasted, they would be willing to pay more. Yet, it is interesting to note the context of this conversation: the community garden was the result of a partnership with inner-city service agencies that worked with homeless youth and adults. Certainly, a number of those present would not have been able to afford local, organic tomatoes from the farmers' market, and the absence of any such discussion of cost was conspicuous. Further, prior to the community garden project, many of the gardeners had not had access to garden space, transportation to a community garden, gardening knowledge, or the resources needed to grow their own food, yet these barriers were eclipsed by discourse stressing that local food was superior because of its taste and quality.

After making these observations in the garden and comparing them with those from our other events, we noted that a relatively homogeneous group attended many of the food-related events in Edmonton and went back through our notes to see if this was discussed during the interviews. People of colour were all but absent from many of the observation events, with one notable exception: the garden where organic tomatoes were the topic of discussion. The gardeners here were much more representative of Edmonton's demographic makeup than those at other events. Yet overall, discussions of race, gender, or class were absent from the interviews, events, and meetings we attended, and we observed how the etiquette of these spaces fostered a cultural politics that did not encourage critical dialogue about who might be excluded. At a number of events and meetings, conversation focussed on the positive and beneficial aspects of the projects being discussed. Arguments for why alternative food was important consistently spoke to how fun, healthy, pleasurable, and economically beneficial it was rather than the barriers to broader participation, such as time, cost, and access to local food. We also noted that the etiquette of these spaces was set through posted rules stating that participants should "focus on the positives" or by the way group leaders led discussions. At public events and meetings, we did not observe conversations about potentially controversial topics, such as diversity or inequality within the AFNs; instead, there was a clear sense that discussing such topics was taboo. Across all sectors, we observed that a focus on the positives seemed to displace discussion of institutional or structural barriers that might hamper broad participation.

Farmers and the Environment: Have You Ever Seen a Thirteen-Striped Gopher?

The farmers we spoke with focussed their civic practices on encouraging consumers to reconnect with their food and their farmers by hosting farm tours and using community supported agriculture (CSA) models. While we expected that environmental degradation would be a motivator of many advocates in AFNs, few participants discussed the environmental impacts of food production or consumption, instead focussing on human health, happiness, taste, the local economy, or (at times) social justice. Overall, farmers brought up the issue of the environment much more frequently and discussed it in much greater detail than others we interviewed or observed. This finding is notable, given the significant implications food and agriculture have for the environment (Carolan 2012) and previous work demonstrating that consumers report choosing local food for environmental reasons (Johnston and Baumann 2010).

Farmers' discourses and civic practices do not differ widely from others in our sample, because they encourage sustainable food consumption through connection, education, and awareness. However, they spoke about the environment not only more frequently but also with much more precision, offering up stories about how they had seen the land change first-hand and how they had been a part of that transformation. Commonly, farmers discussed how they hoped hosting people at their farms would foster a reconnection with the land.[6] While touring Al's farm and checking his cattle, we discussed an off-the-grid retreat he had built for people to stay at while they visited. During our conversation, Al was searching for a word to explain why he had built it, when one of us offered the term "connection," prompting him to discuss reconnection:

> That's a great term, "reconnect." And that is what this is all about. Reconnecting the consumer to the land through the food. When people leave, especially if they're a family, and they say thank you, thank you, thank you. I say, that chicken you bought, when you get back to the city and cook that, remind your kids that you are helping a farm like this to make a living and to sustain itself. It's a personal connection too. It is. And it's a relationship. It's a relationship with a consumer, and the farmer has a relationship with the land, and we're trying to bridge that gap.

Through farm visits and CSA models, the farmers we spoke with hoped to achieve the dual purpose of encouraging people to buy food from their farms and fostering a connection with the land. The idea of environmental stewardship was embedded in the everyday discourses and civic practices of the farmers we interviewed. For instance, farmer Al had a keen eye for birds and small mammals, spotting a rare thirteen-striped gopher that had only recently returned to his farm because of the native clovers and grasses he had planted. Jim, a vegetable farmer, spotted two bald eagles overhead during the interview and remarked on how unusual it was, noting that they lived in the old-growth forest his family had protected from encroaching development. Both Al and Jim had changed their farming practices over the years, moving toward management practices that reduced their environmental impact. As with all the farmers we interviewed, the environment played a central role in their daily lives, directly impacting how they made a living. Underlying these practices was the complicated relationship between economic survival and environmental stewardship. For instance, Jim spoke about how he had resisted removing the old-growth forest on his property despite significant economic incentive over the years. Al, on the other hand, had collaborated with economists to calculate the economic values of the ecological goods and services his farm contributed. Marilyn, who operated her farm as a CSA, struggled to ensure she earned enough profit to survive, and relied on off-farm income to continue. While environmental stewardship was a significant motivator for farmers, these issues were not as prevalent among other participants, who rarely voiced environmental concerns.

The Cultural Politics of Alternative Food Networks

Interviewing and observing actors from civil, state, and market spheres allowed us to compare the political consciousness of a range of actors who participate in reproducing the cultural politics of AFNs and to explore how environmental and social justice concerns were expressed in local food initiatives. Based on Johnston and Baumann's (2010, 139–40) suggestion that environmental issues tend to dominate the food discourse in North America, we expected to hear the same from actors in Edmonton's AFNs. However, the only actors who spoke extensively about the environmental impacts of food and agriculture were farmers. That farmers would discuss the environment is not surprising, given the daily impact the environment has on farmers' lives and the constant interaction they have with the land. However, given the emphasis on reconnection and awareness, we were surprised to note that the connection being (re)established was more frequently between consumer and producer rather than between humans and the environment. While farmers also discussed the dominant discourses of reconnection and awareness, they saw reconnection as forging a relationship between people and the land, and saw food as mediating that relationship.

Overall, actors in all of the groups focussed their civic practices on changing the food system through educating the consumer (educational civic practices); demonstrating alternative ways to grow, buy, and eat better food (demonstrative civic practices); and connecting producers, consumers, and other AFN actors (relational civic practices). The dominant discourses and civic practices focussed on the positive aspects of alternative food, and the etiquette of these activities encouraged neither critical examination of power or equity issues nor consideration of ways in which regulation could promote broader structural changes. Instead, reconnection and awareness displaced consideration of these more critical themes. Similar to other AFN actors, farmers centred their civic practices on educating the consumer and developing relationships with them through market-based activities, such as CSAs and farm tours. Given that none of the other interviews or participant observation events yielded data on environmental concern, there is evidence that farm visits and CSA models are not enough to develop ideologies that would orient daily practices and discourses to encourage environmentally positive practices. Lacking support or sufficient opportunity to imagine, discuss, or pursue alternative approaches to food politics, farmers within AFNs rely heavily on consumers to serve as agents of change through shopping for local food. Here, we offer evidence that connection to the environment is lost in translation even as eaters procure local food.

Building relationships, demonstrating alternatives to the current food system, and teaching people about food are vital components of food system transformation; yet, the findings of our research indicate a key limitation to the civic practices and discourses of eat local initiatives. With consumers positioned as the key drivers of a market-based approach to food system change, AFN actors may fail to address important environmental and social justice issues, because the dominant paradigm remains unchallenged. For instance, the discourses of awareness and reconnection, and the educational, demonstrative, and relational civic practices we observed all have the potential to reproduce neoliberal ideologies. Using this political imaginary, food becomes a commodity, and the marketplace is seen as the ideal locus of decisions about food and agriculture.[7]

Our research demonstrates that actors from different sectors focussed on market-based and consumer-driven approaches to food system change rarely engaged with state or institutional actors. While farmers focussed on the environmental aspects of food and agriculture more than other actors did, overall there was not broad engagement among AFN actors in environmental or social justice issues. Further, we noted an etiquette that discouraged critical dialogue of equity and social justice issues and did not challenge the dominant ideology of the marketplace. This observation speaks to the limitations of "voting with your fork," which can potentially exclude lower-income and marginalized people. Our concern is that focussing almost exclusively on voting with your fork potentially weakens the ability of food system actors to challenge dominant neoliberal ideology, thus reducing the potential for transformative changes to food and agricultural systems.

Are AFNs Transforming the Food System?

Acknowledging the potential for local food initiatives to reproduce dominant neoliberal ideology leads to the question of whether or not these initiatives can be transformative. Exploring the cultural politics of alternative food in California, Guthman (2008) discusses the colour-blind mentalities and universalizing narratives that shape and colour AFNs (387). Instead of asking "Who is at the table?" Guthman (2008) encourages us to examine "Who set the table?" questioning how cultural politics shape who participates in AFNs and how (388). She discusses some of the common AFN phrases, such as "If they only knew," "Getting your hands in the soil," and "Looking your farmer in the eye" and demonstrates that many people do not identify with the narratives used to promote alternative food (387). Guthman (2008) argues that this "romanticized American agrarian imagery erases the explicitly racist ways in which American land has been distributed historically" (390) and ignores the food history that many people of colour have experienced. While Lockie (2013) warns that labelling AFNs as bastions of white privilege is potentially dangerous because it can trivialize the work of non-elite actors in these networks, he suggests that examining "the processes through which social inclusions and exclusions are produced" is critically important (416). Keeping this in mind, we aim to explain how the table keeps getting set this way.

Evidence of similar discourses were found in Edmonton's AFNs, yet our findings do not indicate that class and race are as polarizing as in Guthman's (2008) observations from California. Adam's suggestion that visiting farms is key to changing consumption patterns, Al's discussion of reconnection, and the civic practices of farmers are all indicative of the type of affirmative discourses of awareness and reconnection that we observed. While not as starkly universalizing as those in Guthman's research, discourses in this case study are potentially exclusionary, given Canada's diverse population. For instance, a number of narratives and food histories are excluded from the discourses of reconnection and awareness that dominate local food. For example, knowledge about and use of traditional foods among Indigenous peoples has declined over the last 150 years due to a number of factors, including the residential school system, urbanization, and the loss of traditional land (Turner and Turner 2008). While traditional foods remain an important part of the diets in many Aboriginal communities (Desmarais and Wittman 2014), there are wide variations in rates of food insecurity among communities (De Schutter 2012). In 2012, almost 13 percent of Canadian households experienced some level of food insecurity (Tarasuk, Dachner, and Loopstra 2014), with Aboriginal populations experiencing levels of food insecurity three to six times higher than the average Canadian household (De Schutter 2012). Immigrants also experience higher rates of food insecurity (De Schutter 2012) and have specific experiences of food and agriculture. As Guthman (2008) reminds us, "getting your hands dirty" or "looking your farmer in the eye" demonstrate reconnection to the land for some, but to others this idea brings back no-so-distant memories of slavery and gruelling labour (394). In the Canadian context, this may include residential schools, colonization, slavery, internment, land grabbing, and loss of traditional foods.

As noted previously, many of the events, committees, and meetings we participated in did not reflect the diverse demographic makeup of the Edmonton region. The membership of Edmonton's Food Council, the key body responsible for providing advice to the city about food and agriculture, is particularly illustrative of this point. More importantly, discussions of equity, gender, race, and class were not part of the etiquette or discourse of these AFNs. Overall, although participants were concerned with social justice and sustainability, the etiquette of these public spaces discouraged participants from discussing power relations or questioning whether the existing framing of food politics addressed them. This lack of critical public dialogue is significant, given the findings of other scholars who note that AFNs have been slow to address white privilege and class inequality (Alkon and McCullen 2011; Slocum 2007). These observations corroborate Eliasoph's (2013) and Johnston and Baumann's (2010) conclusion that participation in civic life is often dominated by relatively privileged actors and, as a result, dominant discourses are shaped by the ideologies of those who have greater access to cultural and economic capital. This exclusion of marginalized actors and viewpoints limits the transformative potential of alternative food networks. While the possibility remains that there are parallel food networks populated by visible minorities, marginalized, or non-dominant groups, such as those observed by Gibb and Wittman (2013) in British Columbia, our findings are troubling, given the potential for elites to increase their social and economic capital through participation in AFNs, potentially reproducing and perpetuating existing inequality.

Currently, AFNs are well positioned to work within the neoliberal ideologies of the marketplace, which allows them to make use of significant amounts of cultural and economic capital. In a capitalist model, focussing on the pleasures of local food supports a market-based model. However, emphasizing market and civil activities, without engaging the state or challenging institutional barriers may not bring out the kind of transformative social change that some hope to achieve. We suggest that the cultural politics of AFNs are potentially exclusionary and individualizing, in that they do not address power relations or engage a broad range of actors in promoting environmental sustainability, thereby bringing into question the effectiveness of these approaches. The discourses and civic practices that structure AFNs seem to preclude any critical examination of power relations, foster a belief that the individual consumer is the most appropriate location for social change, and assume that shifting intransigent eating practices is a matter of awareness. The danger of these market-focussed change activities is that they can potentially limit citizen engagement in politics, because people feel as though they have adequately participated simply through their consumption (Szasz 2009). AFNs in Edmonton have been successful in many ways, encouraging a large number of citizens to participate in food and agriculture hearings, and providing new opportunities to purchase, cook, and grow local food. At the same time, the transformative potential of AFNs is limited by taboos against exploring systemic drivers of injustice and barriers to sustainability. In short, we find evidence that AFNs can discourage more radical behaviour through an etiquette that encourages participants to focus almost exclusively on the positive aspects of local food, instead of tackling the challenges. In particular, a tendency to emphasize awareness-based solutions seems to prevent food citizens from accounting for the numerous political, cultural, and economic barriers to localizing the food system. This conclusion is notable, given the findings of other scholars, who suggest that such projects can be both radical and neoliberal (McClintock 2014).

Conclusion

Using contrasting accounts of the significance and success of alternative food networks to situate a case study from the city of Edmonton, we explored the cultural politics of these networks and aimed to address whether or not food politics are as compromised or as transformative as others studies suggest. We demonstrated how a reliance on education focussed on reconnection and awareness cultivates a cultural politics that places the locus for social change in the marketplace. This market-based orientation may exacerbate the tendency to download public services to the private sphere, limiting the ability of local food movements to adequately address broader structural barriers that inhibit the transformation to an environmentally sustainable and socially just food system. We drew attention to discourses that tend to exclude any consideration or illumination of power relations in AFNs— cautionary evidence that the current framing of food politics may be insufficient for significantly transforming the food system. Given these limitations, we remain uncertain as to whether the current tactics of AFNs could foster a more just and sustainable food system. While this case study cannot be generalized to apply to all AFNs, it offers a means of analyzing cultural politics and an indication of how and why actors engage in the public sphere and what the outcomes of this work may be. Further, this case study indicates the need for further analysis of civic engagement both in food studies and beyond.

This case study has important implications for both AFNs and other social movements. Environmental movements often place a strong focus on education, undertaking awareness campaigns that encourage people to take action based on their knowledge of environmental issues. For instance, many initiatives focus on reducing greenhouse gas emissions by fostering awareness about climate change, yet the "lexicon of ABC [attitude, behaviour, change] does not contain within it the terms and concepts required to discuss or debate significant societal transformation" (Shove 2010, 1277). Like AFNs, climate change politics often place a strong emphasis on the role of the consumer as the agent of change. While more than eight out of ten Western Canadians believe climate change is a significant issue (Berdahl 2008), we have yet to see any significant changes to policy or practice. By focussing on education and behaviour, parts of the environmental movement may, like AFNs, be limited in their ability to foster eco-social change.

While our findings indicate a number of potential challenges within AFNs in Edmonton, there are also a number of strengths, which could be further developed to form a movement that adequately addresses power and justice. For instance, educational civic practices could be harnessed to provided anti-racism training, build models of collective action, and teach conflict resolution. The strong relational focus that we observed could create opportunities for a broader range of actors to participate. Instead of only demonstrating alternatives to the current system, critical discussions about how these alternatives might work with, against, and beyond the current system could be facilitated. Given that rates of urbanization are projected to increase to over 70 percent by 2050 (United Nations 2012), AFNs could also explore new ways to develop environmental concern in both urban and rural settings and among producers, consumers, and others. Overall, there are many opportunities for AFNs to transform the food system. By offering a critique of AFNs, we do not intend to encourage those interested in change to abandon the project. Instead, we suggest that developing a more critical gaze with regard to how AFNs are structured and reproduced is just as important as—and indeed, germane to—promoting local food consumption and reconnection. A critical approach would foster civic practices that consider how inequality in the food system emerged in the first place, in addition to creating viable alternatives. There is an inherent value in such reflection: as Žižek writes, "It is time to step back, think and say the right thing. True, we often talk about something instead of doing it; but sometimes we also do things in order to avoid talking and thinking about them" (Žižek, 2009, 11). For those who study and engage in AFNs, we must remain cognizant of the possibility that narrowing our conversations to avoid politically contentious and inflammatory topics might inhibit the development of a food politics that is truly transformative.

Acknowledgements

This research was generously supported by the Social Sciences and Humanities Research Council of Canada (Insight Development Grant: 430-2013-0559). We would also like to extend our gratitude to co-PIs Josée Johnston and John Parkins, to supervisor Hannah Wittman, and to research assistants Tyler Bateman and Charles Levkoe for their helpful discussions, support, and comments during the creation of this chapter.

Notes

1   Neoliberalism is a market-based political ideology that promotes deregulation, reduced government intervention and welfare, privatization, and other mechanisms of market liberalization (McClintock 2014).

2   It is worth noting that extensive transformation is likely not the main goal or intent for many actors within AFNs. Rather, many players in AFNs seek primarily to offer alternatives to the conventional food system.

3   Note that Eliasoph's (2013) work does not examine food- or agriculture-related activities specifically. Instead, she focuses more generally on civic engagement and volunteering in a number of different types of groups.

4   See www.edmonton.ca/Edmonton_Food_Council_members.pdf for photos and biographies of the inaugural members of Edmonton's Food Council. The TOR can be found at: http://www.edmonton.ca/city_government/documents/Amended%20TOR%20Sep%2024%202015.pdf.

5   If sustainability were like "falling off a log," it would be the easy, default option that people would choose without giving it conscious thought or effort (Hawken 1994).

6 Many of the farmers we interviewed used the word "land" interchangeably with the word "environment."

7 As noted by a reviewer of this chapter, many AFNs do not explicitly aim to challenge the dominant market paradigm but, instead, encourage market exchanges that represent alternatives to a "pure" market logic. Recognizing the value of this argument, we stress that our findings nonetheless demonstrate that environmental and social justice challenges and benefits are sidelined by discourses stressing food quality, taste, and other more "individualized" characteristics of local food.

References

Alkon, Alison H. 2008. "Paradise or Pavement: The Social Constructions of the Environment in Two Urban Farmers' Markets and Their Implications for Environmental Justice and Sustainability." *Local Environment: The International Journal of Justice and Sustainability* 13 (3): 271–89. http://dx.doi.org/10.1080/13549830701669039.

Alkon, Alison H. 2013. "Food Justice, Food Sovereignty, and the Challenge of Neoliberalism." Paper presented at Food Sovereignty: A Critical Dialogue. International Conference, Yale University, New Haven, CT, 14–15 September.

Alkon, Alison H., and Christie G. McCullen. 2011. "Whiteness and Farmers Markets: Performances, Perpetuations…Contestations?" *Antipode* 43 (4): 937–59. http://dx.doi.org/10.1111/j.1467-8330.2010.00818.x.

Allen, Patricia, Margaret FitzSimmons, Michael Goodman, and Keith Warner. 2003. "Shifting Plates in the Agrifood Landscape: The Tectonics of Alternative Agrifood Initiatives in California." *Journal of Rural Studies* 19 (1): 61–75. http://dx.doi.org/10.1016/S0743-0167(02)00047-5.

Beckie, Marie A., Lorelei L. Hanson, and Deborah Schrader. 2013. "Farms or Freeways? Citizen Engagement and Municipal Governance in Edmonton's Food and Agriculture Strategy Development." *Journal of Agriculture, Food Systems, and Community Development* 4 (1): 15–31.

Berdahl, Loleen. 2008. "Hot Topics: Western Canadian Attitudes toward Climate Change." *Looking West 2008*. Vancouver: Canada West Foundation. http://cwf.ca/pdf-docs/publications/looking-west-strategic-investments-2008.pdf.

Blee, Kathlenn M. 2012. *Democracy in the Making: How Activist Groups Form*. Oxford: Oxford University Press. http://dx.doi.org/10.1093/acprof:oso/9780199842766.001.0001.

Carolan, Michael S. 2012. *The Sociology of Food and Agriculture*. London: Routledge.

De Schutter, Olivier. 2012. Report of the Special Rapporteur on the Right to Food, Mission to Canada, 6 to 16 May 2012. http://foodsecurecanada.org/sites/foodsecurecanada.org/files/20120321_SRRTF_Aide-m%C3%A9moire_Canada.pdf.

Desmarais, Annette A., and Hannah H. Wittman. 2014. "Farmers, Foodies and First Nations: Getting to Food Sovereignty in Canada." *Journal of Peasant Studies* 41 (6): 1153–73. http://dx.doi.org/10.1080/03066150.2013.876623.

DuPuis, Melanie E., and David Goodman. 2005. "Should We Go 'Home' to Eat? Toward a Reflexive Politics of Localism." *Journal of Rural Studies* 21 (3): 359–71. http://dx.doi.org/10.1016/j.jrurstud.2005.05.011.

Edmonton Community Foundation. 2013. "Edmonton Vital Signs 2013." http://www.vitalsignscanada.ca/files/localreports/2013_EdmontonFood_report.pdf.

Eliasoph, Nina. 1996. "Making a Fragile Public : A Talk-Centered Study of Citizenship and Power." *Sociological Theory* 14 (3): 262–90. http://dx.doi.org/10.2307/3045389.

Eliasoph, Nina. 2011. *Making Volunteers: Civic Life after Welfare's End.* Princeton, NJ: Princeton University Press. http://dx.doi.org/10.1515/9781400838820.

Eliasoph, Nina. 2013. *The Politics of Volunteering.* New York: Polity.

Fairclough, Norman. 2013. "Critical Discourse Analysis and Critical Policy Studies." *Critical Policy Studies* 7 (2): 177–97. http://dx.doi.org/10.1080/19460171.2013.798239.

Ferree, Myra Marx, and David A. Merrill. 2000. "Hot Movements, Cold Cognition: Thinking about Social Movements in Gendered Frames." *Contemporary Sociology* 23 (3): 454–62. http://www.jstor.org/stable/2653932. http://dx.doi.org/10.2307/2653932.

Gibb, Natalie, and Hannah H. Wittman. 2013. "Parallel Alternatives: Chinese-Canadian Farmers and the Metro Vancouver Local Food Movement." *Local Environment* 18 (1): 1–19. http://dx.doi.org/10.1080/13549839.2012.714763.

Goodman, David, Melanie E. DuPuis, and Michael K. Goodman. 2011. *Alternative Food Networks: Knowledge, Practice and Politics.* London: Routledge.

Guthman, Julie. 2008. "'If They Only Knew': Color Blindness and Universalism in California Alternative Food Institutions." *Professional Geographer* 60 (3): 387–397. http://dx.doi.org/10.1080/00330120802013679.

Hawken, Paul. 1994. *The Ecology of Commerce: A Declaration of Sustainability.* New York: HarperBusiness.

Hughner, Renée Shaw, Pierre McDonagh, Andrea Prothero, Clifford J. Shultz, and Julie Stanton. 2007. "Who Are Organic Food Consumers? A Compilation and Review of Why People Purchase Organic Food." *Journal of Consumer Behaviour* 6 (2–3): 94–110. http://dx.doi.org/10.1002/cb.210.

Jackson, Peter. 1991. "The Cultural Politics of Masculinity: Towards a Social Geography." *Transactions of the Institute of British Geographers* 16 (2): 199–213. http://dx.doi.org/10.2307/622614.

Johnston, Josée. 2008. "The Citizen-Consumer Hybrid: Ideological Tensions and the Case of Whole Foods Market." *Theory and Society* 37 (3): 229–70. http://dx.doi.org/10.1007/s11186-007-9058-5.

Johnston, Josée, and Shyon Baumann. 2010. *Foodies: Democracy and Distinction in the Gourmet Foodscape.* London: Routledge.

Johnston, Josée, and Michelle Szabo. 2011. "Reflexivity and the Whole Foods Market Consumer: The Lived Experience of Shopping for Change." *Agriculture and Human Values* 28 (3): 303–19. http://dx.doi.org/10.1007/s10460-010-9283-9.

Johnston, Josée, Michelle Szabo, and Alexandra Rodney. 2011. "Good Food, Good People: Understanding the Cultural Repertoire of Ethical Eating." *Journal of Consumer Culture* 11 (3): 293–318. http://dx.doi.org/10.1177/1469540511417996.

Koç, Mustafa, Rod MacRae, Ellen Desjardins, and Wayne Roberts. 2008. "Getting Civil About Food : The Interactions Between Civil Society and the State to Advance Sustainable Food Systems in Canada." *Journal of Hunger and Environmental Nutrition* 3 (2–3): 122–44. http://dx.doi.org/10.1080/19320240802243175.

Levkoe, Charles Z. 2011. "Towards a Transformative Food Politics." *Local Environment* 16 (7): 687–705. http://dx.doi.org/10.1080/13549839.2011.592182.

Lockie, Stewart. 2013. "Bastions of White Privilege? Reflections on the Racialization of Alternative Food Networks." *International Journal of Sociology of Agriculture and Food* 20 (3): 409–18.

Lynch, Meghan, and Audrey Giles. 2013. "Let Them Eat Organic Cake: Discourses in Sustainable Food Initiatives." *Food, Culture, & Society* 16 (3): 479–93. http://dx.doi.org/10.2752/175174413X13673466711967.

McClintock, Neil. 2014. "Radical, Reformist, and Garden-Variety Neoliberal: Coming to Terms with Urban Agriculture's Contradictions." *Local Environment* 19 (2): 147–71. http://dx.doi.org/10.1080/13549839.2012.752797.

Morgan, Kevin. 2009. "Feeding the City: The Challenge of Urban Food Planning." *International Planning Studies* 14 (4): 341–8. http://dx.doi.org/10.1080/13563471003642852.

Oliver, Pamela E., and Hank Johnston. 2000. "What a Good Idea! Ideologies and Frames in Social Movement Research." *Mobilization: An International Quarterly* 4 (1): 37–54.

Sbicca, Joshua. 2012. "Growing Food Justice by Planting an Anti-Oppression Foundation: Opportunities and Obstacles for a Budding Social Movement." *Agriculture and Human Values* 29 (4): 455–66. http://dx.doi.org/10.1007/s10460-012-9363-0.

Shove, Elizabeth. 2010. "Beyond the ABC: Climate Change Policy and Theories of Social Change." *Environment and Planning A* 42 (6): 1273–85. http://dx.doi.org/10.1068/a42282.

Slocum, Rachel. 2007. "Whiteness, Space and Alternative Food Practice." *Geoforum* 38 (3): 520–33. http://dx.doi.org/10.1016/j.geoforum.2006.10.006.

Szasz, Andrew. 2009. *Shopping Our Way to Safety: How We Changed from Protecting the Environment to Protecting Ourselves*. Minnesota: University of Minnesota Press.

Tarasuk, Valerie, Naomi Dachner, and Rachel Loopstra. 2014. "Food Banks, Welfare, and Food Insecurity in Canada." *British Food Journal* 116 (9): 1405–17. http://dx.doi.org/10.1108/BFJ-02-2014-0077.

Turner, Nancy J., and Katherine L. Turner. 2008. "'Where Our Women Used to Get the Food': Cumulative Effects and Loss of Ethnobotanical Knowledge and Practice; Case Study from Coastal British Columbia." *Botany* 86 (2): 103–15. http://dx.doi.org/10.1139/B07-020.

United Nations. 2012. *World Urbanization Prospect, the 2011 Revisions: Highlights*. New York: United Nations.

Wakefield, Sarah E.L. 2007. "Reflective Action in the Academy: Exploring Praxis in Critical Geography Using a 'Food Movement' Case Study." *Antipode* 39 (2): 331–54. http://dx.doi.org/10.1111/j.1467-8330.2007.00524.x.

Žižek, Slavoj. 2009. *First as Tragedy, Then as Farce*. London: Verso.

CHAPTER 9

Sustenance: Contested Definitions of the Sustainable Diet

Mark Bomford and Samara Brock

A ruddy country gentleman stands proudly behind a comically fat pig in a blurry photo plate at the front of a 1920s homesteading manual. Such hefty volumes could be found in the possession of thousands of agriculturally inexperienced European colonists hoping to achieve affluence on government-issued land grants in Canada in the early twentieth century. While the manuals belied a profound colonial disconnection, casting their readers as pioneers on a fabled *terra nullius*, they also acknowledged and reinforced strong and consistent connections between the health of the new farm and the health of the new farm family. Within the smallholder's homestead, the black loams that gave rise to vigorous crops and verdant pasture were directly connected to the fatness and fitness of both the pig and the humans. Fittingly, these how-to guides bound together their agricultural instructions in the same book as the how-to guides for nutrition, medicine, and health. The homestead manual spanned different domains of knowledge in a way that might satisfy some of today's calls to integrate and reconnect in food networks, whether by state adoption of "joined-up food policies" (Barling, Lang, and Caraher 2002; MacRae 2011), by academic institutions creating discipline-crossing food studies programs (Koç et al. 2012), or by communities and individuals "coming into the[ir] foodshed" (Kloppenburg et al. 1996). Such calls to bridge rifts between place, nature, agriculture, and health; to eliminate "distancing" between food system actors; and to advance more holistic, more complete, and more connected models for food systems (Hinrichs 2003) reveal that the conceptual links between good husbandry and good health found in century-old homesteading manuals were lost somewhere along the way. An important and potentially powerful concept that could serve to reveal agriculture–health linkages in a contemporary context is the sustainable diet (SD). Pulling from the nutritional, agricultural, and social sciences, and from analysis of representative historical debate and methodological trends, this chapter's three parts explore the evolution of the SD concept, some of its contested definitions, its influence, and its potential significance. The first part considers the origins of the SD discourse, reflecting upon earlier controversies that emerged in attempts to define and standardize concepts of "soil quality" and "certified organic."The second part summarizes the emergence of Life Cycle Assessment (LCA) as one popular method for measuring sustainability in agri-food systems, and the creation and application of the Healthy Eating Index (HEI) for measuring human diet quality. The third part analyzes the use of quantitative indicator schemes for assessing SDs, discussing some of the systemic issues related to both the philosophical and methodological underpinnings of measurement, with an emphasis on LCA and the HEI. We conclude that while the SD concept offers a particularly valuable and potentially transgressive framing to think about food systems, the growing efforts to standardize its definition, especially through reliance upon LCA and HEI metrics alone, may serve to erode these qualities.

Evolving Definitions of the Sustainable Diet

Origins of the "Sustainable Diet" Concept

There are long-standing historical examples of writers who drew connections between soil health and human health; however, the first explicit definition of these links in a form that is recognizably consistent with today's writing on SDs comes from Ellen Swallow Richards in the late nineteenth century. Richards's texts and curricular materials for the study of "Human Ecology" at the Massachusetts Institute of Technology note that the conservation and care of soil, water, air, and mineral nutrients in agricultural systems are essential for human nutrition and well-being (Richards and Woodman 1900). After Richards's time, however, such interdisciplinary connections were largely absent from academic publications in the agricultural or nutritional sciences until the mid-1980s, when they were reintroduced by nutritional scientists Joan Gussow and Kate Clancy. Their 1986 paper, "Dietary Guidelines for Sustainability" (Gussow and Clancy 1986), marked the origin of the SD in its contemporary context. The term was a reference to "sustainable agriculture," already the focus of considerable dialogue and debate by 1986. By combining a term from the agricultural sciences and a term from the human nutrition sciences, SD implicitly identified the need to connect two networks and schools of thought that had been the domain of separate and specialized disciplines for several decades. Gussow and Clancy described sustainability in agricultural systems as "not wasteful of such finite resources as top soil, water, and fossil energy" and, in defining nutrition, referred to Contento's goals, namely, to sustain "healthy and productive citizens" (Gussow and Clancy 1986: 1). There were no institutionalized definitions or any consistently used metrics for either "sustainability" or "health" when Gussow and Clancy first proposed this linkage.

Three years later, Gussow and Clancy's concept was developed into a proposed place-specific SD based upon regional food availability for Montana (Herrin and Gussow 1989). The rationale for linking local marketing and agricultural sustainability drew upon arguments advanced by the work of various bioregionalist scholars (Sale 1991). Herrin and Gussow proposed eight menus, two for each season, which met or exceeded the U.S. Department of Agriculture's (USDA) dietary guidelines using foods that could be grown in the state. With no supporting economic or ecological impact analysis for these menus, the authors cautioned that an all-local diet such as they suggested might not meet short-term criteria for affordability or agricultural sustainability. The thrust of these first published menus labelled "sustainable diets," however, was that "local" should be the foremost criterion that would contribute to agricultural sustainability. Before "food miles" had entered the lexicon, Herrin and Gussow's menus contended that a diet based on the seasonal output of nearby farms would promote more sustainable agricultural practices than menus sourced with distant ingredients.

Gussow later investigated the "Mediterranean diet" from a sustainability perspective in a special issue of the *American Journal of Clinical Nutrition* dedicated to the study of this particular dietary pattern (Gussow 1995). The Mediterranean diet remains the topic of considerable investigation today, given its repeated positive correlations to health outcomes in many different studies (Sofi et al. 2008). For Gussow's assessment, again, local stands as the chief sustainability criterion. For example, the article praises the nutritional benefits of a plant-centred diet—such as the pattern described in Crete in the early 1960s—but cautions against replicating such a diet in other areas of the world, as the long-distance transport of crops specific to the Mediterranean would constitute a sustainability compromise (Gussow 1995). In framing the urgency of adopting a more sustainable diet, Gussow portrays the mid-1990s as a time of reckoning. The article generally heeds evidence put forward in a 1993 Worldwatch report, concluding that most nations, and the human species as a whole, had exceeded the earth's carrying capacity (Brown and Starke 1993), with catastrophic population collapse forestalled only by the short-term obscuring effects of cheap oil. The case of long-distance food transportation offered a visible and compelling example of oil dependence in food systems, and it resonated with self-sufficiency and energy conservation ideals associated with both the political left (e.g., bioregionalism, permaculture, and local economic trading systems) and the political right (e.g., neo-agrarian populism and survivalism). While ideals of local self-sufficiency were, and remain, subject to criticism as being analytically and politically misconceived (Whatmore 2009), the concept of the local (as in geographically proximate, distinct from origin designation–focused locality) remains rhetorically robust in alternative food networks and continues to resonate in discussions of agri-food system sustainability and SDs today. The local, however, has only relatively recently ascended into the pantheon of sustainable agriculture criteria, taking its place alongside a range of indicators underwritten by ideals of purity, authenticity, and naturalness. Some of the controversies that emerged in the 1990s regarding two concepts of potential importance to sustainable agriculture in general—"soil quality" and "organic"—provide illustrative precedents that help to contextualize debates in current SD discourse and are discussed below.

Codifying Sustainable Agriculture: "Soil Quality" and "Organic"

Emerging mostly from nutritional sciences journals, early discussion of SDs did not fully engage with the dialogue that was unfolding in the academic literature of the agricultural sciences. Sustainable agriculture, while positioned by early SD proponents as an understood and definable prerequisite for an SD, was politically and academically contested, and its definition was far from finding consensus in the 1980s. Emerging from a broad swathe of socio-political value frames, different proponents for sustainable agriculture advanced different sets of new guiding principles, indicator-driven assessment methods, terminology, and best management practice schemes. Two terms of particular interest to this analysis, "soil quality" and "organic," were both the subject of considerable debate in the 1980s and the 1990s. These debates led to distinctly different outcomes, and it is useful for us to review them before we consider some of the differences that underpin the framing of SDs today.

Soil "health" has been central to many definitions of sustainable agriculture, and, by extension, a sustainable diet (Burlingame and Dernini 2012).

This begs the question of how we assess soil health, and as a proposed way to make this assessment, the "soil quality" (SQ) concept gained several high-profile adherents and critics in the mid-1990s (Sojka, Upchurch, and Borlaug 2003). A committee of the Soil Science Society of America (SSSA) advanced the concept of SQ in the early 1990s, aiming to reconcile the diversity of opinions on what constituted healthy soil. The committee defined SQ in its simplest terms as "the capacity [of soil] to function" (Karlen et al. 1997). The challenge of this definition lay in the inherent heterogeneous multi-functionality of soil. Soil could function simultaneously, for example, as a medium to support crop growth, a carbon sink, a water filtration system, a reservoir of biodiversity, or a substrate for building human habitat. Determining which functions to include or exclude, and how multiple functions might be weighted relative to one another, had the potential to be a subjective, contradictory, and generally confusing exercise. As Robert Sojka, a former USDA research scientist and one of the most vocal critics of the application of the soil quality concept, pointed out, soil has no reference standard for purity (Sojka and Upchurch 1999). Water and air both have a purity baseline, and every contaminant provides a measurable deviation from this reference standard. Soil, by contrast, is structurally, relationally, and functionally heterogeneous, simultaneously performing a range of dynamic functions, some of which may give rise to contradictory endpoints. To illustrate the subjectivity of assigning a baseline purity metric to soil, Sojka and Upchurch give the example of soil's important ecological function as a sink or attenuator for pollutants. A highly functioning (or high-quality) soil could, for example, be one that is heavily contaminated with lead—if such contamination prevented the lead from entering waterways and human bodies. At one point, Sojka and Upchurch suggest that the "health" of a soil is a value-laden, function-specific complex, stating, "even in the productivity context, we feel quality (singular) is undefinable for complex systems as diverse as soils...anything that is infinitely defined is, ultimately, undefined and undefinable" (Sojka and Upchurch 1999: 1042). This criticism could readily be interpreted as suggesting that soil quality is inherently subjective and that attempts to measure it might be futile, but such an interpretation would be inconsistent with Sojka and Upchurch's unflagging defence of expert measurement over forms of citizen science, which generally propels their argument. The article's closing captures this sentiment, stating that "soil science has struggled for over 200 yr [sic] to dispel the image of a second-class technology derived from folk wisdom and superstition. We are concerned that the ascendance of soil science...is severely diminished by photos in our journals of farmers smelling a handful of soil, implying that this is the technical legacy of 200 yr" (Sojka and Upchurch 1999: 1050).

The occasionally vitriolic defence of "value-neutrality" in the agricultural sciences (or, more specifically in this case, edaphology) was the focus of considerable debate in the following years, including a lengthy 2003 article on soil quality, co-authored by Nobel Laureate Norman Borlaug, which pleaded with scientists to steer clear of advocacy work. The authors clearly state, "Objectivity is the purpose of science. Subjectivity is the purpose of values and belief systems. Science is evidence-driven. Values and belief systems are faith or conviction–driven" (Sojka, Upchurch, and Borlaug 2003: 43).

A decade after Borlaug's statement, the term "soil quality" remains in widespread and contextually specific use, but it is unregulated at any national or supranational level (in contrast to both air quality and water quality), and any definition or system of standardization suitable as a basis for legislation remains elusive (Bone et al. 2010). Where related legislation exists, it tends to be framed in terms of water contamination or erosion control in designated areas, staying clear of the SQ term. This contrasts markedly with the evolution and outcomes of the "organic" concept. In the mid-1990s, advocates for scaling up organic agriculture were struggling with accusations that their movement was driven by faith and conviction rather than evidence (Youngberg and DeMuth 2013). Organic advocates found that "sustainable" was politically accepted as a less value-laden term than "organic" and were able to gain credibility and open dialogue with the USDA by positioning the latter under the sustainability rubric (Youngberg and DeMuth 2013). The political processes that gave rise to the National Organic Program (NOP), which enabled rapid market growth for organic food products but also reduced their more complex practices and progressive underpinnings to a pass/fail rule set for production inputs, have been well documented by food scholars. A quote that Julie Guthman attributed to a member of the Organic Crop Improvement Association (OCIA) during the development of the NOP is particularly representative of the drive to remove values from and depoliticize the approach to organic: "[We want to] take the religion out of certification and make it just like getting a driver's license" (Guthman 1998, 144). By most accounts, the NOP was successful in taking the "religion" out of organic, to the extent that many popular food writers and scholars in the 2000s noted that the increasingly common large-scale, "industrial" organic farms had become effectively indistinguishable from their conventional counterparts (Pollan 2001; Youngberg and DeMuth 2013; Goodman,

DuPuis, and Goodman 2011). The successful growth of certified organic sales, increasingly under the ownership and distribution of much larger conventional food conglomerates (DuPuis 2000; Jaffee and Howard 2010), was predicated in part on the simplification, standardization, and depoliticization of its earlier philosophy, which emphasized interconnectedness and whole-system transformation (Youngberg and DeMuth 2013).

The cases of SQ and certified organic are used here to illustrate how attempts to standardize a similarly complex and value-laden term such as "sustainable diet" could potentially unfold. Proponents of SQ attempted to keep the inherent complexity and subjectivity of the concept intact, and in doing so failed to propel it into mainstream recognition or enshrine it as legislation (Bone et al. 2010). Certified organic, by contrast, shed many of its founding values in a manner that has been criticized as an exemplary case of the co-option of a social movement and at the same time achieved mainstream recognition, dedicated legislation, and economic success (Jaffee and Howard 2010). The SD, originally advanced in both qualitative and quantitative terms that spanned disciplinary boundaries, may be on the cusp of becoming enshrined as a concept. Will it follow the path of soil quality or certified organic or, alternatively, find some kind of middle ground where values and robust measurement can coexist? We now turn our attention toward two recently developed assessment methods, namely, Life Cycle Assessment (LCA) and the Healthy Eating Index (HEI), which are gaining increased attention in attempts to quantify contemporary SD proposals.

Approaches to Building a Sustainable Diet Metric: Life Cycle Assessment and the Healthy Eating Index

The Rise of Life Cycle Assessment (LCA) in Agri-food Systems

At the same time as organic producer groups worked with consumer, research, and government organizations to create ostensibly value-neutral standards for certifying organic products, an overarching effort was under way, largely pursued by researchers in the agricultural sciences, to determine sustainability indicators for larger food systems that were both practical and measurable and that could be applicable to any management practice. Life Cycle Assessment (LCA) originated as an analytical tool for forecasting the profitability of different complex processes in the U.S. private sector in the late 1960s (Hunt, Franklin, and Hunt 1996). Following the oil price shocks of the 1970s, growing public interest in energy conservation boosted research into environmental LCAs, which assessed non-market environmental impacts of different complex industrial and manufacturing processes. The first LCAs conducted on agri-food system processes emerged in the early 2000s, and fifteen years later they have become a core methodological approach for metrics-driven sustainability assessment in agri-food systems (Andersson, Ohlsson, and Olsson 1994; Garnett 2013a; Soussana 2014). A comparable whole-system, multi-indicator assessment process in nutrition has been more elusive. The Healthy Eating Index (HEI) has recently emerged—alongside a number of approaches to measure the nutritional quality of a complete dietary pattern—as the preferred "diet" counterpart to the LCA for "sustainable" in measuring an SD (Heller, Keoleian, and Willett 2013; McCullough and Willett 2006). In this section, we briefly outline the origins and growth in the use of LCA and the HEI in their respective subsystems as well as the more recent attempts to link the two as ways to quantifiably assess sustainable and healthy diets.

Following a multi-stakeholder workshop at the University of Michigan in 1999, Martin Heller and Greg Keolian produced the comprehensive report, "Life Cycle–Based Sustainability Indicators for Assessment of the U.S. Food System" (Heller and Keoleian 2000). The report recommended fifty-seven measurable sustainability indicators, spanning five different stages of the food system (input origin, agricultural production, processing and distribution, preparation and consumption, and end of life) and three spheres of sustainability consideration (social, economic, and environmental). The 2000 Heller and Keolian report is an early approach toward a food-system LCA, predating the 2006 specification by the International Standards Organization (ISO 14040) that introduced more robust standards. The report stands as an influential precursor to today's interest in calculating "true cost" accounting of agri-food systems across social, economic, and environmental domains (Sustainable Food Trust 2014). LCAs have now been used to assess different environmental impacts for a range of diets in addition to specific agri-food products, and have identified consistent "hot spots" of high environmental impact (Garnett 2011; Eshel and Martin 2009). The first consistent pattern emerging from such agri-food LCAs is that the production phase (on-farm activity) is found on aggregate to be responsible for equal or greater environmental impacts than all other phases of the food system combined, including post-farm activities such as transportation, processing, and packaging. Second, meat and dairy are consistently identified as the foods with the highest environmental impacts in all categories (Garnett 2011; Garnett 2013b; Eshel et al. 2014; Bajželj et al. 2014; Tilman and Clark 2014). LCAs have been used to assess the relative benefits of specific agricultural practices (e.g., certified organic, conventional, reduced tillage, grass-finished beef, and grain-finished beef), but their highly variable results have provided no consistent endorsement for a particular system on environmental grounds (Heller, Keoleian, and Willett 2013; Lang and Barling 2013; Sustainable Development Commission 2009; Tuomisto et al. 2012).

The rise and acceptance of LCA in food systems has also generated a number of "debunking" cases, portrayed in the media as overturning an environmental folklore that naively assumed the superiority of local and organic foods (Schnell 2013). A report from Saunders, Barber, and Taylor (2006), for example, used LCA to demonstrate that "local" lamb, produced and consumed in the U.K. generated more life-cycle greenhouse gases than "global" lamb, produced in New Zealand and consumed in the United Kingdom. Weber and Matthews (2008) used LCA to assess complete dietary patterns in the United States, and found that the most publicly recognizable metric for local food—"food miles," the distance travelled from farm gate to retail—contributed only 4 percent of the life-cycle greenhouse gas (GHG) emissions to U.S. diets. The authors suggested that even a minor reduction in the consumption of meat in the United States would lead to a much more significant reduction of GHG emissions than any decisions to source food locally (3513). Their paper was released at a time when local food was enjoying considerable positive public and media attention, and it remains the most-cited scholarly article dealing with the "food miles" topic. Organic agriculture received a similar, but somewhat more ambiguous treatment in a 2012 meta-analysis of LCA studies that compared the environmental impact of similar conventional and organic farms (Tuomisto et al. 2012). The authors argued that neither conventional nor organic farms could be generalized as environmentally superior or inferior and that, to advance toward a more sustainable agriculture in the future, farmers might selectively employ both conventional and organic techniques in a contextually specific mix. In a range of studies, LCA has generally cast the agri-food ideals of alternative food networks (local, seasonal, organic, small-scale, family-farmed, and pesticide-free) as being of relatively minor importance in the assessment of environmental impact (Soussana 2014; Van Kernebeek et al. 2014; Schmidt Rivera, Espinoza Orias, and Azapagic 2014). LCAs have tended to support the tenets of high-yield "sustainable intensification," a new, evolving, and contested concept, whose proponents advocate for "freezing the footprint" of agriculture. Contrasted with the "sharing" approach of multi-functional agriculture, which considers the multiple social and ecological benefits that can emerge from low-yielding extensive systems, sustainable intensification embodies the "sparing" approach: increasing yields with all available technologies, so that no new land is converted to agriculture (Godfray and Garnett 2014). Ultimately, assessment of the sustainability of a diet using agri-food system LCA has little to say about the healthfulness of the diet. In order to assess whether a diet is both ecologically sustainable and healthy, agri-food LCA requires a nutritional counterpart.

The Rise of the Healthy Eating Index (HEI)

In parallel with agricultural scientists' efforts to find measurable indicators of sustainability in agricultural systems, food and nutrition scientists have also worked to find readily quantifiable measures for dietary quality (Guenther et al. 2013). An important metric in the current discussion of SDs (particularly in North America) is the Healthy Eating Index (HEI), which was first proposed in a 1995 paper by Eileen Kennedy (Kennedy et al. 1995). The initial HEI formulation drew from earlier work on dietary quality indices, which in turn were derived from federally published diet guidelines and Recommended Dietary Allowances (RDAs) for specific nutrients and vitamins. The application of the HEI provided a unitless index that could be standardized, assessed, and compared among different populations and dietary patterns, and over time (Guenther et al. 2014). While nutritionists have proposed a number of alternative metrics, including some that put greater weight on dietary diversity (Drescher, Thiele, and Mensink 2007), the HEI's relative simplicity and ease of measurement have made it the indicator of choice for studies attempting to model dietary patterns that would simultaneously maximize health benefits and minimize environmental impacts—that is, optimize an SD. While the HEI does not have universal acceptance in nutritional sciences, it is often used in the SD models as a proposed effective counterpart to LCA.

One of the challenges facing the accurate measurement of dietary quality is that foods and nutrients are not eaten in isolation, and the desired health outcomes will be different for each individual. The quality of a diet, like soil quality, is greater than the sum of its parts (Slattery 2008). Despite these acknowledged challenges, the HEI has been taken up by a number of scholars outside of the nutritional sciences and has been used to assess the effects of different food policy interventions, from school lunch programs to food stamps to welfare reforms (Beatty, Lin, and Smith 2014). Like the LCA, the HEI simplifies a complex system, aggregating the measurement of a limited set of criteria into a homogenized abstraction that will not necessarily capture a holistic concept such as "health" particularly well. In a similar fashion to LCAs, the HEI has also been used for "debunking" purposes, raising contradictory evidence against the popular accounts of declining dietary quality. Khoury and co-authors assessed changes in global dietary diversity over the past fifty years and concluded that, while globally available crop diversity had declined, dietary diversity at nearly every national level had increased (Khoury et al. 2014). In the United States, Beatty, Lin, and Smith used the HEI to evaluate dietary quality changes from 1989 to 2008, determining that dietary quality had improved across all income categor-ies, largely due to improvements in the formulations of pre-prepared meals (Beatty, Lin, and Smith 2014). The paper's findings of widespread dietary improvement run contrary to the narratives of dietary deterioration that frame many appeals to adopt more SDs. Despite these contradictions, the continued development and increasing sophistication of both the HEI and LCAs has made the nexus of these two methods—at least in North Amer-ican studies—the de facto assessment tool to determine what constitutes an SD. A meta-analysis conducted in 2013 showed that for university-based research, the LCA-HEI nexus was increasingly the methodology of choice for assessing different SD models (Heller, Keoleian, and Willett 2013), a trend that is also visibly reflected in the keyword query analysis depicted in Figure 9.1. In what ways might the choice of the method—particularly the

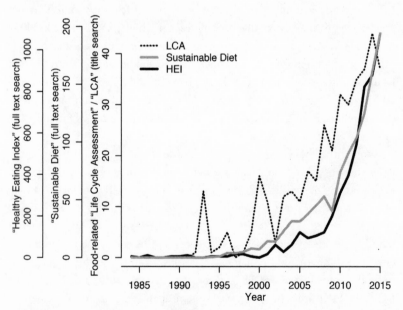

Figure 9.1. Google Scholar results over time for occurrence of "Sustain-able Diet" (grey line), "Healthy Eating Index" (black line), and Life Cycle Assessment (LCA) in agri-food contexts (dashed line).

LCA-HEI nexus—predetermine the kind of diet we deem to be sustainable? The final section of the paper reviews some of the challenges inherent in restricting our definition of SDs to indices such as these.

Sustainable Diets and Challenges of Measurement

Following the food price spikes of 2008, interest in defining, advocating for, and adopting SDs moved beyond the academic literature and into the realm of NGO, private sector, and government interest. The World Wildlife Federation's LiveWell for LIFE campaign, the Culinary Institute of America's Menus of Change initiative, the Walmart-initiated Sustainability Consortium, and revised government nutrition guidelines in the Netherlands, Sweden, and Denmark have all begun to advance different interpretations of SDs in the past five years (Lang and Barling 2013; Clay 2010; Arizona State University and University of Arkansas 2012). A consistent value held common by the majority of proponents from each of these sectors is that definitions of "healthy" and "sustainable" should be standardized, measurable, and directly comparable with one another. The challenge of quantitative comparison of "health" and "sustainability" is that both multi-dimensional terms must be aggregated for comparison, and some of the elements of the terms are incommensurable (Bestwick et al. 2013). In its more general form, the problem of comparing fundamentally incomparable values with one another has been a perennial challenge in efforts to measure social good. An example of this from welfare economics is Amartya Sen's (2004) discussion of the difference between fasting and starving, which could be described as identical and thus comparable biophysical phenomena but which are clearly not equal states of being (see also Nussbaum 2003). In similar discontinuity, the production of a calorie that induces obesity would be treated in the same way by an LCA as a calorie that lifts one from starvation. A quantity of reactive nitrogen that causes eutrophication in a stream might be weighed against a quantity of nitrous oxide released to the atmosphere that contributes to global warming. The selection and aggregation of different elements that make up an index or even a dashboard (whether for health or environmental purposes) require a high level of subjective judgment, and there is ample room for implicit value expression in the process. While quantitative assessment can generate important insights into what creates health or sustainability, there is also danger inherent in such assessments, in that the concepts themselves may come to be defined by their method of measurement, enshrined as unidimensional entities. The following section identifies some of the challenges inherent in attempting to quantify an SD and discusses how the reliance on a single disciplinary viewpoint could undervalue or neglect a wide range of potentially valuable or sustainable farm production practices and dietary patterns.

There are a number of methods, ranging from simple sensitivity analyses to more sophisticated statistical tools, used to test the robustness of parameters, models, and choices embedded in LCAs. Relatively simple sensitivity tests can be employed to identify significant assumptions in agri-food LCAs, especially related to the chosen parameters (e.g., a range of possible values for soil-based GHG emissions), the chosen functional unit (e.g., testing a per-calorie impact versus a per-hectare impact), different system boundaries (e.g., including or not including co-products such as veal calves in a dairy system), or, perhaps most importantly, the weighting of different components in an aggregate index (e.g., the relative risks of eutrophication versus global warming potential). To date, there have been remarkably few sensitivity or uncertainty analyses comparing different complete-diet health and environment indices. A small number of papers presented to the LCA food conferences in 2012 and 2014 have begun to employ this type of analysis and have shown modelled GHG emissions (a common component of agri-food LCAs) to be highly sensitive to both functional unit and parameter choice as well as epistemic uncertainties (Zehetmeier et al. 2014; Van Kernebeek et al. 2014; Kendall and Brodt 2014). Kendall and Brodt's (2014) analysis, for example, showed that the choice of two different functional units (one based on weight and another based on a nutritional score) for the same quantity of rice led to life cycle GHG emissions that had an apparent sevenfold difference. It could be very useful to consider this kind of sensitivity analysis prior to developing recommendations for the adoption of a particular diet type. In the broader field of sustainable development, where similar indices have been used for decades to develop various country rankings, several studies suggest that biases in the inclusion, exclusion, and weighting of different elements of an index make a very significant difference to the outcome of the research (Høyland, Moene, and Willumsen 2012; Morse and Bell 2011). Scholars of sustainable development have written extensively about the problems of "indicatorism" (Whitehouse 2005: 37) and the rise of the "audit culture" (Campbell 2009; Goodman, DuPuis, and Goodman 2011). Statistical comparisons between sustainability indicators suggest that their application may be not only externally problematic but also potentially internally incoherent as well. Jeffrey Wilson's 2007 correlation study examined six of the most popular sustainable development indices that purported to objectively measure and rank country-level sustainability performance (Wilson, Tyedmers, and Pelot 2007). Some indicators had no statistical relationship to each other, some were positively correlated, and some were actually strongly and significantly negatively correlated. The significant negative correlation between, for example, the Ecological Footprint (EF) of nations and the Human Development Index (HDI) of nations (often called the environmentalist's paradox [Raudsepp-Hearne et al. 2010]) suggests that using indices may be less an objective assessment of the "sustainable development" progress of a country, and more a quasi-quantitative statement of normative values (Wilson, Tyedmers, and Pelot 2007). Böhringer's survey of eleven of the leading sustainable development indices concluded that they all contained innate mathematical aggregation errors that rendered them nearly meaningless (Böhringer and Jochem 2007). With respect to concrete policy advice, Böhringer suggested that indexing and ranking was at best "useless," and at worst, "dangerously misleading." Proponents of these indices, conversely, maintain that their application would eliminate the distortions imposed by narrowly conceived economic indicators, such as GDP, and help to "redefine" progress along more holistic lines (Kubiszewski et al. 2013; Bagstad, Berik, and Brown Gaddis 2014). This sentiment is expressed in the specific case of sustainable agriculture and sustainable dietary patterns, particularly in the hope that a rigorous investigation of the full life cycle of production and full benefits of consumption will produce a "true" cost of food, free from marketplace distortions. Experiences from the fields of ecological economics and development studies, however, caution that such measurement approaches are most useful when they are reflexive and continually evolve, and when they are used in concert with other analytical approaches (Neumayer 2000; Goodman, DuPuis, and Goodman 2011).

Boundary and Functional Unit Problems

From both a philosophical and mathematical perspective, the challenge of trying to weight and rank qualitatively incommensurable values (or, more specifically, their chosen indicators, either in absolute or relative terms) with one another is a persistent problem neither LCA nor the HEI solves. The necessary processes of setting a system boundary delineating and classifying discrete elements and their relationships (often involving a choice between different models with different parameters), choosing a functional unit, making the final selection, and weighting and aggregating the impact categories all have significant impacts on the policy recommendations that arise from these methods. Importantly, these processes determine which information is admissible or inadmissible (Sen 1977) and help to explain why there is so much disagreement between the outcomes of different sustainability metrics. Even before grappling with the process of boundary definition or aggregation, an LCA must choose a functional unit. The repercussions of this fundamental choice can be illustrated by the example of the long-distance strawberry that appeared in Gussow's early writings on the kind of environmental harm that an SD would avoid. Gussow reported in her seminal 1986 paper on SDs, "The calculated cost of flying one five-calorie strawberry from California to New York is 435 calories." The origin of this number was David and Marcia Pimentel's book, *Food, Energy, and Society*, which did not specifically examine the changing dynamics of strawberry transport but included sample parameters for caloric expenditures involved in air freight, estimated from figures published in a Kansas Cooperative Extension Service leaflet (Pimentel and Pimentel 2007; Thor, Kirkendal, and Kansas Cooperative Extension Service leaflet 1982). The 5:435 statistic, which continues to be cited today (Pollan 2001), implicitly chooses straw-berry calories as a basic functional unit for analysis, and this choice has significant implications. Like all foods, strawberries provide many benefits (perhaps most notably, pleasure and vitamin C) and incur many costs (per-haps most notably, the health impacts on farm workers from exposure to methyl bromide). The need for calories, however, is not a significant factor influencing consumer demand for strawberries, bringing into question the relevance of choosing strawberry calories as a functional unit of value. If food calories are a questionable representation of the benefit of a strawberry, then fuel calories burned in their transportation (which are largely under-taken by truck in North America, at a caloric ratio of approximately 1:10 for a cross-country trip [Girgenti et al. 2014]) are a similarly questionable representation of their cost. The 5:435 caloric ratio for the strawberry air freight provides a credible (quantified, precise, expert-derived) signifier for "squandering resources," or evidence of a drawing down of natural capital, but upon closer investigation predicts nothing about the inherent sustain-ability of strawberry production, distribution, or consumption, and even less about the sustainability of the food system overall.

Building (and Measuring) Sustainable Food Systems: A Wicked Problem

The problem of a healthy food system—one that might theoretically emerge from a well-chosen SD—has been presented as a "wicked problem" (Hamm 2009, 242). In contrast to a tame problem, which is clear and solvable, a wicked problem is not clearly defined and has no optimum endpoint. This does not mean that attempts to find solutions are pointless; instead, it means that there will be no single solution that solves the problem in its entirety but rather multiple, dynamic, and partial solutions that provide partial relief of the problem(s). Viewed through this lens, it is apparent that a single SD is a contradiction in terms and that SDs will necessarily be diverse not only within their internal composition but also in relation to each other.

According to Morse and Bell, reductionist indicators are insufficient to describe, predict, or solve "wicked" problems with no endpoint (Morse and Bell 2011). Fluid "conversationalist" indicators can instead be reflexively applied to the problem, evolving as different knowledge is produced or considered and values and priorities change. The attempt to measure the sustainability of diets using limited sets of indicators may foreclose opportunities for other desirable trajectories and predetermine a single path forward. Gerrymandering system boundaries, directly comparing incommensurable values, choosing functional units without context, and neglecting opportunity costs are all ways that aggregate metrics, particularly LCAs and the HEI, and may selectively bias the assessment of SDs. This does not imply that these methods have no use; rather, it means that usefulness emerges only when values are explicitly acknowledged and addressed and are open for debate. Unfortunately, composite metrics are often portrayed as objective, value-free representation of fact (Freidberg 2014). Certainly, the apparent authoritative sophistication of the LCA and the HEI presents a compelling picture of the SD that adheres to Norman Borlaug's idealized, evidence-driven, and value-free science discussed in the first section of the paper. However, the metrics being used to assess SDs today have shown indifference to many of the qualities and signifiers that have driven "the quality turn" in food—localness and locality, taste and culture, organic, fair trade, food justice, and others (Garnett 2013a; Freidberg 2013, 2014). As happened in the scaling up of "certified organic," it is easy to imagine that the term "SD" may lose some of the values that were foundational to its early conceptions, such as reconnection between the health of the soil, plants, animals, people, and communities. Regardless of their accuracy or precision, the simplifying necessity of such metrics-based approaches creates a systemic tendency to marginalize the small, diverse, and difficult-to-measure elements of the food system.

Conclusion

Over the last five years, three decades after it was first articulated in the academic literature, the SD concept has gained widespread attention from academics, non-governmental organizations, government organizations, and the private sector. As the concept has moved toward the mainstream, it has also markedly departed from the vision of deeply interconnected, small, diversified, local food systems that were described in Gussow's earliest writing on the topic. The contemporary view of an SD that is expertly and comprehensively measured and optimized to maximize health benefits and minimize environmental costs may, in fact, tend to favour a highly globalized and economically consolidated system, achieving economies of scale and comparative advantage in not only the production of verifiably low-environmental impact and healthy food but also the production of reliable metrics. While the move to create standardized and robust metrics to evaluate SDs has revealed some interesting insights, including the addition of important perspective to the relative environmental impacts of "food miles," the pursuit of value-free indicators may ultimately obscure as much as it reveals. There are numerous methodological uncertainties and subjectivities—which can rapidly translate into value biases—inherent in this quantification turn. Relevant recent precedents can be found for this transition pattern, perhaps the most significant of which was the growth, standardization, and depoliticization of certified organic in the 1990s. Just as organic agriculture shifted from a more connected holistic framing (akin to that expressed in the homesteading manual that opened this chapter) toward a "less religious" empirical frame (which has inadvertently favoured large, distant, and highly specialized "industrial" organic farms), so too may the move to quantify the SD more broadly. By comparison, the contextually specific SQ concept offers a cautionary example of another kind. If the SD fails to find some kind of common basis for generalized comparison and easy communication, it could also fail to scale as either a concept or a practice.

Ultimately, the impossibility of measuring *everything* in a complex system dictates that measurement must always exclude *something*, making the acts of measurement value-laden choices in and of themselves. If these values are obscured through the seemingly neutral façade of numbers, the ability to see, and thus debate, these assumptions may be lost. How can we best ensure that immeasurable things such as connection to place, diversity, culture, and justice remain part of the debate about the future of SDs? Clearly, there is much that can be revealed through new, information-rich food-chain transparency efforts, and citizens are increasingly looking for this kind of information-rich food. However, we must continue questioning whether these numbers, and the values that underlie them, are actually going to lead us toward some version of "the good life." Among the most promising implications of the original SD concept was its transgressive nature, creating both an invitation and an imperative to bring cross-disciplinary perspectives to bear upon a wicked problem that could not be tackled by the approach of any single discipline. Today, the potential perils and pitfalls of quantification efforts could be openly acknowledged in their framing by again bringing different disciplinary perspectives to the conversation. Most importantly, as efforts continue to definitively outline what constitutes a SD, these processes must be understood as linked to underlying values, and these values need be part of the conversation about the future of the SD.

References

Andersson, Karin, Thomas Ohlsson, and Pär Olsson. 1994. "Life Cycle Assessment (LCA) of Food Products and Production Systems." *Trends in Food Science & Technology* 5 (5): 134–8. http://dx.doi.org/10.1016/0924-2244(94)90118-X.

Arizona State University and University of Arkansas. 2012. "The Sustainability Consortium." https://www.sustainabilityconsortium.org/.

Bagstad, Kenneth J., Günseli Berik, and Erica J. Brown Gaddis. 2014. "Methodological Developments in US State-Level Genuine Progress Indicators: Toward GPI 2.0." *Ecological Indicators* 45 (October): 474–85. http://dx.doi.org/10.1016/j.ecolind.2014.05.005.

Bajželj, Bojana, Keith S. Richards, Julian M. Allwood, Pete Smith, John S. Dennis, Elizabeth Curmi, and Christopher A. Gilligan. 2014. "Importance of Food-Demand Management for Climate Mitigation." *Nature Climate Change* 4 (10): 924–9. http://dx.doi.org/10.1038/nclimate2353.

Barling, David, Tim Lang, and Martin Caraher. 2002. "Joined-up Food Policy? The Trials of Governance, Public Policy and the Food System." *Social Policy and Administration* 36 (6): 556–74. http://dx.doi.org/10.1111/1467-9515.t01-1-00304.

Beatty, Timothy K.M., Biing-Hwan Lin, and Travis A. Smith. 2014. "Is Diet Quality Improving? Distributional Changes in the United States, 1989–2008." *American Journal of Agricultural Economics* 96 (3): 769–89. http://dx.doi.org/10.1093/ajae/aat104.

Bestwick, C.S., F.C.G. Douglas, J.L. Allan, J.I. Macdiarmid, A. Ludbrook, and S. Carlisle. 2013. "A Perspective on the Strategic Approach to the Complexity and Challenges of Behaviour Change in Relation to Dietary Health." *Nutrition Bulletin* 38 (1): 50–6. http://dx.doi.org/10.1111/nbu.12007.

Böhringer, Christoph, and Patrick E.P. Jochem. 2007. "Measuring the Immeasurable—A Survey of Sustainability Indices." *Ecological Economics* 63 (1): 1–8. http://dx.doi.org/10.1016/j.ecolecon.2007.03.008.

Bone, James, Martin Head, Declan Barraclough, Michael Archer, Catherine Scheib, Dee Flight, and Nikolaos Voulvoulis. 2010. "Soil Quality Assessment under Emerging Regulatory Requirements." *Environment International* 36 (6): 609–22. http://dx.doi.org/10.1016/j.envint.2010.04.010. Medline:20483160.

Brown, Lester Russell, and Linda Starke. 1993. *State of the World 1993: A Worldwatch Institute Report on Progress toward a Sustainable Society*. Cambridge: Cambridge University Press.

Burlingame, Barbara A., and Sandro Dernini, eds. 2012. *Sustainable Diets and Biodiversity: Directions and Solutions for Policy, Research and Action*. Rome: Food and Agriculture Organization (U.N.).

Campbell, Hugh. 2009. "Breaking New Ground in Food Regime Theory: Corporate Environmentalism, Ecological Feedbacks and the 'Food from Somewhere' Regime?" *Agriculture and Human Values* 26 (4): 309–19. http://dx.doi.org/10.1007/s10460-009-9215-8.

Clay, Jason. 2010. *How Big Brands Can Help Save Biodiversity.* Videoclip of TED Talk. http://www.ted.com/talks/jason_clay_how_big_brands_can_save_biodiversity?language=en.

Drescher, Larissa S., Silke Thiele, and Gert B. M. Mensink. 2007. "A New Index to Measure Healthy Food Diversity Better Reflects a Healthy Diet than Traditional Measures." *Journal of Nutrition* 137 (3): 647–51. Medline:17311954.

DuPuis, E. Melanie. 2000. "Not in My Body: BGH and the Rise of Organic Milk." *Agriculture and Human Values* 17 (3): 285–95. http://dx.doi.org/10.1023/A:1007604704026.

Eshel, Gidon, and Pamela A. Martin. 2009. "Geophysics and Nutritional Science: Toward a Novel, Unified Paradigm." *American Journal of Clinical Nutrition* 89 (5): 1710S–6S. http://dx.doi.org/10.3945/ajcn.2009.26736BB. Medline: 19357219.

Eshel, Gidon, Alon Shepon, Tamar Makov, and Ron Milo. 2014. "Land, Irrigation Water, Greenhouse Gas, and Reactive Nitrogen Burdens of Meat, Eggs, and Dairy Production in the United States." *Proceedings of the National Academy of Sciences of the United States of America* 111 (33): 11996–2001. http://dx.doi.org/10.1073/pnas.1402183111. Medline:25049416.

Freidberg, Susanne. 2013. "Calculating Sustainability in Supply Chain Capitalism." *Economy and Society* 42 (4): 571–96. http://dx.doi.org/10.1080/03085147.2012.760349.

Freidberg, Susanne. 2014. "Footprint Technopolitics." *Geoforum* 55:178–89. http://dx.doi.org/10.1016/j.geoforum.2014.06.009.

Garnett, Tara. 2011. "Where Are the Best Opportunities for Reducing Greenhouse Gas Emissions in the Food System (Including the Food Chain)?" *Food Policy* 36 (January Supplement 1): S23–32. http://dx.doi.org/10.1016/j.foodpol.2010.10.010.

Garnett, Tara. 2013a. "Three Perspectives on Sustainable Food Security: Efficiency, Demand Restraint, Food System Transformation. What Role for LCA?" *Journal of Cleaner Production* 18:10–8. http://dx.doi.org/10.1016/j.jclepro.2013.07.045.

Garnett, Tara. 2013b. "Food Sustainability: Problems, Perspectives and Solutions." *Proceedings of the Nutrition Society* 72 (1): 29–39. http://dx.doi.org/10.1017/S0029665112002947. Medline:23336559.

Girgenti, Vincenzo, Cristiana Peano, Claudio Baudino, and Nadia Tecco. 2014. "From 'Farm to Fork' Strawberry System: Current Realities and Potential Innovative Scenarios from Life Cycle Assessment of Non-renewable Energy Use and Green House Gas Emissions." *Science of the Total Environment* 473–4 (March): 48–53. http://dx.doi.org/10.1016/j.scitotenv.2013.11.133. Medline:24361447.

Godfray, H. Charles J., and Tara Garnett. 2014. "Food Security and Sustainable Intensification." *Philosophical Transactions of the Royal Society of London. Series B, Biological Sciences* 369 (1639): 20120273. http://dx.doi.org/10.1098/rstb.2012.0273. Medline:24535385.

Goodman, David, Melanie E. DuPuis, and Michael K. Goodman. 2011. *Alternative Food Networks: Knowledge, Practice and Politics*. New York: Routledge.

Guenther, Patricia M., Kellie O. Casavale, Jill Reedy, Sharon I. Kirkpatrick, Hazel A.B. Hiza, Kevin J. Kuczynski, Lisa L. Kahle, and Susan M. Krebs-Smith. 2013. "Update of the Healthy Eating Index: HEI-2010." *Journal of the Academy of Nutrition and Dietetics* 113 (4): 569–80. http://dx.doi.org/10.1016/j.jand.2012.12.016. Medline:23415502.

Guenther, Patricia M., Sharon I. Kirkpatrick, Jill Reedy, Susan M. Krebs-Smith, Dennis W. Buckman, Kevin W. Dodd, Kellie O. Casavale, and Raymond J. Carroll. 2014. "The Healthy Eating Index-2010 is a Valid and Reliable Measure of Diet Quality According to the 2010 Dietary Guidelines for Americans." *Journal of Nutrition* 144 (3): 399–407. http://dx.doi.org/10.3945/jn.113.183079. Medline:24453128.

Gussow, Joan D. 1995. "Mediterranean Diets: Are They Environmentally Responsible?" *American Journal of Clinical Nutrition* 61 (6 Supplement): 1383S–9S. Medline:7754992.

Gussow, Joan D., and Katherine L. Clancy. 1986. "Dietary Guidelines for Sustainability." *Journal of Nutrition Education* 18 (1): 1–5. http://dx.doi.org/10.1016/S0022-3182(86)80255-2.

Guthman, Julie. 1998. "Regulating Meaning, Appropriating Nature: The Codification of California Organic Agriculture." *Antipode* 30 (2): 135–54. http://dx.doi.org/10.1111/1467-8330.00071.

Hamm, Michael W. 2009. "Principles for Framing a Healthy Food System." *Journal of Hunger & Environmental Nutrition* 4 (3-4): 241–50. http://dx.doi.org/10.1080/19320240903321219. Medline:23144672.

Heller, Martin C., and Gregory A. Keoleian. 2000. *Life Cycle–Based Sustainability Indicators for Assessment of the US Food System*. Center for Sustainable Systems Report no. CS00-04. Ann Arbor, MI: University of Michigan.

Heller, Martin C., Gregory A. Keoleian, and Walter C. Willett. 2013. "Toward a Life Cycle-Based, Diet-Level Framework for Food Environmental Impact and Nutritional Quality Assessment: A Critical Review." *Critical Reviews in Environmental Science and Technology* 47 (22): 12632–47. http://dx.doi.org/10.1021/es4025113. Medline:24152032.

Herrin, Marcia, and Joan D. Gussow. 1989. "Designing a Sustainable Regional Diet." *Journal of Nutrition Education* 21 (6): 270–5. http://dx.doi.org/10.1016/S0022-3182(89)80146-3.

Hinrichs, Claire C. 2003. "The Practice and Politics of Food System Localization." *Journal of Rural Studies* 19 (1): 33–45. http://dx.doi.org/10.1016/S0743-0167(02)00040-2.

Høyland, Bjørn, Karl Moene, and Fredrik Willumsen. 2012. "The Tyranny of International Index Rankings." *Journal of Development Economics* 97 (1): 1–14. http://dx.doi.org/10.1016/j.jdeveco.2011.01.007.

Hunt, Robert G., William E. Franklin, and R.G. Hunt. 1996. "LCA—How It Came About." *International Journal of Life Cycle Assessment* 1 (1): 4–7. http://dx.doi.org/10.1007/BF02978624.

Jaffee, Daniel, and Philip H. Howard. 2010. "Corporate Cooptation of Organic and Fair Trade Standards." *Agriculture and Human Values* 27 (4): 387–99. http://dx.doi.org/10.1007/s10460-009-9231-8.

Karlen, D.L., M.J. Mausbach, J.W. Doran, R.G. Cline, R.F. Harris, and G.E. Schuman. 1997. "Soil Quality: A Concept, Definition, and Framework for Evaluation (A Guest Editorial)." *Soil Science Society of America Journal* 61 (1): 4–10. http://dx.doi.org/10.2136/sssaj1997.03615995006100010001x.

Kendall, Alissa, and Sonja B. Brodt. 2014. "Comparing Alternative Nutritional Functional Units for Expressing Life Cycle Greenhouse Gas Emissions in Food Production Systems." Paper presented at the 9th International Conference on Life Cycle Assessment in the Agri-Food Sector, 8–10 October 2014, San Francisco CA. http://lcafood2014.org/papers/251.pdf.

Kennedy, Eileen T, James Ohls, Steven Carlson, and Kathryn Fleming. 1995. "The Healthy Eating Index: Design and Applications." *Journal of the American Dietetic Association* 95 (10): 1103–8. http://dx.doi.org/10.1016/S0002-8223(95)00300-2. Medline:7560680.

Khoury, Colin K., Anne D. Bjorkman, Hannes Dempewolf, Julian Ramirez-Villegas, Luigi Guarino, Andy Jarvis, Loren H. Rieseberg, and Paul C. Struik. 2014. "Increasing Homogeneity in Global Food Supplies and the Implications for Food Security." *Proceedings of the National Academy of Sciences of the United States of America* 111 (11): 4001–6. http://dx.doi.org/10.1073/pnas.1313490111. Medline:24591623.

Kloppenburg, Jack, Jr., John Hendrickson, and Garry W. Stevenson. 1996. "Coming in to the Foodshed." *Agriculture and Human Values* 13 (3): 33–42. http://dx.doi.org/10.1007/BF01538225.

Koç, Mustafa, Rod MacRae, Andrea Noack, and Özlem Güçlü Üstündag. 2012. "What Is Food Studies? Characterizing an Emerging Academic Field through the Eyes of Canadian Scholars." In *Critical Perspectives in Food Studies*, edited by M. Koç, J. Sumner, and T. Winson, 4–15. Oxford: Oxford University Press.

Kubiszewski, Ida, Robert Costanza, Carol Franco, Philip Lawn, John Talberth, Tim Jackson, and Camille Aylmer. 2013. "Beyond GDP: Measuring and Achieving Global Genuine Progress." *Ecological Economics* 93 (September): 57–68. http://dx.doi.org/10.1016/j.ecolecon.2013.04.019.

Lang, Tim, and David Barling. 2013. "Nutrition and Sustainability: An Emerging Food Policy Discourse." *Proceedings of the Nutrition Society* 72 (1): 1–12. http://dx.doi.org/10.1017/S002966511200290X. Medline:23217475.

MacRae, Rod. 2011. "A Joined-up Food Policy for Canada." *Journal of Hunger & Environmental Nutrition* 6 (4): 424–57. http://dx.doi.org/10.1080/193202 48.2011.627297.

McCullough, Marjorie L., and Walter C. Willett. 2006. "Evaluating Adherence to Recommended Diets in Adults: The Alternate Healthy Eating Index." *Public Health Nutrition* 9 (1A): 152–7. http://dx.doi.org/10.1079/PHN2005938. Medline:16512963.

Morse, Stephen, and Simon Bell. 2011. "Sustainable Development Indicators: The Tyranny of Methodology Revisited." *Consilience: The Journal of Sustainable Development* 6 (1): 222–39.

Neumayer, Eric. 2000. "On the Methodology of ISEW, GPI and Related Measures: Some Constructive Suggestions and Some Doubt on the 'threshold' Hypothesis." *Ecological Economics* 34 (3): 347–61. http://dx.doi.org/10.1016/S0921-8009(00)00192-0.

Nussbaum, Martha. 2003. "Capabilities as Fundamental Entitlements: Sen and Social Justice." *Feminist Economics* 9 (2–3): 33–59. http://dx.doi.org/10.10 80/1354570022000077926.

Pimentel, David, and Marcia Pimentel. 2007. *Food, Energy, and Society*. 3rd ed. Boca Raton, FL: CRC Press.

Pollan, Michael. 2001. "Behind the Organic-Industrial Complex." *New York Times*, May 13. http://wphna.org/wp-content/uploads/2013/04/01-05-13-Michael-Pollan-Behind-the-Organic-Industrial-Complex-NYTM.pdf.

Raudsepp-Hearne, Ciara, Garry D. Peterson, Maria Tengö, Elena M. Bennett, Tim Holland, Karina Benessaiah, Graham K. MacDonald, and Laura Pfeifer. 2010. "Untangling the Environmentalist's Paradox: Why Is Human Well-Being Increasing as Ecosystem Services Degrade?" *Bioscience* 60 (8): 576–89. http://dx.doi.org/10.1525/bio.2010.60.8.4.

Richards, Ellen Henrietta, and Alpheus Grant Woodman. 1900. *Air, Water and Food from a Sanitary Standpoint*. London: John Wiley and Sons.

Sale, Kirkpatrick. 1991. *Dwellers in the Land: The Bioregional Vision*. Philadelphia, PA: New Society Publishers.

Saunders, Caroline, Andrew Barber, and Greg Taylor. 2006. *Food Miles–Comparative Energy/emissions Performance of New Zealand's Agriculture Industry*. Lincoln, NZ: Lincoln University, Agribusiness and Economics Research Unit.

Schmidt Rivera, Ximena C., Namy Espinoza Orias, and Adisa Azapagic. 2014. "Life Cycle Environmental Impacts of Convenience Food: Comparison of Ready and Home-Made Meals." *Journal of Cleaner Production* 73 (June): 294–309. http://dx.doi.org/10.1016/j.jclepro.2014.01.008.

Schnell, Steven M. 2013. "Food Miles, Local Eating, and Community Supported Agriculture: Putting Local Food in Its Place." *Agriculture and Human Values* 30 (4): 615–28. http://dx.doi.org/10.1007/s10460-013-9436-8.

Sen, Amartya K. 1977. "On Weights and Measures: Informational Constraints in Social Welfare Analysis." *Econometrica* 45 (7): 1539–72. http://dx.doi.org/10.2307/1913949.

Sen, Amartya K. 2004. "Capabilities, Lists, and Public Reason: Continuing the Conversation." *Feminist Economics* 10 (3): 77–80. http://dx.doi.org/10.1080/135 4570042000315163.

Slattery, Martha L. 2008. "Defining Dietary Consumption: Is the Sum Greater than Its Parts?" *American Journal of Clinical Nutrition* 88 (1): 14–5. Medline:18614718.

Sofi, Francesco, Francesca Cesari, Rosanna Abbate, Gian Franco Gensini, and Alessandro Casini. 2008. "Adherence to Mediterranean Diet and Health Status: Meta-Analysis." *British Medical Journal* 337: a1344. http://dx.doi.org/10.1136/bmj.a1344. Medline:18786971.

Sojka, R.E., and D.R. Upchurch. 1999. "Reservations Regarding the Soil Quality Concept." *Soil Science Society of America Journal* 63 (5): 1039–54. http://dx.doi.org/10.2136/sssaj1999.6351039x.

Sojka, R.E., D.R. Upchurch, and N.E. Borlaug. 2003. "Quality Soil Management or Soil Quality Management : Performance versus Semantics." *Advances in Agronomy* 79: 1–68. http://dx.doi.org/10.1016/S0065-2113(02)79001-9.

Soussana, Jean-François. 2014. "Research Priorities for Sustainable Agri-Food Systems and Life Cycle Assessment." *Journal of Cleaner Production* 73: 19–23. http://dx.doi.org/10.1016/j.jclepro.2014.02.061.

Sustainable Development Commission. 2009. "Setting the Table: Advice to Government on Priority Elements of Sustainable Diets." http://lac-repo-live6.is.ed.ac.uk/handle/10023/2213.

Sustainable Food Trust. 2014. "True Cost." *Sustainable Food Trust*. http://sustain ablefoodtrust.org/projects/true-cost/.

Thor, Carl E., and Eric D. Kirkendal, and the Kansas Cooperative Extension Service, Kansas Energy Extension Service, and Transportation Program. 1982. *Energy Conservation in Agricultural Transportation*. Manhattan, KS: Kansas Cooperative Extension Service.

Tilman, David, and Michael Clark. 2014. "Global Diets Link Environmental Sustainability and Human Health." *Nature* 515 (7528): 518–22. http://dx.doi.org/10.1038/nature13959. Medline:25383533.

Tuomisto, H.L., I.D. Hodge, P. Riordan, and D.W. Macdonald. 2012. "Does Organic Farming Reduce Environmental Impacts?—A Meta-Analysis of European Research." *Journal of Environmental Management* 112 (December): 309–20. http://dx.doi.org/10.1016/j.jenvman.2012.08.018. Medline:22947228.

Van Kernebeek, H. R. J., S. J. Oosting, E. J. M. Feskens, P. J. Gerber, and I. J. M. De Boer. 2014. "The Effect of Nutritional Quality on Comparing Environmental Impacts of Human Diets." *Journal of Cleaner Production* 73: 88–99. http://dx.doi.org/10.1016/j.jclepro.2013.11.028.

Weber, Christopher L., and H.S. Matthews. 2008. "Food-Miles and the Relative Climate Impacts of Food Choices in the United States." *Environmental Science and Technology* 42 (10): 3508–13. http://dx.doi.org/10.1021/es702969f. Medline:18546681.

Whatmore, Sarah. 2009. "Bioregionalism." In *The Dictionary of Human Geography*. John Wiley and Sons.

Whitehouse, Chris. 2005. "The Ants and the Cockroach: A Challenge to the Use of Indicators." In *Why Did the Chicken Cross the Road? And Other Stories on Development Evaluation…*, edited by Sarah Cummings, 35–42. Amsterdam: Royal Tropical Institute (KIT), KIT Publishers.

Wilson, Jeffrey, Peter Tyedmers, and Ronald Pelot. 2007. "Contrasting and Comparing Sustainable Development Indicator Metrics." *Ecological Indicators* 7 (2): 299–314. http://dx.doi.org/10.1016/j.ecolind.2006.02.009.

Youngberg, Garth, and Suzanne P. DeMuth. 2013. "Organic Agriculture in the United States: A 30-Year Retrospective." *Renewable Agriculture and Food Systems* 28 (4): 294–328. http://dx.doi.org/10.1017/S1742170513000173.

Zehetmeier, M., M. Gandorfer, H. Hoffmann, U. K. Müller, I. J. M. de Boer, and A. Heißenhuber. 2014. "The Impact of Uncertainties on Predicted Greenhouse Gas Emissions of Dairy Cow Production Systems." *Journal of Cleaner Production* 73: 116–24. http://dx.doi.org/10.1016/j.jclepro.2013.09.054.

CHAPTER 10

From "Farm to Table" to "Farm to Dump": Emerging Research on Urban Household Food Waste in the Global South

Keith Lee and Tammara Soma

Amidst the reality of global hunger, people waste an estimated 30 to 50 percent of food produced for human consumption (Gustavsson et al. 2011). In Canada, $31 billion worth of food is wasted annually, which translates to 2 percent of Canadian GDP and approximately 40 percent of all food available for consumption (Gooch, Felfel, and Glasbey 2014). Similarly, researchers estimate that UK households throw away one-third of the food they purchase, representing economic losses of approximately $21 billion (Quested et al. 2013). Food waste contributes to climate change: landfilled food waste decomposes and produces methane, a greenhouse gas twenty to twenty-five times more potent than $CO2$ (Lundie and Peters 2005). Food waste also has indirect impacts on food production, which requires large inputs of natural resources such as water and oil (for fertilizers and pesticides), and this has significant impacts on climate change. For example, livestock production is responsible for 18 percent of global greenhouse gas emissions, and the agricultural sector alone is responsible for 70 percent of global freshwater withdrawals (Kummu et al. 2012).

While research on food waste is gaining momentum, the topic is still relatively understudied. Existing research has assessed municipal food waste (Evans-Cowley 2011) and investigated organic waste management options (Cofie et al. 2009), but the study of food waste is not limited to the area of waste management. Rather, this interdisciplinary field crosses the boundaries between food studies and waste studies and addresses topics including, but not limited to, food disposal, food safety labelling, modern consumption in the kitchen, food waste infrastructure, and cultural values relating to food waste. Most recently, scholars have explored the causes of household food waste (Evans 2012). Even so, such research has been concentrated in the Global North, and little is known about household food waste in the Global South.

This chapter begins to address this gap in our knowledge of food waste and continues in the tradition of cross-disciplinary collaboration by investigating and analyzing food waste, especially in the growing cities of the Global South. In this chapter we focus on household (post-consumer) food waste and its causes, and begin by providing an overview of the paradoxes and complexities of food waste and related behaviours. Next, we critique current discourses of food waste in developing countries and highlight the importance of household food waste research in the cities of the Global South, identifying rising urban incomes, dietary change, and the growing popularity of modern grocery retail as key factors. We illustrate our argument with vignettes from research in Indonesia and conclude by proposing future avenues for research in household food waste, which must consider the influence of urbanization.

Research Methods and Data

In this chapter, we draw new insights from prior food waste research in the Global North and empirical material from Tammara Soma's fieldwork in Bogor, Indonesia, which took place between May and August 2014. Bogor is the sixth-largest city in Indonesia and is located approximately sixty kilometres south of Jakarta. Indonesia is the fourth-most populous country in the world, and, like many lower-income countries in the region, it is rapidly urbanizing, has a tropical climate, and has poor waste infrastructure (Meidiana and Gamse 2011). Countries such as Indonesia are undergoing rapid transformation and "mega-urbanization" (Firman 2009), and the population defined as the "New Rich" in industrializing Asia increasingly exhibits Westernized consumption patterns in terms of tastes and excessiveness (Goodman and Robinson 2013). Adhikari, Barrington, and Martinez (2006) project that urban food waste in Indonesia will grow by 49 percent between 2005 and 2025, underscoring the urgency of addressing the urban food waste problem.

Soma's study involved immersed field research with low- (n = 7), middle- (n = 7), and high-income (n = 7) families, which involved following them on shopping trips, accompanying them during meal preparation, and conducting multiple semi-structured interviews. Soma also conducted twelve key informant interviews with food retailers and vendors, local government representatives, and a neighbourhood waste collector.

The Complexities of Food Waste

Global food security is often discussed with reference to increasing food production, but improving food security requires a multi-faceted approach that also includes reducing food waste (Godfray et al. 2010). Increasing food production may improve the quantity of food, but this does not necessarily solve the issue of uneven global food distribution, nor does it guarantee its affordability. Research has established that the current level of food production has the capacity to feed not only the world's present population but up to 10 billion people (Holt-Giménez et al. 2012). The call to increase agricultural yields misses a massive opportunity to focus on reducing food waste.

The European Union Council defines waste as "means any substance or object which the holder discards or intends or is required to discard," but defining food waste is not so simple (2008, 9). First, food waste scholars use different terms for it, depending on where in the supply chain it occurs. Wastage that takes place pre-consumer—after harvest and during transportation, distribution, and processing—is commonly referred to as "food losses" or "spoilage," while the term, "food waste," is usually reserved for food discarded by retailers and households (Parfitt, Barthel, and Macnaughton 2010; Gustavsson et al. 2011). In most cases, the definition of food waste encompasses discarded food that is still fit, or was previously fit, for human consumption. Some scholars also include food fed to animals that was originally produced for humans, while others include over-nutrition, arguing that excess calorie intake can be considered wastage (Parfitt, Barthel, and Macnaughton 2010). However, research conducted at the post-consumer, or household, level does not take for granted that food waste refers only to edible portions. Researchers use "avoidable food waste" to refer to matter that is still or was previously edible, and "unavoidable food waste" to refer to inedible organic matter such as egg shells, bones, and cores (OECD 2013; Koivupuro et al. 2012; WRAP 2008). This distinction reflects the subjective nature of food waste, since that which is deemed inedible and discarded by some households (e.g., broccoli stalks) might be considered edible in other households (Lebersorger and Schneider 2011).

The definition of food waste is further complicated in light of O'Brien's (2012, 196–7) argument that food waste is capitalist surplus, "waste" is an imaginary construct, and "discarded food" in some contexts is still considered to be private property under the law. To clarify, he cites the case of Steven De Geynst, a freegan[1] who was charged with "violent robbery" for taking two bags of muffins from a waste container outside a store in Belgium. Similarly, Evans (2011) points out how an object becomes waste not because of its innate characteristics but because of its entry into the waste stream. Based on his findings from the United Kingdom that surplus food regularly finds its way to the bin, rather than being gifted or composted, Evans (2011) equates food waste with surplus food. Discarded food items are thus not necessarily unwanted or unusable, thereby complicating the definition of food waste.

The ultimate fate of discarded food can also complicate the definition and study of food waste. Whereas Evans (2011) argues that composting saves food from wastage, we argue that while composting and other management methods such as anaerobic digestion might divert food waste from landfills, they do not change the fact that food produced for human consumption has not been eaten. In view of this, it is necessary to distinguish between diverting food waste from landfills (diversion) and preventing it from occurring *in the first place* (prevention). Food waste diversion has value, in that it enables some resource recovery in the form of compost or methane and reduces levels of greenhouse gases produced by decomposing food in landfills (Venkat 2012). However, food waste prevention reduces not only the waste of valuable resources used to produce food but also the environmental impacts of activities supporting waste diversion, such as the collection, transportation, and processing of waste (Cleary 2014). This logic is reflected in the traditional waste management hierarchy, which prioritizes prevention over options such as reuse, recycling, or energy recovery through incineration (Cleary 2014).

In this chapter, we consider food waste to be any *discarded organic matter that was intended for consumption by humans, regardless of its ultimate fate*. In other words, food is wasted when it does not fulfil its original purpose of providing human nourishment, regardless of whether it is composted, anaerobically digested, landfilled, or incinerated. Defining food waste independently of how it is managed highlights the importance of at-source waste reduction and helps avoid misperceptions that food waste is not environmentally problematic as long as it avoids landfill or incineration. Despite its desirability, household food waste prevention is challenging, due to the complex nature of household food waste behaviours and the embeddedness of consumers in the broader food system.

Frameworks for Understanding Food Waste

There have been multiple efforts to understand human behaviour and develop models for behavioural change. To date, the dominant mode of thinking, informing policy, and promoting environmentally sustainable behaviour is oriented around individuals—specifically their attitudes, behaviours, and choices. Shove (2010) refers to this mode of thinking as the ABC model of social change, in which **A**ttitudes and values determine what **B**ehaviours individuals **C**hoose to adopt. The ABC model is premised on rational choice theory (Becker 1978) and the theory of planned behaviour (Ajzen 1991). Broadly speaking, these theories focus on individuals' decision-making processes and suggest that society as a whole can be understood as the aggregate of all individuals' actions. These individualistic models posit that individuals' intentions to perform behaviours are the outcomes of rational thought processes involving their attitudes toward different actions and beliefs about their ability to carry out those actions. At the most basic level, proponents of these models suggest that individuals generate waste because they do not consider waste to be "bad" and, consequently, do not choose to reduce the amount of waste they produce.

One weakness of individualistic models of behaviour is how they account for the well-documented attitude–behaviour (or value–action) gap, which refers to how people's behaviours are rarely consistent with their attitudes or knowledge about issues such as the environment. Researchers point to a range of internal factors (e.g., conflicting motivations, perceived control, responsibilities) and external ones (e.g., institutional, economic, social, cultural) to explain the gap and how it might be overcome (Kollmuss and Agyeman 2002). For example, people may have strong environmental values (attitude) and the intention to not waste food (behavioural intention) but may end up discarding food (action) because their children disliked the food. Shove (2010) argues that accounting for the attitude–behaviour gap using the language of internal and external factors treats the latter inadequately— either as simple barriers to behaviour or as influences on an individual's ability (perceived or actual) to perform a behaviour. In this sense, individualistic behavioural models oversimplify the influence of external factors as diverse as physical infrastructure, culture, social norms, lifestyles, policy, technology, and institutions on behaviours such as wasting food.

There is also the issue of precisely which attitudes, intentions, and behaviours should be the focus of such theories. A straightforward application of an individualistic behavioural model to food waste suggests that we should consider individuals' attitudes to food waste and their intentions not to waste food. However, doing so can be problematic because it is unclear whether these intentions should be connected to overall efforts to reduce food waste or specific waste-reducing actions, e.g., preparing and purchasing the right amount of food and managing inventories properly (Quested et al. 2013). In addition, many different attitudes and external factors may influence individuals' food waste-reducing behaviours. They may, for instance, be a function of not only people's attitudes but also social norms, habits, or other facilitating conditions (Quested et al. 2013). The reason for this is that, whereas individualistic models seek to explain one behaviour, the production of food waste is actually the result of multiple behaviours arising from complex interactions between individual and contextual factors (Quested et al. 2013). Individualistic models of human behaviour, while well-developed, thus remain inadequate for confronting contextual factors that construct, condition, and constrain human behaviour.

As a result, frameworks for understanding food waste are required which can better handle the influence of context and capture the multi-behavioural aspect of food waste. To meet this need, some food waste scholars have turned to practice theory. Practice theory focuses not on individual decision making, but on the practices that make up our everyday lives—broadly recognizable activities or groups of behaviours, such as cooking (Warde 2005). Practices depend not only on how individuals carry them out (performance) but also on the meanings of the practices and the physical objects (materials) and know-how (competence) required to perform the practices (Shove and Pantzar 2005). Though practices persist in society over time, they also evolve with variation in their performance, meanings, materials, and competence (Røpke 2009). Practice theory therefore permits an account of how contextual factors such as socio-cultural norms, infrastructure, or institutions influence behaviour without ruling out individual agency. Practice theory has been adopted by scholars as the basis for studies of environmental behaviour, especially in relation to everyday life. Existing research includes studies of showering (Hand, Shove, and Southerton 2005), energy use (Gram-Hanssen 2010), transportation (Watson 2012), and notably, food waste (Ganglbauer, Fitzpatrick, and Comber 2013; Evans 2012; Watson and Meah 2012). In summary, focussing only on individuals' behaviours cannot adequately explain food waste. A more complex, contextual account is required, and practice theory provides the tools to develop one.

Soma's research in Indonesia provides examples that illustrate how the concepts of "materials," "meanings," and "competence" (Shove and Pantzar

2005) help explain why the same practices can vary with place and time. Soma found that wealthier households in Indonesia often own double-door refrigerators or two standard refrigerators, while low-income households have either a small refrigerator or no refrigerator at all (see Figures 10.1 and 10.2). The refrigerator is an example of a *material* element, which alters

Figure 10.1. A double-door fridge in a high-income household (notice the amount of food stored—the freezer section is separate). Photo by Tammara Soma.

Figure 10.2. A fridge in a low-income household, mainly used to cool drinking water and store a few vegetables. Photo by Tammara Soma.

activities related to food storage by influencing the type and amount of food that each household can purchase. With more refrigerator space, it is possible for households to store more food and forget about items in the back of the fridge, which leads to more food waste. At the same time, households with limited refrigerator space have much less time to consume perishables before they go bad. These factors not only affect the possibilities for food waste generation but also alter how and when households do their grocery shopping in the first place.

The influence of *meaning* on practices can be observed when middle-income households that spend a lot of time commuting long distances place greater value on convenience foods that not only provide sustenance but also help them save precious time. The price premium of such pre-prepared foods might also make these consumers feel more "modern" and allow them to assert their middle-class status. Lastly, *competence* affects what is eaten and what is discarded—lower-income households need to know how to cook cheaper cuts of meat such as chicken innards, while an upper-income household used to purchasing whole free-range chicken might not. Different combinations of competencies, meanings, and materials not only form different practices but also create large variations in how different people perform universal practices such as food provisioning and meal preparation.

Practice theory also helps construct a theoretical framework for understanding food waste by showing how it results from multiple preceding behaviours and contexts related to the purchase and consumption of food, such as grocery shopping and meal preparation. Just as "consumption is not itself a practice but is, rather, a moment in almost every practice" (Warde 2005, 137), we argue that disposal is also a (sometimes less visible) moment in almost every practice. Acquiring items for consumption represents a moment in which *materials* (e.g., food) enter into the service of the *practice* (e.g., eating). As the practice is performed, materials are discarded sooner or later, because they are no longer required or fit to serve their purpose. Put another way, in order for an object to be discarded, it must first be acquired. In the context of perishable foods, there is not much time between their acquisition and when they are discarded as food waste. The circumstances under which they were acquired, as well as managed, therefore play a large role in determining foods' ultimate fate. These circumstances are tied to how individuals carry out food-related practices. As suggested by Evans (2012), "the passage of 'food' into 'waste' occurs as a consequence of households enacting ordinary domestic practices and negotiating the contingencies of everyday life," and "disposal (and wasting) is a necessary moment in the competent enactment of domestic practice" (53). Whether or not food becomes waste may in fact be determined as early as the moment it is purchased (Ganglbauer, Fitzpatrick, and Comber 2013).

Practice theory illustrates how individuals' everyday lives comprise the performance of different practices that inherently have temporal and spatial dimensions—they must be performed in a specific place and a specific time. For example, a practice might require an individual to interact with others (e.g., to be at home during family dinners) or make use of particular physical items (e.g., a stovetop for cooking). Practices are thus interconnected with individuals, places, and material objects (Pred 1981). The practices performed by a single individual are also interconnected, because the performance of one reduces the time available to the individual for the performance of another. A simple example is how spending more time working leaves less time for leisure or cooking. Since individuals cannot be in more than one place at one time, and because time is a finite resource, practices must compete with each other for an individual's time and attention (Røpke 2009). Such interconnectedness reveals a complex system of behaviours and relationships that interact to produce practices and, subsequently, individual behaviour; altering any part of the system therefore leads to changes in individual behaviour.

The insights that practice theory offers into the complexities of food waste–related behaviours have allowed scholars to develop frameworks for understanding the causes of household food waste and their linkage to the broader contexts of everyday life. In particular, research has revealed the importance of behaviours related to the practices of household provisioning and meal preparation. These behaviours include the use of a shopping list, checking inventory, planning meals in advance, buying the appropriate amounts, storing food properly, using leftovers, and understanding use-by and sell-by dates, and these practices have been found to be important in reducing household food waste (Quested et al. 2011; Stefan et al. 2013; Williams et al. 2012; WRAP 2008). However, everyday life's contingencies, such as those originating from social relations and busy schedules, can often undermine these waste-reducing behaviours (Evans 2012). For example, Ganglbauer et al. (2013) explain that busy individuals often do not have time to make lists and show how time scarcity is responsible for "opportunistic" shopping behavior, in which individuals make use of an opportune moment for unplanned grocery shopping but do so without being able to check what they have at home first and therefore end up buying too much. Increased perceptions of time scarcity and related desires for convenience can also contribute to the tendency of households to stock up on food in order to insulate themselves from unexpected events that might disrupt their regular grocery routines—but often at the cost of increased spoilage (Watson and Meah 2012). In short, the social and temporal organization of daily life has important implications for household food waste.

More traditional household food waste studies that do not explicitly employ practice theory retain a focus on the individual by asking *who* is generating food waste. These studies suggest that younger households, smaller households, and households with a female primary shopper generate higher quantities of avoidable food waste per capita (Koivupuro et al. 2012; Wenlock et al. 1980; Williams et al. 2012; Hamilton, Denniss, and Baker 2005; Quested et al. 2011; WRAP 2008). The exclusion of income as an important variable on this list is notable—research has not found that more income significantly increases food waste (Koivupuro et al. 2012; Stefan et al. 2013; Williams et al. 2012). The apparent irrelevance of income may simply reflect that none of these studies are from the Global South, suggesting that the effect of income may disappear once it exceeds a certain amount. Soma's research in Indonesia suggests that, up to a particular point, income may increase food waste. She found that food purchases constitute a much higher proportion of low-income households' expenditures, significantly influencing the amount and type of food people can afford and where they shop (e.g., supermarkets versus wet markets).[2] Different income groups also have different gifting and consumption habits, with higher-income groups often receiving and gifting significant amounts of food within their network. These disparities consequently influence the amount of food waste different income groups generate, showing how income may be an important factor influencing food waste in poorer countries.

This contrast in findings about income, together with the fact that all but one of the studies cited in this section are from the Global North, is symptomatic of the lack of household food waste research in the Global South. In the rest of this chapter, we discuss this shortage and deploy practice theory to argue for more research and policy attention to household food waste in the Global South.

Food Waste Narratives: Transgressing the Global North Paradigm

According to United Nations (2012) projections, the global population is expected to reach 9 billion people by 2050, with most of the additional 2.3 billion people coming from developing countries, and all in urban areas. Thus, there is an urgent need to address the issue of urban food waste in the Global South. Currently, the few English-language studies of food waste in developing countries focus primarily on issues of agricultural loss caused by improper storage facilities and other inadequate farming infrastructure (Oelofse and Nahman 2013). The overall lack of post-consumer food waste research in the Global South can be linked to what Gille (2012,

40) problematizes as "distinct and isolated" narratives of food waste in the Global North and South, which she attributes to agro-technological research (Institute of Mechanical Engineers 2013; Hodges, Buzby, and Bennett 2011) and studies by organizations like the UN (Gustavsson et al. 2011). These narratives position food waste in developing countries as an issue of inadequate production and distribution technology, unlike in developed countries, where food wastage ostensibly occurs at the consumer level (Gille 2012). For example, an Institute of Mechanical Engineers (2013) report highlights how developing countries waste more at the farm level by practising "inefficient" small-scale farming and not using modern farming technologies.

However, the dichotomy of these narratives is problematic for two reasons. First, Gille (2012) suggests that food waste in the Global South is framed as a technological issue in order to further Western economic interests by promoting highly technological interventions, such as biotechnology and/or international loans to further mechanize agriculture. Furthermore, this technological framing maintains smallholder farmers' reliance on the alleged superiority of Western experts to increase yield and reduce food loss, all amidst the spread of industrial agriculture throughout the Global South (Moore 2010). This results in the neglect of crucial interrelated socio-economic structures and cultural factors that influence the generation of food waste in the Global South. These include the influence of world trade regulations, corporate retail power, and the dumping of surplus Western produce in the form of food aid (Gille 2012).

Second, the characterization of developing countries as "too poor" to waste food neglects the impact of globalization and urbanization on the consumption and waste practices of a large and growing number of middle- to upper-income households in developing countries (Myers and Kent 2003). For example, a growing number of urban populations in Indonesia are participating in non-agricultural forms of labour (Firman, Kombaitan, and Pradono 2007). Participation in this labour sector is often accompanied by longer commutes, the practice of eating out, and weekly shopping trips to supermarkets as opposed to daily trips to wet markets. Highly consumptive lifestyles often attributed to Western consumers also exist in Asian countries (Hobson 2004), even in lower-income Asian countries (Leichenko and Solecki 2005; Goodman and Robinson 2013; Arai 2001). Hughes and Woldekidan's work (1994) on the emerging middle class in Southeast Asia posits that there are spectrums within middle-class groups ranging from lower-income middle class to upper-income middle class. Hughes and Woldekidan (1994) also note that the middle class spends a smaller proportion of their income on food than poorer people do, and that in developing countries, the middle class has growing access to supermarkets and department stores, which replace traditional open markets and small artisanal shops. In essence, without adequate empirical research, it is premature to assume that consumers in cities of the Global South are not producing large amounts of food waste.

Desperate situations with waste management in cities of the Global South, demonstrate the need for research and policy focus on household food waste. Many countries in the Global South suffer from poor waste collection, and in some cases, as much as 50 percent of waste generated remains uncollected (Parizeau, Maclaren, and Chanthy 2008). Waste is often burned or dumped in rivers or vacant lots (Meidiana and Gamse 2011). The content of organic or biodegradable waste in developing countries is also high, ranging from approximately 50 to 80 percent (Yedla 2012; Oberlin and Szántó 2011; Parizeau, Maclaren, and Chanthy 2008). As food waste decomposes quickly in hot and humid environments and attracts disease-carrying vermin, the issues of uneven waste management and poor sanitation are detrimental to the health and well-being of citizens in many developing countries (Joseph 2006; Konteh 2009). Therefore, addressing the issue of food waste in developing countries should not be limited to the context of agricultural food loss.

There is currently a lack of empirical research and critical analysis on the structural and systemic issues that created the problems of food waste in cities of the Global South. More research on patterns of consumption and wastage in urban areas of developing countries is especially pertinent, given the financial and demographic characteristics and growth of megacities such as Jakarta, Manila, New Delhi, and Bangkok. Ethnographic studies on food waste (Evans 2012) are useful in explorations of the specific cultural frameworks that define and categorize food waste, and further ethnographic studies in the Global South are necessary to explore this phenomenon.

Exploring Urban Food Waste in the Global South: Urbanization and the "New Rich"

We have shown how dominant narratives of food waste in the Global South have neglected the emergence of the new middle classes, whose growing wealth and changing lifestyles cannot be ignored. We suggest that growing affluence in developing urban centres has enabled a mutually reinforcing relationship between dietary transition and modern forms of food retail development (Pingali 2007; Reardon et al. 2003), changing consumer lifestyles in the process. In this section we use practice theory to develop a theoretical framework for understanding how this has taken place and what it means for household food waste. In the process, we draw upon evidence from Soma's research in Indonesia to illustrate the importance of analyzing urban food waste within a Global South context.

Major reports on food waste have identified the need to augment food production to meet the dietary demands of increasing and more affluent urban populations in developing countries (Gustavsson et al. 2011; Institute of Mechanical Engineers 2013; Teng and Trethewie 2012). Pingali's (2007) study on Asian diets found signs of convergence toward a more Western diet, driven by the global interconnectedness of the urban middle class and by globalization. This dietary transition is characterized by increased consumption of wheat, temperate fruits and vegetables, meat, fish, dairy products, and stronger demand for fast food and processed convenience foods. The trend is expected to worsen the incidence of diet-related diseases, such as obesity, and also subject smallholder agriculture to competitive pressures (Pingali 2007), but less is made of the fact that growing preferences for perishable foods can result in more food waste (Parfitt, Barthel, and Macnaughton 2010). This is a problem, considering that many urban households in Indonesia have increased their purchases of perishable goods, including vegetables and imported fruits such as grapes, but constant traffic gridlock and heat increase the risk of spoilage. This illustrates how consumers buy food without recognizing that their purchasing decisions may mean the difference between whether food is wasted or not, as highlighted by practice theory.

The transition to Western diets has both driven and been enabled by the rapid growth of modern, large-format food retailers in the Global South, such as supermarkets and hypermarkets[3] (Pingali 2007). The importance of this process, known as food retail modernization, can be framed in terms of practice theory through recognition that the ways in which grocery stores, as infrastructures of provision, constitute an important material element of practice and that the modernization of these infrastructures of provision is required in order to support Westernized, food-related practices. Both demand- and supply-side factors have contributed to food retail modernization. On the one hand, income growth and rising female labour-force participation rates have driven demand for modern food retailers. On the other hand, the improvement of logistics and inventory management technology has enabled large-scale food retail operations, while widespread retail market liberalization has sparked an influx of foreign direct investment into Asia and Latin America from capital-rich Western retailers like Carrefour,

Tesco, and Walmart (Reardon et al. 2003; Reardon and Timmer 2005). Given our prior discussion of how household practices, such as provisioning and meal-preparation, are linked to household food waste, it follows that changing infrastructures of provision associated with these food-related practices not only enable the dietary transition but can also impact household food waste.

Modern food retail formats have taken, and are expected to continue taking, market share away from incumbent forms of food retail in the Global South, such as family-run neighbourhood grocers and traditional wet markets (Reardon and Hopkins 2006). In Indonesia, for example, the number of supermarkets and hypermarkets grew by 9 percent per year and 27 percent per year, respectively, from 1999 to 2003 (Natawidjaja 2005), and hypermarket revenues grew annually by 22 percent on average from 2004 to 2008, presaging the decline of traditional markets (Pandin 2009, cited in Kato, Ota, and Yamashita 2010). One key reason for their growth in popularity is the one-stop-shopping convenience they provide, which is particularly alluring to consumers whose time is increasingly scarce and valuable. This group includes not only the increasingly affluent but also women who have entered the labour force while remaining responsible for domestic practices such as meal preparation (Reardon et al. 2003). Prior to the advent of modern food retail, grocery shopping was an arduous task, involving frequent trips to multiple traditional, more specialized, food retailers (Deutsch 2010), but the convenience of modern, large-format stores, coupled with growing time scarcity, has encouraged middle-class consumers to concentrate their grocery shopping activities by going less frequently and to fewer places (Watson 2012). Where consumers might have purchased food in small amounts on an as-needed basis every day at traditional markets or from mobile vegetable vendors,[4] they might now visit modern grocery stores once per week, buying everything they need at once (Sonesson et al. 2005). Due to the increased challenge of managing larger perishable food inventories, bigger per-trip purchases have, in turn, been found to increase household food waste (Williams et al. 2012). Practices of meal provisioning thus evolve over time as a result of changing interlinkages among households' grocery shopping destinations and practices, the spatial-temporal organization of their everyday lives, and their dietary preferences. In the process, the amount of household food waste is likely to grow.

Household practices of provisioning and meal preparation can also change with shifts in the materials and meanings experienced when consumers enter modern, large-format stores. Here, changes to the materials involved in food-related practices is evident in the differences in products sold in supermarkets and hypermarkets—qualities, quantities, packaging, and pricing are all different from other retail formats, especially more traditional options such as neighbourhood grocers, mobile food vendors, and wet markets. This is especially reflected in the ways in which modern food retailers employ advertising and promotions, such as bulk discount offers, and manipulate in-store environments to encourage unplanned purchasing (Chandon and Wansink 2012) and increase revenues with little regard for whether this increases food waste or not. Retail modernization and urbanization play important parts in the social and temporal organization of daily lives by altering where, when, and how frequently households shop for groceries.

Patterns of urbanization may also affect everyday life and food waste by affecting the ability of individuals to be in particular places at certain times in order to perform practices. Research shows how everyday practices, such as the need to take care of children, interact with factors such as housing affordability and transportation to create specific demands on the ways in which families move around and use their time effectively (Jarvis 2005). Given that household provisioning and meal preparation are also necessary and time consuming, and exert similar demands on individuals' time resources and mobility, urban planning and issues of accessibility may also have ramifications for food waste. Soma's research in Bogor provides an illustration: in one family, a woman prepared dinner for her husband, who commutes daily to Jakarta, without realizing that he had to work late and had already eaten at work. This example illustrates the potential for practices such as family meals to be disrupted by social contingencies, increasing the chance of food wastage. In addition, many households in Bogor have traditionally been able to purchase food daily from mobile vegetable vendors. However, vegetable vendors often start selling around 6:00 a.m. and finish their neighbourhood rounds by 2:00 p.m. Meanwhile, an increasing number of Bogor's residents work in Jakarta and leave by 5:00 a.m. to avoid the traffic, returning only around 7:30 p.m. An interview with a vegetable vendor revealed that his sales had shrunk due to competition with supermarket prices and people's earlier commute times. He also expressed that heavier traffic has made it more dangerous for cart vendors, which means that they must now avoid certain neighbourhoods for their own safety. Furthermore, mobile vegetable vendors are not permitted within elite gated developments in the greater Bogor area at all. Traditionally, customers of mobile vegetable vendors purchase small quantities—just enough to cover a day's worth of meals. This practice reduces the chances of overpurchasing and therefore can lead to less food wasted from not being used in time. This example illustrates how housing development and imbalances between regional jobs and housing also have consequences for the practices of meal provisioning.

Urbanization and retail modernization in the Global South are still ongoing and have taken place far more briskly than in the Global North. The processes and possibilities described above are indicative of how the oft-mentioned rise of the new middle classes and the spread of Western consumerist lifestyles are embedded in the spread of what Leichenko and Solecki (2005) call "consumption landscapes." Although Leichenko and Solecki use the term to refer specifically to suburban housing development in the Global South, we interpret the term as also reflecting how urbanization is bound up with lifestyle change and new modes of consumption. Of special concern is the way in which modern, large-format retail development is closely tied to suburbanization and urban sprawl. On the fringes of Jakarta, the processes that drive suburbanization can also contribute to the spread of modern, large-format food retail. Liberalization of the real estate market has encouraged speculative development of new towns by private property developers (Firman 2004) selling prospects of modernity and Western-style living to attract affluent residents, who expect modern amenities, including hypermarkets and supermarkets. In addition, fiscal decentralization of the Indonesian state in the 1990s has encouraged local authorities to invite large retailers to open stores in order to boost local tax revenues and economic development (Vander Stichele, Van der Wal, and Oldenziel 2006), suggesting the continued proliferation and growth in popularity of hypermarkets and supermarkets. Such trends, together with the linkages to food waste we have described above, show that urbanization is not only a process that physically transforms individuals' surroundings but also necessarily leads to a transformation of their daily lives by altering the ways in which everyday practices are performed. As just one of the outcomes of this broader transformation under way in the Global South, changing household food waste patterns warrant more research and policy attention than they currently attract.

Conclusion

Food waste is still emerging as a topic of academic inquiry. Existing research in this area tends to have two main foci: early supply-chain food losses in developing countries, and household food waste in developed countries. As part of a broader practice turn among scholars of environmental behaviour, household food waste is increasingly being studied using practice theory as a lens. Practice theory sheds light on the complexity of behaviours related to food waste that individualistic behavioural models ignore, showing in particular how household food waste originates from multiple behaviours related to the practices of food provisioning and meal preparation. It also shows how the performances of these behaviours are inextricable from the social-temporal organization of daily life. However, these patterns and causes of food waste are unlikely to be exclusive to the Global North, given the emergence of a growingly affluent and urban middle class in the Global South. Nonetheless, existing research about food waste in the Global South is limited to a handful of narratives about agricultural food losses and the need for improved technology, to the neglect of post-consumer food waste. Using practice theory to extend existing frameworks for understanding food waste, we have highlighted the growing salience of household food waste research in developing countries, focusing on the processes of rapid urbanization and income growth and their connections to the emergence of global supermarket chains and transnational big-box retailers. This has transformed the urban food retail landscape, giving increasingly affluent urban consumers unprecedented access to large quantities and varieties of food products at ever lower prices (Coyle 2006).

We have offered some initial possibilities for how food retail modernization might impact household food waste, especially in the Global South. Future research should attempt to corroborate these suggestions, as well as attempt to understand how the shifting food retail landscape interacts with other aspects of urbanization, such as changing land use patterns and transportation infrastructure, to affect everyday practices related to food waste. Not discussed here was the possibility that income-driven time scarcity may reduce the extent to which households prepare meals at home and increase demand for convenience foods and meals outside the home. As such, research on food waste from restaurants and food processing will be important as well. Overall, such research will be vital for understanding and predicting broader trends in food waste and improving strategies for its reduction and management. Not only is there a need to cross boundaries between academic disciplines as diverse as sociology, geography, urban planning, psychology, economics, and marketing for the study of food waste, but also, we must problematize the assumptions about the occurrence of food waste in the Global North and Global South.

Acknowledgements

This research was supported by the Pierre Elliott Trudeau Foundation, the Social Sciences and Humanities Research Council of Canada, and the Dr. David Chu Asia Pacific Scholarship, University of Toronto. We would also like to thank the entire editorial team, anonymous reviewers, and especially Jordon Lazell for feedback on initial drafts of the chapter.

Notes

1 Freegans are members of an anti-consumerist movement who eat only food that has been discarded by others.

2 Wet markets sell fresh foods in an open, multi-stall format. They are different from Western farmers' markets in that stall owners generally do not produce the foods they sell.

3 Hypermarkets are differentiated from supermarkets by their larger floor areas, where grocery sales are combined with a large variety of other goods, including household items, clothing, and electronics.

4 Mobile vegetable vendors are vendors who go through neighbourhoods selling fresh produce and also various meats, either from weaved baskets strung on long sticks carried on their shoulders, from pushed carts, or, more recently, from motorcycles.

References

Adhikari, Bijaya K., Suzelle Barrington, and José Martinez. 2006. "Predicted Growth of World Urban Food Waste and Methane Production." *Waste Management & Research* 24 (5): 421–33. http://dx.doi.org/10.1177/0734242X06067767. Medline:17121114.

Ajzen, Icek. 1991. "The Theory of Planned Behavior." *Organizational Behavior and Human Decision Processes* 50 (2): 179–211. http://dx.doi.org/10.1016/0749-5978(91)90020-T.

Arai, Kenichiro. 2001. "Only Yesterday in Jakarta: Property Boom and Consumptive Trends in the Late New Order Metropolitan City." *Japanese Journal of Southeast Asian Studies* 38 (4): 481–511.

Becker, Gary S. 1978. *The Economic Approach to Human Behavior*. Chicago: University of Chicago Press.

Chandon, Pierre, and Brian Wansink. 2012. "Does Food Marketing Need to Make Us Fat? A Review and Solutions." *Nutrition Reviews* 70 (10): 571–93. http://dx.doi.org/10.1111/j.1753-4887.2012.00518.x. Medline:23035805.

Cleary, Julian. 2014. "A Life Cycle Assessment of Residential Waste Management and Prevention." *International Journal of Life Cycle Assessment* 19 (9): 1–16. http://dx.doi.org/10.1007/s11367-014-0767-5.

Cofie, Olufunke O., Pay Drechsel, S. Agbottah, and Rene van Veenhuizen. 2009. "Resource Recovery from Urban Waste: Options and Challenges for Community-Based Composting in Sub-Saharan Africa." *Desalination* 248 (1–3): 256–61. http://dx.doi.org/10.1016/j.desal.2008.05.063.

Coyle, William. 2006. "A Revolution in Food Retailing Underway in the Asia-Pacific Region." *Amber Waves* 3 (4): 22–9.

Deutsch, Tracey. 2010. *Building a Housewife's Paradise: Gender, Politics, and American Grocery Stores in the Twentieth Century*. Chapel Hill: University of North Carolina Press.

European Union. 2008. "Directive 2008/98/EC of the European Parliament and of the Council on Waste and Repealing Certain Directives." *Official Journal of the European Union*: L312/3-30. http://eur-lex.europa.eu/LexUriServ/Lex UriServ.do?uri=OJ:L:2008:312:0003:0030:en:PDF.

Evans, David. 2011. "Blaming the Consumer–Once Again: The Social and Material Contexts of Everyday Food Waste Practices in Some English Households." *Critical Public Health* 21 (4): 429–40. http://dx.doi.org/10.1080/09581596 .2011.608797.

Evans, David. 2012. "Beyond the Throwaway Society: Ordinary Domestic Practice and a Sociological Approach to Household Food Waste." *Sociology* 46 (1): 41–56. http://dx.doi.org/10.1177/0038038511416150.

Evans-Cowley, Jennifer. 2011. "Evaluating Food Systems in Comprehensive Planning: Is the Mississippi Gulf Coast Planning for Food?" *Journal of Agriculture, Food Systems, and Community Development* 2 (1): 104–26. http:// dx.doi.org/10.5304/jafscd.2011.021.009.

Firman, Tommy. 2004. "New Town Development in Jakarta Metropolitan Region: A Perspective of Spatial Segregation." *Habitat International* 28 (3): 349–68. http://dx.doi.org/10.1016/S0197-3975(03)00037-7.

Firman, Tommy. 2009. "The Continuity and Change in Mega-Urbanization in Indonesia: A Survey of Jakarta–Bandung Region (JBR) Development." *Habitat International* 33 (4): 327–39. http://dx.doi.org/10.1016/j. habitatint.2008.08.005.

Firman, Tommy, Benedictus Kombaitan, and Pradono Pradono. 2007. "The Dynamics of Indonesia's Urbanisation, 1980–2006." *Urban Policy and Research* 25 (4): 433–54. http://dx.doi.org/10.1080/08111140701540752.

Ganglbauer, Eva, Geraldine Fitzpatrick, and Rob Comber. 2013. "Negotiating Food Waste: Using a Practice Lens to Inform Design." *ACM Transactions on Computer-Human Interaction* 20 (2): 11.1–11.25. http://dx.doi. org/10.1145/2463579.2463582.

Gille, Zsuzsa. 2012. "From Risk to Waste: Global Food Waste Regimes." *Sociological Review* 60 (S2): 27–46. http://dx.doi.org/10.1111/1467-954X.12036.

Godfray, Charles J.H., John R. Beddington, Ian R. Crute, Lawrence Haddad, David Lawrence, James F. Muir, Jules Pretty, Sherman Robinson, Sandy M. Thomas, and Camilla Toulmin. 2010. "Food Security: The Challenge of Feeding 9 Billion People." *Science* 327 (5967): 812–8. http://dx.doi.org/10.1126/sci ence.1185383. Medline:20110467.

Gooch, Martin, Abdel Felfel, and Caroline Glasbey. 2014. *"$27 Billion" Revisited The Cost of Canada's Annual Food Waste*. Guelph, ON: Value Chain Management Centre, George Morris Centre. http://vcm-international.com/ wp-content/uploads/2014/12/Food-Waste-in-Canada-27-Billion-Revisited-Dec-10-2014.pdf.

Goodman, David S., and Richard Robinson. 2013. *The New Rich in Asia: Mobile Phones, McDonald's and Middle Class Revolution*. London: Routledge.

Gram-Hanssen, Kirsten. 2010. "Standby Consumption in Households Analyzed With a Practice Theory Approach." *Journal of Industrial Ecology* 14 (1): 150–65. http://dx.doi.org/10.1111/j.1530-9290.2009.00194.x.

Gustavsson, Jenny, Christel Cederberg, Ulf Sonesson, Robert Van Otterdijk, and Alexandre Meybeck. 2011. *Global Food Losses and Food Waste: Extent, Causes and Prevention*. Rome: United Nations Food and Agriculture Organization. http://agriskmanagementforum.org/taxonomy/term/339.

Hamilton, Clive, Richard Denniss, and David Graham Baker. 2005. "Wasteful Consumption in Australia." Canberra: Australia Institute. http://www.tai.org.au/documents/dp_fulltext/DP77.pdf.

Hand, Martin, Elizabeth Shove, and Dale Southerton. 2005. "Explaining Showering: A Discussion of the Material, Conventional, and Temporal Dimensions of Practice." *Sociological Research Online* 10 (2): N.p. http://dx.doi.org/10.5153/sro.1100. https://ideas.repec.org/a/sro/srosro/2004-70-2.html.

Hobson, Kersty. 2004. "Researching 'Sustainable Consumption' in Asia-Pacific Cities." *Asia Pacific Viewpoint* 45 (2): 279–88. http://dx.doi.org/10.1111/j.1467-8373.2004.00237_45_2.x.

Hodges, Richard J., Jean C. Buzby, and Ben Bennett. 2011. "Postharvest Losses and Waste in Developed and Less Developed Countries: Opportunities to Improve Resource Use." *Journal of Agricultural Science* 149 (Suppl S1): 37–45. http://dx.doi.org/10.1017/S0021859610000936.

Holt-Giménez, Eric, Annie Shattuck, Miguel Altieri, Hans Herren, and Steve Gliessman. 2012. "We Already Grow Enough Food for 10 Billion People… and Still Can't End Hunger." *Journal of Sustainable Agriculture* 36 (6): 595–8. http://dx.doi.org/10.1080/10440046.2012.695331.

Hughes, Helen, and Berhanu Woldekidan. 1994. "The Emergence of the Middle Class in ASEAN Countries." *ASEAN Economic Bulletin* 11 (2): 139–49. http://dx.doi.org/10.1355/AE11-2A.

Institute of Mechanical Engineers. 2013. "Global Food: Waste Not, Want Not." London: Institute of Mechanical Engineers. http://www.imeche.org/docs/default-source/reports/Global_Food_Report.pdf?sfvrsn=0.

Jarvis, Helen. 2005. "Moving to London Time: Household Co-ordination and the Infrastructure of Everyday Life." *Time & Society* 14 (1): 133–54. http://dx.doi.org/10.1177/0961463X05050302.

Joseph, Kurian. 2006. "Stakeholder Participation for Sustainable Waste Management." *Habitat International* 30 (4): 863–71. http://dx.doi.org/10.1016/j.habitatint.2005.09.009.

Kato, Hironori, Tetsuo Ota, and Yuko Yamashita. 2010. "Destination Choice for Shopping: Evidence from Jakarta, Indonesia." Paper presented at the 15th HKSTS International Conference, Hong Kong, December. http://www.trip.t.u-tokyo.ac.jp/kato/WP/2010/2010wp_e9.pdf.

Koivupuro, Heta-Kaisa, Hanna Hartikainen, Kirsi Silvennoinen, Juha-Matti Katajajuuri, Noora Heikintalo, Anu Reinikainen, and Lotta Jalkanen. 2012. "Influence of Socio-Demographical, Behavioural and Attitudinal Factors on the Amount of Avoidable Food Waste Generated in Finnish Households." *International Journal of Consumer Studies* 36 (2): 183–91. http://dx.doi.org/10.1111/j.1470-6431.2011.01080.x.

Kollmuss, Anja, and Julian Agyeman. 2002. "Mind the Gap: Why Do People Act Environmentally and What Are the Barriers to Pro-environmental Behavior?" *Environmental Education Research* 8 (3): 239–60. http://dx.doi.org/10.1080/13504620220145401.

Konteh, Frederick Hassan. 2009. "Urban Sanitation and Health in the Developing World: Reminiscing the Nineteenth Century Industrial Nations." *Health & Place* 15 (1): 69–78. http://dx.doi.org/10.1016/j.healthplace.2008.02.003. Medline:18359263.

Kummu, M., H. de Moel, M. Porkka, S. Siebert, O. Varis, and P.J. Ward. 2012. "Lost Food, Wasted Resources: Global Food Supply Chain Losses and Their Impacts on Freshwater, Cropland, and Fertiliser Use." *Science of the Total Environment* 438: 477–89. http://dx.doi.org/10.1016/j.scitotenv.2012.08.092. Medline: 23032564.

Lebersorger, S., and F. Schneider. 2011. "Discussion on the Methodology for Determining Food Waste in Household Waste Composition Studies." *Waste Management* 31 (9–10): 1924–33. http://dx.doi.org/10.1016/j.wasman.2011.05.023. Medline:21705207.

Leichenko, Robin M., and William D. Solecki. 2005. "Exporting the American Dream: The Globalization of Suburban Consumption Landscapes." *Regional Studies* 39: 241–53. http://dx.doi.org/10.1080/003434005200060080.

Lundie, Sven, and Gregory M. Peters. 2005. "Life Cycle Assessment of Food Waste Management Options." *Journal of Cleaner Production, Environmental Assessments and Waste Management* 13 (3): 275–86. http://dx.doi.org/10.1016/j.jclepro.2004.02.020.

Meidiana, Christia, and Thomas Gamse. 2011. "The New Waste Law: Challenging Opportunity for Future Landfill Operation in Indonesia." *Waste Management & Research* 29 (1): 20–9. http://dx.doi.org/10.1177/0734242X10384013. Medline: 20935025.

Moore, Jason W. 2010. "The End of the Road? Agricultural Revolutions in the Capitalist World-Ecology, 1450–2010." *Journal of Agrarian Change* 10 (3): 389–413. http://dx.doi.org/10.1111/j.1471-0366.2010.00276.x.

Myers, Norman, and Jennifer Kent. 2003. "New Consumers: The Influence of Affluence on the Environment." *Proceedings of the National Academy of Sciences of the United States of America* 100 (8): 4963–8. http://dx.doi.org/10.1073/pnas.0438061100. Medline:12672963.

Natawidjaja, Ronnie S. 2005. "Modern Market Growth and the Changing Map of the Retail Food Sector in Indonesia." Paper presented at Pacific Food System Outlook (PFSO) 9th Annual Forecasters Meeting, May. https://www.researchgate.net/publication/248708443_Modern_Market_Growth_and_Changing_Map_of_Retail_Food_Sector_in_Indonesia/file/9c96051e173f350498.pdf.

O'Brien, Martin. 2012. "A 'Lasting Transformation' of Capitalist Surplus: From Food Stocks to Feedstocks." *Sociological Review* 60 (S2): 192–211. http://dx.doi.org/10.1111/1467-954X.12045.

Oberlin, Aisa S., and Gábor L. Szántó. 2011. "Community Level Composting in a Developing Country: Case Study of KIWODET, Tanzania." *Waste Management & Research* 29 (10): 1071–7. http://dx.doi.org/10.1177/0734242X11402871. Medline:21558081.

OECD. 2013. *Greening Household Behaviour*. Paris: Organisation for Economic Co-operation and Development. http://www.oecd-ilibrary.org/content/book/9789264181373-en.

Oelofse, Suzan H.H., and Anton Nahman. 2013. "Estimating the Magnitude of Food Waste Generated in South Africa." *Waste Management & Research* 31 (1): 80–6. http://dx.doi.org/10.1177/0734242X12457117. Medline:22878934.

Pandin, M.L. 2009. "The Portrait of Retail Business in Indonesia: Modern Market." *Economic Review* 215:1–6.

Parfitt, Julian, Mark Barthel, and Sarah Macnaughton. 2010. "Food Waste within Food Supply Chains: Quantification and Potential for Change to 2050." *Philosophical Transactions of the Royal Society of London. Series B, Biological*

Sciences 365 (1554): 3065–81. http://dx.doi.org/10.1098/rstb.2010.0126. Medline:20713403.

Parizeau, Kate, Virginia Maclaren, and Lay Chanthy. 2008. "Budget Sheets and Buy-in: Financing Community-Based Waste Management in Siem Reap, Cambodia." *Environment and Urbanization* 20 (2): 445–63. http://dx.doi.org/10.1177/0956247808096122.

Pingali, Prabhu. 2007. "Westernization of Asian Diets and the Transformation of Food Systems: Implications for Research and Policy." *Food Policy* 32 (3): 281–98. http://dx.doi.org/10.1016/j.foodpol.2006.08.001.

Pred, Allan. 1981. "Social Reproduction and the Time-Geography of Everyday Life." *Geografiska Annaler. Series B, Human Geography* 63 (1): 5–22. http://dx.doi.org/10.2307/490994.

Quested, Tom, E. Marsh, D. Stunell, and A.D. Parry. 2013. "Spaghetti Soup: The Complex World of Food Waste Behaviours." *Resources, Conservation and Recycling* 79: 43–51. http://dx.doi.org/10.1016/j.resconrec.2013.04.011.

Quested, Tom, A.D. Parry, S. Easteal, and R. Swannell. 2011. "Food and Drink Waste from Households in the UK." *Nutrition Bulletin* 36 (4): 460–7. http://dx.doi.org/10.1111/j.1467-3010.2011.01924.x.

Reardon, Thomas, and Rose Hopkins. 2006. "The Supermarket Revolution in Developing Countries: Policies to Address Emerging Tensions Among Supermarkets, Suppliers and Traditional Retailers." *European Journal of Development Research* 18 (4): 522–45. http://dx.doi.org/10.1080/09578810601070613.

Reardon, Thomas, and C. Peter Timmer. 2005. "The Supermarket Revolution with Asian Characteristics. " Paper presented at the International Conference on Agricultural and Rural Development in Asia, Makati City, The Philippines, November. ftp://ftp.cgiar.org/ilri/ICT/Theme%203/SEARCA%20Reardon-Timmer%20November%202005%20for%20conference%20participants.doc.

Reardon, Thomas, C. Peter Timmer, Christopher B. Barrett, and Julio Berdegué. 2003. "The Rise of Supermarkets in Africa, Asia, and Latin America." *American Journal of Agricultural Economics* 85 (5): 1140–6. http://dx.doi.org/10.1111/j.0092-5853.2003.00520.x.

Røpke, Inge. 2009. "Theories of Practice—New Inspiration for Ecological Economic Studies on Consumption." *Ecological Economics* 68 (10): 2490–7. http://dx.doi.org/10.1016/j.ecolecon.2009.05.015.

Shove, Elizabeth. 2010. "Beyond the ABC: Climate Change Policy and Theories of Social Change." *Environment & Planning A* 42 (6): 1273–85. http://dx.doi.org/10.1068/a42282.

Shove, Elizabeth, and Mika Pantzar. 2005. "Consumers, Producers and Practices Understanding the Invention and Reinvention of Nordic Walking." *Journal of Consumer Culture* 5 (1): 43–64. http://dx.doi.org/10.1177/1469540505049846.

Sonesson, Ulf, Frida Anteson, Jennifer Davis, and Per-Olow Sjödén. 2005. "Home Transport and Wastage: Environmentally Relevant Household Activities in the Life Cycle of Food." *AMBIO: A Journal of the Human Environment* 34 (4): 371–5. http://dx.doi.org/10.1579/0044-7447-34.4.371.

Stefan, Violeta, Erica van Herpen, Ana Alina Tudoran, and Liisa Lähteenmäki. 2013. "Avoiding Food Waste by Romanian Consumers: The Importance of Planning and Shopping Routines." *Food Quality and Preference* 28 (1): 375–81. http://dx.doi.org/10.1016/j.foodqual.2012.11.001.

Teng, Paul, and Sally Trethewie. 2012. "Tackling Urban and Rural Food Wasteage in Southeast Asia: Issues and Interventions." Policy Brief No 17. Singapore: RSIS Centre for Non-Traditional Security (NTS) Studies. http://www.rsis.edu.sg/wp-content/uploads/2014/07/PB121001-NTS-PB17.pdf.

United Nations. 2012. *World Urbanization Prospects: The 2011 Revision: High-lights.* (Document ESA/P/WP/224.) New York: UN. http://desa.un.org/unup/pdf/WUP2011_Highlights.pdf.

Vander Stichele, Myriam, Sanne Van der Wal, and Joris Oldenziel. 2006. *Who Reaps the Fruit? Critical Issues in the Fresh Fruit and Vegetable Chain.* Amsterdam: Stichting Onderzoek Multinationale Ondernemingen (SOMO).

Venkat, Kumar. 2012. "The Climate Change and Economic Impacts of Food Waste in the United States." *International Journal on Food System Dynamics* 2 (4): 431–46.

Warde, Alan. 2005. "Consumption and Theories of Practice." *Journal of Consumer Culture* 5 (2): 131–53. http://dx.doi.org/10.1177/1469540505053090.

Watson, Matt. 2012. "How Theories of Practice Can Inform Transition to a Decarbonised Transport System." *Journal of Transport Geography* 24 (September): 488–96. http://dx.doi.org/10.1016/j.jtrangeo.2012.04.002.

Watson, Matt, and Angela Meah. 2012. "Food, Waste and Safety: Negotiating Conflicting Social Anxieties into the Practices of Domestic Provisioning." *Sociological Review* 60: 102–20. http://dx.doi.org/10.1111/1467-954X.12040.

Wenlock, R.W., D.H. Buss, B.J. Derry, and E.J. Dixon. 1980. "Household Food Wastage in Britain." *British Journal of Nutrition* 43 (1): 53–70. http://dx.doi.org/10.1079/BJN19800064. Medline:7370218.

Williams, Helén, Fredrik Wikström, Tobias Otterbring, Martin Löfgren, and Anders Gustafsson. 2012. "Reasons for Household Food Waste with Special Attention to Packaging." *Journal of Cleaner Production* 24 (March): 141–8. http://dx.doi.org/10.1016/j.jclepro.2011.11.044.

WRAP. 2008. "The Food We Waste." Banbury, UK: Waste and Resources Action Programme (WRAP).

Yedla, Sudhakar. 2012. "Replication of Urban Innovations—Prioritization of Strategies for the Replication of Dhaka's Community-Based Decentralized Composting Model." *Waste Management & Research* 30 (1): 20–31. http://dx.doi.org/10.1177/0734242X10380116.

CHAPTER 11

A Meta-Analysis on the Constitution and Configuration of Alternative Food Networks

Lani Trenouth, Serhiy Polyakov, Ankit Gupta,
and Konstantinos Zougris

Over the last thirty years, there has been increasing interest in food studies spanning a range of disciplines. This can be seen in the upsurge in academic publishing on food-related topics in an expanding array of academic journals, as well as in the growing number of university courses and programs with food as a focus or as a lens through which to view other topics. Research within the domain of food studies is being approached from a wide range of disciplines, and scholars are negotiating and crossing conventional disciplinary boundaries, borrowing conceptual frameworks from other fields and experimenting with new methodological approaches. In this chapter, we bring together the myriad knowledges from a wide range of disciplines and put them into conversation with one another in order to map out academic knowledge of one key concept in food studies. We focus on the amorphous concept of "alternative food networks" (AFNs), in all its various permutations,[1] and review the state of the art of research and academic knowledge on this concept. Our purpose is to contribute to the ongoing development of academic thought and practice on AFNs by applying a quantitative text analysis method to a collection of journal articles in order to facilitate an understanding of recurrent topical themes that form the conceptual undergirding of AFNs. Our main interest here is in the semantic variations in the "alternativeness" of alternative food networks.

The qualifier "alternative" is commonly understood as a state of being that is different from the normal, the mainstream, or the conventional. However, a cursory review of the literature within the growing field of food studies

reveals that despite its prevalent use there is a lack of consensus on the meaning and deployment of the term "alternative." Going further, Goodman and
his co-authors (2013) refer to the term AFNs as "convenient collective labels
for what are, in fact, incredibly heterogeneous sets of organizational forms
of food provisioning" (428). Some scholars have pointed to the ambiguity
and ambivalence of "alternative" as constraining scholarly development in the
domain of food studies. For instance, Goodman (2003) points to a need to
(re)conceptualize AFNs; Sonnino and Marsden (2006) call for new conceptual tools to explore the nature and dynamics of the "alternative sector"; and
Tregear (2011, 420) asserts that the unclear and inconsistent use of concepts
in AFN research has led to "a problematic state of knowledge in this field."
That Tregear makes her argument almost a decade after Goodman called
for a reconceptualization indicates there has been insufficient progress on
resolving this issue.

Despite the apparent lack of consensus on the meaning and manifestation
of alterity in food, there are at least two notable scholarly conversations surrounding AFNs toward which academics have gravitated. First, some scholars have suggested that, despite an academic turn toward consumption, much
of the AFN literature has emanated from a distinctly production-oriented
point of departure (Goodman and DuPuis 2002; Goodman 2004; Tregear
2011)—a contention which Van der Ploeg and Renting (2004) strongly dis-
pute, citing examples of research from the Dutch context.

Second, a number of scholars characterize differences in academic
thought on AFNs along geographic lines. DuPuis and Goodman (2005)
suggest that U.S. literature on AFNs often normatively "echo[es] food
activist rhetoric," while literature on the European context is more concerned with local value chains and the maintenance of rural livelihoods.
Similarly, Holloway and his co-authors (2005) also suggest a broad distinction between European and North American alternatives, in that the former
tend to fall into the interstitial spaces left open by mainstream food system
activities, whereas the latter are often oppositional activities resisting the
status quo of the conventional system. These proposed distinctions based on
geography suggest that "alternative" food practices and understandings of
these practices vary widely across places and peoples.

Unresolved debates and contradictions surrounding AFNs remain; the
"alternative" in alternative food networks is a fuzzy concept, lacking precise
and fixed meaning, thereby making it difficult to describe what is and what
is not included. Yet, we depend on common understandings and definitions,
and we use linguistic shorthands, in order to build upon existing knowledge,

as well as to develop and share new knowledge. By moving toward semantic convergence of the language used to convey knowledge, academics and practitioners alike could more easily converse with the abstracted concepts used to represent AFNs. The distillation and mapping of the scholarly knowledge related to AFNs presents one way to help move toward greater lexical and conceptual convergence by making visible (and visual) the semantic divergences, hidden biases and assumptions, or underexplored linkages between different interpretations of AFNs. Furthermore, the ways in which AFNs are conceptualized and understood not only has implications for the theory of food studies but also impacts policy and practice.

In this chapter, we apply a meta-analytical approach belonging to the family of quantitative content analysis. Using a technique called latent semantic analysis (LSA), we parse out themes within academic knowledge of the concept of AFNs, with the goal of understanding the thematic structure and dynamics of the existing literature. LSA is a technique for discovering and analyzing latent relationships between words, concepts, and individual documents within a larger collection of documents. This quantitative textual analysis method allows us to gain a critical distance from which to understand the contours of the scholarly landscape.

In keeping with the themes of this book—conversations and border crossing—our methodological choice itself is found at the intersection of information retrieval, bibliometrics, and psychology, and here we apply it for the first time to the domain of food studies.[2]

Transgressing Disciplinary Boundaries to Converse with Emergent Methods

Content analysis is an empirical research methodology consisting of a family of techniques that are used to systematically synthesize a collection of texts[3] in order to extract manifest and latent content and to analyze emergent patterns (Holsti 1969; Krippendorff 1969; Neuendorf 2002; Krippendorff 2004). Facilitated by the expansion in the processing power of computational software, computer text analysis emerged in the late 1950s and the 1960s as a result of a growing interest in mechanical translation, abstraction, and information retrieval systems (Krippendorff 2004).

Quantitative computer text analysis is a collection of methods used to identify units of text for analysis and to extract from the texts quantitatively measureable features (coded content categories, word counts, dictionary counts, or parts of speech) for inferential statistical analysis. The most basic measure in quantitative text analysis is word frequency count. The assumption of this method is that those words used most often reflect the theme or topic of the text unit. However, the simplicity of this approach may lead to incorrect inferences. For example, a wide range of synonyms can be used throughout a document and thus may lead the researchers to under-estimate the importance of a concept (Weber 1990). Also, word frequency counts may not account for the ways that some words can have multiple meanings.

One method that can be used for circumventing these problems in quantitative text analysis is latent semantic analysis. LSA is a bridge between the field of automated content analysis and the field of information retrieval, where it was first introduced in the late 1980s (Deerwester et al. 1990; Dumais 2007). Since its development, LSA has been applied to a range of fields, such as psychology (Mehl 2006), the theory of meaning (Landauer 2007), real estate (Winson-Geideman and Evangelopoulos 2013), geography (Parr and Lu 2010), business (Sidorova et al. 2008), and operation management (Kulkarni, Apte, and Evangelopoulos 2014). We argue that this method can advance the domain of food studies by facilitating the mapping of knowledge and relationships between themes so that the current conceptual and thematic state of the field can be better understood.

LSA uses mathematical algorithms to extract meaningful terms (not merely the most frequent) from a collection of documents and detect themes based on word usage. The objective of LSA is to uncover underlying meanings in a collection of texts, which may or may not be readily apparent to readers, especially when they are dealing with a large volume of documents (Landauer 2007). A pre-defined set of keywords or coding structure is not necessary with LSA, as is the case with many content analysis methods, because the mathematical algorithms this method uses allow themes to emerge from the collection of documents without direct human influence.

Much more sophisticated than a simple word count analysis, LSA is able to determine the significance of words and underlying meanings even when various synonyms are used to describe the same concept. Therefore, this method is also able to reveal latent relationships between articles despite the varying linguistic preferences of authors. The main purpose of LSA is not to group or cluster documents based on similarity of their content; rather, it is to identify several themes throughout a collection of documents. The relationships between the documents and the themes that emerge from them are made visible through LSA in which each document includes multiple themes in varying degrees of prominence.

The algorithms of LSA calculate weighed relationships between three key variables—documents,[4] terms,[5] and themes[6]—and provide a framework for deeper text analysis at virtually any desired level of abstraction, according to the needs of the study (Zhu and Ghodsi 2006).

In LSA, there is no a priori optimum number of themes to parse out of any given collection of documents. The optimal number of themes is determined in part by the level of abstraction needed to achieve the analytical objectives of the study and in part by the specifics of a collection of documents, such as the number of documents included and the number of meaningful terms that are extracted (Evangelopoulos et al. 2012). For example, if the granularity (level of abstraction) is too coarse, there may be too few themes to allow for useful interpretation, and if the granularity is too fine, there may be too many themes to be interpretable (i.e., the complexity of the information in the text can not be adequately synthesized for human interpretation). To facilitate the selection of the optimum number of themes, a statistical test as described by Zhu and Ghodsi (2006) can be applied to the data to identify several possible recommendations. From these statistically generated recommendations, each at different levels of granularity, an analyst conversant in the subject matter being studied can select the most appropriate number of themes and level of abstraction.

While a rich and detailed understanding of the meaning of a document or collection of documents can be garnered through qualitative efforts of a domain expert, it remains a laborious and time-consuming effort and is particularly challenging when the collection of documents to be addressed is large. The advantage of LSA is that it can process and analyze large data sets, which would not be feasible with a qualitative approach. Furthermore, in a domain such as food studies, which is both divergent and atomized in terms of topics and disciplines, it may be difficult to comprehensively grasp the entirety of a domain that can contain thousands of articles. In other words, disciplinary inclinations and blind spots may still be present—despite the most rigorous of qualitative analyses—because of the limited capacity of a single person, or even a group of people, to achieve the same breadth of understanding possible with computer-assisted quantitative methods. The advantage of the LSA method used here is that its mathematical approach can help to reduce the influence of natural biases that domain experts may hold, based on their disciplinary background, expertise, or involvement in certain academic communities; it is one way to provide a different vantage point from which to view a body of work.

Data Collection, Processing, and Analysis

Along with the apparent vagueness of the AFN concept, the inspiration for this study was the frequent interchangeability of the nouns that follow "alternative food" in academic literature (e.g., "network," "initiative," or "system"). This, however, posed some challenges in the data collection process and necessitated a complex and iterative approach to collecting data and completing our analysis (see Figure 11.1, representing our visualization process). In total, we carried out two rounds of data collection and three rounds of LSA. Initially, we searched eight large electronic journal databases[7] using the various permutations of "alternative food"[8] found in food studies. In some databases, this yielded thousands of results many of which were irrelevant to this study. Through a laborious and often manual process of exclusion and refinement, such as removing articles related to ecology or food science, the number of relevant hits was reduced to a total of 625 unique articles.

Running a first application of LSA on the abstracts yielded a series of new search terms,[9] for an expanded second round of data collection. The sum of the first and second rounds of data collection culminated in the compilation of 2,075 unique articles, which formed the full collection of documents to which LSA was applied. The rationale for this dual-stage process was to use "alternative food" as a starting point without excluding articles that did not explicitly employ the qualifier "alternative" but were nonetheless centred on the same topics. In other words, the first round of data collection gathered articles that touched on various themes and

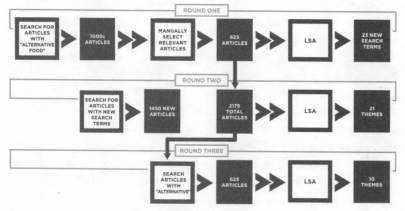

Figure 11.1. Simplified data collection and analysis flow chart.

explicitly labelled them as "alternative," whereas the second round identified articles that were focussed on these same themes but might not necessarily label them as "alternative."

For all three rounds of data analysis, the articles were treated to a series of pre-processing text normalization steps[10] typical of quantitative text analysis, and then the methods of rotated LSA[11] were performed on the titles, keywords, and abstracts of all articles in the collection. The first round of LSA was applied to the initial 625 articles that explicitly used the term "alternative food" in the title or abstract in order to reveal the most relevant search terms, which were then used in the second round of data collection.

A second round of LSA was carried out on the full collection of 2,075 articles. To determine the optimal number of themes, we used a dimensionality detection test (Zhu and Ghodsi 2006). In this case, according to the dimensionality detection test, the optimal numbers for this particular set of 2,075 articles were ten, twenty-one, thirty-three, and forty-five themes. After examining the different arrays of themes for each level of abstraction (i.e., ten, twenty-one, thirty-three, and forty-five themes) we ultimately selected twenty-one themes that best represented the body of research on and around the concept of AFNs. Finally, a third round of analysis was carried out on a subset of the full collection that used the word "alternative" in the title, keywords, or abstract. We applied the same process for the subset of 325 articles, using the term "alternative" explicitly, and found that ten themes best represented this collection. For each round of analysis, the title we assigned to each theme was determined by a review of the top-loaded terms, titles, and abstracts, which are indicative of the most prominent concepts within a particular theme.

We made choices in the processes of deciding the number of themes to parse out of the collection, labelling the themes, and selecting the search terms for the second round of data collection—other thematic configurations and labels are possible, especially given a different set of analytical objectives (e.g., a higher level of abstraction). However, we remain confident that the configurations we present below accurately represent the constitution and configuration of present research on and around AFNs.

To better understand the dynamics of research on AFNs, we also analyzed the spikes in frequency in term usage over time, using a "burst detection" algorithm developed by Kleinberg (2002). The objective of this algorithm is to identify terms that demonstrate a sudden and large increase in usage, rather than a gradual increase, and to identify the span of time for which they remained "bursty." This can provide further information on what themes and topics were popular and over what period.

The Intellectual Landscape and Dynamics of "Alternative" Food

The 2,075 research articles identified for this study were published between 1981 and 2013 in 462 unique journals. The smaller and more focussed "alternative" collection was composed of a subset of 325 articles that used the word "alternative" in the title, keywords, or abstract and were published between 1996 and 2013 in 110 different journals. Using the results from these two collections, we examined the data in multiple ways to assess the intellectual landscape and dynamics of the "alternative food" concept.

Intellectual Landscape

The range of themes detected by LSA on and around the concept of "alternative food" is rather broad (Figure 11.2). This graph reflects the outcome of the LSA theme detection of the entire collection of 2,075 articles and depicts all twenty-one themes identified and the conceptual linkages among them. What follows is a description and discussion of some general tendencies exhibited by the results from this data and from the analysis of the subset of articles forming the "alternative" collection.

In order to better understand how the themes related to one another, we mapped the semantic relationships among them as expressed through document cross-loading[12] (Figure 11.2). Each circle represents a theme, the size of which is proportional to the number of documents (journal articles) in that theme. A line connecting two themes indicates that there are articles common to both themes, and the thickness of the line is proportional to the number of articles belonging to the two themes. Document cross-loading demonstrates linkages between themes, and when many documents are cross-loaded onto two themes it can be said that the themes are more strongly linked than themes for which there are no, or few, cross-loaded documents. For instance, there are many articles that belong to both "Politics, Justice, and Food Movements" and "Fair Trade," much fewer belonging to both "Politics, Justice, and Food Movements" and "Climate Change," and virtually no articles belonging to both "Politics, Justice, and Food Movements" and "School Food and Nutrition Programs."

Here we remind our readers that while the theme labels we have applied reflect the *most prominent* topics of each theme, the labels are neither exhaustive nor exclusionary descriptions of the themes or all the documents

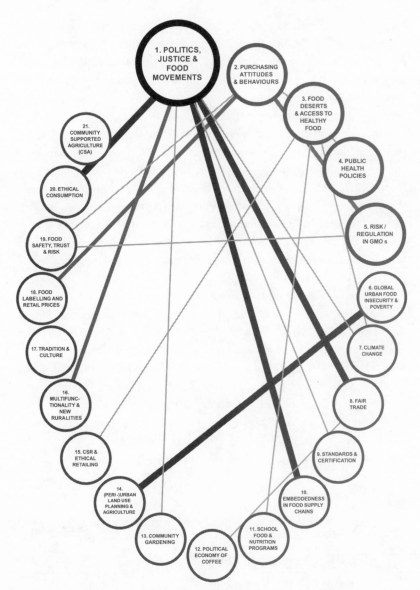

Figure 11.2. Themes and their relationships (full collection).

included in the theme. For example, in the case of "Political Economy of Coffee," coffee was highly prominent among the vast majority articles included in this theme, but not all articles loaded onto this theme were on coffee. Some articles were centred on other commodities but used similar language and conveyed similar latent meanings as the articles specifically addressing coffee. On the other hand, the theme "Politics, Justice, and Food Movements" is the best description we could derive for a rather large and somewhat eclectic grouping, which included a large number of conceptual papers.

Since the LSA approach employed allows an article to have membership in multiple themes, quite a number of articles were found to belong to more than one theme—which is to be expected, given the multidisciplinarity, interdisciplinarity, and overlapping topics in the domain of food studies research. In order to render the graph more readable, we have included only the lines for which there is a cross-loading of a minimum of ten articles. That is, the thinnest line linking two themes in the above graph has at least ten articles loaded onto each theme. The number of shared articles may be interpreted as a degree of association or overlap between the themes, where the more shared articles means a stronger link.

The theme "Politics, Justice, and Food Movements" was by far the largest, with 389 articles, more than double the number of the next largest theme (see Table 11.1). This theme is most strongly linked to "Fair Trade," "Embeddedness in Food Supply Chains," and "Ethical Consumption," as shown by the large degree of article cross-loading. Quite a number of the articles in the "Politics, Justice, and Food Movements" theme are theoretical or conceptual and take a critical theory perspective on a range to topics, which might explain why this theme is the largest and most highly linked. Furthermore, because "Politics, Justice, and Food Movements" includes. many more articles than some of the other themes, it may mean that it

Table 11.1. *Top ten largest themes.*

Theme	# Articles
Politics, Justice, and Food Movements	389
Purchasing Attitudes and Behaviours	180
Food Deserts and Access to Healthy Food	135
Public Health Policies	110
Risk and Regulation in GMOs	162
Global Urban Food Insecurity and Poverty	116
Climate Change	108
Standards and Certification	104
Embeddedness in Food Supply Chains	94
Fair Trade	85

includes a number of subthemes not sufficiently coherent to be detected by LSA and/or highly transversal elements, which are not easily detected by LSA if they are highly pervasive across the entire collection.

In "Purchasing Attitudes and Behaviours," organic foods and genetically modified organisms (GMOs) figure predominantly, and the theme has quite a large number of articles in common with "Risk and Regulation in GMOs," which would indicate an interest in the influence of these two qualities on consumer food purchasing. There are surprisingly few articles cross-loaded among "Purchasing Attitudes and Behaviours," "Food Labelling and Retail Prices," "CSR[13] and Ethical Retailing" and "Ethical Consumption," which might be explained by differences in disciplinary interests or lexicon. "Purchasing Attitudes and Behaviours" is dominated by articles from the interdisciplinary field of consumer studies, while many of the articles in "Food Labelling and Retail Prices" were published in marketing and economics journals with a focus on retail and business and these articles tend to be somewhat older than those in the other themes.

While both "CSR and Ethical Retailing" and "Ethical Consumption" include articles that address the concept of ethics in food, articles in the former theme are published in a broader base of interdisciplinary journals, and the content is more business oriented, with an interest in supply chains. The latter theme includes articles published in journals that have a stronger disciplinary focus on geography, sociology, and consumer culture, and the articles tend to be more influenced by ideas of political consumerism, reflexivity, and values. Nonetheless, there might be some fruitful, but as yet underexplored avenues of research between these themes and opportunities to put their ideas into conversation with one another. In particular, it may be informative to explore the epistemological and disciplinary divides and parallels between "CSR and Ethical Retailing" and "Ethical Consumption."

Both "Risk and Regulation in GMOs" and "Global Urban Food Insecurity and Poverty" contain a large number of articles on the African context, with the former theme focussing on the acceptability of genetically modified crops in African countries and the latter focussing on issues of food insecurity more broadly. That "Global Urban Food Insecurity and Poverty" is strongly linked to "(Peri)-Urban Land Use Planning and Agriculture" may reflect a tendency to view urban agriculture in African countries as a coping strategy of the urban poor; a deeper qualitative look into the full content of the cross-loaded articles would help to confirm or reject this inference.

Somewhat surprisingly, the fairly narrow topic of "Political Economy of Coffee" was a separate theme and not subsumed within "Fair Trade," and further qualitative study would be necessary to unpack the reasons why; however there are at least two plausible explanations. The first might be related to the sheer volume of academic publications on coffee that touched upon issues of fair trade, organic production, standards and certifications, consumer preferences, etc., but which explored the topic using relatively homogeneous language thereby ensuring that coffee emerged as a separate theme. For example, by measure of trade value in 2011, coffee is the eighth-most traded commodity in the world,[14] and is dominant among all fair trade crops (Raynolds 2000). Second, many of the articles in "Fair Trade" are also cross-loaded with "Politics, Justice, and Food Movements," and the tone of the more central articles in "Fair Trade" also take a critical perspective. Conversely "Political Economy of Coffee" does not have any articles cross-loaded with "Politics, Justice, and Food Movements," and articles in this theme tend to be more instrumentalist and use a case study approach.

The theme of "Embeddedness in Food Supply Chains" is strongly represented by the works of just a few authors, which may indicate either that a few authors and papers are very influential or that the theme does not yet attract a wide group of scholars. While social embeddedness focuses on relationships of reciprocity, trust, and connectivity, the term "embeddedness" as it is currently used in food studies refers to the interplay and relationships among people, product, and place. This concept is often deployed in empirical and conceptual work on food relocalization as well as "quality" or "artisanal" food as a means of product differentiation and distinction. It is a concept used predominantly by a handful of European authors who often co-author works together, most notably Roberta Sonnino, Terry Marsden, Jonathan Murdoch, and Jo Banks. A deeper, more qualitative look into this theme, and perhaps a temporal and spatial mapping of the diffusion of the concept of embeddedness, would help to further our understanding of why just a few authors dominate despite the fact that the theme has been circulating more widely in academic thought in food studies since 2000.

The separation between "Community Gardening" and "(Peri-)Urban Land Use Planning and Agriculture" is initially curious. That there are some papers cross-loaded to both "Community Gardening" and "Politics, Justice, and Food Movements" indicates an interest in social justice among some of the authors of papers on community gardening, while there is no such link between "(Peri-)Urban Land Use Planning and Agriculture" and "Politics, Justice, and Food Movements." Quite a number of the papers in "Community Gardening" are case studies in the North American context, with a handful of European examples, whereas "(Peri-)Urban Land Use Planning and Agriculture" features a much larger representation of the Global South. Finally, while the papers in "Community Gardening" are particularly interested in both health and social impact, and are very much focussed on the community, "(Peri-)Urban Land Use Planning and Agriculture" contains articles more oriented toward planning, land use and agriculture, so this might reflect an action-versus-management divide. "Community Supported Agriculture" (CSA) is somewhat of an outlier, as it is linked neither strongly nor moderately to any other theme; this may be because there are relatively few articles in this theme, as compared to the others, and these articles are very coherent with one another in their language and latent meanings.

Given the strong academic interest in both local and organic food, the apparent absence of these as key themes is particularly striking. However, because LSA disambiguates themes based on what *differentiates* their constituent articles from one another, the absence of "local" and "organic" as unique and separate themes underscores their ubiquity throughout the entire collection. In other words, articles addressing local food and organic food are so pervasive throughout the other categories that there is insufficient difference among the articles within the themes emerging out of the literature for local or organic to form their own separate themes. At a higher level of abstraction of, say, three to four themes, it is possible that local and/or organic might emerge as separate themes.

Locating Alterity within the Collection

The discussion above provides an overview of the multiple framings and understandings of AFNs that can be parsed out of the domain of academic research on them; while some of the themes are more readily recognizable as conceptually linked to alterity, others evince more ambiguous connections. LSA offers a means, through term loadings onto each theme, to mathematically assess how central or important a concept is to a particular theme. We looked at how highly the stemmed word "altern" was loaded onto each theme in order to determine the centrality of this concept within that theme. Of the twenty-one themes described above, "altern" is highly loaded on the themes of "Politics, Justice, and Food Movements" and "Embeddedness in Food Supply Chains," and moderately loaded on "Ethical Consumption" and "Community Supported Agriculture." Therefore, according to the LSA dimensions of meaning, these four themes contain articles for which "altern" is central. In this regard, LSA allowed us to reveal the semantic relatedness of these themes with the concept of alterity.

We applied the same data processing and visualization techniques described above to the subset of articles which explicitly used the qualifier "alternative" (see Figure 11.3). Because a subset of only 325 out of 2,075

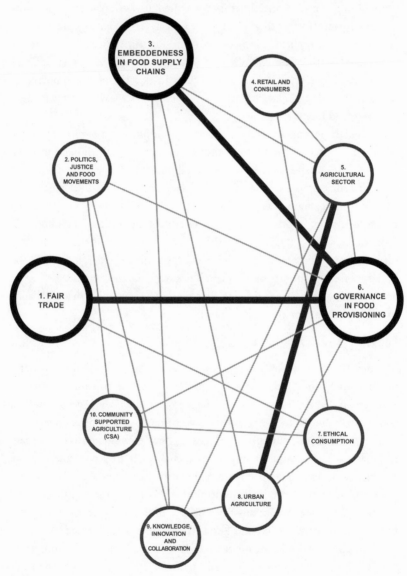

Figure 11.3. Themes and their relationships ("alternative" collection).

articles formed this collection, our conclusions are somewhat more tentative than for the full collection. The ten themes shown in the figure below represent the range of topics that include academic articles explicitly using the term "alternative food."

Five themes from the full collection also emerged from the "alternative" sub-collection, namely "Fair Trade," "Embeddedness in Food Supply Chains," "Politics, Justice, and Food Movements," "Ethical Consumption," and "Community Supported Agriculture." The other five themes in the "alternative" collection did not match those in the full collection enough to for us to consider them analogous, and one theme "Knowledge, Innovation, and Collaboration" emerged as a completely new theme from the "alternative" collection. This new theme is composed of articles that are concerned with innovation networks and new modes of knowledge creation and dissemination within the business world, mostly in Europe and primarily with a focus on "quality" and local products.

In the analysis of the "alternative" subcollection, the number of articles in each theme is relatively even, and unlike in the full collection, "Politics, Justice, and Food Movements" does not dominate, nor is it the most interlinked theme. "Governance in Food Provisioning," on the other hand, is linked to six out of ten of the themes, indicating that there is a particular interest of the intersection of governance with other themes that are expressly deemed as alternative by a number of authors. There seems to be a high interest in the governance element in both "Fair Trade" and "Embeddedness in Food Supply Chains"—more so than in the other themes, as shown by the patterns of document cross-loading. Yet when the themes of the top fifty most-cited papers in the collection are considered, governance falls somewhere in the middle—meaning that while governance is discussed in conjunction with many themes, articles on governance are only moderately influential, at least according to citation counts.

"Knowledge, Innovation, and Collaboration" is fairly well connected, but the lack of a significant link with "Retail and Consumers" indicates an underdeveloped research opportunity. And as with the full collection, we do not see a significant number of articles that speak to both "Politics, Justice, and Food Movements" and "Ethical Consumption." The lack of a strong link between these two themes is somewhat perplexing, in that "alternative" food is often portrayed as (among other things) appealing to the more politically and ethically minded. Yet on the other hand, weakness of the linkage may be attributed to a consumer–citizen divide, whereby ethical consumption is seen as an individual act driven by personal consumer values and choices, and justice and social movements are seen as more concerned with citizenship, collective action, and structural issues.[15] Nonetheless, this division calls for deeper analysis of the content of these themes, using a qualitative approach to better understand where and how they converge and diverge.

Dynamics

To explore the temporal dynamics of this collection of literature, we used term burst analysis to examine publishing patterns.

Figure 11.4 shows the visualization of the term bursts for the period over which a particular term showed a high degree of popularity in usage. For instance, "urban" and "citi" (city) were frequently used over the fourteen years between 1981 and 1995, whereas "movem" (movement) had a much shorter lifespan, only one year, but was significantly more "bursty," as indicated by the thickness of the lines.

The burst period of "urban," "citi," "household," and "secur" (security) between 1981 and 1996 coincides with the relative predominance of articles

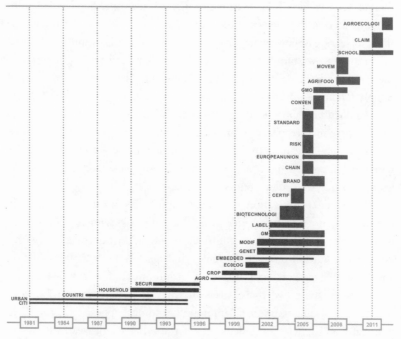

Figure 11.4. Temporal visualization of term bursts, 1981–2013.

from the "Global Urban Food Insecurity and Poverty" theme, especially in the mid-1990s (50 percent of all publications in 1995). This likely reflects an increase in concern about a rapidly urbanizing global population and the recognition that food insecurity was quickly becoming a critical urban issue. Subsequently, publications in the "Global Urban Food Insecurity and Poverty" theme accounted for only 10 percent of articles published.

The topic of genetic modification suddenly spiked between 2001 and 2009, evidenced by term burst patterns. This spike coincided with a burst in in the topic of labelling from 2002 to 2005 and quite a large burst of interest in risk and standards in 2005. It is likely that these term bursts are related, considering that risk and regulation loaded highly on the theme "Risk and Regulation in GMOs". The relation is further supported, given the high cross-loading of articles between "Risk and Regulation in GMOs" and "Purchasing Attitudes and Behaviours"—yet, curiously, there was no strong link to "Food Labelling and Retail Prices." According to publication patterns in the analyzed document collection, interest in GMOs has declined in more recent years.

Bursts of "brand" and "chain" overlap with each other in a short burst from 2005 to 2007, also coinciding with bursts in "standard" and "risk"; however, attributing any linkage based on the data here would be purely speculative. A deeper analysis into the contents of the papers published in this period would be necessary for any definitive conclusions to be drawn. In addition, the burst patterns of "risk," "standard," "brand," and "chain" are not clearly linked to any particular publication trend. There was a spike in publications in the theme "Purchasing Attitudes and Behaviours," which may be linked; but again, further analysis would be needed before an association could be either confirmed or rejected.

Finally, in 2008, there was a short but significant burst in the term "movem" ("movement/s"). This may be linked to the theme "Politics, Justice, and Food Movements," which had a large share of the publications in that year. But again, a more qualitative reading of the articles using these terms and published in this period is required before drawing any definitive conclusions. More broadly, "Politics, Justice, and Food Movements" had a significant spike in 2000, with about 40 percent of the articles published that year belonging to this theme. After dropping back down to 19 percent, it has seen a consistently high proportion of the publications, roughly between 14 and 25 percent, which is nearly double that of the next-largest theme.

Conclusions and Further Research

Our aim in this chapter has been to present a bird's-eye view of the contours and dynamics of academic knowledge on and around "alternative food," as expressed in published journal articles. Through a meta-analysis using the quantitative text analysis method of LSA, we identified twenty-one themes emerging from the diverse range of articles in the collection of academic literature on and around the concept of "alternative" food networks. These themes represent the range of semantic variation of academic knowledge on the topic of AFNs, whereby the centrality of the concept of alterity is more immediately apparent in some themes than in others. According to our multi-staged analysis of the full collection of documents and the "alternative" sub-collection, we determined that the themes in which alterity is most central are (1) "Politics, Justice, and Food Movements," (2) "Embeddedness in Food Supply Chains," (3) "Ethical Consumption," (4) "Community Supported Agriculture," and (5) "Governance in Food Provisioning."

The array of linkages among the twenty-one themes, as revealed through document cross-loading, revealed a handful of themes that are strongly linked semantically with other themes. These are (1) "Politics, Justice, and Food Movements" with "Fair Trade," (2) "Politics, Justice, and Food Movements" with "Embeddedness in Food Supply Chains," (3) "Politics, Justice, and Food Movements" with "Ethical Consumption," and (4) "Global Urban Food Insecurity and Poverty" with "(Peri-)Urban Land Use Planning and Agriculture." In the "alternative" sub-collection, the strongest thematic interlinkages are "Governance in Food Provisioning" with "Embeddedness in Food Supply Chains" and "Governance in Food Provisioning" with "Fair Trade."

The conceptual mapping of AFNs we provide here could be enriched with additional layers of analysis on organic food and local food by applying the same methodological process as carried out in this study. Other possibly fruitful avenues of further research are an exploration of the absence of linkages (i.e., cross-loadings) where they might have been expected (e.g., "CSR and Ethical Retailing" and "Ethical Consumption"), or an examination of why two themes emerged as separately from one another (e.g., "Political Economy of Coffee" and "Fair Trade").

Visualization of the temporal dynamics of term bursts shows a relative stability in term usage between 1981 and 1996, followed by a significant increase in the number of terms which became bursty and a decrease in the length of time over which they were bursty. The burst patterns show that there was a shift in academic publishing around 1996 and a peak of diversity in bursty terms around 2004–05. An examination of the articles published around these years would likely yield further insights into the dynamics of knowledge on AFNs.

While the variable deployment of the term and concept of "alternative food" was the inspiration for this study, it was also the source of the challenges in carrying it out. Attempting to understand the intellectual landscape and dynamics of a particular phenomenon, while simultaneously allowing the scope of inclusion to emerge organically based on the content of the collection itself, proved to be especially challenging. Here, our strategy was to build the data set by starting with "alternative food," identify the primary terms emanating from that collection, and then expand the data set using these terms as keywords for further searching to expand the collection. The fuzziness of the notion of alterity generates difficulties in concept operationalization for empirical research, especially for ontologically oriented inquiry. This is likely to remain a thorny issue until greater lexical convergence is found within food studies, indeed, if this is even possible. On the other hand, efforts to decrease fuzziness through more explicit operationalization of the AFN concept by academic authors when they choose to use it in their writing would offer a notable contribution to the advancement of food studies.

Beyond the implications for academic theory, the semantics of the concept of AFNs and the current state of ambivalence and ambiguity has an impact on the realm of practice. The way in which AFNs are conceptualized influences policy making and decision making for both rural/urban development and food system planning at the micro and meso levels. For example, a particular "alternative" food provisioning or consumption practice is likely to be handled differently by policy makers if it is conceptualized as "fringe," "oppositional," "counter-cultural," "interstitial," "innovative," or simply "alternate." Regulatory frameworks can facilitate or impede the development of local food procurement for schools or an enabling environment for small and medium-sized food producers and processors, depending on how the AFN under consideration is framed and understood.

As demonstrated here, AFNs are conceptualized in a wide variety of ways and variably associated with many related concepts. How AFNs are constructed—the semantic of the concept—ultimately has implications on both theory and practice. We are not advocating for a singular understanding of AFNs, as we see value in diversity of ontologies and epistemologies of AFNs. We are, however, adding our voices to the calls for a disambiguation of AFNs by reducing semantic divergence and increasing convergence in lexical connotations. Or, at the very least we are advocating for academics to be increasingly reflexive in their use of the qualifier "alternative" and to be more explicit as to what that qualifier means in the context of their argument.

Notes

1 For the sake of simplicity, and while recognizing linguistic limitations and inaccuracies, we will use the term "alternative food network" to refer to the full breadth of the concept under investigation in this chapter. Other terms sometimes used include "alternative food initiatives," "alternative food projects," "alternative food systems," "alternative food movements," "alternative food economies," "alternative agri(-)food networks," "alternative agrofood networks," "alternative food chains," "alternative food geography," "alternative food economy," among others.

2 The authors have found only one other comprehensive overview of the related research topic of community food systems—conducted by Campbell, Carlisle-Cummins, and Feenstra (2013) using a qualitative approach. However, since the starting point of their study was different (AFNs rather than community food systems), their results are not comparable to the results presented here.

3 Krippendorff (2004: 18–9) notes that "other meaningful matter" in the form of art, images, maps, sounds, signs, symbols, and numerical records may be considered as "texts" for the purpose of content analysis.

4 A document is an article used in the analysis, and a collection of documents is the full suite of documents used in the analysis.

5 A term is a keyword found in a document and used for the analysis; this may or may not coincide with author-provided keywords.

6 A theme is a principle object of attention running through the document, for example, an idea, object, phenomena, activity, process, structure, substance, and so on (Taylor and Joudrey, 2009).

7 These journal databases were EBSCO Host, Emerald, ISI Web of Science, JSTOR, SAGE, ScienceDirect, Scopus, and Springer Link.

8 The terms used were "alternative food," "alternative agri-food," "alternative agri-food," "alternative agrofood," and "alternative agro-food."

9 The new search terms were "artisan food," "civic food," "community gardens," "community supported agriculture," "direct marketing," "direct purchase," "ethical consum*," "fair trade," "farmers' market," "food desert," "food justice," "food miles," "food movement," "food provision," "genetically modified," "informal food," "local food," "moral econom*," "multifunctional agriculture," "organic certification," "organic food," "quality food," "school food," "short food supply chain," "slow food," "sustainable food," "terroir," "traditional food," and "urban agriculture."

10 Such steps include harmonizing spellings (for example, between British English and American English) and ensuring term consistency (for instance, U.S., U. S., US, and United States were all replaced by UnitedStates (without space); and agri-food, agrifood, agro-food, and agro-food were harmonized as agri-food).

11 For more on the particular technique of "rotated LSA" used here, see Sidorova et al. (2008).

12 "Loading" is the degree to which an article or term is representative of a theme. For example, highly loaded documents or highly loaded terms are the most

characteristic of that theme. Individual documents are normally "cross-loaded" onto more than one theme, meaning that they speak to more than one theme.

13 Corporate social responsibility.

14 FAOSTAT, http://faostat.fao.org/site/342/default.aspx.

15 Our gratitude to Josée Johnston, who drew our attention to this possibility.

References

Campbell, David C., Ildi Carlisle-Cummins, and Gail Feenstra. 2013. "Community Food Systems: Strengthening the Research-to-Practice Continuum." *Journal of Agriculture, Food Systems, and Community Development* 3 (3): 121–38. http://dx.doi.org/10.5304/jafscd.2013.033.008.

Deerwester, Scott, Susan T. Dumais, George W. Furnas, Thomas K. Landauer, and Richard Harshman. 1990. "Indexing by Latent Semantic Analysis." *Journal of the American Society for Information Science* 41 (6): 391–407. http://dx.doi.org/10.1002/(SICI)1097-4571(199009)41:6<391::AID-ASI1>3.0.CO;2-9.

DuPuis, Melanie E., and David Goodman. 2005. "Should We Go 'Home' to Eat? Toward a Reflexive Politics of Localism." *Journal of Rural Studies* 21 (3): 359–71. http://dx.doi.org/10.1016/j.jrurstud.2005.05.011.

Dumais, Susan T. 2007. "LSA and Information Retrieval: Getting back to Basics." In *Handbook of Latent Semantic Analysis*, edited by Thomas K. Landauer, Danielle S. McNamara, Simon Dennis, and Walter Kintsch, 293–322. Mahwah, NJ: Lawrence Erlbaum Associates.

Evangelopoulos, Nicholas, Xiaoni Zhang, and Victor R. Prybutok. 2012. "Latent Semantic Analysis: Five Methodological Recommendations." *European Journal of Information Systems* 21 (1): 70–86. http://dx.doi.org/10.1057/ejis.2010.61.

Goodman, David. 2003. "The Quality 'Turn' and Alternative Food Practices: Reflections and Agenda." *Journal of Rural Studies* 19 (1): 1–7. http://dx.doi.org/10.1016/S0743-0167(02)00043-8.

Goodman, David. 2004. "Rural Europe Redux? Reflections on Alternative Agro-Food Networks and Paradigm Change." *Sociologia Ruralis* 44 (1): 3–16. http://dx.doi.org/10.1111/j.1467-9523.2004.00258.x.

Goodman, David, and E. Melanie DuPuis. 2002. "Knowing Food and Growing Food: Beyond the Production-Consumption Debate in the Sociology of Agriculture." *Sociologia Ruralis* 42 (1): 5–22. http://dx.doi.org/10.1111/1467-9523.00199.

Goodman, David, E. Melanie DuPuis, and Michael K. Goodman. 2013. "Engaging Alternative Food Networks: Commentaries and Research Agendas." *International Journal of Sociology of Agriculture and Food* 20 (2): 425–31.

Holloway, Lewis, Moya Kneafsey, Laura Venn, Rosie Cox, Elizabeth Dowler, and Helena Tuomainen. 2005. "Possible Food Economies: Food Production-Consumption Arrangements and the Meaning of 'Alternative.'" Working paper no. 25. London: Cultures of Consumption, and ESRC-AHRC Research Programme. http://www.consume.bbk.ac.uk/working_papers/HollowayPossible foodeconomiesrevised.doc.

Holsti, Ole R. 1969. *Content Analysis for the Social Sciences and Humanities.* Reading, MA: Addison-Wesley.

Kleinberg, Jon. 2002. "Bursty and Hierarchical Structure in Streams." In Proceedings of the Eighth ACM SIGKDD International Conference on Knowledge Discovery and Data Mining—KDD '02, 91–101. New York: ACM Press. http://dx.doi.org/10.1145/775047.775061.

Krippendorff, Klaus. 2004. "Reliability in Content Analysis." *Human Communication Research* 30 (3): 411–33. http://dx.doi.org/10.1111/j.1468-2958.2004. tb00738.x.

Krippendorff, Klaus. 1969. "Models of Messages: Three Prototypes." In *The Analysis of Communication Content*, edited by G. Gerbner, O.R. Holsti, K. Krippendorff, G.J. Paisly, and Ph.J. Stone, 69–106. New York: Wiley.

Kulkarni, Shailesh S., Uday M. Apte, and Nicholas E. Evangelopoulos. 2014. "The Use of Latent Semantic Analysis in Operations Management Research." *Decision Sciences* 45 (5): 971–94. http://dx.doi.org/10.1111/deci.12095.

Landauer, Thomas K. 2007. "LSA as a Theory of Meaning." In *Handbook of Latent Semantic Analysis*, edited by Thomas K. Landauer, Danielle S. McNamara, Simon Dennis, and Walter Kintsch, 3–34. Mahwah, NJ: Lawrence Erlbaum Associates.

Mehl, Matthias R. 2006. "Quantitative Text Analysis." In *Handbook of Multimethod Measurement in Psychology*, edited by Michael Eid and Ed Diener, 141–56. Washington, DC: American Psychological Association. http://dx.doi. org/10.1037/11383-011.

Neuendorf, Kimberly A. 2002. *The Content Analysis Guidebook*. Thousand Oaks, CA: Sage.

Parr, David A., and Yongmei Lu. 2010. "The Landscape of GIScience Publications 1997–2007: An Empirical Investigation with Latent Semantic Analysis." *Transactions in GIS* 14 (5): 689–708. http://dx.doi.org/10.1111/j.1467-9671. 2010.01228.x.

Raynolds, Laura. 2000. "Re-embedding Global Agriculture: The International Organic and Fair Trade Movements." *Agriculture and Human Values* 17 (3): 297–309. http://dx.doi.org/10.1023/A:1007608805843.

Sidorova, Anna, Nicholas E. Evangelopoulos, Joseph S. Valacich, and Thiagarajan Ramakrishnan. 2008. "Uncovering the Intellectual Core of the Information Systems Discipline." *Management Information Systems Quarterly* 32 (3): 467–82.

Sonnino, Roberta, and Terry Marsden. 2006. "Beyond the Divide: Rethinking Relationships between Alternative and Conventional Food Networks in Europe." *Journal of Economic Geography* 6 (2): 181–99. http://dx.doi.org/10.1093/ jeg/lbi006.

Taylor, Arlene G., and Daniel N. Joudrey. 2009. *The Organization of Information*. Englewood, CO: Libraries Unlimited.

Tregear, Angela. 2011. "Progressing Knowledge in Alternative and Local Food Networks: Critical Reflections and a Research Agenda." *Journal of Rural Studies* 27 (4): 419–30. http://dx.doi.org/10.1016/j.jrurstud.2011.06.003.

Van der Ploeg, Jan Douwe, and Henk Renting. 2004. "Behind the 'Redux': A Rejoinder to David Goodman." *Sociologia Ruralis* 44 (2): 234–42. http://dx.doi. org/10.1111/j.1467-9523.2004.00272.x.

Weber, Robert Philip. 1990. *Basic Content Analysis*. Newbury Park, CA: Sage.

Winson-Geideman, Kimberly, and Nicholas E. Evangelopoulos. 2013. "Topics in Real Estate Research: 1973–2010: A Latent Semantic Analysis." *Journal of Real Estate Literature* 21 (1): 59–76.

Zhu, Mu, and Ali Ghodsi. 2006. "Automatic Dimensionality Selection from the Scree Plot via the Use of Profile Likelihood." *Computational Statistics & Data Analysis* 51 (2): 918–30. http://dx.doi.org/10.1016/j.csda.2005.09.010.

Commentary on Part III: "Un-doing" Food Studies: A Case for Flexible Fencing

Josée Johnston[1]

The preceding chapters all deal with the topic of "un-doing." Certainly this theme has a lot of intuitive appeal. Many of us in the field of food studies are deeply critical and oriented toward social justice. The idea of tearing down walls, kicking over barricades, and creating a bit of trouble appeals to many of us. While there is much to be gained from this impulse, in this brief commentary, I'm going to make a slightly different kind of argument. I'm going to argue that while food scholars should certainly listen to their impulse to "un-do," we must at the same time strategically think through where and when it is useful to erect a fence.

To further my case about the utility of flexible fencing, I draw an analogy with rotational grazing systems.[2] For ranchers following this system, the goal is not to do away with all fences that contain livestock and let the cows (or chickens or pigs) run wild and free across the countryside. Instead, the goal is to use a system of flexible fencing to control access to pasture. Cows may be left on a relatively restricted area of pasture for a set amount of time (a day, or even less), and then the fence is moved in order to move the animals to a different spot of the pasture. This system is widely recognized as sustainable (since it uses animal fertilization and traction to build soil and encourage plant growth), but it requires a lot of labour and skill. Ranchers need to know when and how often to move their fences. They must understand how to move the animals frequently without causing undue stress, and they must have an intimate knowledge of the land the animals are grazing on, as well as variable conditions, such as weather and water sources.

While there are limits to my rotational grazing metaphor, I contend that food scholarship would do well to take inspiration from these systems and their flexible use of temporary fences. By *selectively* erecting fences and thinking carefully about when and where a boundary is needed, we can push food studies to build greater knowledge about the industrialized globalized food system, as well as the many alternatives that are bubbling up to challenge it. To make this point more concrete, I will briefly discuss two instances where flexible fences can be a useful metaphor for marking out a path for food scholars.

Temporary Fence #1. Academic Disciplines

The first "fence" involves the relation of food studies to conventional disciplines, such as sociology, history, economics, and anthropology. There is much to criticize about these traditional disciplines and their tendencies toward insularity and specialization. As sociologist Bill Carroll (2013) writes, in an eloquent critique of disciplinary ossification in sociology: "Disciplinary procedures that police the borders may actually limit our capacity to comprehend a complex reality that is always social, psychological, political, cultural, economic, historical, and geographical. The result is fragmented knowledge that may be useful for managing and reproducing an institutional order...but that is incapable of informing the transformative practices needed to move beyond that deeply problematic way of life" (11).

Carroll's argument is erudite and convincing, and certainly the papers that precede this commentary all speak to the knowledge dividends that accrue when disciplinary boundaries are challenged. Bomford and Brock's chapter speaks to the importance of connecting literatures on health with scholarship on sustainability. More generally, their writing speaks to the utter lunacy of discussing diets that are "healthy" for individuals without simultaneously considering the health of supporting ecological systems—even though this division makes perfect sense from a disciplinary perspective. Relatedly, Lee and Soma's paper illustrates how a topic of vital social importance—food waste—has fallen through the disciplinary cracks. Further, when food waste has been studied, it has been contained within a problematic disciplinary binary separating those who study wasteful consumers in the Global North from those who examine on-farm waste in food systems in the Global South.

Certainly, there is much to be gained from approaches that study food from multiple or interdisciplinary perspectives. Likely, we can all agree on the problematic tendency for academics (from across all fields) to hive away their knowledge in proprietary disciplinary "silos." However, the language of silo is useful here, as it is also a meaningful agricultural referent. A silo is a stable, solid structure (often a tower, and often constructed out of metal) used to protect grain from airborne impurities, weather, and infestation by pests, such as rats. The key word here is "protect." Simply put, sometimes silos are useful and even vital to our well-being. So, too, are disciplines. Sometimes, a disciplinary home can protect our intellectual development, providing useful things such as stable employment; intellectual comrades who can exchange ideas on shared methods, literature, and theories; and a relatively stable framework for knowledge accumulation and dissemination. Arguably, the complex methodological technique used in the chapter by Trenouth and co-authors—latent semantic analysis—could not have been developed without disciplinary specialization, even though, ironically, this technique is used to chart the meanings of "alternative" food *across* disciplines. My point here is not to romanticize disciplines, or even to suggest that food studies become its own discipline. Rather, it is to suggest that it is useful to see disciplines as temporary fences that we can selectively employ to accumulate knowledge and methodological techniques that are valuable for studying food, *and* food system transformation. In this way, it is clear that although the Carroll quote I have enlisted above provides a useful caution against academic specialization, it is overly pessimistic and totalizing.

Disciplinary frameworks can be, and have been, used to inform the transformative practices needed to critique an unjust and unsustainable food system as well as to develop alternatives. For example, we need specialized scientific training and study in order to document the food system's connection to climate change and develop much-needed agricultural alternatives. To use a social scientific example closer to home, my own discipline of sociology has developed a corpus of scholarship on classed taste stratification and classification, drawing from the work of French sociologist Pierre Bourdieu (1984). In my own research, this body of scholarship has greatly enriched my own thinking on the cultural dimensions of social inequality and the role that food plays in naturalizing inequities so that consuming "good food" (e.g., organic, green, local, healthy, foodie) comes to serve as a classed and moral boundary marker (e.g., Johnston and Baumann 2014; Johnston, Szabo, and Rodney 2011; Johnston, Rodney, and Szabo 2012). The marshalling of sociological energy into the puzzle of food, culture, and inequality has been productive and enlightening. At the same time, it's useful to see the disciplinary fence as temporary and selective. For example, I have much to learn from psychological literature on taste boundaries, as well as from boundary-disrupters within my own discipline. As a case in point,

Michael Carolan's (2011, 2014) work on "taste" challenges conventional sociological accounts, encourages us to think beyond "we can tell" (representational knowledge), and a develops a concept of taste "ecologies" that incorporate feelings and experiences of food. He also creatively incorporates interviews with food "taste makers" in the food industry to shed light on how industrial foodscapes actively shape taste preferences. This work challenges the common food truism that "good" food (e.g., local, natural, organic) will "naturally" attract caring consumers (e.g., "if only people could taste a home-grown tomato!") and, instead, lends credence to the idea that sustainable food cannot simply be something we know about; rather, it has to be something we feel, practice, perform, and develop a taste for (Carolan 2014).

Temporary Fence #2. Alternative Food

The second temporary fence I will defend is the marker surrounding "alternative" food. The "alternative" marker is contentious and often ill-defined. A useful finding from Trenouth and co-authors' method of latent class analysis is the fact that the definition of "alternative" food is often more clear-cut when it is used in theoretical literature and more ambiguous when it is employed with regard to on-the-ground, real-life food struggles. Relatedly, Sprague and Kennedy's chapter shows that identifying "alternative" food is highly difficult in food praxis, and they critique the various ways in which alternative food networks embody elements from conventional capitalism, especially the over-sold idea of making change through commoditization ("voting with your fork") rather than more radical strategies of citizenship, collective action, and the disruption of structural power hierarchies.

There are certainly many reasons to be skeptical, then, of the concept of alternative food. However, there is also an argument to be made for retaining an interest in this term. As I wrote with my colleague Kate Cairns:

> In a recent conversation about food politics with a food studies scholar, she balked at the use of the term "alternative." For her, there was no point talking about "alternative" food projects in a world where Wal-Mart sells organics and non-profit food projects form partnerships with grocery store chains. While we certainly understand this point, we are reluctant to abandon terminology designed to identify what is different—a taxonomy that guides us towards projects that are not the corporate, capitalist "business as usual." Why? Because if everything is now located in the "mushy middle" of do-good capitalism, how can scholars and activists figure out which strategies are most

useful for working towards greater food system sustainability and social justice? How can we call out the "greenwashers" and the cynical corporate do-gooding, and distinguish this from more substantive social movement efforts? Obviously there are no easy answers to these questions, but it seems that that some kind of boundaries are required—both analytically and politically (Johnston and Cairns 2013, 403).

Building on this argument, I contend that seeing the label "alternative" as a kind of flexible fence encourages us to keep our eye on the ball of food system transformation. To be clear, "alternative" is not a synonym for "perfect." The critiques of depoliticization and consumer fetishization made by Sprague and Kennedy, for example, are endemic to many "alternative" food projects (e.g., DeLind 2011). However, we on the socially progressive, sustainability-oriented, justice-oriented left (academics *and* consumers) are continually in danger of throwing out the baby with the bathwater when the lived experience of social change doesn't live up to our ideals. When Walmart sells organic, we deem it meaningless. When Starbucks sells fair trade, we stop believing. When "local food" colonizes the signage at Whole Foods Market (even over bins of long-distance California produce), we feel defeated. These are all understandable responses, but it is important that we not abandon the hard-slogging intellectual and emotional work of drawing and redrawing the line between "alternative" and corporate "green/fair-trade washing," even if that work is never-ending and the boundaries are only temporarily demarcated.

So, *how* do we erect fence posts around "alternative" food? In their wide-reaching and theoretically rich book, *Alternative Food Networks*, Goodman, DuPuis, and Goodman (2012) provide a framework for moving beyond a naïve "food as saviour" versus an overly pessimistic account. As such, their work provides several important guidelines for thinking about the constitution of "alternatives." First, they advocate a reflexive approach that carefully considers the "alterity" of a food project rather than assuming, for example, that everything local is virtuous or everything homemade is soulful. For Goodman and his co-authors (2012), "alterity" rejects a priori assumptions of a food project's "goodness" and is, instead, about attempting to find "new ways of doing things," coexisting with a powerful system of capitalist agriculture, and "trying to change it from within" (9). Second, Goodman and his co-authors (2012) advance a nuanced and materialist idea of power in relation to alternative food system debates. This means that power is not only seen as a disciplinary force but is also concentrated in large bureaucracies

Commentary on Part III **297**

and corporations (86–7), such as the world's largest ten food and beverage companies (e.g., Coca-Cola, Nestlé, Unilever), which Oxfam (2013) has critiqued in its report, "Behind the Brands." Adding to these criteria, I would add that race and gender inequities are additional factors to consider in relation to food system stratification and transformation (e.g., Alkon and Agyeman 2011; Cairns and Johnston 2015; Allen and Sachs 2007).

In short, food scholars can honour and retain our impulse to "un-do," remaining critical and sceptical, and defending the academic privilege *and responsibility* to deconstruct and critique the world around us. At the same time, we can recognize when boundaries are useful, when it is important to skillfully and reflexively build fences. These fences are useful analytically, as I have shown in the case of disciplinary boundaries, but they are also important politically, as we struggle to maintain solidarity around emergent hopes for a more sustainable, socially just food system. As Alkon and Agyeman (2011) write, the point is not to "chastise the food movement, but to work toward building a stronger and deeper critique of industrialized agriculture" and to "nurture fertile soil in which a polyculture of approaches to a just and sustainable agriculture can thrive" (4).

Notes

1 Thanks to Michael Carolan, Michael Goodman, and Emily Huddart-Kennedy for reading drafts of this commentary.
2 Systems of rotational grazing became prominent in the public eye through the charismatic (and libertarian) work of Joel Salatin—a rancher who appeared in the wildly successful film *Food Inc.* Others preceded and inspired Salatin's work, notably Alan Savory, who founded a system of land management for grasslands that he terms "holistic management." See http://www.savoryinstitute.com/.

References

Alkon, Alison Hope, and Julian Agyeman, eds. 2011. *Cultivating Food Justice: Race, Class and Sustainability.* Cambridge, MA: MIT Press.

Allen, Patricia, and Carolyn Sachs. 2007. "Women and Food Chains: The Gendered Politics of Food." *International Journal of Sociology of Food and Agriculture* 15 (1): 1–23.

Bourdieu, Pierre. 1984. *Distinction.* Cambridge, MA: Harvard University Press.

Cairns, Kate, and Josée Johnston. 2015. *Food and Femininity.* London: Bloomsbury.

Carolan, Michael. 2011. *Embodied Food Politics.* Burlington, VT: Ashgate.

Carolan, Michael. 2014. "Affective Sustainable Landscapes and Care Ecologies: Getting a Real Feel for Alternative Food Communities." *Sustainability Science* 10 (2): 317–29. http://dx.doi.org/10.1007/s11625-014-0280-6.

Carroll, William K. 2013. "Discipline, Field, Nexus: Re-Visioning Sociology." *Canadian Review of Sociology* 50 (1): 1–26. http://dx.doi.org/10.1111/cars.12000.

DeLind, Laura B. 2011. "Are Local Food and the Local Food Movement Taking Us Where We Want to Go? Or Are We Hitching Our Wagons to the Wrong Stars?" *Agriculture and Human Values* 28 (2): 273–83. http://dx.doi.org/10.1007/s10460-010-9263-0.

Goodman, David, Melanie DuPuis, and Michael Goodman. 2012. *Alternative Food Networks: Knowledge, Practice and Politics.* New York: Routledge.

Johnston, Josée, and Kate Cairns. 2013. "Searching for the 'Alternative,' Caring, Reflexive Consumer." *International Journal of Sociology of Food and Agriculture* 20 (3): 403–8.

Johnston, Josée, and Shyon Baumann. 2014. *Foodies: Democracy and Distinction in the American Foodscape.* 2nd ed. New York: Routledge.

Johnston, Josée, Alexandra Rodney, and Michelle Szabo. 2012. "Place, Ethics, and Everyday Eating: A Tale of Two Neighbourhoods." *Sociology* 46 (6): 1091–108. http://dx.doi.org/10.1177/0038038511435060.

Johnston, Josée, Michelle Szabo, and Alexandra Rodney. 2011. "Good Food, Good People: Understanding the Cultural Repertoire of Ethical Eating." *Journal of Consumer Culture* 11 (3): 293–318. http://dx.doi.org/10.1177/1469540511417996.

Oxfam. 2013. "Behind the Brands." London: 166 Oxfam Briefing Paper. http://www.oxfam.org.

PART IV: SCALING LEARNING IN AGRI-FOOD SYSTEMS

CHAPTER 12

Transitioning Toward Sustainable Food and Farming: Interactions between Learning and Practice in Community Spaces

Jennifer A. Braun and Eva A. Bogdan

Food is increasingly becoming a powerful arena in the struggle for a more ecologically and socially just society. There is growing recognition that the choices people make around food have significant environmental and social impacts, both on their communities and around the globe. If a shift from unsustainable practices is to be achieved, scholars argue, profound personal and social changes are required, and transformative learning theory is useful for understanding some of these processes (e.g., Kerton and Sinclair 2010; Lankester 2013; Tarnoczi 2011).

To better understand the iterative relationship between learning and practice in community spaces, we draw upon both transformative learning theory and social practice theory to analyze the complex learning processes, contexts, and motivations that influence behavioural change in agri-food systems. By bringing these two theories into conversation, and by revealing the influence of friends, family, and peers as communities of practice (CoP) (Wenger 1998, Wenger and Snyder 2000)—which are integral for the successful and continuous commitment to more sustainable agri-food practices—we challenge the notion that transformative learning is individualistic.

In this chapter, we apply a comparative qualitative case study method to examine the relationship between learning and practice in two different contexts: producers' stewardship practices in the Alberta Environmental Farm Plan (EFP) program and women's food practices in a rural Alberta community. These two case studies are examples of the ways in which food systems are an essential link between ecosystems and human populations.

Agriculture and food consumption are two of the most important drivers of environmental pressures, especially habitat change, climate change, water use, and toxic emissions (United Nations Environment Programme 2010). Practices reproduced in any society, including those in food production and consumption, are outcomes of complex processes over which no single actor has control (Shove, Pantzar, and Watson 2012). Therefore, approaches that target individual attitudes, behaviours, and choices to create change neglect the extent to which state and other actors influence everyday life, both currently and historically, through the shaping of options, the design of technology and infrastructure, and the promotion of institutions that maintain the status quo (Shove 2010). A sustainable agri-food system—a cornerstone to environmental sustainability—requires uptake and circulation of environmentally friendly practices in community spaces.

We begin with a brief review of literature on transformative learning and social practice theory, followed by methods and a description of the cases. Next, we present evidence from each of the two case studies, that relates to our emergent three-part analysis: transformative learning and change as either incremental or rapid in response to crisis; the importance and influence of CoPs; and the residual and ripple effects of learning and practices. We conclude with a discussion on transformative processes for transitioning toward sustainable agri-food systems.

Transformative Learning

Cultural canon, socio-economic structures, ideologies and beliefs, and the practices they support can foster conformity and impede socially and environmentally responsible action. Transformative learning theory examines how adults learn to negotiate and act on their own purposes, values, feelings, and meanings—rather than those they have uncritically assimilated from others—to gain greater control over their lives as socially responsible decision makers (Mezirow 1997). Transformative learning demands that people become aware of how they come to knowledge and of the values that lead them to their perspectives (Mezirow 1997; Taylor and Cranton 2012).

Transformative learning occurs when an individual's frame of reference, or structure of assumptions, shifts to one that is "more inclusive, differentiating, permeable (open to other viewpoints), critically reflective of assumptions, emotionally capable of change, and integrative of experience" (Mezirow 2000, 19), leading an individual toward "an informed and reflective decision to act" (Mezirow 1996, 163–4). Once set in their assumptions, adults tend to think and act without questioning their frame of reference and to reject ideas that do not fit into it or the way they interpret their surroundings or experiences. A shift in frame of reference can occur through critical reflection on the assumptions upon which habits of mind or points of view are based (see Figure 1 in Tarnoczi 2011). Habits of mind are durable, "broad, abstract, orienting, habitual ways of thinking, feeling, and acting influenced by assumptions" (Mezirow 1997, 5–6) that structure the way we interpret our experiences (for example, anthropocentrism). Habits of mind become articulated in a specific point of view that is changeable and is composed of specific attitudes, beliefs, feelings, and value judgments that filter interpretation (Mezirow 1997), for example, regarding wetland protection.

Shifts in assumptions can occur through involvement in communicative learning or instrumental problem solving (Mezirow 1997). Communicative learning involves two or more people attempting to understand the meaning of what is being communicated in their discourse by assessing the interpretations or justifications that stem from underlying assumptions (Mezirow 1997). Communicative learning occurs when the following change: (1) insight into one's own interests, (2) insights into the interests and experiences of others, (3) communication strategies and methods through sharing knowledge, and (4) social mobilization (Diduck and Mitchell 2003; Kerton and Sinclair 2010; Lankester 2013; Sinclair, Diduck and Fitzpatrick 2008; Tarnoczi 2011).

Instrumental learning involves learning how to manipulate or control people or the environment to enhance performance through (1) scientific and technical knowledge, (2) legal, administrative, and political procedures, (3) social and economic knowledge, and (4) evaluation of potential risks and impacts (Diduck and Mitchell 2003; Kerton and Sinclair 2010; Lankester 2013; Sinclair, Diduck and Fitzpatrick 2008; Tarnoczi 2011). While communicative and instrumental learning are pathways for transformative learning, they may not include the degree of change that would qualify them as transformative.

Learning can occur through several processes: altering or expanding an existing point of view, establishing a new point of view, and lastly, transforming habit of mind by becoming aware and critical of one's assumptions and beliefs (Mezirow 1997). Transformative learning can occur at a slow and incremental pace but can also be triggered by an externally imposed "disorienting dilemma" (Mezirow 1990, 13), such as a sudden or dramatic event. Personal transformations can cause changes that lead a person to have a different impact on his or her environment, translating individual transformative learning into broader social change. Furthermore, becoming critically reflective of the assumptions of oneself and others is fundamental for effective collaborative problem posing, redefining, and solving, as well as adapting to change (Mezirow 1990).

One major critique of Mezirow's theory is that it has been too driven by rationality, with not enough attention to the way that individuals come to know and learn, such as through emotions or embodied forms of knowing (Taylor 2001). Other critiques point to this theory's excessive focus on the individual and inattention to social transformation, relationships, or context (Merriam, Caffarella, and Baumgartner 2007; Taylor 2007). These learning scholars have argued for a stronger focus on the importance of body, emotion, and relationships.

Thus, we consider how bodies and relationships come together as CoP in specific social contexts and tactile spaces. Tactile spaces stimulate the senses (e.g., touch, taste, smell) and incubate lived experiences of the social and natural worlds and create opportunities for instrumental, communicative, and transformative learning to occur through the exchange of different forms of knowledge (Carolan 2007). We found that community, collective action, and relationships, while sometimes challenging and messy, were critical for transforming knowledge and practices in the food system.

Social Practice Theory

Social practice theory departs from analyses that tend to overemphasize either structure or agency as the source of the problem and/or solution, and instead describes the world as constructed and ordered by social practices (Warde 2005). The principal implication of a theory of practice is that the sources of changed behaviour lie in the development and enactment of practices themselves. Thus, behaviour is determined not by individual agency, nor by societal structures alone, but rather everyday practices like shopping, cooking, or eating. As Giddens (1984) observed, "The basic domain of study of the social sciences…is neither the experience of the individual actor, nor the existence of any form of societal totality, but social practices ordered across space and time" (2). In this view, sustainable patterns of food consumption, for example, are not understood as the result of individuals' attitudes, values, and beliefs constrained by various contextual barriers, but rather as embedded within and occurring as part of larger social practices (Warde 2005).

In turn, the performance of numerous social practices is seen as part of "the routine accomplishment of what we identify as 'normal' ways of life" (Shove 2004, 117). Practices are "the source and carrier of meaning, language and normativity" (Schatzki 2001, 12) and are "centrally organized around shared practical understanding" (Schatzki 2001, 2). In this view, attention is diverted from individual decision making toward the "doing" of different social practices (Hargreaves 2011). Importantly, practice theory emphasizes that it is through these engagements with practices that individuals come to understand the world around them and to develop a more or less coherent sense of self (Warde 2005). It should be noted that this theory does not mean individuals are passive victims of the dictates of practice, but instead conceives of them as skilled agents who actively negotiate and perform a wide range of practices in the course of everyday life (Hargreaves 2011). Bringing about more sustainable patterns of production or consumption, therefore, does not depend solely on a top-down, undemocratic process of persuading individuals to make different or "better" decisions, but instead on understanding the social practices that constitute everyday life, and the ways in which they can be reworked or transformed to acknowledge the social, economic, and environmental concerns, contexts, and constraints in people's lives.

If people are "faithful carriers of practices" (Shove, Pantzar, and Watson 2012, 98), then how are practices reproduced? How do they become defective? According to Shove and her co-authors (2012), practice consists of three basic elements: *materials* (objects, infrastructure, tools, and the body itself); *competencies* (skills, know-how, technique); and *meanings* (the social and symbolic significance of participation). Practices exist, persist, or disappear when the links between these three elements are created, sustained, or broken by practitioners. *Competencies* and *meanings* can be significantly shaped by transformative learning and thus contribute to changed practice over time. There are two distinct aspects in the reproduction of circuits of practice (Reckwitz 2002): first, practice-as-entity (practice as a block or pattern created by the interdependencies between the three basic elements), which is then filled out and reproduced through the second aspect, practice-as-performance (practice as immediacy of doing; see Chapter 2 by Szanto, Wong, and Brady in this book for an exploration of food as performance).

Through routinized practices, individuals sustain a sense of ontological security (i.e., stable mental state), and reproduce their social life (Giddens 1984). When an event occurs that is not consistent with the meaning of one's life, ontological security is threatened. This is similar to Mezirow's "disorienting dilemma," triggered by an event that opens up a possibility for transformative learning. In this chapter, we examine such instances and the changes in individual's practices and subsequent collective practices.

According to Giddens (1984), it is the reflexive monitoring of not just individuals' but also others' activities, as well as the contexts that are a continuing feature of everyday action. This is noteworthy since critical reflection is also important in Mezirow's transformative learning theory. Giddens and Mezirow agree: both call for a critical examining of actions. We therefore use criteria outlined for each theory to examine the magnitude of learning, whether it be transformative or less extensive in the case of instrumental and communicative learning.

A challenge with social practice theory is that it has undergone a number of waves of change, creating a diversity of approaches with varied and conflicting conceptions and research strategies. That said, all practice approaches are bounded by conceptualizing the field of practices as consisting of a crucible wherein phenomena occur, such as human activity, power, language, social institutions, knowledge, meaning, science, and historical transformation (Schatzki 2001). Social practice theory raises a series of radically different questions about how to create more sustainable patterns of consumption (Hargreaves 2011), and arguably production, including those related to food and agriculture. The focus no longer rests on individuals' attitudes, behaviours, and choices, but instead on how practices form, reproduce, or become defective among the carriers of practice, who form a CoP.

Communities of Practice (CoP)

CoPs are "groups of people informally bounded together by shared expertise and passion for a joint enterprise [who] share their experiences and knowledge in free-flowing, creative ways that foster new approaches to problems" (Wenger and Snyder 2000, 139–40). Theories of CoP examine how people learn socially from their peers within communities (Wenger 1998) and has provided a useful lens through which to view farmers and their practices (Oreszczyn, Lane, and Carr 2010) as well as community members engaging in cooking activities (Terrenghi, Hilliges, and Butz 2007). Wenger and Snyder (2000) argue that participating in CoPs is essential for learning because communities are the basic building blocks of a social learning[1] system. When CoPs do not form, knowledge and practices may be lost.

Within the CoP literature, an emphasis is often put on the social learning that occurs when people engage with one another, often from diverse perspectives and experiences to develop a common framework of understanding and basis for joint action (Schusler, Decker, and Pfeffer 2003, 311). The development of a new, shared world view through social learning is an example of transformative learning (Cundill and Fabricius 2009). CoPs play a significant role in prompting individuals to critically reflect on their own and each other's assumptions of the world, which is an important part of learning that enhances sustainability (Lankester 2013). For Pahl-Wostl, Mostert, and Tàbara (2008) social learning includes relationships between social agents and between socio-ecological systems, emphasizing collaboration in moving toward sustainability.

The process of understanding perspectives or points of view other than one's own, or "decentration" (Mezirow 1981, 15) can result in shared subjectivity that transcends pursuit of individual drives (Hoverman et al. 2011). In turn, the experience of shared subjectivity lends itself to the development of empathy, responsibility, transparency, trust, and accountability and can alter relationships to people, animals, and land. Hoverman et al. (2011) found that "just as the process of knowledge formation is a social process, so too is creating or agreeing on a new understanding of the world that incorporates new perspectives into the accepted view of social truth" (29). If we trust a social network, we will likely believe the knowledge it produces, thereby accepting its version of truth or reality (Carolan 2006b).

Methods

Since learning is always "situated" (Lave and Wenger 1991) and practices occur within a specific time and space (Shove, Pantzar, and Watson 2012), we apply a case study method approach that involves an empirical investigation of a phenomenon within its real-life context (Flyvbjerg 2001; Yin 2014). The case study method is ideal for examining a set of complex interactions, rather than relationships between variables, thereby enhancing our understanding of the richness and nuances of social life.

Every province in Canada and the Yukon Territory has an EFP program (Agriculture and Agri-Food Canada 2009). In Alberta, over 12,000 producers have participated to date. Based on the principles of adult education, the EFP is a business and risk-management tool that enables farmers to voluntarily perform a self-assessment of their farming operation to identify environmental risks relating to water, soil, air, and biodiversity (AEFP 2012). Producers develop a farm plan to mitigate or eliminate risks based on suitable beneficial management practices (BMPs). We chose this case study because it provides an opportunity to examine the process of transitioning to sustainable farming practices. The case study draws on secondary data from EFP media articles[2] (n = 74) from 2006 to 2013, which are based on interviews with producers participating in the Alberta EFP program.

The second case study examines the gardening, cooking, and canning practices of women in Stony Plain, a rural Albertan community. This case study highlights the women's learning around food and agriculture and provides insight into everyday household food procurement, preparation, and preservation practices. Data for this project was collected as part of research on traditional food practices of rural women in Alberta (Braun 2014). This research involved extensive participant observation and fifteen in-depth, semi-structured qualitative interviews and a focus group conducted with the women and their (adult) children.

These two case studies provide opportunities to explore the interplay between transformative learning and social practices in growing and preparing food shaped by, and circulated among, community. They also differ in a number of ways. In the EFP study, participants are from a wide geographic range in Alberta and are mostly male, whereas the second study consisted of women from a small community. In addition, the EFP program has evolved as part of a formal government initiative, whereas the practices of the rural Albertan women are informal and "everyday." The EFP media articles highlight only success stories and the interviewees from Stony Plain self-selected to participate in the study. Although these case studies were methodologically distinct, a qualitative analysis approach allowed us to reconcile these differences. The emergent analysis drew strength from this diversity and constructed new insights by working across these two distinct studies and indeed, by looking at learning across spaces of production and consumption.

Transitions Toward Sustainable Food Practices and Farming

In this section, we explore how learning and practices interact to encourage a transition toward sustainable food practices and farming among our interviewees in community spaces. We also explore the role of CoPs in this process where friends, family, and peers served as carriers and conduits of practices.

Change: Sudden or Incremental

The experience of direct personal hardship as well as indirect learning from others who experience difficulties can create disorienting dilemmas and serve as opportunities for learning and motivation for changing practices (Lankester 2013; Mezirow 1990). In our case studies, the occurrence of environmental or health problems often had deep and profound impacts on individuals and entire families.

In agriculture, a producer's values, shared meanings and social norms, underlying beliefs and assumptions, and relationships shape his or her system of farming (Alberta Research Council 2006; Carolan 2005). A crisis, such as a drought, can trigger shifts in perceptions and practices, which farmers Glen and Kelly Hall faced in the 1980s: "So for us, that whole big picture water system became very clear.... A lot of what we've wrapped our heads around over the last three decades [since the drought] is that by looking after the land and the water and being good stewards, it then looks after you" (AEFP 6 December 2012, paras. 17, 28). The couple made several changes in their farming practices: protecting watersheds and leaving half the grass un-grazed, for which "people look at [them] funny" (para. 11) (*meaning*); conservation tilling to reduce erosion and conserve moisture; and planting shelterbelts (*materials*). The environmental crisis alerted these ranchers to the value of good water sources and consequently they sought ways of educating (*competences*) themselves through the EFP on how to manage those sources: "That EFP experience was a good reflection on our practices and it helped us to realize what we were doing right.... Our focus really became water once we looked at that whole Farm Plan" (para. 23).

This example illustrates instrumental learning, in which new practices were adopted in response to a disorienting dilemma, to enhance environmental performance through the application of scientific and technical knowledge, and had positive impacts on water, land, and neighbours' farming operations downstream. Learning became transformative as the couple moved away from mainstream grazing practices to more sustainable ones. Glen and Kelly examined their role as stewards of the land and critically reflected on farming practices. In addition, the couple continued "building on [their] initial success" (AEFP 6 December 2012, para. 25), indicating they were set on a pathway for further reflection on sustainability. Such changes in ways of thinking and acting have also been found in other agricultural research as evidence of transformative learning (Lankester 2013; Tarnoczi 2011).

Altered perceptions and beliefs can result in a change of practices, but the opposite can also occur—that is, change in practices can result in shifts in perceptions and beliefs. As such, learning is an iterative process; learning leads to changed practices, which in turn, leads to new learning and new practices (Mezirow, 2000). Michel-Guillou and Moser (2006) found that when producers adopt new practices because of social influences, it "seems to trigger interest in the environment, particularly in terms of conceptualizing the environment and of assessing the farmers' own capacity for action" (227). This finding is unique in that it demonstrates how action and routinization can lead to reflection and changes in perceptions, but is consistent with social practice theory. In the context of EFP, this suggests that producers initially motivated by social or economic factors to implement stewardship practices may incrementally internalize sustainability-oriented attitudes, beliefs, feelings, and value judgments or point of view, and if repeated, ultimately transform their frame of reference.

Incremental learning was also a key finding in our other case study. Ang, a mother of three, went through a series of small shifts in points of view that resulted in a significant transformation in her food practices and beliefs about food over time. When she was pregnant with her first child, she moved out to rural Alberta to be closer to her in-laws. Ang did not grow up with any type of gardening or canning background, and was surprised when she discovered the copious amounts of fresh, healthy, and delicious food her mother-in-law could get from her home garden: "I couldn't get over the fact that when you plant one row of carrots, how many freaking carrots you got. I just had no concept of that until the first year I did the garden with my [mother in law]. There was that much food coming out of the garden!... And that's where I got into making my own baby food; I could use all the extras from the garden and make baby food all year long."

Ang ascribes her desire to have her own small garden at home, can all of her own baby food, bake her own bread, and cook from scratch, as well as the learning that occurred through interactions with her mother-in-law. Ang explained, "Gardening is important because it's [the produce] just fresher and we know where our food came from. And that's what I wanted to do when I found out we were having our son—I canned all my own baby food. I never ever bought one jar from the store because I knew it had acid and all those yucky things in it, so I just wanted my kids to eat fresh out of the garden.... I think it's important to know where your food comes from and to know what you're eating and that it's not laced with chemicals."

Gaining knowledge (*competencies*) and evaluating potential risks of chemicals set the stage for further reflection on sustainability and gave Ang motivation to continue learning about the ingredients (and their side effects) in processed food, which led to more insights into, and questioning of, mainstream food production practices.

Another interesting transformation that occurred in Ang's life is her active participation in the buying, and later selling, of goods (*materials*) at the farmers' market. She began attending the farmers' market with her mother-in-law. She then started selling small amounts of homemade cupcakes on the weekends, and found that she loved the relationships (*meaning*) she was able to build with customers and fellow vendors. Further, the positive interactions and convivial environment of the farmers' market has kept Ang baking treats each week to sell, despite having three small children at home, and a husband who works full time. This example illustrates communicative learning with Ang's mother-in-law, then enhanced communicative *competence* at the farmers' market, as well as the inklings of social mobilization by recruiting other members of her family in gardening. Ang also demonstrates enhanced instrumental learning by replacing her habitual practices with new *competencies*: gardening, preparing food from scratch, and selling it. Eventually, the incremental changes lead to a transformation.

Furthermore, through all of these transformative learning experiences, Ang became a producer (gardening, canning much of her own produce, and selling at the farmers' market) and consumer (of different kinds of products) as a result of her changing orientation toward food practices and beliefs about the food system. This was certainly not the case for all of the women interviewed; some gardened and canned out of necessity, others dabbled in either canning or gardening over the years, and a majority of them had not personally experienced any sort of disorienting dilemma about their food. The motivations were varied across the lives of the women, but the most significant changes occurred in the women who had undergone some critical transformative moments with their children or community, which is further elaborated on in the next section.

Communities of Practice as Carriers and Conduits of Practices

Family, friends, colleagues, and peers can constitute a CoP, and through mutual engagement, shared repertoire, and joint enterprise, these communities can become carriers of particular practices (Shove, Pantzar, and Watson 2012; Wenger and Snyder 2000). Getting together allows for collaborative activities, but also sharing a lived experience, creating tactile spaces that "embed and embody individuals within the social and natural worlds; a move that, in turn, nurtures new intelligibilities and behaviours toward others and the environment" (Carolan 2007, 1265). Social networks and relationships in both case studies emerged as fundamental to processes of transformative learning. In this section, we explore multiple scales of social embeddedness, the importance of community, and the critical role of family in sharing knowledge and shaping sustainable agri-food practices.

Without the relationships and social networks formed in Stony Plain (the Stony Plain Women's Institute, the Multicultural Heritage Centre, churches, other local charities, farmers' markets, and friendship circles), some of the women would not be as active in their gardening, cooking, and canning as they are today. Some of the older generation also volunteer with the Multicultural Heritage Centre's children's programs, and teach grade four and five students how to use local crab apples to make jams and jellies. Throughout the course of our research, it became evident that food practices, learning, and community involvement were indeed iterative and mutually reinforcing. Another example is the involvement of several women volunteering to cook for the community soup kitchen. They became involved in this practice through their social networks at the Stony Plain Women's Institute. The learning and subsequent changes in practices were not always transformative according to Mezirow's criteria, but through community networks and the influence of peers, food practices were able to be shared for the greater nourishment of the Stony Plain community. Participation in the local farmers' market was a space that allowed Ang to embody her transformative learning experiences by producing, consuming, and selling locally made, fresh, natural food products.

Relatedly, the articles on EFP indicate that producers are embedded in multiple levels of social influences: family and friends who may also be part of the farming operation; fellow farmers who may even be part of a producer value chain; commodity organizations such as Potato Growers of Alberta and Alberta Beef Producers; neighbours; consumers; institutions such as financial and real estate; municipal, provincial, and federal government programs; and environmental organizations. Producers expressed a sense of belonging to community through phrases such as "shared responsibility," "world working together," "coordinated responses," and "we're all in it together." This mirrors findings in the literature on the critical role of social factors affecting uptake and maintenance of stewardship practices (including Carolan 2005, 2006a, 2006b; Oreszczyn, Lane, and Carr 2010). The EFP workshops provided opportunities for discussion and exchange between producers. Formal workshops and programs bringing producers together to learn and share their experiences are pivotal for changing agricultural practices (Lankester 2013). For example, a survey on environmental stewardship in Alberta found that BMP adoption was 23 percent higher on farms where someone had attended a farm conservation workshop or training program (Government of Alberta 2012).

The implementation of BMPs from farm plans may not have been solely a result of a transformative learning experience. Other factors may have been equally important, such as government-sponsored financial incentives that farmers receive for adopting more sustainable farming practices. However, we argue that financial incentives do not negate the subsequent and ongoing learning and changed perceptions that occurred for EFP participants, as evidenced by numerous personal stories in the media articles. In addition, finances are necessary for purchasing (farm) *materials* and possibly for obtaining *competencies* (e.g., registering for a course or travelling to a farm demonstration). Workshops and programs draw from a diversity of people and can create a space for people to safely explore and confront various viewpoints and interests through dialogue (communicative learning), form new social connections, and develop new CoPs supportive of values that are environment-oriented (Hoverman et al. 2011; McLachlan and Yestrau 2009). Informal gatherings in local coffee shops and community restaurants also provided opportunities for knowledge exchange (ARC 2006; Lankester 2013).

Another overlapping theme across both case studies was the significant influence of family. Almost all of the producers interviewed in the AEFP media articles mentioned the significance of their spouse or families, and children were a key consideration when farmers reflected on their role as stewards of the land. The well-being of their children was a motivator even for producers who did not consider themselves environmentalists: "We borrow this world from our kids and they will borrow it from the next generation. I'm not a tree-hugger, but I believe we should all play our part so everyone has a chance to enjoy it" (AEFP 15 May 2009, para. 6).

Family was not only a source of motivation for transforming practices but also a medium for sharing knowledge: "[My wife] would learn something at a workshop, share that information with me, and then we would get the kids excited about making environmental improvements. There was education happening on multiple levels" (AEFP 3 December 2007, para. 2). EFP workshop facilitator Dan Moe noted that it was common to see several family members become involved in learning about and developing a plan for changing agricultural practices: "We've seen couples take on the process as a team, and we've even seen whole families getting involved" (AEF 24 December 2007, para. 11). Family, as demonstrated in this case study, is an important type of CoP for communicative learning, and for changing or preserving certain agricultural practices (Oreszczyn, Lane, and Carr 2010).

Children were a key variable and influence for the women of Stony Plain when changing their procurement and preservation practices. Recall the changes that Ang made to her food preparation and consumption as a result of her children's health and well-being. In this case study, it was often the mothers who had a transformative experience that resulted in a changed practice, but it was often embedded within the family, and sometimes within larger social networks.

Further, the desire to garden, cook, and preserve was fostered, in part, by the presence of a strong and influential "food role model" in the family. The conditions needed to create, sustain, and extend not only the technical skills but the appreciation and enduring desire for fresh, homemade, inexpensive, and unprocessed food were often created in the context of the home, together with a particular family member. For example, a mother and daughter baked traditional Austrian food together: "[It's] something that we do together and it's just a bonding thing, and you have some wine and you make some cookies: it's just a good social thing."

Our two case studies show that different layers of communities and social influences were essential to fostering and sustaining practices related to the production and consumption of food. It is difficult to identify any type of transformative experience and subsequent practice change as an exclusively individualistic and isolated endeavour. Changed perspectives, norms, and sustained commitment to more sustainable activities are intimately linked with larger communities. We argue that this is particularly true whenever food is present. Food is inherently social—not just when consumed but also when produced.

Ripple Effects: To Community and Beyond

Participatory experiences increase the sense of integration into the wider community and society, promoting an "active public-spirited character" (Held 1987, cited in Hoverman et al. 2011, 31). Such "ripple or spillover effects" that extended beyond the immediate communities and spaces were repeatedly found in our case studies. The findings from the Stony Plain case study indicate that sustained participation in gardening, cooking, and canning practices created larger ripple effects that reverberated into other areas of the participants' lives. Cooking good food at community soup kitchens, teaching children to use local food to make jam, and selling high-quality, preservative-free products at the farmers' market are just a few examples of the ways the women are contributing to a more healthy and sustainable food environment in their communities. Other ripple effects among the women included a strong conservation ethic and aversion to waste, increased participation in community food-related activities, and finally an acute awareness (among some participants) of local land issues and other problems with the conventional food system. Without an overtly political or critical agenda, and before it was trendy or ethical to do so, the women in Stony Plain were acting as thoughtful and committed food citizens, and continue to be in their own ways.

EFP media articles captured spillover effects where food, commodity, environment, producer, and consumer repeatedly blended together: "I don't think you can run a business without really knowing your environmental impact. We have to make sure, especially farmers, that we can keep producing food. That's the way we look at it—it's not just about making money, it's about feeding people" (AEFP 11 January 2013, para. 15). The EFP media articles capture the shift from recognizing food as not just a product of a competitive food industry but also a form of nourishment. Food was not mentioned in the first two years of the EFP media articles, except for one article in 2006. At the onset of the 2008–09 food crisis, as the concept of a "sustainable diet" emerged (see Bomford and Brock in this collection), a keyword search revealed that forty-three of the seventy-four EFP articles mentioned food, and of those, almost half (n = 21) mentioned food in the context of consumers, sustainability, welfare, and safety. These results are reflective of recent emphasis for farmers and the food industry in general to adapt to societal demands, not only to reduce environmental impacts but also to influence animal welfare, safety, and quality issues (Alberta Farm Animal Care 2012; Domaneschi 2012).

Not surprisingly, consumer support for farming was one of the most frequent topics in the EFP articles in the last two years. Agriculture is increasingly operating in the context of a tightening social license where the latitude that producers and agri-food industry are allowed to exploit resources for their private purposes is being qualified and enclosed (Martin and Williams 2011). The former Alberta EFP program coordinator, Perry Phillips explains how this can create opportunities for savvy farmers: "More and more the agricultural industry is realizing this is a partnership with the food industry in supplying consumer expectations" (AEFP 7 October 2011, para. 12). The Potato Growers of Alberta is one of EFP's greatest success stories to date and exemplifies the power of CoPs to create change. To fulfill shareholder requests, the Potato Growers of Alberta made EFP a standard for demonstrating environmental stewardship across the Prairie provinces. As a result, they are able to sell through McCain Foods and are receiving top dividends by meeting consumer demand for potatoes grown using environmentally responsible practices (AEFP 15 February 2013). Such shifts in the agri-food system are opportunities for producers' and consumers' shared values on sustainability to meet in the marketplace (for more research on the role of marketplace, see Chapter 5 by Lowitt, Mount, Khan, and Clément in this collection).

Both of our case studies demonstrate how transformative learning contributed to sustainable food and farming practices that had ripple and spillover effects on other areas of the participants' lives and on the lives of others who are not necessarily part of the immediate CoP. While learning is situated, the impacts of learning can clearly spread into other spaces and manifest in (collective) social practice changes as well as products that support environmentally sustainable practices.

Conclusion

In this chapter, we examined and compared two case studies by drawing upon transformative learning theory and social practice theory in our analysis of food systems change. These case studies provided an opportunity to explore some new and interesting theoretical conversations about transformative learning, social practices, and broader change for social and environmental sustainability.

Transformative learning theory is a useful tool in understanding the process of changed behaviour oriented toward more ethical and sustainable practices, but it is incomplete because it does not account for the already existing social practices ordered across time and space. Transformative learning does not occur in a vacuum, but occurs within communities who have certain norms, expectations, and meanings attached to their routine behaviours, like cooking from scratch, ensuring children are adequately and nutritiously fed, or conserving water for irrigation and habitat. Indeed, learning, shifting perceptions, and changed behaviour occur in an iterative process that is sometimes incremental and sometimes triggered, enhanced, or halted by a disruptive event or a disorienting dilemma, as we saw from our case study examples. However, there is much more going on in these processes than simply a seamless transformative experience, and it is important to consider these transformations as embedded within and shaped by larger social practices.

A social practice theoretical framework allows us to understand how the world is constructed and ordered. It is neither individual behaviour nor societal structures that exclusively affect behaviours, but rather everyday practices made up of the materials, meanings, and competencies that hold them together. We looked at specific food and stewardship practices that served as sustainable exemplars, their evolution, the significant influences of transformative learning in that process, and how they are continually nested in, and influenced by, larger CoPs.

By applying CoP theory, we argued that transformative learning in regards to food cannot be abstracted and isolated from its social context. Food in and of itself transgresses many boundaries: it is a biological necessity, a cultural marker, and a social and political symbol for many of the problems we see within today's society. Food is an infinite source of pleasure and delight, but often that joy is entirely bound up with the communities with which that food is produced and shared. These findings are important because they speak to the necessity of a more holistic and socially focused approach to both social and environmental sustainability.

Current interventions seeking to "solve" our environmental and related social crises tend to be top-down, undemocratic, and individual-focused. Within the current neoliberal context, practices like paying for ecosystem services, "greenwashing" consumer products, and downloading responsibility onto individuals (precautionary consumption, feeding the "organic child") are perhaps missing the importance of the larger influence of social learning, CoPs, and personal relationships as sites of change. For example, simple strategies that seek to educate and inform the population about environmental degradation, while useful and necessary, are limited. These strategies do not take into account the context within which unsustainable practices are created and fostered, nor do they consider the complex relationships that can either foster or eliminate (un)sustainable practices. Also, they do not give space for community as sites of social learning, and as a critical factor in the uptake or disregard of more environmentally friendly practices. By examining practices of individuals and communities engaged in the pursuit of social and environmental sustainability, and the learning processes and transformations that have facilitated their transition, we hope to bring a new perspective to the discussion of how change is happening in the agri-food system.

Acknowledgments

We would like to thank Dr. Mary Beckie for her assistance and mentorship as we co-wrote this paper. I (Jennifer) would like to acknowledge SSHRC for their funding of my MSc research project.

Notes

1   Social learning is characterized by an iterative process of "reflective practice, utilization of diversity, shared understanding, and experimentation" (Rodela, Cundill, and Wals 2012, 16).

2   The EFP media articles are available at http://www.albertaefp.com.

References

Agriculture and Agri-Food Canada (AAFC). 2009. *Environmental Farm Planning in Canada: A 2006 Overview.* http://publications.gc.ca/collections/collection_2011/agr/A125-15-2011-eng.pdf.

Alberta Environmental Farm Plan (AEFP). 2012. *Developing an EFP: Main Reasons to Complete an EFP.* http://www.albertaefp.com.

Alberta Research Council (ARC). 2006. *Study on Identifying Rural Sociological Barriers to Adoption.* Edmonton, AB: ARC.

Alberta Farm Animal Care (AFAC). 2012. *Social License, Trust Critical as Industry Shapes New Future of Farm Animal Care.* http://lcc.afac.ab.ca/conferences/2012/SociallicenseshapeslivesockcareMarch262012formatfax_000.pdf.

Braun, Jennifer A. L. 2014. "Against the Odds: The Survival of Traditional Food Knowledge in a Rural Alberta Community." *Canadian Food Studies* 1 (1): 54–71.

Carolan, Michael S. 2005. "Barriers to the Adoption of Sustainable Agriculture on Rented Land: An Examination of Contesting Social Fields." *Rural Sociology* 70 (3): 387–413. http://dx.doi.org/10.1526/0036011054831233.

Carolan, Michael S. 2006a. "Do You See What I See? Examining the Epistemic Barriers to Sustainable Agriculture." *Rural Sociology* 71 (2): 232–60. http://dx.doi.org/10.1526/003601106777789756.

Carolan, Michael S. 2006b. "Social Change and the Adoption and Adaptation of Knowledge Claims: Whose Truth Do You Trust in Regard to Sustainable Agriculture?" *Agriculture and Human Values* 23 (3): 325–39. http://dx.doi.org/10.1007/s10460-006-9006-4.

Carolan, Michael S. 2007. "Introducing the Concept of Tactile Space: Creating Lasting Social and Environmental Commitments." *Geoforum* 38 (6): 1264–75. http://dx.doi.org/10.1016/j.geoforum.2007.03.013.

Cundill, Georgina, and Christo Fabricius. 2009. "Monitoring in Adaptive Co-management: Toward a Learning Based Approach." *Journal of Environmental Management* 90 (11): 3205–11. http://dx.doi.org/10.1016/j.jenvman.2009.05.012. Medline:19520488

Diduck, Alan, and Bruce Mitchell. 2003. "Learning, Public Involvement and Environmental Assessment: A Canadian Case Study." *Journal of Environmental Assessment Policy and Management* 5 (3): 339–64. http://dx.doi.org/10.1142/S1464333203001401.

Domaneschi, Lorenzo. 2012. "Food Social Practices: Theory of Practice and the New Battlefield of Food Quality." *Journal of Consumer Culture* 12 (3): 306–22. http://dx.doi.org/10.1177/1469540512456919.

Flyvbjerg, Bent. 2001. *Making Social Science Matter: Why Social Inquiry Fails and How It Can Succeed Again.* Cambridge: Cambridge University Press. http://dx.doi.org/10.1017/CBO9780511810503.

Giddens, Anthony. 1984. *The Constitution of Society.* Cambridge: Polity Press.

Government of Alberta (GoA). 2012. *Environmentally Sustainable Agriculture Tracking Survey: Executive Summary.* http://www1.agric.gov.ab.ca/$Department/deptdocs.nsf/all/aesa6467/$FILE/2012esa.pdf.

Hargreaves, Tom. 2011. "Practice-ing Behaviour Change: Applying Social Practice Theory to Pro-environmental Behaviour Change." *Journal of Consumer Culture* 11 (1): 79–99. http://dx.doi.org/10.1177/1469540510390500.

Held, D. 1987. *Models of Democracy*. Cambridge: Polity Press.

Hoverman, Suzanne, Helen Ross, Terence Chan, and Bronwyn Powell. 2011. "Social Learning through Participatory Integrated Catchment Risk Assessment in the Solomon Islands." *Ecology and Society* 16 (2): 17–38. http://hdl.handle. net.login.ezproxy.library.ualberta.ca/10535/7590.

Kerton, Sarah, and John A. Sinclair. 2010. "Buying Local Organic Food: A Pathway to Transformative Learning." *Agriculture and Human Values* 27 (4): 401–13. http://dx.doi.org/10.1007/s10460-009-9233-6.

Lankester, Ally J. 2013. "Conceptual and Operational Understanding of Learning for Sustainability: A Case Study of the Beef Industry in North-Eastern Australia." *Journal of Environmental Management* 119: 182–93. http://dx.doi. org/10.1016/j.jenvman.2013.02.002. Medline:23500021

Lave, Jean, and Etienne Wenger. 1991. *Situated Learning: Legitimate Peripheral Participation*. Cambridge: Cambridge University Press. http://dx.doi. org/10.1017/CBO9780511815355.

Martin, Paul, and Jacqueline Williams, eds. 2011. *Defending the Social Licence of Farming: Issues, Challenges and New Directions for Agriculture*. Victoria, Australia: CSIRO Publishing.

McLachlan, Stéphane M., and Melisa Yestrau. 2009. "From the Ground Up: Holistic Management and Grassroots Rural Adaptation to Bovine Spongiform Encephalopathy across Western Canada." *Mitigation and Adaptation Strategies for Global Change* 14 (4): 299–316. http://dx.doi.org/10.1007/ s11027-008-9165-2.

Merriam, B. Sharran, Rosemary S. Caffarella, and Lisa M. Baumgartner. 2007. *Learning in Adulthood: A Comprehensive Guide*. San Francisco: John Wiley and Sons.

Mezirow, Jack. 1981. "A Critical Theory of Adult Learning and Education." *Adult Education Quarterly* 32 (1): 3–24. http://dx.doi.org/10.1177/07417136 8103200101.

Mezirow, Jack. 1990. How Critical Reflection Triggers Transformative Learning. *Fostering Critical Reflection in Adulthood*, 1–20.

Mezirow, Jack. 1996. "Contemporary Paradigms of Learning." *Adult Education Quarterly* 46 (3): 158–72. http://dx.doi.org/10.1177/074171369604600303.

Mezirow, Jack. 1997. "Transformative Learning: Theory to Practice." *New Directions for Adult and Continuing Education* 74: 5–12. http://dx.doi.org/10.1002/ ace.7401.

Mezirow, Jack. 2000. "Learning to Think Like an Adult." In *Learning as Transformation: Critical Perspectives on a Theory in Progress*, edited by Jack Mezirow, 3–33. San Francisco: Jossey-Bass.

Michel-Guillou, Elisabeth, and Gabriel Moser. 2006. "Commitment of Farmers to Environmental Protection: From Social Pressure to Environmental Conscience." *Journal of Environmental Psychology* 26 (3): 227–35. http://dx.doi. org/10.1016/j.jenvp.2006.07.004.

Oreszczyn, Sue, Andy Lane, and Susan Carr. 2010. "The Role of Networks of Practice and Webs of Influencers on Farmers' Engagement with and Learning about Agricultural Innovations." *Journal of Rural Studies* 26 (4): 404–17. http://dx.doi.org/10.1016/j.jrurstud.2010.03.003.

Pahl-Wostl, Claudia, Erik Mostert, and David Tàbara. 2008. "The Growing Importance of Social Learning in Water Resources Management and Sustainability

Science." *Ecology and Society* 13 (1): 24–27. http://www.ecologyandsociety. org/vol13/iss1/art24/.

Reckwitz, Andreas. 2002. "Toward a Theory of Social Practices: A Development in Culturalist Theorizing." *European Journal of Social Theory* 5 (2): 243–63. http://dx.doi.org/10.1177/13684310222225432.

Rodela, Romina, Georgina Cundill, and Argen E.J. Wals. 2012. "An Analysis of the Methodological Underpinnings of Social Learning Research in Natural Resource Management." *Ecological Economics* 77: 16–26. http://dx.doi. org/10.1016/j.ecolecon.2012.02.032.

Schatzki, Theodore K. 2001. "Introduction: Practice Theory." In *The Practice Turn in Contemporary Theory*, edited by Theodore K. Schatzki, Karine Knorr Cetina, and Eike von Savigny, 1–14 London: Routledge.

Schusler, Tania M., Daniel J. Decker, and Max J. Pfeffer. 2003. "Social Learning for Collaborative Natural Resource Management." *Society & Natural Resources* 16 (4): 309–26. http://dx.doi.org/10.1080/08941920390178874.

Shove, Elizabeth. 2004. "Challenging Human Behaviour and Lifestyle: A Challenge for Sustainable Consumption." In *The Ecological Economics of Consumption*, edited by Lucia A. Reisch and Inge Røpke, 111–32. Cheltenham, UK: Edward Elgar.

Shove, Elizabeth. 2010. "Beyond the ABC: Climate Change Policy and Theories of Social Change." *Environment & Planning A* 42 (6): 1273–85. http://dx.doi. org/10.1068/a42282.

Shove, Elizabeth, Mika Pantzar, and Matt Watson. 2012. *The Dynamics of Social Practice: Everyday Life and How It Changes*. London: Sage. http://dx.doi. org/10.4135/9781446250655.n1.

Sinclair, A. John, Alan Diduck, and Patricia Fitzpatrick. 2008. "Conceptualizing Learning for Sustainability through Environmental Assessment: Critical Reflections on 15 years of Research." *Environmental Impact Assessment Review* 28 (7): 415–28. http://dx.doi.org/10.1016/j.eiar.2007.11.001.

Tarnoczi, Tyler. 2011. "Transformative Learning and Adaptation to Climate Change in the Canadian Prairie Agro-ecosystem." *Mitigation and Adaptation Strategies for Global Change* 16 (4): 387–406. http://dx.doi.org/10.1007/ s11027-010-9265-7.

Taylor, Edward W. 2001. "Transformative Learning Theory: A Neurobiological Perspective of the Role of Emotions and Unconscious Ways of Knowing." *International Journal of Lifelong Education* 20 (3): 218–36. http://dx.doi. org/10.1080/02601370110036064.

Taylor, Edward W. 2007. "An Update of Transformative Learning Theory: A Critical Review of the Empirical Research (1999–2005)." *International Journal of Lifelong Education* 26 (2): 173–91. http://dx.doi.org/10.1080/02601370 701219475.

Taylor, Edward W., and Patricia Cranton. 2012. *The Handbook of Transformative Learning: Theory, Research, and Practice*. San Francisco: John Wiley and Sons.

Terrenghi, Lucia, Otmar Hilliges, and Andreas Butz. 2007. "Kitchen Stories: Sharing Recipes with the Living Cookbook." *Personal and Ubiquitous Computing* 11 (5): 409–14. http://dx.doi.org/10.1007/s00779-006-0079-2.

United Nations Environment Programme. 2010. Assessing the Environmental Impacts of Consumption and Production: Priority Products and Materials. A

Report of the Working Group on the Environmental Impacts of Products and Materials to the International Panel for Sustainable Resource Management. http://www.unep.fr/shared/publications/pdf/DTIx1262xPA-PriorityProd uctsAndMaterials_Report.pdf.

Warde, Alan. 2005. "Consumption and Theories of Practice." *Journal of Consumer Culture* 5 (2): 131–53. http://dx.doi.org/10.1177/1469540505053090.

Wenger, Etienne C. 1998. *Communities of Practice: Learning, Meaning, and Identity.* Cambridge: Cambridge University Press. http://dx.doi.org/10.1017/ CBO9780511803932.

Wenger, Etienne C., and William M. Snyder. 2000. "Communities of Practice: The Organizational Frontier." *Harvard Business Review* 78 (1): 139–46.

Yin, Robert K. 2014. *Case Study Research: Design and Methods.* Thousand Oaks, CA: Sage.

CHAPTER 13

Pedagogical Encounters: Critical Food Pedagogy and Transformative Learning in the School and Community

Jennifer Sumner and Cassie Wever

Food and pedagogy are central to human development and closely linked in fundamental ways. As humans evolved, they learned which foods were safe to eat, where and when to find food and—momentous for our species—how to grow it. Babies learn to appreciate different foods, manipulate eating utensils, and participate in family rituals associated with food. Immigrants learn how to navigate new foodways, prepare new fruits and vegetables, and engage in new styles of food shopping. Young people setting up house learn to budget for weekly food expenditures, cook new recipes, and avoid wasting food.

Clearly, pedagogical encounters with food are a common occurrence, often creating and recreating open-ended opportunities for learning. These encounters can be positive, such as discovering a new cuisine, choosing to eat locally, or mastering the art of breadmaking. But they can also be negative, such as binge eating to cope with unhappiness or dieting to meet unrealistic body-image expectations. Because we need to eat every day, we never lack for opportunities to learn through our encounters with food.

Both food and pedagogy have long been recognized as catalysts for personal and social change. For example, learning about the plight of farmers from the global south has prompted many people to forgo conventional coffee and drink fair trade products. Two related concepts can help us to understand the relationship between the pedagogical process and change, particularly with reference to food. The first is critical food pedagogy (Sumner 2015), a pedagogical approach that discourages acceptance of the status quo and encourages critique of our unsustainable food system and the creation of alternatives that are more environmentally, socially, and economically sustainable. The second is transformative learning (Mezirow 1991, 1994), a form of learning that occurs in the face of a disorienting dilemma and results in a fundamental shift in world views.

We begin this chapter by examining these two key concepts and linking them with a number of pedagogical encounters with food both within and beyond educational institutions. Within educational institutions, we discuss student nutrition programs, farm-to-school relationships, and school gardens. Within the community, we examine a variety of pedagogical sites: food festivals, farmers' markets, community-supported agriculture programs, and community gardens. We contend that these pedagogical encounters can teach people about our current unsustainable food system and pave the way for the personal and social changes so necessary to the creation of more sustainable alternatives.

Critical Food Pedagogy and Transformative Learning

Food and pedagogy are basic to our existence, but until recently, they have seldom been used in conjunction with one another. Flowers and Swan (2012) noted that the connection between food and pedagogy had been relatively neglected, which they found surprising. In the last few years, however, food studies has begun to recognize the importance of teaching and learning as it matures as an interdisciplinary field, with explorations of the role of education in the food justice movement (Barndt 2012), in community gardens (Walter 2013), and in regards to everyday practices (e.g., see Chapter 12 by Braun and Bogdan in this book). In turn, the field of education is starting to grapple with issues of food, such as food literacy (Sumner 2013) and critical consumption (Jubas 2014).

The marriage of food and pedagogy opens up new spaces that are just beginning to be explored. Within food studies, for example, Flowers and Swan (2012) use the plural term "food pedagogies" to mean aggregations of education, teaching, and learning about all aspects of food by a variety of agencies, actors, and media. Their definition includes intended or emergent change in behaviour, habit, emotion, cognition, and/or knowledge. Catalyzing such change starts with an understanding and critique of the industrial food system, which has been shown to value profits over health and to lead to a nutritionally deficient "industrial diet" (Winson 2013). Nurturing understanding and critique, in turn, requires not just any type of pedagogy, but a critical pedagogy that understands education as a political process and "seeks to illuminate how education and learning (teachers as well as learners) are implicated in structures and practices that both reinforce and challenge injustices" (Butterwick 2005, 257). Applying critical pedagogy to the case of food produces what has been termed "critical food pedagogy" (Sumner 2015), which involves approaching the subject of food with a critical attitude, on the part of the teacher as well as the learner. This approach is in keeping not only with the principles of critical pedagogy, but also with the ethos of food studies, which involves "a critical perspective in perceiving existing problems as resulting from the normal operation of the food system and everyday practices" (Koç, Sumner, and Winson 2012, xiii). Such a perspective can counter the neoliberal ideology supporting the current dysfunctional food system and raise critical consciousness about more sustainable alternatives. It also helps to avoid the kind of unreflexive localism that can perpetuate the status quo through co-optation, exploitation, oppression, and unsustainability (Born and Purcell 2006; DeLind 2011; Levkoe 2011).

Critical food pedagogy also involves cultivating an emancipatory approach with respect to food, which can help individuals and social groups develop new types of knowledge that will inform actions that contribute to resistance, greater freedom, and agency to shape their world (see Tisdell 2005). This emancipatory approach has its roots in the work of Brazilian educator Paulo Freire (1996), who encouraged learners to "read the world" and challenge the social structures that oppressed them. His "pedagogy of the oppressed" promoted a form of consciousness raising that he called *conscientization*, which "refers to learning to perceive social, political, and economic contradictions, and to take action against the oppressive elements of reality" (17). In this way, critical food pedagogy supports personal and social changes associated with agency. The most profound changes are linked to another key concept— transformative learning.

Transformative learning entails learning that results in a fundamental change of world view. Unlike other forms of learning, it involves a "deep, structural shift in basic premises of thought, feelings and actions" (TLC 2013). The concept was developed by adult educator Jack Mezirow (1991), who proposed that when humans found themselves confronted with a disorienting dilemma, some went through a critical reflection process that ended with a shift in consciousness. Mezirow (1994, 224) went on to identify phases in the transformative learning process, beginning with a disorienting dilemma (such as a death in the family, divorce, or being fired), followed by self-examination and critical assessment, and culminating in an exploration of new options and a renegotiation of current relationships and the cultivation of new ones, all from a new perspective. According to the Transformative Learning Centre (TLC 2013), "transformative learning makes us understand the world in a different way, changing the way we experience it and the way we act in our day-to-day lives. Transformative learning has an individual and a collective dimension, and includes both individual and social transformation."

Transformative learning has been studied in conjunction with alternatives to the current food system. For example, Levkoe (2006) found that food justice movements could be important sites of transformative learning, while Mündel (2007) investigated transformative learning among farmers in Alberta as they transitioned to more sustainable agriculture, finding that they needed to learn a different way of being in the world. Kerton and Sinclair (2010) concluded that buying local food was a pathway to transformative learning for consumers in Atlantic Canada.

While transformative learning encompasses a type of learning that results in a shift in world view, critical food pedagogy is a broader term that includes many sorts of learning, as well as education and teaching about food. Both concepts can catalyze personal and social change that is more holistic and inclusive, making pedagogical encounters with food ripe with possibilities for creating more sustainable food systems.

Pedagogical Encounters with Food

Flowers and Swan (2012) have observed that "not only is food an *object* of learning, but it is also a *vehicle* for learning" (423). In other words, we can learn about food (e.g., how to prepare a non-GMO dinner or how to avoid foods with a high pesticide load), and we can learn through food (e.g., how to raise healthy children or how to care for the environment). The encounters described below exemplify learning about and through food in a range of sites in educational institutions and the broader community, and highlight opportunities for transformative learning and critical food pedagogy. It is important to note, however, that not all pedagogical encounters produce personal or social change. Many forms of teaching, learning, and education support the status quo. This reality highlights the importance of critical food pedagogy and transformative learning as catalysts for the kind of change that will encourage critique of the current industrial food system and the creation of more sustainable alternatives.

Pedagogical Encounters in the School

There are many opportunities for learning about food and through food in educational institutions at all levels, with some of them supporting the status quo and some of them challenging vested interests and catalyzing personal and social change. This learning may occur through formal curriculum or informal teaching related to food and food systems, or may only be revealed through a closer, critical examination of how food is or is not provided, talked about, advertised, grown, or processed at institutions. Callenbach (2005) writes, "An overlapping term, 'hidden curriculum,'...points to the fact that schools transmit not just 'knowledge' but also norms and values.... Sometimes the hidden curriculum's lessons are not intentional, but reveal unspoken, and often unconscious, values: the soda machine in the hallway outside the classroom where nutrition is being taught is hidden curriculum" (42).

Whether food is implicitly or explicitly included in an educational curriculum, learning in regards to food is still occurring: for example, if and how food is valued, what counts as food and nutrition, and what role food plays in establishing relationships and a sense of community.

From the kindergarten classroom to the university campus, the school food environment plays an important role in both explicit and hidden learning. The school food environment consists of the food available to students through vending machines, canteens, cafeterias, and school meal or snack programs. Some scholars point out that the school food environment also includes the food advertising that may exist inside or around a school and what the food environment immediately adjacent to the school is like, such as the kind of food available for students to purchase during off-campus lunch breaks (Winson 2008). The school food environment itself presents rich opportunities for critical food pedagogy, from questioning the availability of healthy food options in schools to the environmental impacts of packaged versus "litterless lunches." For example, Winson (2008) found that the types and price of food in Ontario secondary schools can be influenced by the options that eating establishments in close proximity to the school are providing. Student tuck shops reduced the prices of their junk food snacks in order to remain competitive with these establishments and to capture revenue from students (and, in some cases, for fundraising purposes)—a situation that raises critical questions regarding the priorities dictating school food.

Unique opportunities exist to include food in learning at all levels of education. The next two sections address a few of the main institutional sites through which students experience a pedagogical encounter with food.

Pedagogical Encounters with Food in Elementary and High Schools

While food is often included as a component of health and physical education in the kindergarten-to-grade-12 curriculum (e.g., Ontario Ministry of Education 2010), with some mention in other curriculum areas, much of the pedagogy associated with food reinforces the status quo, such as Agriculture in the Classroom programs (sponsored by agribusiness), pizza days, and selling chocolate bars to fund school projects. This section will focus on sites of learning where food transgresses curriculum boundaries and opens up opportunities for critical engagement: student nutrition policy and programs, farm-to-school relationships, and, in particular, school gardens.

1. Student Nutrition Policy and Programs

School nutrition policies represent one way of modifying the school food environment (e.g., see McKenna 2010; Ontario Ministry of Education 2013), which not only impacts students' food-related behaviour (Taylor, Evers, and McKenna 2005), but also provides opportunities for pedagogical encounters. These policies play out in sites such as school cafeterias. Lunchtime at school can consist of frantically consuming packaged food over a short noon break, sitting down to a lengthy homemade meal, or not eating anything at all. Mullally et al. (2010) found that a school nutrition policy guiding what foods could be present in elementary schools in Prince Edward Island was associated with positive and healthy changes in student food consumption. Such transformation is particularly important given the increasing prevalence of obesity and overweight in Canadian children and the associated health impacts (Healthy Kids Panel 2013). It is also important in terms of cultivating positive attitudes toward food, normalizing certain kinds of food and promoting understanding of different cultures.

Implementing a Student Nutrition Program (SNP), especially in combination with school nutrition policy, can also have pedagogical implications. An SNP is "a program that offers a healthy breakfast, morning meal, snack and/or lunch to students before, during or after each school day" (FoodShare 2014). SNPs exist in every province of Canada and, depending on the specific program, are supported through not-for-profit organizations (e.g., Breakfast for Learning 2013), volunteers, teachers, parents, staff, and public funding. While providing good, healthy food to children and youth has a positive impact on learning and development, there are deeper lessons at stake that provide fodder for critical inquiry and transformative learning. As Briggs (2005) observes, "The way that meals are served and eaten is part of the hidden curriculum that tells students what the school really believes about food. Does the school model a belief that mealtime is part of living a healthy life? Standing in industrial cafeteria lines, allotting too little time for lunch, and combining lunch with recess teach kids that meals are something to rush through on the way to somewhere else" (246). She points to examples of school meal programs that have successfully integrated senior citizens as table hosts in family-style dining, thus building community and fostering intergenerational learning.

2. Farm-to-School Relationships

The term "farm-to-school" encompasses a range of relationships among schools, farms, and farmers. In some instances, "farm-to-school" signifies a direct marketing relationship whereby farmers supply fresh, local food to a school cafeteria or classrooms (Vallianatos, Gottlieb, and Haase 2004). In other examples, a school builds relationships with one or more farms and farmers, potentially taking students on field trips to the farm, bringing farmers into the classroom, and celebrating the local foods grown in the area through school events (Vallianatos, Gottlieb, and Haase 2004). Farm to Cafeteria Canada is a national network that promotes, supports, and links farms to cafeteria programs, policy, and practice from coast to coast (Farm to Cafeteria Canada 2012). One of the programs in their network, the Farm to School Manitoba Healthy Choice Fundraiser, operates as an alternative to school fundraising initiatives that typically involve selling chocolate bars or magazine subscriptions. Schools and daycares can schedule fundraisers anytime between September and December. Interested parents and community members place their order for a $10 or $20 bag of Manitoba-grown produce, and the school keeps 50 percent of the proceeds. The program encourages educators to take advantage of the learning opportunities presented by the fundraiser, suggesting lesson topics such as healthy food choices, Manitoba agriculture, and sustainable food systems (Farm to School 2014).

Farm-to-school programs have the potential to build fertile ground for transformative learning experiences by connecting students and the adults in their lives with good food and the people who grow it, as well as the local environment and community. These learning experiences can be explicitly critical, as observed in the case in The Food School at Centre Wellington District High School in Fergus, Ontario (Food School 2014). The school runs a series of courses on the growing and preparation of food, serving student-prepared meals in a school café. The school builds relationships with local farmers and takes students on field trips to see where their food is grown, with the mission to "highlight a hopeful, insightful and tasty food alternative" and foster "critical and confident food growers and consumers." Citing such influences as Michael Pollan, Vandana Shiva, and The Stop Community Food Centre in Toronto, the program also incorporates the actual growing of food onsite in a school garden.

3. School Gardens

Depending on the space and resources available, school gardens can consist of growing seedlings in a classroom, container gardens, a small raised bed, or a larger vegetable or market garden. They may be started for any number of reasons, including the desire to build community, educate, increase students' access to nature, and support the local food movement (see Nowatschin 2014). A number of the direct and indirect pedagogical benefits associated with school gardens have been well documented in the literature. School gardens have been shown to directly improve academic outcomes in subjects such as math, science, and the language arts, as well as in other areas (see Williams and Dixon 2013 and Lieberman and Hoody 1998 for reviews). They have also been linked to improved skills and attitudes that benefit learning, such as student enthusiasm and positive attitudes toward school; social, physical, personal, and moral development; and student bonding and community building (Blair 2009; Williams and Dixon 2013). In addition, school food gardens have been successfully used to teach about food and nutrition by improving the efficacy of nutrition programs and steering students' preferences toward the consumption of fruits and vegetables (McAleese and Rankin 2007; Morris and Zidenberg-Cherr 2002).

Williams and Brown (2012) argue that our current model of education utilizes a mechanistic metaphor. They focus on school gardens as sites for an alternative pedagogy with seven guiding principles: "cultivating a sense of place, fostering curiosity and wonder, discovering rhythm and scale, valuing biocultural diversity, embracing practical experience, nurturing interconnectedness, and awakening the senses" (14). From their experiences creating and teaching in school gardens, along with their research and theoretical grounding, they assert that school gardens present a practical means for transformative, interdisciplinary learning for sustainability. This is supported by Breunig (2013), who examined the impacts of integrated environmental studies programs, a form of interdisciplinary curriculum-based pedagogy in Ontario secondary schools, on students' pro-environmental and pro-social attitudes and behaviours. Food education emerged as a theme motivating attitudinal and behavioural changes. Breunig noted in particular that experiential learning in the form of gardening and farming impelled students to make pro-environmental and pro-social food choices. Based on her findings, Breunig's other recommendations for transformative learning experiences include students preparing a weekly locavore meal and visiting local farmers. Furthermore, she encourages the adoption of food-specific environmental education curriculum in all grades as one means to transform students' environmental attitudes and behaviours.

In terms of critical food pedagogy, proponents of school gardens link them to a form of learning that runs counter to the industrial paradigm of education described by Taylor (2010) as well as the industrial food system discussed above. Capra (2009) defines this learning as ecological literacy, or "our ability to understand the basic principles of ecology and to live accordingly" (244). He goes on to specify that a form of learning emphasizing the interconnectedness of people, the environment, and food production teaches "[the] fundamental facts of life—that one species' waste is another species' food; that matter cycles continually through the web of life; that the energy driving the ecological cycles flows from the sun; that diversity assures resilience; that life, from its beginning more than three billion years ago, did not take over the planet by combat but by networking" (244). Such an education serves to reconnect students to the source of their food and the ecological cycles upon which we all depend, countering the disconnect between food and the consumer that epitomizes the corporate food economy (Levkoe 2006). Empirical evidence from Chawla et al. (2014) suggest that some students working in a school food garden took away profound ecological lessons. One student stated, "It all connects one way or another, so I figure that I'm helping the environment, it's helping the garden, I'm helping myself. It's not that everything is about me, it's that everything is about everything else" (9). Another stated, "I like it [the school garden] because I know it all works together, just a big old complete cycle. It calms me down. It makes me feel relaxed, at ease. It reminds me of who I am, and I don't have to worry about anything else" (9). While an explicit critique of the current food system may or may not be included in a school garden program, depending on the educator involved, intimate learning about the source of one's food can form the basis for future critical questions: Who grew this food? Where did it come from? Did they use compost or synthetic fertilizers? How did it get to me? What impact does my food have on the environment and the people that produce it?

Not surprisingly, Nowatschin (2014) found that school gardens in Canada are often initiated and run by not-for-profit and/or community or parent organizations in partnership with the school. In many other cases, they are operated by a particularly dedicated teacher. This raises issues regarding the sustainability of these pedagogical sites, as well as questions around sources of funding and maintenance. For school gardens and other food-related activities to truly become embedded in the landscapes of Canadian elementary and high schools and remain vibrant sites for critical and transformative pedagogical encounters with food, provincial governments and school boards must create supportive policies and dedicated funding for infrastructure, teacher training, and potentially paid garden and/or food education coordinators.

Pedagogical Encounters with Food in Post-secondary Education

Many of the food-based pedagogical opportunities in post-secondary education can also support the status quo, such as residence meal plans that include fast-food chains, ubiquitous soda-vending machines that displace water fountains, and curricula supported by multinational food corporations. However, a growing number of encounters with food in post-secondary settings provide critical pedagogical openings. For example, attending university or college may provide students with their first opportunity to grocery shop independently, explore the local farmers' market, or discover cultural cuisines that are new to them. On some campuses, students and faculty have established farmers' markets and community gardens. Other institutions are running full-fledged campus farms. For example, McGill Food and Dining Services (MFDS) has been working with students in the McGill Food Systems Management project to reimagine institutional food. They now incorporate Local Food Days and Meatless Mondays into their cafeterias, offer culinary workshops and teaching and research opportunities related to food, and source fresh produce from McGill's MacDonald Campus Farm (McGill Food and Dining Services 2014). In their strategic plan they state, "Uniquely among sustainable approaches to institutional food, MFDS simultaneously seeks to nurture in students an appetite for learning about and connecting with the food they eat. For many students, University is an opportunity to develop a new independence in making their own food choices. At this critical time, MFDS strives to promote the development of healthy relationships with food and farming, with a focus on sustainability and nutrition" (Rhodes and Laperle 2014). In order to achieve their goals, MFDS has worked with students, faculty, and staff at McGill, as well as corporate food service providers, demonstrating the capacity for transformative change even within highly established institutional systems.

Courses with an explicitly critical focus on food are becoming more prevalent in post-secondary institutions. What was once a sparse offering is now much richer; students can enrol in the "Pedagogy of Food" at the Ontario Institute for Studies in Education, "Food Policy Development in Canada" at York University, or any of a variety of food-related courses in the Faculty of Land and Food Systems at the University of British Columbia. In Ontario alone, there are a significant number of options. For example,

Fleming College students can obtain a graduate certificate in Sustainable Agriculture, complete with on-farm practical experience, and Ryerson University offers a certificate in Food Security through a continuing education program. Those completing a Bachelor of Science in Agriculture at the University of Guelph can pursue a major in Organic Agriculture, while at Trent University students can pursue a Bachelor of Arts or a Bachelor of Sciences in Sustainable Agriculture and Food Systems. Many of these offerings, such as the first-year course called Food Matters at the University of Toronto's New College, encourage students to critically examine methods of food production, distribution, and consumption, consider alternatives to the status quo, and relate their conceptual learning to personal experiences. Galt et al. (2013) discuss their approach to fostering transformative learning in a food systems course at the University of California, Davis, and highlight the efficacy of this critical, self-reflective method. Coupled with experiential learning, such as farm visits and the opportunity for practical food-related projects and papers, courses such as these have incredible potential to transform student learning and perspectives on food and its myriad of interconnected issues.

Pedagogical Encounters in the Community

Within the larger community, pedagogical encounters with food occur in an endless number of sites every day. While many of these sites can reinforce the status quo, such as food courts in malls, chain grocery stores, and fastfood outlets, others present formidable challenges. For example, food festivals, farmers' markets, community supported agriculture (CSA) programs, and community gardens provide opportunities for learning and change.

Food Festivals

Food festivals offer food and fun in a festive atmosphere—an ideal environment for learning. Ethnic food festivals (such as A Taste of Little Italy or Taste of the Danforth in Toronto) teach people about new foods, multiculturalism, and appreciation of other cultures. Local food festivals showcase local food producers, who teach people about local products, sustainable production methods, and *terroir*—"the notion that the taste of food is affected by a region's soil, its climate, its landscape, its hours of sunlight— that the place where food is made is inextricably linked to what it is" (Elton 2010, 167). Specific foods can also be highlighted, as in the garlic festival in Stratford or the Bala cranberry festival in Ontario, which can teach people about the history, importance, and preparation of the star attraction. Some food festivals provide little space for critical food pedagogy and transformative learning, while others open the door to these concepts. For example, the grassroots food festival called Foodstock was organized to raise money and awareness to resist the "mega-quarry" planned for over 2,300 acres of prime farmland in south-central Ontario. Over 28,000 people gathered in the rain to sample local foods prepared by chefs from across Canada and to register their resistance to farmland destruction. Dubbed by the Canadian Chefs Congress (2012) as "the largest culinary protest in the history of Canada," this food festival helped to raise awareness about the future of food system sustainability. In the words of celebrity chef Michael Stadtländer, who helped to organize the event, "We have to protect land that can grow food.... We're just at the dawn of localism, and after seeing the drought, hurricanes and floods that have happened in the United States, I think we had better secure where our food comes from" (quoted in Bain 2011).

Farmers' Markets

Farmers' markets have long been a part of human history and have always engendered pedagogical encounters of the alimentary kind. Their existence in North America was seriously challenged by the rise of supermarkets in the last half of the twentieth century, but farmers' markets have experienced a resurgence through government initiatives (e.g., the Ontario government's greenbelt legislation, which spurred the establishment of new farmers' markets) and what Cummings, Galin, and Murray (1998) described as "the desire of community residents to have a shopping experience closer to the food producer and the community—a more personal approach. New Markets were established, older Markets revitalized, and a new customer base was introduced to the Farmers' Market experience" (7). Farmers' markets offer seasonal or year-round learning opportunities. Market-goers can learn about such varied topics as cheesemaking, apple harvesting, lambing, and cider pressing. They can ask questions, weigh the answers, and make choices, often in consultation with the primary producers. While farmers' markets are not without problems and contradictions (e.g., see Smithers, Lamarche, and Joseph 2008), they are nevertheless on the front lines of the relocalization of food and will play a vital role in a more sustainable food system. They also offer opportunities for critical food pedagogy and transformative learning. Their very existence—replete with tactile experiences, face-to-face engagement, and olfactory discoveries—challenges the global corporate food system, with its faceless, placeless food that is shrink-wrapped in the sterile confines of the supermarket aisle. In addition, as public spaces, they provide an opportunity for community organizing and change—citizens can set up a booth and collect signatures, hand out literature, and engage with market-goers on a range of community issues.

Community Supported Agriculture

Community supported agriculture (CSA) can be understood as an arrangement whereby "customers buy a farmer's crops in advance of the season and receive produce throughout the season" (Koç, Sumner, and Winson 2012, 381). Begun in Japan in the 1960s (where the original term—"teikei"—literally means partnership, but philosophically means "food with the farmer's face on it" [Van En 1995, 1]), the movement spread to North America and the rest of the world. As a springboard for critical food pedagogy, CSAs provide "a social and economic alternative to the conventional, large-scale, corporately managed food system," with farmers gaining a reliable market and financial support of members prior to each season and members receiving weekly shares of fresh, locally grown produce (DeLind and Ferguson 1999, 191). In essence, CSAs offer a working alternative to the global corporate food system—an alternative that does not specialize in increasing the distance between producers and consumers, thus concealing "the circumstances in which food may be produced" (Sage 2012, 297). CSAs may also include educational materials in their baskets, such as recipes, which help to overcome the deskilling associated with the so-called "convenience foods" of the global corporate food system. They can also become spaces for critical food pedagogy and transformative learning as people meet to pick up produce, attend CSA socials, or contribute sweat equity. For example, one study of a CSA in Michigan highlighted women's participation in CSAs as "a quiet form of activism" (DeLind and Ferguson 1999, 196–7) that did not involve tearing down the current food system, but looked to build something new, especially new relationships with food and the environment. As a form of direct marketing, CSAs can also be transformative as they become "an important facet of a more sustainable, locally based food system" (Kolodinsky and Pelch 1997, 129), resulting in what Van En (1995) has referred to as "agriculture supported community."

Community Gardens

Community gardens have become particularly fecund sites for pedagogical encounters. The American Community Garden Association (2012 in Walter 2013) describes community gardens as "any piece of land gardened by a group of people…. It can be urban, suburban, or rural. It can grow flowers, vegetables or community. It can be one community plot, or can be many individual plots. It can be at a school, hospital, or in a neighborhood. It can also be a series of plots dedicated to 'urban agriculture' where the produce is grown for a market" (523). To this description, Draper and Freedman (2010) add that "community gardens are used by, and beneficial for, individuals of any age, race, ethnicity, and socioeconomic status, as well as the disabled and nondisabled alike" (458). Community gardens also exhibit a variety of types: individual plots, communal plots, or plots that provide employment.

Although community gardens have been cultivated in North America for over a century, they have taken on a new importance with the rise of the local food movement. In doing so, they have come to serve a range of social objectives besides growing food, such as providing gardening and nature experience, offering training or employment opportunities, and developing community cohesion (Parker, Fournier, and Reedy 2007), as well as creating space for community organizing, building social capital, and promoting public health outcomes such as enhanced nutrition and physical activity (Twiss et al. 2003). Wakefield et al. (2007) also note contributions in terms of mental health, security, and safety in local communities and local ecology and sustainability.

One commonality among community gardens is the recognition of their deep association with learning. Indeed, for some, learning is the purpose and primary component of community gardens (see Holland 2004; Pelletier et al. 1999). This learning "is not only cognitive, but also emotional, spiritual, sensory and physical," as well as "collective, constructivist, synergistic and transformative" (Walter 2013, 534). In his study of learning in community gardens, Walter (2013) found evidence of individual learning in the form of informal learning, incidental learning, self-directed learning, experiential learning, non-formal learning, and even formal learning. He also found evidence of collective learning, with opportunities to learn about food security, environmental sustainability, community resilience, social justice, and cultural identity.

Given their association with the local food movement, community gardens can also be understood as sites of critical food pedagogy and transformative learning. While earlier incarnations of community gardens may have reinforced dominant ideologies (e.g., Victory gardens in Canada and the United States during the Second World War), Walter (2013) contends that, after the 1960s, they "more readily embraced a public pedagogy of contestation and resistance" (524). He describes how the taste of "'real,' chemically clean, freshly picked food" can result in a "sensory and culinary epiphany," which may lead to "further examinations of diet, corporate food production, human health and the culture of eating and growing local food" (530). He also notes that community gardens can have a more radical role in terms of decolonization, cultural identity, environmental justice, and anti-racist education.

Furthermore, Levkoe (2006) reports that the experience of creating, looking after, and even defending a community garden can be transformative. Walter (2013, 530) agrees, describing a shift in the perception of the environment associated with some community gardeners—moving from an understanding of the environment as an object or a place, to "a view characterized by the interconnectedness of humans and environment" (530). In sum, it is clear that community gardens matter, not only as opportunities for individual and community development, but also as sites for critical pedagogical encounters.

Conclusion

While food is a worthy pedagogical subject in and of itself, it can also become an entry point for learning about larger issues, such as sustainability, community development, ecological cycles, globalization, human rights, and climate destabilization. In this way, eating is not just about putting fuel in the body; eating can also be a pedagogical act, as well as a social, political, cultural, and ecological act (Sumner 2008) that involves learning about and through food in the search for sustainable alternatives. This linkage is strengthened by the recognition that food has deep material and symbolic power and has become "a focus of contention and resistance to a corporate takeover of life itself" (McMichael 2000, 32).

Clearly, many pedagogical encounters with food are neither critical nor transformative, but support the status quo. Even alternatives such as fair trade and organic food are being undermined by large corporate interests determined to capture the price premium associated with these products. However, the examples in this chapter illustrate how the dynamic concepts of critical food pedagogy and transformative learning can work together to harness the power of food, catalyze learning, and promote personal and social change toward more sustainable food systems. Within the school and the community, the application of these concepts can galvanize food and learning for a more sustainable future—they can raise awareness, change behaviour, foster new attitudes, encourage resistance, and forge new relationships. But they are not always successful. The industrial food system is deeply entrenched, with the industrial diet becoming normalized and "socially acceptable—indeed, highly desirable" (Winson 2013, 287). In the face of such entrenchment, and the kind of learning promoted by multinational food corporations through mass advertising, change is difficult and slow. But learning is not static—as the examples in this chapter demonstrate, we can also unlearn the lessons of the industrial food system through everyday pedagogical encounters with food. This highlights the need for pedagogical encounters that encourage a critical attitude, cultivate emancipatory agency, and provide disorienting dilemmas that can lead to transformative change.

Finally, the individual learning associated with pedagogical encounters with food can only take us so far when deep, systemic change is required to overcome the problems of the industrial food system. As Guthman (2011) observes, education is only part of the solution—those who want to teach people to make better food choices should spend more time reforming the policies that allow bad food in the first place. This observation calls for understanding critical food pedagogy as a social process that entails collective action and political mobilization, such as lobbying, protests, boycotts, buycotts, petitions, letter writing, and food literacy campaigns. For this reason, it is paramount to make linkages, build relationships, and form alliances among individuals, groups, and organizations associated with food to reach the critical mass that is essential for demanding, developing, and implementing the kind of policies that can create lasting change.

References

Bain, Jennifer. 2011. "Chefs, Farmers Unite for Foodstock," *Toronto Star*, 17 September. http://www.thestar.com/life/food_wine/2011/09/17/chefs_farmers_unite_for_foodstock.html.

Barndt, Deborah. 2012. "Catalyzing Creativity: Education and Art Feed the Food Justice Movement." In *Critical Perspectives in Food Studies*, edited by Mustafa Koç, Jennifer Sumner, and Anthony Winson, 65–88. Don Mills, ON: Oxford University Press.

Blair, Dorothy. 2009. "The Child in the Garden: An Evaluative Review of the Benefits of School Gardening." *Journal of Environmental Education* 40 (2): 15–38. http://dx.doi.org/10.3200/JOEE.40.2.15-38.

Born, Branden, and Mark Purcell. 2006. "Avoiding the Local Trap: Scale and Food Systems in Planning Research." *Journal of Planning Education and Research* 26 (2): 195–207. http://dx.doi.org/10.1177/0739456X06291389.

Breakfast for Learning. 2013. "Our Story." http://www.breakfastforlearning.ca/about-us/our-story/.

Breunig, Mary. 2013. "Food for Thought: An Analysis of Pro-environmental Behaviours and Food Choices in Ontario Environmental Studies Programs." *Canadian Journal of Environmental Education* 18: 155–72.

Briggs, Marilyn. 2005. "Rethinking School Lunch." In *Ecological Literacy: Educating Our Children for a Sustainable World*, edited by Michael K. Stone and Zenobia Barlow, 241–49. San Francisco: Sierra Club Books.

Butterwick, Shauna. 2005. "Feminist Pedagogy." In *The International Encyclopedia of Adult Education*, edited by Leona M. English, 257–62. New York: Palgrave Macmillan Publishers.

Callenbach, Ernest. 2005. "The Power of Words." In *Ecological Literacy: Educating Our Children for a Sustainable World*, edited by Michael K. Stone and Zenobia Barlow, 41–44. San Francisco: Sierra Club Books.

Canadian Chefs Congress. 2012. "Foodstock." http://canadianchefscongress.com/food-activism/mega-quarry/foodstock/.

Capra, Fritjof. 2009. "The New Facts of Life: Connecting the Dots on Food, Health, and the Environment." *Public Library Quarterly* 28 (3): 242–8. http://dx.doi.org/10.1080/01616840903110107.

Chawla, Louise, Kelly Keena, Illène Pevec, and Emily Stanley. 2014. "Green Schoolyards as Havens from Stress and Resources for Resilience in Childhood and Adolescence." *Health & Place* 28: 1–13. http://dx.doi.org/10.1016/j.healthplace.2014.03.001. Medline:24691122

Cummings, Harry, Kora Galin, and Don Murray. 1998. "Farmers' Markets in Ontario and Their Economic Impact." School of Rural Planning and Development, University of Guelph. http://www.agrinewsinteractive.com/features/farmersmarkets/farmersmarkets.html.

DeLind, Laura B. 2011. "Are Local Food and the Local Food Movement Taking Us Where We Want To Go? Or Are We Hitching Our Wagons to the Wrong Stars?" *Agriculture and Human Values* 28 (2): 273–83. http://dx.doi.org/10.1007/s10460-010-9263-0.

DeLind, Laura B., and Anne E. Ferguson. 1999. "Is This a Women's Movement? The Relationship of Gender to Community-Supported Agriculture in Michigan." *Human Organization* 58 (2): 190–200. http://dx.doi.org/10.17730/humo.58.2.lpk17625008871x7.

Draper, Carrie, and Darcy Freedman. 2010. "Review and Analysis of the Benefits, Purposes, and Motivations Associated with Community Gardening in the United States." *Journal of Community Practice* 18 (4): 458–92. http://dx.doi.org/10.1080/10705422.2010.519682.

Elton, Sarah. 2010. *Locavore: From Farmers' Fields to Rooftop Gardens—How Canadians Are Changing the Way We Eat.* Toronto: HarperCollins Publisher.

Farm to Cafeteria Canada. 2012. "What is Farm to Cafeteria?" http://www.farmtocafeteriacanada.ca/about-us/what-is-farm-to-cafeteria/.

Farm to School. 2014. "Farm to School Manitoba Healthy Choice Fundraiser". http://www.farmtoschoolmanitoba.ca/.

Flowers, Rick, and Elaine Swan. 2012. "Introduction: Why Food? Why Pedagogy? Why Adult Education?" *Australian Journal of Adult Learning* 52 (3): 419–33.

Food School. 2014. "Farm". http://foodschool.ca/farm.

FoodShare. 2014. "Student Nutrition." http://www.tpsn.net/what-is-a-student-nutrition-program.

Freire, Paulo. 1996. *Pedagogy of the Oppressed.* New York: Continuum Press.

Galt, Ryan E., Damian Parr, Julia Van Soelen Kim, Jessica Beckett, Maggie Lickter, and Heidi Ballard. 2013. "Transformative Food Systems Education in a

Land-Grant College of Agriculture: The Importance of Learner-Centred Inquiries." *Agriculture and Human Values* 30 (1): 129–42. http://dx.doi.org/10.1007/s10460-012-9384-8.

Guthman, Julie. 2011. *Weighing In: Obesity, Food Justice, and the Limits of Capitalism.* Los Angeles: University of California Press.

Healthy Kids Panel. 2013. "No Time to Wait: The Healthy Kids Strategy." http://www.health.gov.on.ca/en/common/ministry/publications/reports/healthy_kids/healthy_kids.pdf.

Holland, Leigh. 2004. "Diversity and Connections in Community Gardens: A Contribution to Local Sustainability." *Local Environment* 9 (3): 285–305. http://dx.doi.org/10.1080/1354983042000219388.

Jubas, Keila. 2014. "If I Am What I Eat, Who Am I? How Critical Shopping Teaches Adults about Food, Identity and Social Change." In *Food Pedagogies*, edited by Elaine Swan and Rick Flowers, 131–46. London: Ashgate.

Kerton, Sarah, and A. John Sinclair. 2010. "Buying Local Organic Food: A Pathway to Transformative Learning." *Agriculture and Human Values* 27 (4): 401–13. http://dx.doi.org/10.1007/s10460-009-9233-6.

Koç, Mustafa, Jennifer Sumner, and Anthony Winson. 2012. *Critical Perspectives in Food Studies.* Don Mills, ON: Oxford University Press.

Kolodinsky, Jane M., and Leslie L. Pelch. 1997. "Factors Influencing the Decision to Join a Community Supported Agriculture (CSA) Farm." *Journal of Sustainable Agriculture* 10 (2–3): 129–41. http://dx.doi.org/10.1300/J064v10n02_11.

Levkoe, Charles Z. 2011. "Towards a Transformative Food Politics." *Local Environment* 16 (7): 687–705. http://dx.doi.org/10.1080/13549839.2011.592182.

Levkoe, Charles Z. 2006. "Learning Democracy through Food Justice Movements." *Agriculture and Human Values* 23 (1): 89–98. http://dx.doi.org/10.1007/s10460-005-5871-5.

Lieberman, Gerald A., and Linda L. Hoody. 1998. *Closing the Achievement Gap: Using the Environment as an Integrating Context for Learning. Results of a Nationwide Study.* Poway, CA: Science Wizards.

McGill Food and Dining Services. 2014. "Feeding McGill." http://www.mcgill.ca/foodservices/sustainability/feeding-mcgill.

McAleese, Jessica D., and Linda L. Rankin. 2007. "Garden-Based Nutrition Education Affects Fruit and Vegetable Consumption in Sixth-Grade Adolescents." *Journal of the American Dietetic Association* 107 (4): 662–5. http://dx.doi.org/10.1016/j.jada.2007.01.015. Medline:17383272

McKenna, Mary L. 2010. "Policy Options to Support Healthy Eating in Schools." *Canadian Journal of Public Health* 101 (Suppl 2): S14–7. Medline:21133196

Mezirow, Jack. 1994. "Understanding Transformation Theory." *Adult Education Quarterly* 44 (4): 222–32. http://dx.doi.org/10.1177/074171369404400403.

Mezirow, Jack. 1991. *Transformative Dimensions of Adult Learning.* San Francisco: Jossey-Bass.

Morris, Jennifer L., and Sheri Zidenberg-Cherr. 2002. "Garden-Enhanced Nutrition Curriculum Improves Fourth-Grade School Children's Knowledge of Nutrition and Preferences for Some Vegetables." *Journal of the American Dietetic Association* 102 (1): 91–3. http://dx.doi.org/10.1016/S0002-8223(02)90027-1. Medline:11794509

McMichael, Phillip. 2000. "The Power of Food." *Agriculture and Human Values* 17 (1): 21–33. http://dx.doi.org/10.1023/A:1007684827140.

Mullally, Megan L., Jennifer P. Taylor, Stefan Kuhle, Janet Bryanton, Kimberly J. Hernandez, Debbie L. MacLellan, Mary L. McKenna, Robert J. Gray, and Paul J. Veugelers. 2010. "A Province-Wide School Nutrition Policy and Food Consumption in Elementary School Children in Prince Edward Island." *Canadian Journal of Public Health* 101 (1): 40–3. Medline:20364537

Mündel, Karsten. 2007. "'Walking Through Your Old Way of Thinking': The Learning Dimensions of Farmers' Transitions to Sustainable Agriculture." PhD diss., University of Toronto.

Nowatschin, Elizabeth. 2014. "Educational Food Landscapes: Developing Design Guidelines for School Gardens." MLA thesis, University of Guelph. https://dspace.lib.uoguelph.ca/xmlui/handle/10214/8057.

Ontario Ministry of Education. 2010. "The Ontario Curriculum Grades 1–8: Health and Physical Education Interim Edition." http://www.edu.gov.on.ca/eng/curriculum/elementary/healthcurr18.pdf.

Ontario Ministry of Education. 2013. "Healthy Schools: New School Food and Beverage Policy." http://www.edu.gov.on.ca/eng/healthyschools/policy.html.

Parker, Martin, Valérie Fournier, and Patrick Reedy. 2007. *The Dictionary of Alternatives*. New York: Zed Books.

Pelletier, David L., Vivica Kraak, Christine McCullum, Ulla Unsitalo, and Robert Rich. 1999. "Community Food Security: Salience and Participation at Community Level." *Agriculture and Human Values* 16 (4): 401–19. http://dx.doi.org/10.1023/A:1007651801471.

Rhodes, Laura, and Mathieu Laperle. 2014. "An Appetite for Sustainability: McGill Food and Dining Services Strategic Plan 2010–2013." https://www.mcgill.ca/files/foodservices/appetiteforsustainability.pdf

Sage, Colin. 2012. *Environment and Food*. New York: Routledge.

Smithers, John, Jeremy Lamarche, and Alun E. Joseph. 2008. "Unpacking the Terms of Engagement with Local Food at the Farmers' Market: Insights from Ontario." *Journal of Rural Studies* 24 (3): 337–50. http://dx.doi.org/10.1016/j.jrurstud.2007.12.009.

Sumner, Jennifer. 2015. "Learning to Eat with Attitude: Critical Food Pedagogies." In *Food Pedagogies*, edited by Elaine Swan and Rick Flowers, 201–14. London: Ashgate.

Sumner, Jennifer. 2013. "Adult Education and Food: Eating as Praxis." In *Building on Critical Traditions: Adult Education and Learning in Canada*, edited by Tom Nesbit, Susan Brigham, Nancy Taber, and Tara Gibb, 194–203. Toronto: Thompson Educational Publishing Inc.

Sumner, Jennifer. 2008. "Eating as a Pedagogical Act: Food as a Catalyst for Adult Education for Sustainability." *Kursiv - Journal fuer politische Bildung* 4: 32–7.

Taylor, Ken. 2010. "RSA Animate: Changing Education Paradigms." October. http://youtu.be/zDZFcDGpL4U.

Taylor, Jennifer P., Susan Evers, and Mary McKenna. 2005. "Determinants of Healthy Eating in Children and Youth." *Canadian Journal of Public Health* 96 (Suppl 3): S20–6, S22–9. Medline:16042160

Tisdell, Elizabeth J. 2005. "Emancipatory Education." In *The International Encyclopedia of Adult Education*, edited by Leona M. English, 205–10. New York: Palgrave Macmillan.

TLC. 2013. "About the Transformative Learning Centre." Transformative Learning Centre. http://tlc.oise.utoronto.ca/About.html.

Twiss, Joan, Joy Dickinson, Shirley Duma, Tanya Kleinman, Heather Paulsen, and Liz Rilveria. 2003. "Community Gardens: Lessons Learned from California Healthy Cities and Communities." *American Journal of Public Health* 93 (9): 1435–8. http://dx.doi.org/10.2105/AJPH.93.9.1435. Medline:12948958

Vallianatos, Mark, Robert Gottlieb, and Margaret Ann Haase. 2004. "Farm-to-School: Strategies for Urban Health, Combating Sprawl, and Establishing a Community Food Systems Approach." *Journal of Planning Education and Research* 23 (4): 414–23. http://dx.doi.org/10.1177/0739456X04264765.

Van En, Robyn. 1995. "Eating for Your Community: Towards Agriculture Supported Community." *Context (Ibadan)* 42 (Fall): 29–31.

Wakefield, Sarah, Fiona Yeudall, Carolin Taron, Jennifer Reynolds, and Ana Skinner. 2007. "Growing Urban Health: Community Gardening in South-East Toronto." *Health Promotion International* 22 (2): 92–101. http://dx.doi.org/10.1093/heapro/dam001. Medline:17324956

Walter, Pierre. 2013. "Theorising Community Gardens as Pedagogical Sites in the Food Movement." *Environmental Education Research* 19 (4): 521–39. http://dx.doi.org/10.1080/13504622.2012.709824.

Williams, Dilafruz R., and Jonathan D. Brown. 2012. *Learning Gardens and Sustainability Education: Bringing Life to Schools and Schools to Life.* New York: Routledge.

Williams, Dilafruz R., and P. Scott Dixon. 2013. "Impact of Garden-Based Learning on Academic Outcomes in Schools: Synthesis of Research between 1990 and 2010." *Review of Educational Research* 83 (2): 211–35. http://dx.doi.org/10.3102/0034654313475824.

Winson, Anthony. 2013. *The Industrial Diet: The Degradation of Food and the Struggle for Healthy Eating.* Vancouver: UBC Press.

Winson, Anthony. 2008. "School Food Environments and the Obesity Issue: Content, Structural Determinants, and Agency in Canadian High Schools." *Agriculture and Human Values* 25 (4): 499–511. http://dx.doi.org/10.1007/s10460-008-9139-8.

Commentary on Part IV: Scaling Learning in Agri-food Systems

Mary A. Beckie

Learning through food, as both a product and a practice, is at the core of food studies, and whether we identify as educators or students, we are all learners in the broad effort to create more sustainable agri-food systems. The two chapters in this section delve into theoretical examination of important and overlapping subthemes—critical pedagogy, the iterative relationship between learning and practice, transformative learning, and communities of practice—with analysis of examples from individual, community, and institutional levels. It is the growing number of opportunities for learning at, between, and beyond these levels that is influencing important changes in the way we think about and practice food.

Granted, there is still *a lot* of work to be done, but it appears that awareness of problems associated with the conventional food system is growing and that the alternative agri-food movement is gaining ground. Yet I would agree with Marsden and Franklin (2013) that the scholarship of this movement is at a critical juncture and needs to "address more rigorously questions of convergence and scaling out" (637) if we are to play a more substantial role in radically transforming agri-food systems. This will require a willingness to reach beyond our knowledge borders, the boundaries of our disciplines and our communities of practice, to engage in more open discussion and learning with those of different, and sometimes conflicting, views and approaches, in order to develop integrated, context-relevant solutions. While borders and boundaries have their purpose, as outlined elsewhere in this book, restrictive and less permeable boundaries can create insularity that constrains the learning processes and changes in practices needed in the transition toward a more resilient agri-food system. Using insights gained from the chapters in this section as a springboard, I aim to contribute to this conversation by examining other pedagogical opportunities for transformative learning and change, and how boundary processes can contribute to scaling learning and innovation in agri-food systems.

Before I begin, I should briefly explain my rather unconventional path to food studies, the boundaries I had to cross, and where my work is currently situated. Prior to doing an interdisciplinary doctorate on sustainable agriculture and rural development, I studied biology and molecular genetics, and was involved for several years in agricultural biotechnology research and teaching. It was while working in this field that I was invited to take part in a meeting on international agricultural issues, hosted by Oxfam and the National Farmers Union, which changed the course of my career, and my life. Listening to other presentations, I realized that I knew very little about what was happening in agriculture outside of the lab. It was truly a "disorienting dilemma" that triggered my leaving the world of biotechnology to begin a process of re-education about agri-food systems. My work over the past fifteen years has evolved from investigations of organic farming and marketing systems, to the broader study of alternative agri-food systems in sustainable community development, and the role of government, citizen engagement, and the social economy. My research and teaching is interdisciplinary, community-based, and most often in partnership with community representatives. I am a firm advocate of constructivist approaches as a means to transformative learning and social change.

Transformative Learning Through Engagement

Both chapters in this section use a constructivist lens to look at food as a platform for transformative learning and change. There is a growing body of evidence from learning and behavioural science supporting the value of constructivist approaches, which focus on experiential, situated learning for elevating critical consciousness and longer-term behavioural change over positivist approaches (for an overview, see Fried and Associates 2012). These processes of meaning making can occur informally, as in the case study of rural women, or through structured initiatives such as student nutrition programs. These and other examples woven throughout the chapters provide evidence of opportunities for "critical food pedagogy" within academic institutions and the wider community. Sumner and Wever underline the importance of this form of pedagogy in fostering critical examination of the ·

food system as well as the emancipatory agency that can lead to individual and broader social change. Braun and Bogdan make a novel contribution to this topic by bringing together social practices and transformative learning theories to examine the iterative relationship between learning and practice, and how transformative changes in perception and practice occurring at the individual level are influenced by and can also influence communities of practice; for example, farmers' participation in the Alberta Environmental Farm Plan program, particularly when learning with other farmers, can change consciousness and consequently shape farming practices.

Shifting mindsets by encouraging openness, engagement with others and different situations, reflection, and learning is central to constructivist approaches. In addition to the pedagogical encounters described in these chapters, in recent years there has been a growing appetite for community service learning (CSL) and study abroad programs within educational institutions. These experiential learning opportunities are designed to provide "real world" experiences that engage the head, heart, and hands in bridging the theory-practice divide. Time for reflection is critical to designing and participating in these learning opportunities, which can result in personal transformation. For the past five years, I have helped to coordinate a study abroad course on sustainable urban agriculture in Cuba, which is widely recognized as a world leader in agro-ecology and urban agriculture (Funes et al. 2002; Koont 2011). In this seven-week study abroad program, students learn about the agricultural transformation that has taken place in Cuba over the past twenty-five years, work side by side with Cuban farmers, and become immersed in Cuban culture, history, and language. The emphasis of this program is on experiential learning (both instrumental and communicative), international collaboration, and solidarity building. Participation in the program is not without its challenges, which include limited material resources (from food options to gardening tools), living and working in a group situation (and in a tropical climate), collective decision-making, and immersion in a different culture and language. For many, it is the dilemma of experiencing and collectively confronting these challenges that is at the root of significant personal transformation, some more immediate than others, which has motivated them to be more proactively engaged in agri-food systems and wider social change in their own communities.

Engagement is also the theme of community-university partnerships, which are becoming an increasingly common approach to community-based research. These partnerships "blend the intellectual assets and questions of the academy with the intellectual expertise and questions of the public" (Holland 2005, 11). Engaged research is particularly advantageous in addressing emerging or complex social issues, such as the development of sustainable agri-food systems, where there are a wide range of views and a plurality of knowledge. Contrary to the traditional hierarchical model of knowledge construction, which views academics as "society's primary generators and transmitters of knowledge" (Holland 2005, 12), the core elements of engaged scholarship are reciprocity and benefit for both academic scholarship and society. To achieve this, barriers between academics and practitioners need to be broken down, encouraging mutual respect and the development of shared approaches. Forming a research partnership among groups with different methodologies and goals is challenging; academic expectations and career demands for publications are often counter to practitioners' goals for developing on-the-ground solutions and influencing policy changes. Common interests may bring the partnership together, but a good deal of time and effort is required to ensure that the partnership is structured and executed in a way that is sensitive to the context, needs, and objectives of all participants. These are boundary-crossing opportunities that open up a space for transformative learning, and for individual and organizational change.

Boundaries and Boundary Processes

Knowledge emerges out of complex social processes, through the discontinuous, diffuse and value-bound interactions of different actors and networks; it is a process of both interpretation and negotiation (Long and Villareal 1994, 49).

The concept of boundaries is used in a variety of disciplines to refer to cognitive, relational, physical, and/or temporal limits that define entities as separate from one another (e.g., cultures, political jurisdictions, professions, and academic disciplines). Boundaries enable groups to develop and share knowledge and practices, and hence become differentiated from one another. Boundaries that are rigid can, however, limit the flow of knowledge across communities, thereby constraining learning and changes in practice that lead to more radical innovation. But boundaries are also contested and negotiated, and boundary processes create new opportunities for learning through interactions that can arise spontaneously or deliberately (Wenger 2000).

Social learning has become a prominent focus in the alternative agri-food movement, as we re-examine underlying assumptions and values and look to develop more sustainable agri-food systems. Social learning involves the co-production of knowledge through a participatory process of social change. Resilient food systems are characterized by continuous social learning, where trial and error and joint problem-solving builds up community capacity to cope with hardship and unexpected changes, such as those which occurred in Cuba in the late 1980s (Funes et al. 2002). Following the collapse of the Soviet Bloc in Eastern Europe, Cuba's major trading partner, the country experienced a dramatic drop in access to imported foods as well as the fuel, agro-chemicals, and machinery needed to support the industrial, export-oriented agricultural model that was prevalent since the 1960s. As a result, Cuba underwent a severe food crisis. Food rations were put in place and daily caloric intake dropped from over 2,400 to 1,800 as it became difficult to transport food grown in rural areas to the cities where over 70 percent of the population lived. In response to this crisis, Cuba embarked on a nation-wide effort to transition toward low external-input, ecologically based farming methods and a more localized food system. This required extensive collaborative learning and radical changes in social practices, involving farmers, government, education and research institutions, NGOs, and citizens (Rosset et al. 2011). The agricultural transformation that has taken place in Cuba illustrates that social practices can undergo radical changes when institutions and organizations facilitate sharing of knowledge, combined with action on the ground, and allow success and failure to be experienced through experimentation.

Agricultural research and education institutions have played a key role in shaping the industrialization and modernization of agriculture and food systems that has taken place over the past 100 years. Scientific advances in technology and technique that have emerged from these institutions have contributed to significant increases in production and labour efficiency. Productivism, or the singular emphasis on increasing yield as a policy outcome, has been the dominant model in agricultural institutions in Canada since their establishment in the early 1900s, when there was a move away from the social relations of production toward a number of specialized scientific disciplines. As a result, agricultural colleges encompass a range of applied sciences focused on the biophysical aspects of production, but representation of the social sciences is generally limited to agricultural economics, in which prevailing neoclassical theory supports the productivist model. Outside of these institutions, food studies has emerged as an interdisciplinary field in which agri-food practices, and the socio-cultural and political context they are embedded in, are critically examined. A number of social science disciplines contribute to food studies, but collaboration with the natural or applied sciences is rare. Continuing to challenge theories and approaches prevalent within the dominant agri-food paradigm by fostering critical pedagogy is an important focus for food studies, but we also need to be reflexive about our assumptions and practices related to social equity and environmental justice. In order to scale learning and innovation for sustainable agri-food system development, we need to be "flexible, porous and open to collaboration and convergence" (Marsden and Franklin 2013, 637) beyond our knowledge boundaries.

Conclusions

Awareness of the range of problems associated with the industrialized and globalized food system, and the need for change, has grown significantly over the past twenty-five years. Alternative agri-food initiatives have been blossoming worldwide. This can be linked, in part, to the growth of formal and informal learning opportunities being generated within educational institutions and the wider community, which has allowed communities to innovate, often in response to the disorienting dilemmas that arise as a result of the disruptive experiences of the industrial food system. It is clear that designing and participating in pedagogical encounters and boundary processes can be challenging, both in the immediate learning situation but also in the context of the dominant positivist and productivist paradigms. Those espousing alterative views and practices must confront entrenched hierarchies and institutional practices, and possess the ability to be reflexive and open to reaching beyond our boundaries for true interdisciplinary collaboration and social change.

References

Fried, Jane, and Associates. 2012. *Transformative Learning through Engagement: Student Affairs Practice as Experiential Pedagogy*. Stirling, VA: Stylus Publishing.

Funes, Fernando, Luis García, Martin Bourque, Nilda Pérez, and Peter Rosset. 2002. *Sustainable Agriculture and Resistance: Transforming Food Production in Cuba*. Oakland, CA: Food First Books.

Holland, Barbara A. 2005. "Reflections on Community-Campus Partnerships: What has been Learned? What are the Next Challenges?" In *Higher Education Collaboratives for Community Engagement and Improvement*, ed. P.A. Pasque, R.E. Smerek, B. Dwyer, N. Bowman, and B.L. Mallory, 10–18. Ann Arbor, MI: The National Forum on Higher Education for the Public Good; http://files.eric.ed.gov/fulltext/ED515231.pdf.

Koont, Sinan. 2011. *Sustainable Urban Agriculture in Cuba*. Gainesville: University Press of Florida. http://dx.doi.org/10.5744/florida/9780813037578.001.0001.

Long, Norman, and Magdalena Villareal. 1994. "The Interweaving of Knowledge and Power in Development Interfaces." In *Beyond Farmer First*, ed. Ian

Scoones and John Thompson, 41–51. London: International Institute for Environment and Development.

Marsden, Terry, and Alex Franklin. 2013. "Replacing Neoliberalism: Theoretical Implications of the Rise of Local Food Movements." *Local Environment* 18 (5): 636–41. http://dx.doi.org/10.1080/13549839.2013.797157.

Rosset, Peter Michael, Braulio Machín Sosa, Adilén María Roque Jaime, and Dana Rocío Ávila Lozano. 2011. "The Campesino-to-Campesino agroecology movement of ANAP in Cuba: social process methodology in the construction of sustainable peasant agriculture and food sovereignty." *Journal of Peasant Studies* 38 (1): 161–91. http://dx.doi.org/10.1080/03066150.2010.538584. Medline:21284238

Wenger, Etienne. 2000. "Communities of Practice and Social Learning Systems." *Organization* 7 (2): 225–46. http://dx.doi.org/10.1177/135050840072002.

Acknowledgements

When we first conceived of this edited book project, the most common advice we received was not to do an edited book project, because of the amount of time and work it would require. On the contrary, this project has been incredibly valuable and personally meaningful for all of us. We have learned so much from this process, developing our thinking and building and consolidating relationships with a growing network of food studies researchers in Canada and beyond. *Conversations in Food Studies* is an attempt to put into practice what we imagine food studies to be—a collaborative, critical, and interdisciplinary practice. The project spanned three years and involved over forty authors and hundreds of individuals who participated in various ways. The number of people that contributed to this book is far too long to list, but we want to acknowledge the support of some key individuals, without which this book would not have been possible.

We want to begin by thanking all of the book's authors and commentators, who not only contributed their writing but also were involved in developing ideas, providing feedback, and editing chapter drafts. We thank you all for trusting us as editors and having faith in the collective process. Specifically, we appreciate the support from Mustafa Koç who helped advise us through this process.

There were also a number of individuals that contributed to the various parts of the book, and while their names do not appear in the final author list, we greatly appreciate their contributions: Ulrich Teucher and Alexander Sayok, Erin Nelson, Warren Dodd, Frances Dietrich-O'Connor, Chris Yordy, and Ryan Hayhurst. There were also a number of additional reviewers that helped to provide feedback on specific chapters: Nicholas Evangelopoulos, Jordon Lazell, and Elaine Power. Thank you to Carla Kay, who provided copy-editing support for the project.

We gratefully appreciate the ongoing support provided by the Canadian Association for Food Studies/l'Association canadienne des études sur l'alimentation, including the board members and conference organizers. During our first meeting about the book, we were grateful to have the guidance of experienced book editors, food studies scholars, and activists: Annette Desmarais, Hannah Wittman, and Patricia Allen. We would also like to acknowledge the support of the Manitoba Alternative Food Research Alliance and the Social Sciences and Humanities Research Council. Finally, we want to thank the University of Manitoba Press for their ongoing support for this project, and, specifically, the helpful comments of two anonymous reviewers, as well as the guidance and support of Glenn Bergen and Jill McConkey.

Contributors

Colin Anderson is a researcher at the Centre for Agroecology, Water and Resilience at Coventry University in the United Kingdom. His research focuses on working with communities and social movements in collaborative community development and advocacy projects using participatory action research methods. This engaged research contributes to the development of thinking and action related to food systems, community development, food sovereignty, activism, and knowledge mobilization, and especially focuses on the workings of power, resilience, and regeneration in these areas.

Mary A. Beckie is an associate professor in the Faculty of Extension, at the University of Alberta. Her work focuses on sustainable community development, particularly as it relates to agri-food systems and the role of government, citizen engagement, and the social economy. Recent research projects have explored municipal sustainability planning, commercial urban agriculture, farmers' markets, and the emergence of local and regional food systems. While much of this work is situated in Western Canada, Dr. Beckie has also conducted research on sustainable agriculture and localized food systems in Europe, the Midwest United States, and most recently in Cuba, Sri Lanka, and India.

Eva Bogdan has been studying and practising at the cross-section of society and environment for fifteen years, with all of its complexities and wonders, by which she continues to be fascinated and challenged. Bogdan feels very fortunate to have had the opportunity to be involved in agriculture from "field to plate" and beyond to research and policy. As a PhD student at the University of Alberta (Department of Sociology), she is researching perceptions and responses to flood management in Alberta and more broadly, how diverse sets of values, viewpoints, and interests are deliberated and decided on in a democratic approach to natural resource management.

Mark Bomford has spent the last eighteen years—as a farmer, educator, advocate, and leader—immersed in creating sustainable food systems. Bomford was the founding director for the Centre for Sustainable Food Systems at the University of British Columbia, where he launched an interdisciplinary program and a thriving 60-acre teaching and research farm on campus. Prior to his work at UBC, Bomford worked in the non-profit sector, establishing school gardens, new farms and food enterprises, and a range of international urban agricultural programs. Bomford joined Yale University as the director for the Yale Sustainable Food Program in late 2011.

Jennifer Brady is a faculty member in the Department of Applied Human Nutrition at Mount Saint Vincent University in Halifax, Nova Scotia. Her work explores the history and professionalization of dietetics as a feminized profession and its relationships with home economics, food, science, and feminism. More broadly, her work spans critical feminist perspectives of gender, food, nutrition, fatness, health, social justice, and the body.

Jennifer Braun is a PhD student in the Department of Sociology at the University of Alberta. Her substantive research interests include rural farmwomen, food production, and power in the Western Canadian Prairies. Particularly, she is focused on the ways in which decision-making power is distributed, negotiated, and practised in the production of food and what those implications are for women and larger food policy. Her other research interests include looking at the responsibilization of mothers for their children's health, particularly as it relates to childhood obesity in the Global North.

Samara Brock has worked in sustainable food systems for over a decade with a variety of food-focused NGOs in Canada, Cuba, and Argentina, as a food systems planner for the City of Vancouver, and as a program officer at the Tides Canada Foundation funding NGOs focused on food, fisheries, and climate change issues. She is currently pursuing her PhD at the Yale School of Forestry and Environmental Studies.

Robyn Bunn is a PhD student in interdisciplinary studies from the University of British Columbia Okanagan. Her work focuses on collective organizing and community-based approaches to food justice, as well as other related issues of social justice that involve food systems. Currently, she is planning a communal farm in the Okanagan, and is a member of a local collective working with migrant agricultural labourers.

Kirsten Valentine Cadieux directs the sustainability and environmental studies programs at Hamline University, where she studies and teaches about how groups work together to justify and organize land uses and food practices. She investigates the political ecology and everyday dynamics of land uses related to food, and the ways that different sectors work towards improvement in food systems, focusing on practices used by food policy groups and food movement actors to incorporate their values into food supply chains and to evaluate the efficacy of their strategies. Valentine is particularly interested in the use of collaborative knowledge tools to solve food system problems, and in the use of food justice and sustainability frameworks to repair social and ecological problems created by prior food-related land uses.

Chantal Clément is finishing her PhD in political science at Carleton University. Her dissertation focuses on collaborative governance opportunities to support sustainable local food systems in rural municipalities in Canada and the EU. Clément also teaches food politics at Carleton, is a researcher for Project SOIL, and has most recently undertaken research to examine the role and place of family farms in twenty-first century Canada.

Anaïs Détolle is currently finishing her PhD in social and cultural analysis and teaching at Concordia University. For her master's in anthropology, she researched the topic of Provençal food and, through those encounters in the field, she has developed an interest in the construction of food traditions and *terroir*-food production. Therefore, for her PhD research, she is examining changing food traditions in Quebec, via the study of one of the province's iconic drinks: ice cider.

Arthur "Gill" Green earned a PhD in geography from McGill University where he was a McGill Major Fellow and a USINDO Sumitro Fellow. His work examines property issues from an interdisciplinary perspective. He is an educator, researcher, and consultant with experience working on food system issues in Central America, Sub-Saharan Africa, and Southeast Asia. He worked as an extension agent in Central Africa and has done extensive consulting for international organizations on agroforestry and natural resource management. His research interests include human-environment interaction, political ecology, food security, and access to property in post-conflict and post-disaster scenarios. His research on post-conflict property management was featured in an official event at the 2012 Rio+20 United Nations Conference on Sustainable Development. From 2012 to 2014, he served as the chair of the Department of Geography, Earth, and Environmental Science at Okanagan College in British Columbia.

Ankit Gupta is a doctoral candidate at the School of Interactive Arts and Technology at Simon Fraser University. He is part of the CZSaw Visual Analytics group at SFU. He is the lead developer for CZSaw, a tool for entity-based text analysis. His research interests are in visual analytics for text and in human-computer interaction for supporting analytical activity.

Robert Jennings is currently finishing his master's in urban studies at the INRS Centre Urbanisation Culture Société, Concordia University. He has spent the last six years working in the restaurant and hospitality industry in Montreal and Aix-en-Provence, France. This experience and his studies have led him to work on Bring-Your-Own-Wine restaurants. He is mainly interested in qualitative research on subjects related to gentrification, geographies of consumption, and the public domain.

Josée Johnston is associate professor of sociology at the University of Toronto. Her major substantive interest is the sociological study of food, which is a lens for investigating questions relating to consumer culture, politics, gender, and the environment. She is the co-author of *Foodies* (2nd edition, 2015) with Shyon Baumann, and the co-author of *Food and Femininity* (2015) with Kate Cairns. She has published articles in venues including *American Journal of Sociology*, *Journal of Consumer Culture*, *Signs*, *Theory and Society*, and *Gender and Society*.

Emily Huddart Kennedy is an assistant professor of environmental sociology at Washington State University. Her research examines citizen engagement in environmental issues with a focus on how people get involved in individual and collective action.

Ahmed Khan is a former research fellow with UNEP-IEMP in Beijing and currently a postdoctoral researcher at Saint Mary's University. Khan's research interest lies in understanding human-nature interactions and seeking innovative governance mechanisms toward global environmental and economic change.

Mustafa Koç is a professor of sociology at Ryerson University. His research and teaching interests involve food studies, food security and food policy, globalization, and sociology of migration. He was among the founders of the Centre for Studies in Food Security, Food Secure Canada and the Canadian Association for Food Studies. His publications include For Hunger-proof Cities (1999), Interdisciplinary Perspectives in Food Studies (2008), and Critical Perspectives in Food Studies (2012, 2016).

Keith Lee is a doctoral candidate in the Department of City and Regional Planning at the University of California, Berkeley (at the time of writing), whose dissertation research investigates the linkages between retail development and food waste in Seoul, South Korea. His broader research interests encompass the effect of urban development on urban metabolism in the cities of East and Southeast Asia, focusing on food consumption and waste and their immediate and distanced impacts. As an interdisciplinary scholar, Lee's work draws upon approaches and concepts from planning, industrial ecology, sociology, and geography. His research is driven by a desire to explore the role urban planners can play in addressing the issues of overconsumption and environmental degradation.

Charles Z. Levkoe is the Canada Research Chair in Sustainable Food Systems and an assistant professor in the Department of Health Sciences at Lakehead University. His research focuses on grassroots activism, policy, and the growth of regional food networks in Canada. He has been active in investigations at the intersections of food sovereignty movements and community-campus engagement.

Kristen Lowitt is currently a postdoctoral fellow in the Sustainable Futures Research Laboratory at McGill University. Lowitt is particularly interested in socio-ecological approaches to understanding the linkages between food systems, food security, and rural livelihoods and development.

Wanda Martin is a nurse educator and researcher at the University of Saskatchewan. Her focus is on public health, applied food systems research, health equity, and complex adaptive systems. She is also the president of the Saskatchewan Public Health Association.

Victoria Millious is a PhD candidate at Queen's University. Her dissertation research examines the materiality and agency of breast milk in contemporary North America with a focus on how the concepts of nostalgia, purity and immunity inform perinatal and postpartum knowledges.

Phil Mount is the principal investigator of Project SOIL, associate director of Just Food, associate researcher with the Laurier Centre for Sustainable Food Systems, and associate editor at *Canadian Food Studies/La Revue canadienne des études sur l'alimentation*. Phil's research and practice intersects on an agroecological demonstration farm, where local and regional food systems meet informal and social economies of food, and inform the transition to sustainable food systems.

Erika Mundel is a farmer and food activist. The focus of her academic work has been on food movements, critical public health, and Indigenous food systems and health.

Alan Nash teaches courses on the geography of food at Concordia University, where he is a professor in the Department of Geography, Planning and Environment. With a research interest in Montreal and its restaurants, his work on this topic has been published in *Food, Culture and Society*, *Material Culture Review/Revue de la culture matérielle*, and the *Oxford Symposium on Food and Cookery*.

Serhiy Polyakov is an electronic resources specialist at Weill Cornell Medicine - Qatar. He earned a PhD in information science from University of North Texas. His work examines the use of latent semantic analysis in text mining and information retrieval. He has experience as a researcher in the NSF's funded Comparative Assessment of Peer Review project and in other projects in the fields of digital libraries, information retrieval, and learning object repositories. His interests include information systems, metadata, and ontology development.

Karen Rideout is a food systems researcher and policy analyst with a focus on food and culture, public health, food policy, equity, and environmental health.

Steffanie Scott is associate professor in the Department of Geography and Environmental Management at the University of Waterloo, and is engaged in research on sustainable food systems in China and Canada. She is past president of the Canadian Association for Food Studies and is past co-chair of the Waterloo Region Food System Roundtable. Her research focuses on agri-food system sustainability, ecological food production, and rural-urban interfaces. She has published in *Agriculture and Human Values*, *Food Policy*, *Canadian Food Studies*, and *Journal of Agriculture, Food Systems, and Community Development*, among other journals. Recently, she has been teaching herself Chinese vegetarian cooking.

Tammara Soma is a food system planner and a Trudeau Scholar. She is a doctoral candidate in the Department of Geography and Planning at the University of Toronto (at the time of writing). Her research in Bogor, Indonesia, investigates how factors such as culture, income, and urbanization influence household food consumption and wasting practices. It is the interplay between structure and culture that have led her to explore the potential roles of urban planners in creating resilient cities by improving strategies for the prevention, reduction, and management of food waste. The ultimate goal of her research is to make food system consideration an essential factor in urban planning in both the Global North and the Global South. Soma's doctoral work is funded by the Pierre Elliott Trudeau Foundation and the Social Sciences and Humanities Research Council. Her fieldwork in Indonesia is also funded by the Dr. David Chu Scholarship in Asia Pacific Studies and the International Development Research Centre.

Cathryn Sprague recently completed her master's of science at the University of Alberta. Her research interests include food politics, citizen engagement, and food policy. She is also co-founder of Reclaim Urban Farm and an avid cyclist.

Jennifer Sumner teaches in the Adult Education and Community Development Program at OISE/University of Toronto, where she has developed a course called The Pedagogy of Food. Her research interests include sustainable food systems, cooperatives, globalization, and critical pedagogy. She is the co-editor of *Critical Perspectives in Food Studies* (Oxford University Press, 2012) and the editor of *Learning, Food and Sustainability: Sites for Resistance and Change* (Palgrave/Macmillan, forthcoming).

David Szanto is a researcher, artist, and teacher, taking an experimental approach to gastronomy through design, ecology, and performance. Past projects include meal events representing the urban foodscapes of Berlin and Montreal, the immersive sensory environment, *Displace (Mediations of Sensation)*, and *Orchestrer la perte/Perpetual Demotion*, a food-and-robotics installation at the Musée d'art contemporain de Montréal. Having previously taught at Concordia University and l'Université du Québec à Montréal, he is currently professor-at-large with the University of Gastronomic Sciences's Eco-Gastronomy Project. David has served two terms as vice president of the Canadian Association for Food Studies and is an associate editor of its peer-reviewed journal, *Canadian Food Studies/La Revue canadienne des études sur l'alimentation*.

Lani Trenouth is a Marie Curie Early Stage research fellow in the PURE-FOOD project 2011–2014. She is a doctoral candidate at Wageningen University and is based at the University of Latvia. Her research is centred on exploring alterity in food systems and the meanings and motivations of consumers' food consumption practices in Latvia using quantitative, qualitative, and visual research methods.

Penny Van Esterik is professor emerita of anthropology, recently retired from York University, Toronto, where she taught nutritional anthropology, advocacy anthropology, and feminist theory. Her fieldwork was primarily in Southeast Asia (Thailand and Lao PDR). She is a founding member of WABA (World Alliance for Breastfeeding Action) and has developed advocacy materials on breastfeeding and women's work and breastfeeding as infant food security, in addition to academic publishing.

Matt Ventresca is a postdoctoral fellow in the School of History and Sociology at the Georgia Institute of Technology. His work interrogates the numerous intersections of sport, masculinities, and the body with an emphasis on how these connections materialize through the media and scientific research programs.

Cassie Wever obtained a masters in environmental studies from York University with a concurrent certificate in environmental and sustainability education. Her major research focused on critical food pedagogy in FoodShare's School Grown program. Her research interests include the intersections of food, transformative learning experiences, social justice, and ecological thinking. Wever teaches courses in foraging and organic gardening, has worked as a research assistant with the Nourishing Communities research group, and is the current coordinator of Citizenship and Community-Based Learning in Student Life at the University of Guelph.

Carmen C. Wong is a constant outsider and performance maker who creates work in various site-responsive contexts. She is a practice-based-researcher in the field of theatre and performance studies at the University of Warwick (UK). Recurring motifs in her explorations include belonging and memory; materiality, affect and the sensorium; and restaging food micro-ethnographies. Her gastro-performance series, evolved since 2009 has propagated a Tactile Eating workshop and a variety of projects that examine performances by, with, and around food and its eaters.

Konstantinos Zougris is an assistant professor of sociology at the Division of Social Sciences at the University of Hawaii-West O'ahu. His research interests are primarily in the areas of hybrid methodology, global and comparative societies, digital sociology, economic sociology, and quantitative data analysis.